The Financial Times Guide to Exchange Traded Funds and Index Funds

FINANCIAL TIMES

In an increasingly competitive world, we believe it's quality of thinking that will give you the edge – an idea that opens new doors, a technique that solves a problem, or an insight that simply makes sense of it all. The more you know, the smarter and faster you can go.

That's why we work with the best minds in business and finance to bring cutting-edge thinking and best learning practice to a global market.

Under a range of leading imprints, including *Financial Times Prentice Hall*, we create world-class print publications and electronic products bringing our readers knowledge, skills and understanding, which can be applied whether studying or at work.

To find out more about Pearson Education publications, or tell us about the books you'd like to find, you can visit us at **www.pearsoned.co.uk**

The Financial Times Guide to Exchange Traded Funds and Index Funds

How to Use Tracker Funds in Your Investment Portfolio

David Stevenson

**Financial Times
Prentice Hall
is an imprint of**

Harlow, England • London • New York • Boston • San Francisco • Toronto • Sydney • Singapore • Hong Kong
Tokyo • Seoul • Taipei • New Delhi • Cape Town • Madrid • Mexico City • Amsterdam • Munich • Paris • Milan

PEARSON EDUCATION LIMITED

Edinburgh Gate
Harlow CM20 2JE
Tel: +44 (0)1279 623623
Fax: +44 (0)1279 431059
Website: www.pearsoned.co.uk

First published in Great Britain in 2010

ISBN: 978-0-273-72783-5

British Library Cataloguing-in-Publication Data
A catalogue record for this book is available from the British Library

Library of Congress Cataloging-in-Publication Data
A catalog record for this book is available from the Library of Congress

10 9 8 7 6 5 4 3 2
13 12 11 10

Typeset in 9pt Stone Serif by 30
Printed and bound by Ashford Colour Press, Gosport

The publisher's policy is to use paper manufactured from sustainable forests.

Contents

Acknowledgements

Over the last few months ETFs and index tracking funds have become something of an obsession, encouraging in me something of the anorak – many a dinner has started with 'I bet you didn't know there's an ETF that tracks . . . .' Fill in the missing exotic asset class or market and then imagine the pained look on the face of the person opposite me. Precisely because of this anorak-like behaviour I think its important I acknowledge the patience and support of my editor at the FT, Matthew Vincent, who was also kind enough to write the Foreword for this book. I sense that a curry or two might be in order as part payment for his support!

I'd also like to thank Pearson Education's Chris Cudmore, who was very patient with me – we first discussed this proposal a great many moons ago and Chris has always been enormously positive in steering this project away from the inside of my head into hard copy. Alongside Chris I think that Melanie Carter from Pearson also deserves great credit for pushing me to do what I like least – spell out in painstaking detail the exact sources of my data, tables and graphs and generally reminding me to acknowledge all my original sources.

The various contributors to this book also deserve a huge vote of thanks. James Norton at Evolve Financial Planning has been on the receiving end of much of that obsessive lunchtime chatter about ETFs, as has Fundamental's Rob Davies, although both I suspect are as equally fascinated by index funds as I am. Much the same could be said for Paul Amery of Index Universe, who's a real treasure trove of information and analysis on ETFs – his website is a must. Dr Stephen Barber from stockbrokers Selftrade manages to keep a slightly more discreet distance from we ETF obsessives, rightly recommending a broader look at the investment universe, and again I owe many thanks, as I do to Stockcube's Mark Glowrey and Tarquin Coe.

Finally I'd also like to thank my old friend Dr Mike Mason, who has had the patience and fortitude to feign an interest in this book even though it's absolutely not about anything Green or world saving. And most importantly of all to Vanessa and the mob, Rebecca and Zac plus Hettie and Jake. Oh yes, and Mum!

Publisher's acknowledgements

We are grateful to the following for permission to reproduce copyright material:

The CFA Institute for extracts from Bogle, John C., 'The Relentless Rules of Humble Arithmetic', *Financial Analysts Journal*, Nov/Dec 2005. © 2005, CFA Institute. Reproduced and republished by permission of the CFA Institute. All rights reserved; Stockcube Plc for graphs on pp.63, 181, 182, 184, 185, 186, 187, 188, 189, 190, 191 and 192; William Bernstein for the bullet points on p.109 and Table 4.6 on p.110 (www.efficientfrontier.com); Barclays Capital for Table 7.1 on p.146, from Bond, Tim (ed.), Barclays Capital Guilt Study; Hay House for Figure 10.1 on p.200, from Stein, B. and DeMuth, P., *Yes, You Can Supercharge Your Portfolio! Six Steps for Investing Success in the 21st Century* (New Beginnings Press, 2008).

In some instances we have been unable to trace the owners of copyright material, and we would appreciate any information that would enable us to do so.

Foreword

Shortly after 4pm on 11 May 1997, Garry Kasparov further furrowed his customarily furrowed brow. He then shook his head in a rare display of apparent disbelief. He desultorily played bishop takes rook on e7. Seconds later, he rose from his chair, stretched out his arms, and strode away from the table. The world chess champion had resigned in the decisive sixth game of his challenge match against IBM's super computer, Deep Blue. For the first time, man had lost to machine.

To chess players, and to programmers in the field of artificial intelligence, this was a seismic event. To chess-playing investors, however, it was arguably to be expected – because, in the field of investment management, computer-run index-tracking funds had been outperforming humans for years.

In a study of the returns from UK equity unit trusts and open-ended investment companies (Oeics) between April 1975 and December 2002, Keith Cuthbertson, Dirk Nitzsche and Niall O'Sullivan of London's Cass Business School found that only 2 per cent of these actively managed funds outperformed their benchmark indices. Nor is this a peculiarly UK failing. Over the years, similar academic research has come to a similar conclusion: both the average US and UK fund manager consistently fails to beat a comparable benchmark index.

So it is no surprise that index-tracking exchange traded funds (ETFs) – for which computer models, rather than fallible humans, select stocks to sample or replicate index performance – are now a major growth industry. In the US, ETF manager Vanguard has conducted its own research to support its business model. It found that only 'a small percentage – 7 per cent – of actively managed balanced funds have been able to consistently outperform their policy benchmarks'. It now manages approximately $1tn of investors' money and – with only an IT department rather than legions of fund managers to pay – it charges these investors an average of just 0.2 per cent a year. These facts are not unconnected. Market performance, and market forces, will out.

Vanguard launched its first index trackers for UK investors – as conventional funds rather than ETFs – in the summer of 2009, with the lowest charges ever seen in this country: 0.15 per cent for a fund replicating FTSE All-Share performance. It promised ETF versions to follow. Competition between fund managers soon escalated.

Weeks later, HSBC slashed the fees across its seven-strong UK-based index tracking range to 0.25 per cent, having previously charged between 1 and 0.5 per cent. Then, in August, it launched its first European ETF tracking the FTSE 100 index with a total expense ratio (TER) of 0.35 per cent. HSBC's rationale was simple: research conducted by its Global Asset Management arm found that 95 per cent of financial advisers would either 'significantly or moderately increase' their exposure to index tracking funds over the coming three years. With ETFs charging less, and paying advisers no commission, there is almost literally nothing in it for them. Evidently, though, there is a lot in these ETFs for their clients.

So this book on the use of ETFs in private investors' portfolios could not be better timed. Having read the early drafts, I can assure readers that it is far more than a technical exercise in cheerleading for Deep Blue and its ETF-managing computer progeny. Its author is a self-confessed technophile – although, as the commissioning editor of his Adventurous Investor column in the *Financial Times Weekend Money* section, I am yet to discover any evidence of a mastery of the 'spell-check' function on his own PC. What I have discovered in this book, however, and in his weekly columns, is an insightful and balanced view on the pros and cons of index tracking for long-term investors.

Clear explanations and examples abound: of the failings of actively managed funds even in bear markets, where human intervention should win out (a majority of active managers outperformed the market in just three of six US bear markets and in two of five European bear markets), but also of the failings of some index trackers and ETFs, where tracking error and less competitive charges make them serial losers (one non-ETF tracker underperformed the FTSE All-Share Index by an average 2.4 per cent a year). This is not a black and white analysis.

Where this book truly excels, however, is in its non-technical demonstration of the use of ETFs for diversifying your portfolio. With just a handful of ETFs, bought at low cost through an execution-only stockbroker, a private investor can gain the lowest-cost exposure to all major asset classes and thereby reduce the risk – and improve the returns – from any portfolio. With ETFs tracking fundamental indices – collections of shares selected by the strength of company fundamentals rather than their size or expensiveness – a private investor can even hope to outperform benchmarks by a small margin.

When you come to realise, as I did in the course of reading, that it's your choice of asset class rather than your fund manager's choice of shares that makes the most difference to performance – accounting for 94 per cent of the variability in a portfolio's total return, against just 4 per cent – you understand the value of ETFs. And when the numbers are as clear-cut as they are in this book, you don't need a super computer to do the maths. Checkmate.

Matthew Vincent
Editor, *FT Money*
2 September 2009

1

Introduction

'It's amazing how difficult it is for a man to understand something if he's paid a small fortune not to understand it.'

John Bogle paraphrasing Upton Sinclair

'Money often costs too much.'

Ralph Waldo Emerson

Welcome to the revolution – Investing 2.0

Ask yourself how you invest.

In 2001 I did just that – I looked at my long list of then failing investments and asked myself what I was really investing in. Two obvious 'facts on the ground' sprang up at me as I scanned the sorry list of assets – I had invested first in individual stocks, lots of them, and then second, funds, the vast majority of which were conventional unit trusts. In fact I had lots and lots of those funds and to judge by their performance, my strategy was not terribly successful, although to be fair not many investors were having a good time in 2001.

The important bit is that this list of assets comprised my future pension pot and so I repeated that question: what exactly was the strategy here? My initial conclusion seemed to be that I liked buying cheap stocks and investing in good fund managers.

Neither of these 'strategies' was or is a bad idea – buying distressed, cheap bargain stocks has in the past produced some extraordinary results and backing very successful managers like Bill Miller in the US and Neil Woodford in the UK has been a good idea. But I started to worry that maybe I was taking too much risk.

What would happen if those individual, distressed stocks really did blow up and the share price collapsed? Maybe they would issue three profits warnings in a row and then proceed to implode in value? What would happen if anything untoward happened to the fund managers?

A reliance on stock selection, star fund managers and the even more suspect practice of attempting to time the market convinced me, as a private investor, that something was amiss. I was taking too much risk with not enough potential return.

I am prepared to argue that what is true for me is true for other investors. Dr Stephen Barber of Selftrade – and author of a later chapter – suggests that for most of the time his investors tend to trade in individual stocks and star funds. But is this too much of a risk? Do we all think that we are better at investing than we think we are?

When you look at the US market, it is interesting to see what the Americans do. Investors do buy individual stocks, like me, and they did chase star fund managers, but they also increasingly use another investment approach that involves two very simple ideas: buying individual shares is suspect and that you need to be invested in either a whole sector or a market. For the US investors the best way to buy this 'diversification' across sectors and markets is not via a fund actively managed by someone famous like Bill Miller but through a fund that tracks a particular sector/market/asset. The thinking behind what we would call asset class investing was and is simple, namely that because virtually every theme, sector, market, even investment strategy is bound to be tracked somewhere by an index – the index provision business has been a very successful place to be over the last decade – it should be relatively easy to set up a fund that tracks that index.

The idea is brilliantly simple. De-risk your portfolio by avoiding individual stocks and fund managers and buy only the big theme or asset class by tracking it in a fund.

It is also hugely disruptive for the established way of doing things – it is an investing revolution that does away with two of the hallowed core principles of modern investing (individual stock selection and hiring fund managers actively to manage your funds) and replaces them with a simpler, more transparent, cheap concept involving a fund that tracks an index. As we will discover in this book, that revolution – I like to call it Investing 2.0 – is sweeping the US markets and is about to make its impact felt here in Europe as well.

What follows in this book is not a complicated story, although some of the underlying theory is a little tricky in places. The structures that have emerged out of this theory are also not that complicated as innovations go. However, it is fair to say that index tracking can, on first appearance, look confusing if only because of the use of hundreds of difficult-to-understand acronyms. Cut through the acronyms and you'll discover that this asset class investing is simply about tracking key markets, sectors and themes by using a fund that mirrors the underlying index.

Of course, it gets a lot more complicated the more you understand how you should use these funds in a reasoned and cautious way – that's why I have written this book – but the bottom line, at least in my view, is simple: namely that index trackers really are the single best innovation in the last 50 years for private investors. Sadly, until very recently the revolution I have just begun to outline looked like it was going to remain a Stateside phenomenon; over here, in the UK, by contrast, nothing much seemed to be happening. A few tracker unit trusts had been launched and the iShares fund group (owned at the time by Barclays) had just started issuing the listed tracker funds (called exchange traded funds or ETFs), but by and large investing was still based on active fund management and rampant stock picking and tipping.

Fast-forward just a few years – to 2009 – and everything seems to be changing. An amazing explosion of new investment products has kick-started the slightly moribund fund industry – there are now hundreds and hundreds of index tracking funds here in the UK and even independent financial advisers (IFAs) and private investors are making the switch. The asset class investing revolution is now an important part of investment strategies in the UK and European markets.

Why asset class investing will change the way we invest

This revolution may sound enormously exciting but it will amount to nothing unless it helps to change the behaviour of investors – both private and institutional – and provides real benefits for all. Luckily the evidence is that this new world of investing is going to change everything – index or tracker products are slowly gaining market traction and although most small investors probably don't know what an ETF is, more and more experienced investors with bigger portfolios are beginning to build them into the core of their portfolios.

In a recent survey for the European Asset Allocation Summit, more than 100 top institutions were asked to forecast the big trends in investing over the next year (2009). The results were mildly illuminating as there were various comments about equities and commodities on the rebound. But the interesting statistic was that the key product they were nearly all going to buy more of was something called exchange traded funds – stock market listed index funds structured tracking a key index.

Advisers, be they IFAs or wealth advisory managers, are also beginning to recommend these products. This is prompted in part by an increasing recognition that the salad days of investment advising (and high fees) could soon be over and that advisers might actually have to specialise in providing investment advice rather than just sell insurance policies or pensions. Investors of all kinds are beginning to ask awkward questions – why are you, my adviser, making big fees from commissions on actively managed funds but failing to deliver superior outperformance (called alpha in the trade)?

A whole series of changes in behaviour is under way in the business of investment – that's what this book is partly about, detailing the revolution and how you can use it to your advantage.

Inside we will encounter a number of core principles that are repeated again and again. We will show you why index tracking funds are transparent and cheap, and detail the huge choice of markets and assets on offer. Index tracking funds allow you to take a more strategic view of your investments and help build a diversified portfolio. They also cut through the variability of active fund management and give you the returns from holding the asset class. And they tend to produce better returns than most active fund managers.

That last statement is absolutely crucial. Index funds may be cheaper, they may be more transparent and they may help foster wide diversification within a portfolio, but the reason that so many American investors and institutions buy into them is because they deliver better results than traditional forms of fund management and stock picking.

The believers

As with all innovations, index tracking funds have sparked a large amount of controversy. Many active fund managers hate the whole concept of passively managed asset class investing, while many advisers do not feel inclined to recommend something that does not make them any money in trail commission.

On the other side of the debate it has to be conceded that fans of index funds have a certain, almost religious tone to their declarations in which there is a battle of faiths between the new schools, the indexers, versus the established school, the orthodoxy, represented by your mainstream fund manager who actively manages a portfolio.

Fans of indexing invite further comparison with evangelicals by having a slightly embattled tone to their declarations, invoking images of a titanic struggle against a very powerful and rich adversary in the shape of the conventional investment business. But the almost messianic zeal of the believers in Investing 2.0 should not hide the fact that there is a real battle going on and that an uncomfortable fact sits at the heart of this investing revolution.

Do funds actively managed by avowed stock pickers – the preferred route into investing for the vast majority of investors – actually deliver the goods? Is the 'norm' actually a bad idea, built upon very shaky foundations?

The most important fact in favour of indexing focuses on hard statistical analysis. This huge wealth of data has been developed by a collection of fairly sceptical academic economists who have been scouring the data sets on fund returns for the last 40 years. It is their research into the supposed benefits of active fund management that has chipped away at the legitimacy of the active fund management community and helped build the foundations for a new approach to investing called asset class investing.

The fall and decline of the active fund manager

There are a relatively small number of people who actively manage their own portfolios by investing directly in individual shares; until very recently, the vast majority of investors (private and institutional) used funds actively run by a manager. This fund manager would probably belong to one of the big asset management groups. In the US and UK, for instance, about 70 per cent of institutional funds are actively managed and this rises to over 90 per cent for retail funds. Put it another way – of the 14,304 mutual funds currently trading in the US, 13,796 of them are actively managed.

Clearly the fund management industry is convinced that using a fund manager to actively manage is essential and that it delivers the 'goods' in terms of returns. The only niggly problem is that the statistics, as mined by professional economists, don't add up. In fact, academic economists have been scrutinising the performance of active fund managers for decades now, with the first crucial paper produced by Michael Jensen dating back to 1968.[1]

Although some controversy still rumbles on, the majority of studies now conclude that actively managed funds on average underperform their passively managed counterparts. Study after study has revealed a huge discrepancy between actively and passively managed (i.e. index tracking) funds. This huge weight of evidence was nicely summed up by Rex Sinquefield, boss of Dimensional fund management, an index tracking investment firm. 'Researchers uncovered considerable evidence that past prices were of little benefit in forecasting future prices in ways that would earn excess profits; that fundamental data was too quickly reflected in prices to allow such data to be used for beat-the-market purposes; and, most importantly for us, that professional money managers could simply not outperform markets in any meaningful sense.'

Sinquefield's words summarise well some of the key observations from the research world: that the past isn't much use in forecasting the future, that by and large prices set by the market are sensible and 'efficient', and that it is devilishly difficult for money managers to use that past data or those largely efficient markets and make any extra return. If he had made reference to Michael Jensen's paper he might also have noted when managers do outperform the market, they do so largely by taking on extra risk. And that is exactly what most private investors don't realise they are doing when they think they are buying a nice, safe, diversified actively managed fund.

As well as Sinquefield's view, there is now a long list of studies showing that hiring a fund manager is not always the right thing to do. I've detailed some of them below:

Gruber in 1996, for example, found that over the period 1985–1994 the average mutual fund underperformed the passive market index by about 65 basis points per year.[2] Carhart in 1997 confirmed that net returns are negatively correlated with expense levels, i.e. that the more actively managed a fund, the higher the expenses and the lower the returns.[3] Carhart also discovered that the more actively a mutual fund manager trades, the lower is the fund's net return to investors. The University of Chicago professor also studied all the mutual funds that existed any time between 1961 and 1993 and found that, on average, actively managed funds underperformed their index by 1.80 per cent per year.

In yet another study of equity mutual funds, Elton et al., examined all funds that existed over the period 1965–1984 – a total of 143 funds.[4] These funds were then compared to a set of index funds – big stocks, small stocks and fixed income – that most closely corresponded to the actual investment choices made by the mutual funds. The result: on average those actively managed funds underperformed the index funds by a whopping 159 basis points a year. Not a single fund generated positive performance that was statistically significant.

It is also worth noting the first major study of bond market performance, by Blake, Elton and Gruber, in which they examined 361 bond funds starting in 1977, comparing various active bond fund management strategies with a simple 'buy the index' idea.[5] The authors found that active funds on average underperformed the index tracking strategies by 85 basis points a year.

Carhart returned to the fray with what is regarded as the definitive study, which looked at a total of 1,892 funds that existed any time between 1961 and 1993. After adjusting for the common factors in returns, an equal-weighted portfolio of the funds underperformed by 1.8 per cent per year.

This research has even found support in journalistic circles – an article in *The Wall Street Journal* reported that the average mutual fund underperformed its risk-adjusted benchmark by 140 basis points (1.4 per cent) a year.[6]

For many years this research focused on the work of American academics, but in the 1990s the British economists started examining the subject. One of the first was Dr Jonathan Fletcher in what was a fairly seminal paper called 'An examination of UK unit trust performance within the Arbitrage Pricing Theory framework'.[7]

Dr Fletcher's paper looked at a sample of 101 British unit trusts within something called the Arbitrage Pricing Theory framework and then looked at performance data. His conclusion was that 'there appears to be little relationship between performance and the investment objective, size and expenses of the trusts. Also portfolio strategies using past trust performance to rank the trusts fail to generate significant abnormal returns relative to two different benchmark portfolios'.

The bottom line? Active fund management didn't seem to work. More research at the start of the twenty-first century continued to examine statistics, such as the Elton et al., study mentioned earlier.[8]

Another, much more recent paper by Keith Cuthbertson, Dirk Nitzsche and Niall O'Sullivan looks at another key aspect of active fund management: do active fund managers consistently outperform or do they eventually revert to mean, while still charging their relatively higher fees?[9] Their conclusion is that 'only around 2 per cent of all funds truly outperform their bench-marks. ... For different investment styles, this pattern of very few genuine winner funds is repeated for all companies, small companies and equity income funds. ... the majority (around 75–85 per cent) of UK mutual funds neither underperform nor outperform their benchmarks.'

Don't trust the manager

The message from this long list of studies (and there are many, many more) seems to be clear: the 'beat-the-market' efforts of professional fund managers achieve the exact opposite, namely they increase risk, increase cost and reduce returns. In almost any leading developed world asset class, the only consistently superior performer is the market itself.

As one analyst at Dimensional summed it up: 'Almost no one would wager millions of dollars on the flip of a coin, no matter how fair the flip. Similarly, it does not make sense to wager large sums of money on an active manager whose performance is erratic at best, when an index fund closely tracks the performance target. For any year, the return for an equity fund can be predicted only to be within the S&P 500 return –7.5 per cent, approximately equal to the standard deviation of S&P 500 returns. Even though drift is random, the volatility of active manager drift is almost half as large as the volatility of the stock market.'[10]

It is also worth noting one additional set of observations – that even the best active fund managers are not consistent, i.e. they have good years but also lots of bad years which can destroy your wealth. A key US study looked at the most successful fund managers in a five-year period, starting in 1989; it then looked at their performance in the next five-year period starting in 1994. Looking at international fund managers, for instance, in 1989, their five-year results were 20.60 per cent per annum, yet in the five years starting in 1994 that performance had dropped to a dreadful 9.37 per cent per annum. Another fascinating study – by Vanguard, a fund manage-ment group big into indexing funds – looked to see whether excellent past performance was predictive of great, or even above-average, future per-formance. Their research showed that even if one's strategy was to buy the top 20 equity funds from the previous year, there is almost no chance they will be in the top 20 again and about a 40 per cent chance that they will be worse than the average fund in the subsequent year.

So there is a consensus among academics: active fund managers are not good at consistently, over long periods of time, beating the benchmark index. In fact, they are so bad at it, most of the time you would be better off finding a vehicle – an index tracking fund, for instance – that simply tracks the index.

Active fund management costs more

However, any analysis of why active fund managers are not always a good idea has to recognise the work of a small band of eminent economists who have spent much of the last 20 years examining the costs of active fund management. In a paper called 'The Cost of Active Investing', the economist Kenneth French compares the fees, expenses and trading costs paid on actively managed funds and then compares them with an estimate of what would be paid if everyone invested in a vehicle that could track the benchmark index.[11] 'Averaging over 1980 to 2006 I find investors spend 0.67 per cent of the aggregate value of the market each year searching for superior returns. Society's capitalised cost of price discovery is at least 10 per cent of the current market cap. Under reasonable assumptions, the typical investor would increase his average annual return by 67 basis points over the 1980–2006 period if he switched to a passive market portfolio.' He adds ominously: 'This estimate is conservative.'

This paper is a hugely compelling tour de force of the pitfalls of active fund management and is worth sticking with a bit longer in this run-through of the pitfalls of active fund management. French examines overtrading via turnover measures – his hypothesis is that active fund managers trade too often and as trading costs money these expenses sap returns. According to French: 'Market turnover is above 110 per cent in the 1920s. It reaches a high of 143 per cent in 1928, then plunges with the market to 52 per cent in 1932. By 1938 it is below 20 per cent. In light of recent experience, it is perhaps surprising that annual turnover remains close to or below 20 per cent from 1938 to 1975. Turnover rises fairly steadily over the next three decades, however, from 20 per cent in 1975 and 59 per cent in 1990, to an impressive 173 per cent in 2006 and 215 per cent in 2007.'

French concludes that the cost of active investing was $7.0bn in 1980, $30.5bn in 1993 and $101.8bn in 2006. Thus, in 2006 investors searching for superior returns in the US stock market 'consume more than $330 in resources for every man, woman and child in the United States'. And just in case you thought that your average actively managed retail fund manager was bad enough, pity the poor hedge fund investor: 'The value-weight average fee on US equity-related hedge fund assets in 2007 is 4.63 per cent and the average fund of fund fee is 1.85 per cent. Since fund of fund investors must pay both their own funds' fees and the fees of the underlying hedge funds, the typical fund of fund investor does not break even in 2007 unless US equity-related hedge funds generate average abnormal returns of 6.48 per cent. There are $458.6bn invested in hedge funds at the beginning of 2007, so even if we ignore the other costs they incur, hedge funds must take $29.7bn in abnormal profits from other US equity investors for their fund of fund clients to break even.'

CMH – the Costs Matter Hypothesis

The job of translating all this wealth of academic analysis has fallen to a small number of dedicated Investing 2.0 evangelicals in the US. The most prominent of these is John Bogle, a master at explaining what is wrong with active fund management and why passively tracking an index (maybe via his firm's funds) is the right way to go. He also argues that the costs of active fund management are destroying the wealth of America, as detailed by French's paper above.

Perhaps his most powerful attack came at the 60th Anniversary Conference of the *Financial Analysts Journal* in February 2005 at Pasadena, California. His message to the gathered audience of US academics was that costs matter. He developed his own thesis to describe it: the Costs Matter Hypothesis, a companion theory to the Efficient Markets Theory which we will encounter in the next chapter. His research was focused on 'gross return in the financial markets, minus the costs of financial intermediation (advisers, brokers and fund managers) equals the net return actually delivered to investors'. Echoing some of French's work, Bogle discovered that during 2004:

- revenues of investment bankers and brokers came to an estimated $220bn;
- direct mutual fund costs came to about $70bn;
- pension management fees amounted to $15bn, annuity commissions to $15bn;
- hedge fund fees came to about $25bn;
- fees paid to personal financial advisers totalled maybe another $5bn;
- the grand total was 'approximately $350bn, all directly deducted from the returns that the financial markets generated for investors before those croupiers' costs were deducted'. He also estimated that in 1985 these costs were a 'mere' $50bn.

The big problem, according to Bogle, was that all these escalating costs did not actually deliver the goods. 'Let's look at the record,' he demanded. 'Over the past 20 years, a simple, low-cost, no-load stock market index fund delivered an annual return of 12.8 per cent – just a hair short of the 13.0 per cent return of the market itself. During the same period the average equity mutual fund delivered a return of just 10.0 per cent, a shortfall to the index fund of 2.8 per centage points per year, and less than 80 per cent of the market's return. Compounded over that period, each $1 invested in the index fund grew by $10.12 – the *magic* of compounding *returns* – while each $1 in the average find grew by just $5.73, not 80 per cent of the market's return but a shrivelled-up 57 per cent – a victim of the *tyranny* of compounding *costs*. And that's before taxes.'

Bogle then implored investors to focus on another measure of returns – asset-weighted returns, i.e. the actual returns of funds based on the flow of funds (see Table 1.1). This is a crucial concept – by and large investors *increase* their payments into investment plans while markets are booming and *decrease* them during a bear market (falling markets) – they do not always invest in a linear, fixed, regular amount.

'The *asset-weighted* returns of mutual funds – quite easy to calculate by examining each fund's quarterly cash flows – lag the standard *time-weighted* returns by fully 3.7 percentage points per year,' claims Bogle. 'Adding that shortfall to the 2.8 percentage point annual lag of time-weighted returns of the average equity fund relative to the 500 index fund over the past two decades, the *asset-weighted* returns of the average equity fund stockholder fell a total of 6.5 per centage points *per year* behind the index fund.'

Using his own 'humble arithmetic', Bogle then spelled out what effect these extra costs might have on future returns. 'If the stock market is kind enough to favour us with a total return of 8 per cent per year over that period,' Bogle argued, 'and if annual mutual fund costs are held to 2½ per cent, the return of the fund investor will average 5½ per cent. By the end of the long period, a cost-free investment at 8 per cent would carry an initial $1,000 investment to a final value of $148,800. However, the 5½ per cent net return for the investor would increase his cumulative wealth by only $31,500. In effect, the amount paid over to the financial system, also compounded, would come to $116,300.'

Table 1.1 Asset-weighted expense ratios of active versus index mutual funds (as of 31 December 2007)

	Actively managed funds – basis points or 1/100ths of 1%	Index funds (bps)	Difference (bps)
Large cap US equity	84	19	65
Mid cap US equity	107	28	79
Small cap US equity	111	32	79
US sector	99	49	50
US real estate	110	26	84
International Developed markets	100	31	69
International emerging markets	129	43	86
US corporate bond	67	21	45
US government bond	58	22	36

Source: Vanguard calculations using data from Morningstar

Bogle's work has been taken one step further by a rather less well-known American analyst, Geoff Considine, who runs a small research firm called Quantext Inc – among many endeavours, Considine's team helps to build simple, easy-to-use portfolios for a low-cost American broking service called FolioFN. In a remarkable paper entitled 'The Humble Arithmetic of Portfolio Management', Considine takes Bogle's analysis and builds on it, adding other real-world costs that sap returns for the average private investor.

Looking at stock market returns between 1983 and 2003, Considine suggests the S&P 500 market returned an average annual return of 13 per cent, from which private investors had to deduct 'average fund lag', which includes poor management and high expenses of 3 per cent per annum, plus bad timing by investors (they invested when markets were close to their peak and withdrew money when they were at the bottom), which costs 3.7 per cent, and finally the net effect of inflation, which was around 3 per cent per annum. The final real return was just 3.3 per cent per annum. The average index fund would yield just under 9.8 per cent per annum by contrast.

But Considine is alive to another more important reality about most private investors – we diversify! We rarely shove all our money into just one market or just one fund – we tend to spread it out over different funds, which in academic theory is actually a good idea, as we will soon discover. Considine looks at a typical 60 per cent equities/40 per cent bonds return over the same period and estimates that annual returns were actually closer to 7.8 per cent per annum. Deduct the 'fund lag' – this time just 1.5 per cent because bond managers tend to be more efficient and charge less in fees – bad timing of 3 per cent and inflation of 3 per cent, and hey presto, the average real return is just 0.3 per cent per annum. Opt for a financial adviser who uses index tracking funds (and charges a 1 per cent annual fee), doesn't market time (sticks with long-term buy-and-hold strategies) and that same portfolio of 60 per cent equities and 40 per cent bonds could yield a real return of 3.5 per cent per annum. Considine's bottom line? Index tracking works, but it works even better if you diversify.

The remorseless rise of the indexers

This detour into academic research on active fund managers and their fees isn't just an exercise in showing how many academic papers it is possible to read. Rather this academic research is the bedrock of a new way of looking at investing. If stock picking by fund managers is largely pointless and counterproductive and it costs us all a lot of money, why bother? If you can receive better returns by finding a vehicle that invests in the benchmark used by these star managers – something like the FTSE 100, for instance – why not use this approach as the basis for building a new kind of portfolio that is full of different asset classes and markets, all via index tracking vehicles of various forms and guises?

A few years ago I made the leap – I dumped all my actively managed funds and started investing in index tracking vehicles, in my case these exchange traded funds. I haven't entirely given up stock picking – I can't quite resist the bug – but index tracking funds now sit at the heart of my portfolio.

There are now a large number of academics, asset allocators and fund managers who are committed to ETFs. This circle even has its own in-house journals, the best of which is *The Exchange Traded Funds Report*, which is published monthly from the US. This is a trade journal for the hardy band of indexers, but in recent years it has grown in status and confidence – where once it would report on just a few new fund launches every month, now it reports on dozens or even hundreds every few weeks. One of its main contributors is Paul Amery, who will look at the intricacies of ETFs and index funds in Chapter 5 of this book.

The January 2009 edition of the journal contains a review of 2008. The stories in this edition should give some insight into how significant indexing has become. In order of importance what follows are the latest 'developments'. These are detailed by the newspaper's editor, Matt Hougan:

▪ More and more cash is flowing into the exchange traded fund sector in the US – ETFs in the US attracted more than $100 billion in net positive cash flows through to 31 October 2008.

▪ ETFs now regularly account for 30 per cent of the total trading volume on US equity exchanges and on some days this rises to over 40 per cent.

▪ Here's the single biggest paradox. Although the ETF movement was spawned by the wave of academic research into the pitfalls of active fund management, a small number of tracker providers have confounded their peers by using an ETF structure – an index tracker – to actively trade a portfolio of shares. This is seen by most ETF providers as a slightly bizarre, even heretical phenomenon, but it demonstrates just how hugely varied the sector is in composition in the US.

▪ The big boys in fund management are jumping on board the indexing movement – even Pimco, the giant US bonds specialist, has decided to launch its own index tracker. Invesco Perpetual, another funds powerhouse, has embraced the revolution via its purchase of Powershares and there are rumours that other big names like Janus are not far away from launching tracker funds.

▪ A bold prediction is that within the not too distant future index tracking ETFs will exceed funds under management of the active boys and girls.

Index funds are not just becoming *part* of the mainstream in American investing – in some niche markets, like commodities for instance, they are *the mainstream*. Index tracking funds, and especially the ETF, are now the main component of many US institutions' investing strategy.

The hard data on this American triumph, especially through the use of ETFs, comes from provider iShares, once part of Barclays. The current MD Deborah Fuhr follows the whole ETF investment space and has kept an eye on the revolutionary growth of index trackers. According to Ms Fuhr's analysis, as of January 2009 there were globally more than 1,539 ETFs with 2,580 listings and assets under management of $633bn, via 86 different managers and 42 exchanges around the world – she reckons that there were 414 new fund launches in 2008 alone, with plans for 570 new launches in 2009.

Another big statistic jumps out from her detailed analysis – the average daily trading volume in US dollar terms increased by 94 per cent to

$17.5bn YTD, with the biggest growth in Europe where, Fuhr observes, although net sales of traditional mutual funds was –$505m, net sales of ETF index trackers was positive at $61m in one of the worst investing periods in investment history. One of the most interesting stats centres on the use of ETFs by institutions and advisers – back in 1997 just 109 advisers used ETFs, now that number has grown up 1,564. That massive increase in demand has prompted the ETF providers to launch all manner of specialised, niche funds tracking everything from Vietnam equities through to forestry product companies.

iShares, for instance, as it stands at the time of writing (January 2009), offers 19 different developed world equity trackers, 10 emerging markets trackers, 5 property funds, 2 infrastructure funds, 3 green funds including a forestry fund and one that invests in the water sector, 3 funds that follow indices that screen according to Islamic criteria, and 16 fixed interest funds including 4 inflation linked gilt trackers, 8 conventional gilt trackers and 4 corporate bond funds. And that's just one major provider in the UK – rivals including Lyxor, Deutsche DBX, Powershares, SPA and ETF Securities (a specialist in commodity funds) offer an equally wide range of index tracking funds.

The above is just for ETFs – these are not the only structures and vehicles launching unprecedented choice. Later in this book we will look at differing products, all built around the simple idea of tracking an index. Other funds and investment vehicles include:

- traditional mutual fund trackers, or unit trust trackers as they are known in the UK;
- trackers that are built around structured derivatives and go under the title of listed structured products or exchange traded notes (ETNs) in the US or certificates in Europe;
- traditional structured products that track an index;
- commodity trackers packaged as exchange traded commodities or ETCs;
- swaps used by big institutions where a counterparty guarantees to pay out the return of an index.

Within these structures different types of 'tracking' have also emerged. With index tracking funds you can:

- short a market using inverse trackers that give greater returns as markets or assets fall;
- leverage up returns, giving investors more than the increase in the underlying index;

- track a portfolio of different indices or asset classes in one fund;
- within specialised markets like commodities even track futures prices, with durations ranging from one month to one year.

The innovation is staggering but there is one big constant – the choice is huge. If your aim is to build a diversified portfolio of assets and markets, your first choice is probably to use trackers as the building blocks.

Why you need to use index tracking funds in your portfolio and how this book can help you

Most opening chapters to books on investment consist of a quick exposition of what lies ahead – a roadmap for the reader. We have started our journey in a slightly more unusual manner by diving straight into one of the most difficult debates in modern economics – I make no apologies for this because it is crucial that readers understand that using indexing and tracking funds is about a very different type of investing.

Nearly all the best investment strategies are based on simple-to-understand principles. Value investors, for instance, have stayed hugely influential because of the elegant theories and suggestions first articulated by Ben Graham in the 1930s. Graham does still have huge relevance, but markets have developed and investing has become a much more popular affair, with every nook and cranny now exploited by countless clever investors, strategies or hedge funds. In this new world Graham's thinking still resonates in some respects, but markets have become much more transparent and efficient. That forces investors to think in fresh and challenging ways and that's where the new world of asset class investing using trackers comes in – it is also making a huge impact because of its basic, easy-to-understand principles. If one could reduce the huge complexity of thinking and research into just a few slogans, they would probably be these:

Active fund managers don't deliver the returns we all need

Everyone needs to diversify cheaply, efficiently and with minimum hassle

The easiest way to diversify is through index tracking funds

Trackers are cheap and do the job

That last slogan is not, truth be told, the most revolutionary or the most challenging, but it does sum up the simple cost effectiveness and flexibility of trackers. As we will discover in this book, trackers have countless, day-to-day advantages over actively managed funds or even individual shares. A bigger list of these common-place virtues might include the following:

- They can be easily purchased, cleared and held in a brokerage or custo-dial account – they are liquid.
- Investors can go long or short using new forms of tracker index funds.
- Most listed tracker funds are lendable and marginable.
- They are transparent and offer investors a clear understanding of the underlying portfolios on a daily basis – exchange listed funds can be traded in real time with continuous pricing.
- They can be used in a strategic way to increase market exposure to key trades and market views as well as part of a core portfolio.
- They are cheap and effective at tracking key markets and asset classes – according to research from Barclays the average total expense ratio (TER) for equity-based ETFs in Europe is 46 basis points or 0.46 per cent per annum compared with 191 bps (1.91 per cent) for the average actively managed equity fund.
- There is a huge choice of funds available, offering massive diversifica-tion benefits for an investor looking to diversify their portfolio.
- They can be used in a tactical sense – by day traders or even money market managers looking to access money market instruments or gilts and bonds.

We toyed around with turning all these advantages into a later chapter on its own, but rather than fill an entire chapter with these virtually self-evident advantages, this book attempts to dig a little deeper and flesh out the argument of why you need to use index tracking funds. By the time you've finished reading it, hopefully you will be able to understand the thinking behind trackers and index funds, comprehend the different struc-tures (including their weaknesses and strengths) and work out how to use them on an everyday basis within a sensibly diversified portfolio.

That narrative 'arc' or journey – constructed to help you build a better portfolio – starts in the next chapter, where we take a step backwards and look first at the theory that spawned all these index tracking vehicles and this new style of asset class investing. 'A quick primer in the theory' spins through an elegant theoretical construct called the Efficient Markets Hypothesis and looks at the challengers to this new orthodoxy – in partic-ular we focus on the academics who have been digging away at the inefficiencies of markets and what that tells us about winning future strategies. We'll also take a look at precisely what an index is – we'll look at our own FTSE 100 – and how they are actually constructed.

In Chapter 3 we take that journey in the development of the thinking behind index funds right up to the current day, looking at the sheer variety of funds and structures, running through all the different types of index tracking funds you might encounter as you build your portfolio. We make no apologies for the fact that in this journey you will encounter a blizzard of acronyms and jargon, but stick with it, because the diversity of products and structures offers enormous advantages.

In Chapter 4 we take a slight detour and delve into the world of commodity index tracking funds – this most alternative of asset classes has boomed in recent years as new fund structures have emerged that allow investors to invest in everything from carbon credits to coffee, by going long or short. This commodities boom has spawned a whole new sub-culture of funds and investors, complete with its own peculiar language.

We return to the mainstream of index tracking funds in Chapter 5, written by indexing guru Paul Amery from Index Universe. He takes all these structures and products (including commodity-based funds) and puts them under the microscope. The chapter picks out some issues to look out for, examines risks inherent in complex subjects like counterparty risk and asks some probing questions about the construction of indices.

Chapter 6 picks up on some debates first encountered in Chapter 2 and takes us on a quick detour into the world of fundamental index funds in the company of fund manager Rob Davies, from the Munro Fund, who runs his own dividend-weighted unit trust. He reminds us of the academic work that provides the foundation for this growing niche and tests out whether funds that use measures like dividends or book value really do provide extra returns.

Building your portfolio

By Chapter 7 we are ready to get into the nitty gritty of how you might use index funds in your portfolio. James Norton, a financial planner and investment director at Evolve Financial Planning, kicks off our investigation of how to build the better portfolio by examining why asset allocation is so important and why you might need something called a glidepath for future success.

In Chapter 8 Dr Stephen Barber of stockbrokers Selftrade looks at how you might juggle different investing styles and themes in a portfolio – how you might, for instance, juggle momentum investing with emerging markets or even alternative assets.

By and large most investors using index funds use a fairly conventional buy-and-hold, long-term investing approach, but a small band of hardy souls – chief among them Mark Glowrey from research firm Investors Intelligence – adopts a much more aggressive approach. In Chapter 9 Glowrey and Tarquin Coe examine how you might use ETFs by overlaying technical analysis to construct a portfolio that is much more short term focused and tactical.

In Chapter 10 we start to look at what asset class investing might mean for private investors. We look at some common issues and challenges encountered when trying to build a portfolio – should you rebalance frequently and should you use only index tracking funds? Are equities really such a good idea in volatile markets? How much do you need to diversify? All these questions and more will be tackled in this penultimate chapter.

In the final chapter we put some flesh on these bones and detail a set of model portfolios built on key indices or markets. These model portfolios are not the very best or most optimised portfolios, but they are easy to build and should provide you with the outline or backbone of a portfolio that should last over the long term. Whether they make you any money we can't predict – they are not tips! Markets are volatile and mostly fairly random creatures, but by using some of the principles outlined in this book you should at least have a well thought through portfolio, full of cheap and efficient trackers that will do most of the heavy lifting for you.

The very last section of the book is our Essential 25, which is not some music hit parade but a look at the key 25 markets or indices you should seriously consider buying exposure to. With each of the Top 25 we will detail the index, how it is built, past returns and risks and examine the funds available to track this index.

Full circle

One last observation: what am I doing with my portfolio all these years on since that epiphany back in 2001? It is jam packed full of ETFs and index tracking funds, but I haven't entirely kicked the active management habit or the stock-picking addiction. I use a core of trackers – ETFs – but I still layer it with some cheap stocks and I still use very specialist managers in niche markets where I sense that trackers might prove difficult (a discussion we'll have in the next chapter when we examine the limits of efficient markets).

My personal bottom line? Index tracking ETFs work for me but I don't use them exclusively. I still think other approaches have some validity. Are index tracking funds the answer to all our investing problems? Of course not, but they are still the best way of capturing key trends and markets in a cheap, efficient and diversified manner. Ignore them at your peril!

2

A quick primer on the theory – or how we got here

'An "efficient" market is defined as a market where there are large numbers of rational, profit-maximizers actively competing with each trying to predict future market values of individual securities, and where important current information is almost freely available to all participants.'

Eugene Fama[1]

'There is an old joke, widely told among economists, about an economist strolling down the street with a companion when they come upon a $100 bill lying on the ground. As the companion reaches down to pick it up, the economist says "Don't bother – if it were a real $100 bill, someone would have already picked it up".'

Lo in Lo (1997)

Step back in time to the era of progressive rock, Marc Bolan and the slow but steady collapse of Western capitalism at the hands of wayward unions and the British miners in particular. In 1973 American writer and academic Burton Malkiel wrote *A Random Walk Down Wall Street*, a book that is now rightly regarded as an investment classic. The Random Walk thesis and its more developed sibling, the Efficient Markets Hypothesis (EMH to the uninitiated), are both crucial to an understanding of modern investment theory.

At their core sits a simple proposition that suggests that the past movement or direction of the price of a stock or overall market cannot be used to predict its future movement. Put simply, these theories argue that both logic and available evidence suggest that markets by and large get it right when it comes to pricing a share or a market, that you as an investor cannot beat that outcome most of the time and that the best, cheapest and most efficient thing to do is to follow the market by copying it via an index fund. If this quick summary suffices as an explanation, you should probably skip this chapter and start to examine the structures on offer.

As we will discover in this brief saunter around the most hotly contested bit of the investment economics war zone, this theory – EMH – has huge ramifications for all investors, suggesting as it does that attempting to stock pick is no worse than betting on the horses. More importantly, this theory and its various spin-offs have played a crucial part in the development of the index/tracker fund revolution.

But there are some nagging doubts – common sense suggests that buying cheap shares is a great idea and that when markets are booming, popular momentum stocks are the place to be. If so, you are asking all the right questions – not everyone in the investment economics wonderland has entirely bought into the efficient markets grand narrative, and if these renegades are right there is an awful lot of money to be made at the margins, mining the inefficiencies of a market that is clearly not perfect.

It is a hugely compelling debate and features some of the modern masters of academic finance – great names like Burton Malkiel and Eugene Fama, who in turn draw on slightly less well-known but influential figures such as French mathematician Louis Bachelier and English statistician Maurice Kendall.

This roll call of economic greats starts though with the genesis of a painfully simple idea, namely that of the random walk.

Taking a random walk on the wild side

Although the story that unfolds in the next few pages largely belongs to the current generation of award-winning American economists – notably Burton Malkiel and Eugene Fama – the development of the Efficient Markets Hypothesis has its roots in the work of a number of earlier, leading theoreticians and investment researchers, all puzzled by the seemingly 'random' distribution of prices in a very liquid market like the stock market. The first attempt to sketch an outline of what became known as the random walk of share prices came from a French mathematician, Louis Bachelier, who penned a dissertation called 'The Theory of Speculation' in 1900.

Bachelier deserves a book all by himself – he is one of those classic mathematicians whose work was initially rejected by the mainstream but was eventually revealed to be decades ahead of its time. Bachelier also has the disadvantage that he outlined the precepts of Brownian random motion not in 'trendy' physics – five years ahead of Einstein's celebrated study of the phenomenon – but in the dreary world of finance, a subject of much distaste to many bourgeois, capitalist-hating French intellectuals. His view is summed up in one key observation, namely that 'there is no useful information contained in historical price movements of securities', although his more pungent observation that 'the mathematical expectation of the speculator is zero' is possibly more relevant to modern investors endlessly chasing elusive profits from hot tips. Just in case the lay reader was in any doubt as to Bachelier's view of speculators, the opening paragraph of his 1900 dissertation nails its colours firmly to the mast, stating that 'past, present and even discounted future events are reflected in market price, but often show no apparent relation to price changes'.

In these simple words Bachelier outlined the foundation stone of modern investment economics – in his view share prices change unpredictably based on the result of unexpected information appearing in the market. Many observers have taken this simple idea and suggested that his theory requires that share price changes move randomly for no rational reason. Bachelier, by contrast, maintained that it is not the changes in share prices that are random but the news that influences that pricing that is random. In essence news is unpredictable – that is its definition after all, it is new(s)– and so investors behave rationally by reacting to this unpredictable news. The unpredictable prompts the eminently predictable!

Bachelier's work lay largely dormant and unnoticed for many decades until the work of another theoretician came to prominence, that of Maurice Kendall, one of those wonderfully talented statisticians that Britain seems to excel at. A genuine polymath – much of his most influential work derives from his spell as head of the World Fertility Survey – Kendall turned his attentions in 1953 to the long-term distribution of returns from shares as well as the price of cotton and wheat, across 19 different indices or markets. Elroy Dimson and Massoud Mussavian, in their review of the rise of the EMH, note that Kendall and his team of researchers were by now using relatively advanced computer processing technology to study long series of price returns.[2] Kendall's assumption was that this new technology could 'analyse an economic time series by extracting from it a long-term movement, or trend, for separate study and then scrutinising the residual portion for short-term oscillatory movements and random fluctuations' (Kendall, 1953).[3] According to Dimson and Mussavian, when 'Kendall examined 22 UK stock and commodity price series, however, the results surprised him. Looking at what statisticians call serial correlations – repeated analysis of the relationships between a series of outcomes – Kendall concluded that 'this series looks like a wandering one, almost as if once a week the Demon of Chance drew a random number from a symmetrical population of fixed dispersion and added it to the current price to determine the next week's price ... The data behave almost like wandering series'.

In 1959 American astrophysicist M. F. Maury Osborne drew upon Kendall's observations and outlined a hypothesis that share prices follow a geometric Brownian motion – it is also worth noting that Osborne worked in detail on the study of risk and extremely unlikely events and was the first to identify what later became known as fat tail risk or events, i.e. big financial crashes that are supposed to be very unlikely but in reality prove to be depressingly common and frequent.

One key insight from the Random Walk Theory made its mark, notably that because price movements will not follow any pattern or trend, you cannot use past price movements to predict future price movements – don't try to second guess the market because you will fail as randomness and reversion to mean will be your undoing! The logic of the random walk idea also suggests that if the flow of information is 'unimpeded', i.e. news channels do their job unhindered and information is immediately reflected in stock prices, then tomorrow's price change will reflect only tomorrow's news and will be independent of the price changes today.

In 1973 in his seminal book *A Random Walk Down Wall Street* Burton Malkiel famously summed up the idea that 'experts' cannot add any value to this random walk by suggesting that 'a blindfolded chimpanzee throwing darts at *The Wall Street Journal* could select a portfolio that would do as well as the experts'.[4] From these building blocks – suggesting that returns from shares are fundamentally random – all that was needed was a causal theory to explain the motives behind participants in this random market. Enter the Efficient Markets Hypothesis.

Many of the basics of this unifying theory came via a diehard fan of Bachelier's work, noted US economist Paul Samuelson. His 1965 paper began with the observation that 'in competitive markets there is a buyer for every seller. If one could be sure that a price would rise, it would have already risen'. According to Dimson and Mussavian, Samuelson asserted that 'arguments like this are used to deduce that competitive prices must display price changes... that perform a random walk with no predictable bias'. Samuelson explains that 'we would expect people in the market place, in pursuit of avid and intelligent self-interest, to take account of those elements of future events that in a probability sense may be discerned to be casting their shadows before them'.[5]

Samuelson's work started to lay out the conceptual building blocks of this new hypothesis of efficient markets. Although the maths that sit behind this theory are as elegant as they are sometimes impenetrable to the untrained eye, the Efficient Markets Hypothesis is not, in truth, a complicated concept to understand. At the core of the theory sits one key assertion – that an 'efficient market is one that quickly adjusts prices to reflect all available public information about the future prospects of an investment',[6] a familiar idea from the random walk thesis. When it comes to setting a price for a stock or a bond, potential buyers and sellers use the best information available to them. Add up all these individual approximations and estimations and you have the market price of a stock which is equivalent to the market's estimation of the 'fair' price.

Although no one academic completely developed the elegant framework that sits behind the EMH, one economist – a certain Eugene Fama – stands head and shoulders above the rest. If you feel so inclined you can easily download his seminal research paper from 1970, 'Efficient capital markets: a review of theory and empirical work'.[7]

In this relatively short work he outlines the key attributes of the EMH, including the idea that:

- 'the primary role of the capital market is allocation of the economy's capital stock';
- the market requires accurate signals to correctly allocate scarce resources, or as Burton Malkiel puts it in a later paper, 'when information arises, the news spreads very quickly and is incorporated into the prices of securities without delay. Thus, neither technical analysis, which is the study of past stock prices in an attempt to predict future prices, nor even fundamental analysis, which is the analysis of financial information such as company earnings, asset values, etc., to help investors select 'undervalued' stocks, would enable an investor to achieve returns greater than those that could be obtained by holding a randomly selected portfolio of individual stocks with comparable risk';[8]
- the outcome of this allocative framework is a market in which prices always fully reflect the available information, i.e. an efficient market;
- an 'efficient' market is thus defined as a market where there are large numbers of rational, profit maximisers, actively competing, with each trying to predict future market values of individual securities, and where important current information is almost freely available to all participants;

■ in an efficient market at any point in time the actual price of a security will be a good estimate of its intrinsic value;

■ if a market is efficient, no information or analysis can be expected to result in outperformance of an appropriate index or benchmark.

Proof for this framework is now the subject of academic orthodoxy, but the early pioneers focused on two specific examples. The first was called 'event studies' – in essence how the market reacted to specific news-based events in the subsequent pricing of shares. Dimson and Mussavian, in their review of this new orthodoxy, reveal the conclusion reached by Fama and his team – that 'the market appears to anticipate the information, and most of the price adjustment is complete before the event is revealed to the market. When news is released, the remaining price adjustment takes place rapidly and accurately'. A study by Fama et al. (1969), in particular, demonstrates that prices reflect not only direct estimates of prospective performance by the sample companies but also information that requires more subtle interpretation.[9]

These studies nailed the first leg of the Efficient Markets Hypothesis – what later became known as the weak efficient market. Fama and his comrades then moved on to a tougher nut – surely insiders trading on their exclusive knowledge (their inside track) would be able to make extra returns. If Fama could prove that even this failed to produce extra profits consistently over time, then he could prove what became known as a strong form of efficient markets. This particular proof was not to come from Fama though – researchers around the world had been studying the returns of fund managers whose job it was to capture this inside track and make a quick buck with their funds. Dimson and Mussavian report on the key research from Michael Jensen in 1968 that analysed 115 fund managers' performance over the period 1955–1964.[10] On a risk-adjusted basis, he finds that any advantage that the portfolio managers might have is consumed by fees and expenses. Even if investment management fees and loads are added back to performance measures, and returns are measured gross of management expenses (i.e. assuming research and other expenses were obtained free), Jensen concludes that *'on average the funds apparently were not quite successful enough in their trading activities to recoup even their brokerage expenses'*.[11]

With this research Fama had found his proof for not only a weak form of market efficiency but a strong one. A number of different forms of efficient markets were now presented to a sceptical world.

- A 'weak' efficient market claims all past market prices and data are fully reflected in securities prices. The bottom line? Don't bother trying to use clever systems to predict price movements as they will fail.

- 'Semistrong' argues that all publicly available information is fully reflected in the share price. This attacks the arguments of value investors by suggesting that fundamental analysis is misguided, i.e. that a share has an intrinsic value based on, say, its assets securities prices.

- The 'strong' form asserts that all information is fully reflected in a share's price. In other words, even insider information is of no use.

In essence, Fama's concept of the EMH suggests that because stock markets are vibrant, hugely liquid spaces, flooded with tens of thousands of intelligent, well-paid and well-educated investors seeking to make a return on the market by looking for a system or trying to find cheap shares, information becomes dispersed ever more quickly and efficiently and the pricing that results becomes ever more accurate and thus efficient.

Efficient markets, rational actors?

Crucially, although most commentators and the general public have assumed that this theory requires all market participants to be rational, EMH theoreticians have never believed this to be true. According to Fama, markets can be efficient even when a group of investors is almost completely irrational – all you need are more rational players like traders to exist who will make money by trading on or 'arbitraging away' those combined inefficiencies.

To understand this subtle distinction let's assume that a room full of schoolchildren is set the challenge to establish a market in a share certificate about which most of them know very little. They might all approach this irrationally, investing in each piece of paper their own behavioural biases and fantasies. Some unrealistic prices may appear based on the perceptions of the underlying value of these shares, but all an efficient market requires is one knowledgeable actor or trader in the room to effectively take advantage of the other players and establish a fair price or market clearing price. That arb, as they are called, might make a killing and some other children might feel deeply aggrieved – but an efficient price eventually emerges notwithstanding these problems and emotions.

Another key attribute mistakenly pinned on the EMH world view is that a share's price accurately represents the value of the underlying business based on certain key fundamentals like the profit rate or the assets on the balance sheet. Efficient market theorists make no such claim – the EMH simply suggests that the share price of a company represents only an aggregation of the probabilities of all future outcomes for the company, based on the best information available at the time, with all the market participants. To return to our room full of children, the price that is established is not a right one as such, i.e. an objective analysis of the value of the share, but simply the price based on the willingness to pay of participants in that room based on their own (frequently mistaken) perceptions of future value plus one key knowledgeable efficient market maker. As one commentator put it: 'EMH does not require a stock's price to reflect a company's future performance, just the best possible estimate or forecast of future performance that can be made with publicly available information. That estimate may still be grossly wrong without violating EMH.'

One last crucial clarification – in reality, markets are neither perfectly efficient nor perfectly inefficient. All markets are efficient to a certain extent, some more so than others. The key observation here is that where news/information flows are less efficient, the less efficient the market will be and the more likely it will be that discrepancies will emerge. A classic example of this phenomenon is in emerging markets space, in places like China or Russia. Crucial market information comes from insiders such as the company management, who do not always completely level with their wider shareholder base. Governments can also interfere with market processes, favour insiders or rivals and generally corrupt the information flows that a free market depends on. And not all these opaque markets are in the developing world – arguably the private equity space for one depends on varied information flows plus insider knowledge that cannot be efficiently and speedily recognised in the publicly listed share price. But – and here is the key observation – the bigger this market grows, and the more obvious these pricing inefficiencies are, the more professional traders will emerge who will arbitrage out or trade away these inefficiencies, making themselves a large amount of profit (note that EMH theorists recognise that arbitrage-based professionals can indeed make a profit via inefficiency) and deepening the pool of liquidity in the market, making it in turn more conventional and more efficient over time. The key conceptual point here is that as markets grow, they become more efficient and liquid, and as they mature those inefficiencies decline as more arbs emerge to make money out of the dwindling inefficiencies.

The critics

Many varied lines of attack against the EMH have emerged over the last few decades, some emanating from within the EMH school, others from outside schools based around classic value investing or behavioural economics influenced by modern cognitive pyschology. Some economists, mathematicians and market practitioners do not believe that man-made markets are inherently efficient, especially when there are good reasons for that inefficiency, including the slow diffusion of information, the undue power of some market participants (e.g. financial institutions) and the existence of apparently sophisticated professional investors. It is worth understanding the huge range of these critical voices because they have all helped shape various interesting and unorthodox indexing investment strategies – strategies that have in turn ended up in novel ETFs and tracker funds.

One of the earliest attacks on the EMH looked at the way that markets react to surprising news – this is perhaps the most visible flaw in the Efficient Market Hypothesis (called underreaction to new information by its observers). For example, news events such as surprise interest rate changes from central banks are not instantaneously taken account of in stock prices, but rather cause sustained movement of prices over periods ranging from hours to months. Recent work by Lo and MacKinlay (1999), for instance, finds that this phenomenon is clearly observable, leading them to reject the random walk thesis.[12] Even Malkiel himself, a great defender of the Efficient Markets Hypothesis in public debates – accepts that 'there does seem to be some momentum in short-run stock prices'. Malkiel also points to research from Lo, Mamaysky and Wang (2000), who find, through the use of sophisticated statistical techniques that can recognise patterns, that some of the stock-price signals used by 'technical analysts', such as 'head and shoulders' formations and 'double bottoms', may actually have some modest predictive power, i.e. that they can predict prices in the short term.[13]

You do not have to use technical analysis to understand the overall outline of this 'inefficient' phenomenon – investors see a share price rising and are drawn into the market in a kind of 'bandwagon effect'. Robert Shiller (2000) also described the late 1990s, stock market boom (or should we say bubble) as the result of psychological contagion leading to irrational exuberance. Behaviouralist economists like James Montier at investment bank SocGen offer their own explanation for this short-run momentum – a tendency for investors to underreact to new information and distinguish statistical significance from economic significance. EMH enthusiasts certainly seem to accept that this phenomenon can exist, but Eugene Fama found that underreaction to information is about as common as overreaction and that 'post-event continuation of abnormal returns is as frequent as post-event reversals', i.e. the inefficiency can work both ways and is not a workable trading strategy. The killer rebuttal, though, to the whole 'momentum' as strategy argument is also the most obvious – once you have spotted the phenomenon and try to make a profit from it, the pattern begins to fade away, or as Malkiel puts it, 'many predictable patterns seem to disappear after they are published in the finance literature'.

Another take on the behavioural oddities of investors comes courtesy of those who observe a discrepancy between EMH and actual, real markets at their most extreme, where irrational behaviour becomes the norm, i.e. as a bubble starts to burst. Towards the end of a crash, markets go into free fall as participants extricate themselves from positions regardless of the unusually good value that those positions represent. Perhaps the most biting attack comes via something called the Grossman–Stiglitz paradox – if markets really are that efficient and everyone knows, no one will bother to beat the market and the market will begin to wither. In their 2001 Nobel Economics award 'for their analyses of markets with asymmetric information', Joseph Stiglitz and Sanford Grossman claimed that the very idea of efficient markets is inherently paradoxical – if a market was 'informationally efficient' (all relevant information was reflected in market prices), then no single agent would have sufficient incentive to acquire the information on which prices are based. Markets may as well be run by computers in the background, banishing all human experts to day jobs serving hamburgers at McDonald's!

These discrepancies and theoretical attacks are dwarfed, however, by a more thorough criticism of supposedly efficient markets which suggests that repeated patterns do in fact occur in markets that are clearly not efficient and that this ever present reality offers investors numerous opportunities to make a profit. The simplest way of understanding this is to look at the small number of investors who have outperformed the market over long periods of time, in a way which it is statistically unreasonable to attribute to good luck, including investment sages such as Warren Buffett, Peter Lynch, Bill Miller and Anthony Bolton, until recently head of the star fund at Fidelity. These investors' strategies are, to a large extent, based on identifying markets where prices do not accurately reflect the available information, in direct contradiction to the EMH which explicitly implies that no such opportunities exist.

Warren Buffett in particular has on several occasions stated that the EMH is not correct, maintaining that 'I'd be a bum on the street with a tin cup if the markets were always efficient' and that 'the professors who taught efficient market theory said that someone throwing darts at the stock tables could select a stock portfolio having prospects just as good as one selected by the brightest, most hard-working securities analyst. Observing correctly that the market was frequently efficient, they went on to conclude incorrectly that it was always efficient'. Some rigorous academic evidence for Buffett's contentions comes from a big Vanguard study on the importance of asset allocation and diversification in fund management.[15] The report mainly supports classic efficient market theories' suspicion of stock picking as an art form, but it does state that *'a small percentage – 7 per cent – of actively managed balanced funds have been able to consistently outperform their policy benchmarks'*. A grand total of 7 per cent may not sound much, but in a very diverse and well-populated market full of thousands of fund managers, that is actually an awful lot of successful fund managers with a great long-term track record. Either these fund managers are practising some mysterious form of market magic or the Efficient Markets Hypothesis has some pretty big holes in it.

More risk, greater returns

How do these star managers produce their super-sized returns? Many mainstream investment economists maintain that these star fund managers simply capitalise on a series of factors (as they are known) which contribute extra risk, and extra rewards, for those sophisticated enough to know where to look. This nuanced view accepts that you can make extra returns but only by taking on more risk, and that this extra risk is found only in certain places within the efficient market.

One of these additional forms of factor risk has been called the size risk by economists – this simply suggests that smaller companies grow faster than bigger companies and thus produce greater returns. Thus any strategy that focuses on small caps or even tiny micro-caps (sub £10m in market cap) will produce exceptional returns over certain periods of time – even Burton Malkiel, in his study of the critiques of EMH, points to data since 1926 which suggests that small-company stocks in the United States have produced rates of return over one percentage point larger than the returns from large stocks (citing another study by Keim, 1983).[16]

Fama and French (1992) have also broken with some of their peers and backed this concept.[17] They examined data from 1963 to 1990 and divided all shares into deciles according to their size as measured by total capitalisation.

The results, according to the two professors, showed a clear tendency for the deciles made up of portfolios of smaller stocks to generate higher average monthly returns than deciles made up of larger stocks. It is worth quickly noting one key caveat made by Malkiel, an erstwhile supporter of Fama and French's work except when it comes to the scale effect – he notes that 'from the mid-1980s through the decade of the 1990s, there has been no gain from holding smaller stocks. Thus, a researcher who examined the ten-year performance of today's small companies would be measuring the performance of those companies that survived – not the ones that failed'.

Another extra form of risk is sometimes called distress risk, although it is also known as the value premium. This is the risk of owning companies that the market perceives as being in some form of financial trouble. While none of us would choose to invest in a single company in potentially big trouble – that distress could be defined as a poor balance sheet or falling earnings or even loss – indices of 'value' stocks have historically offered very high returns precisely because most investors follow the crowd and target what are called growth companies, i.e. companies growing fast, that sport expensive share prices relative to their profits. From this simple observation – noted time and time again by analysts for 50 years – has emerged a whole new branch of the efficient markets school. This schism even has its own moniker – the fundamentalists – and a belief system that suggests that key measures of value (using key balance sheet and profit measures) are crucial to explaining why some shares do better than others.

The rise of fundamentals-based index investing

The hard work digging into the numbers that 'prove' the value premium comes from French and Fama. In 1997 French looked at data on the entire universe of US stocks for the period 1964–2000 (see Table 2.1). He found that small cap stocks that were also good 'value' produced returns of 15.66 per cent compared with 'poor value' (growth) small caps which gave just 10.15 per cent. Likewise for larger companies that were good 'value' – they returned 14.28 per cent compared with 11.49 per cent for low-value peers. French and Fama's bottom line – take on extra risk and invest in both the size premium and the value effect and you can earn an additional 4–7 per cent per year.

Table 2.1 Historical simulation results (in US dollars)

Time span	Index	Annual compound return	Annual standard deviation
1964–2000	Fama French US Large Value Index	14.28%	17.83%
	S&P 500 Index	11.90%	15.92%
	Fama/French US Large Growth Index	11.49%	18.65%
1964–2000	Fama/French US Small Value Index	15.66%	25.89%
	CRSP 6 – 10 Index	13.35%	25.52%
	Fama/French US Small Growth Index	10.15%	30.40%
1975–2000	Fama/French International Value Index	18.26%	20.61%
	International Small Company Index	18.07%	27.44%
	MSCI EAFE Index	13.69%	20.58%

Source: Fama/French, cited at www.dfaus.com/library/articles/index_enhanced_funds

Figure 2.1 presents an even more fascinating paradox – it establishes an inverse relationship between profitability and average share returns. The bottom line? Value stocks and small cap stocks that are less profitable than faster growing equivalent stocks produce greater share price returns. In effect this analysis suggests that efficient markets don't behave in quite the way economists first imagined.

As fundamental indexing fund management firm Dimensional puts it: 'Everything we have learned about expected returns in the equity markets can be summarized in three dimensions. The first is that stocks are riskier than bonds and have greater expected returns. Relative performance among stocks is largely driven by the two other dimensions: small/large and value/growth. Many economists believe small cap and value stocks outperform because the market rationally discounts their prices to reflect underlying risk. The lower prices give investors greater upside as compensation for bearing this risk.'[18]

Another variant on this idea of the value premium is to look at what some called cheap stocks, or bombed-out shares to you and I – shares that have crashed in price. A strong school of contrarian thinking suggests that buying these unpopular stocks can produce huge long-term outperformance for those willing to be patient, mainly because markets overreact in

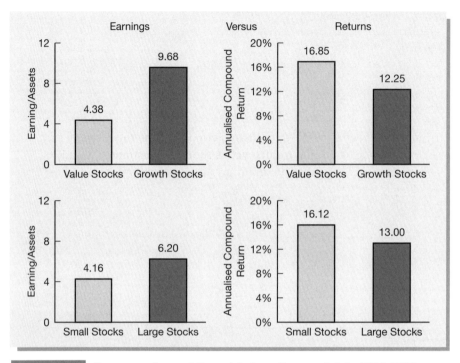

Figure 2.1 Company size and financial strength annual data 1964–2000

Notes: Earnings/assets through 1999 due to availability.

Source: Fama/French, cited at www.dfaus.com/library/articles/index_enhanced_funds

their punishment of certain shares and eventually the market is forced to admit the error of its ways by marking up prices. DeBondt and Thaler (1995), for example, argue that investors are subject to waves of optimism and pessimism which cause prices to crash below their fundamental value (the value of assets for instance) – give the market a few years and these prices revert to mean and reward the brave contrarian.[19] Looking at very long-term horizons they found that 'stocks which have underperformed the most over a three- to five-year period average the highest market-adjusted returns over the subsequent period, and vice versa'.

Dividend payouts also feature prominently in the arguments of value investors who attack the Efficient Markets Hypothesis on a number of fronts. Academics like Jeremy Siegel at Wharton Business School and James Montier, an analyst at French investment bank SocGen, argue that buying high-yielding stocks cheaply makes analytical sense – Montier has produced evidence that close to 80 per cent of medium-term returns from holding shares can be attributed to the actual dividend payout and the market's expectation of future higher dividend payouts.

But Fluck, Malkiel and Quandt (1997) discovered in their analysis that investors 'who simply purchase a portfolio of individual stocks with the highest dividend yields in the market will not earn a particularly high rate of return' – simply buying the highest yielders does not always produce abnormal returns.[20] Critics of this blind, buy-all high-yielders approach also like to point to 'Dogs of the Dow Strategy'. This US-based strategy involves buying the ten stocks in the Dow Jones Industrial Average with the highest dividend yields. Over many periods of time this strategy has produced some exceptional results, yet as soon as the strategy found its way into mutual funds, that premium mysteriously disappeared. Malkiel observes that 'such funds have generally underperformed the market averages during the 1995–99 period'.[21]

Yet another camp of fundamentals-based investors looks specifically to shares with low price–earnings multiples – that is where the stream of profits, expressed as earnings, is at a low multiple to the share price. In many studies these low price to earnings (PE) shares appear to provide higher rates of return than those shares with high PE ratios, i.e. where the share price is many more times greater than the low level of earnings. Nicholson (1960), Ball (1978) and Basu (1977) have all published papers looking at this particular market inefficiency and their results tend to confirm the view of the behaviouralist-inclined economists who think that investors tend to be overconfident of their ability to project high earnings growth and thus overpay for 'growth' stocks (for example, Kahneman and Riepe, 1998). Similar results have been shown for price/cash flow multiples, where cash flow is defined as earnings plus depreciation and amortisation (Hawawini and Keim, 1995).

This constant hum of research and debate has given shape to a whole new way of building indices – fundamentally weighted index funds mapped in detail by Rob Davies in Chapter 6 in this book. Its simple outline and form has been defined by Fama, now adviser to Dimensional: 'I agree that stock picking is gambling,' says Fama. 'I don't agree that the only legitimate indexing approach is holding the market portfolio.' Fama clearly articulates a view that simply 'buying the market' is itself buying a rather arbitrary portfolio of stocks. 'It gives a heavy weighting to financially healthy stocks and a light weighting to distressed stocks. Don't get me wrong: it's hard to fault a market index approach. But if there's more than one type of risk driving returns, it's possible for investors to use a wider range of strategies to gain greater expected returns – all within the bounds of indexing.'[22]

The efficient markets purists' counter attack

'I am convinced that Benjamin Graham (1965) was correct in suggesting that while the stock market in the short run may be a voting mechanism, in the long run it is a weighing mechanism. True value will win out in the end. And before the fact, there is no way in which investors can reliably exploit any anomalies or patterns that might exist. I am skeptical that any of the "predictable patterns" that have been documented in the literature were ever sufficiently robust so as to have created profitable investment opportunities and after they have been discovered and publicized, they will certainly not allow investors to earn excess returns.'

Burton Malkiel[23]

Academics supportive of the Efficient Markets Hypothesis in its purer forms do not dispute the weight of evidence that suggests some kind of value premium exists, especially if it is combined with the size risk. But as Burton Malkiel puts it, 'these findings do not necessarily imply inefficiency. They may simply indicate failure of the capital asset pricing model to capture all the dimensions of risk' – see the box on the CAPM on page 38. They also wonder aloud whether this observed past phenomenon is that relevant to current markets – according to Malkiel, Fama and French's own data suggests 'the period from the early 1960s through 1990 may have been a unique period in which value stocks rather consistently produced higher rates of return'. In other words, what worked in the past may not be relevant to current markets, and even if it does still exist, it is nigh on impossible to capture through any sensible investment policy.

Fluck, Malkiel and Quandt (1997) recognised that the price-reversal strategy mentioned above does seem to exist – over a 13-year period during the 1980s and early 1990s they simulated a strategy of buying stocks that had had particularly poor returns over the past three to five years.[24] According to Malkiel, his team found that 'stocks with very low returns over the past three to five years had higher returns in the next period, and that stocks with very high returns over the past three to five years had lower returns in the next period'. Crucially, though, they also found that 'returns in the next period were similar for both groups, so they could not confirm that a contrarian approach would yield higher-than-average returns. There was a statistically strong pattern of return reversal, but not one that implied inefficiency in the market that would enable investors to make excess returns', i.e. the phenomenon of means reversion might work but it would be very difficult to run it as a trading strategy.

This cynicism about the ability of investors to actually capture these inefficiencies received some support from a study by Schwert (2001), which pointed out that the investment firm of Dimensional Fund Advisors actually began a mutual fund that selected value stocks quantitatively according to the Fama and French (1993) criteria (the firm's academic consultant is Eugene Fama).[25] The abnormal return of such a portfolio (adjusting for beta, the capital asset pricing model measure of risk) was a negative 0.2 per cent per month over the 1993–1998 period, according to Schwert.

An exchange at a symposium about a decade ago between Robert Shiller, an economist who is sympathetic to the argument that stock prices are partially predictable but sceptical about market efficiency, and Richard Roll, an academic financial economist who is also a portfolio manager, beautifully demonstrates this debate about actually capturing these supposed inefficiencies (Roll and Shiller, 1992). After Shiller stressed the importance of inefficiencies in the pricing of stocks, Roll responded as follows:

> 'I have personally tried to invest money, my clients' money and my own, in every single anomaly and predictive device that academics have dreamed up. … I have attempted to exploit the so-called year-end anomalies and a whole variety of strategies supposedly documented by academic research. And I have yet to make a nickel on any of these supposed market inefficiencies … a true market inefficiency ought to be an exploitable opportunity. If there's nothing investors can exploit in a systematic way, time in and time out, then it's very hard to say that information is not being properly incorporated into stock prices.'[26]

The point here is that while many investment economists are willing to concede that there some efficiencies, they doubt whether these form a pattern and that if they do persist, whether these patterns will self-destruct in the future, as so many have done once they have been observed.

This almost philosophical notion that once a regular pattern has been observed, it ceases to exist by the very act of recognition and cognition is beautifully summed up in the following example from Burton Malkiel.

> 'Suppose there is a truly dependable and exploitable January effect, that the stock market – especially stocks of small companies – will generate extraordinary returns during the first five days of January. What will investors do? They will buy on the last day of December, and sell on January 5. But then investors find that the market rallied on the last day of December and so they will need to begin to buy on the next-to-last day of December; and because there is so much 'profit taking' on January 5, investors will have to sell on January 4 to take advantage of this effect. Thus, to beat the gun, investors will have to be buying earlier and earlier in December and selling earlier and earlier in January so that eventually the pattern will self-destruct.'

Some factors that produce extra risk and possible extra returns

Equity factors

Market	Stocks have higher expected returns than fixed income.
Size	Small company stocks have higher expected returns than large company stocks.
Price	Lower-priced 'value' stocks have higher expected returns than higher-priced 'growth' stocks.

Fixed income factors

Maturity	Longer-term instruments are riskier than shorter-term instruments.
Default	Instruments of lower credit quality are riskier than instruments of higher credit quality.

The single strongest argument made by efficient markets purists is, then, perhaps the simplest – if it is so obvious, why don't lots and lots of professional investors make super-sized profits as a result? Surely, this argument goes, professional fund managers should be busy trading away these inefficiencies and thus consistently beating the markets. The reality, as we discovered in the previous chapter, is that the vast majority of 'expert' fund managers singularly fail to capture these returns. Perhaps the best summary comes from Jack Tryenor, who wrote the following in the *Financial Analysis Journal* in 1981.

> *'I believe in a third view of market efficiency, which holds that the securities market will not always be either quick or accurate in processing new information. On the other hand, it is not easy to transform the resulting opportunities to trade profitably against the market consensus into superior portfolio performance. Unless the active investor understands what really goes on in the trading game, he can easily convert even superior research information into the kind of performance that will drive his clients to the poorhouse . . . why aren't more active investors consistently successful? The answer lies in the cost of trading.'*[27]

The Capital Asset Pricing Model (CAPM)

This is an economic model that describes the relationship between risk and return. It allows an investor to work out the rate of return on an asset like a share, if it is to be added to an already well-diversified portfolio, given a certain level of risk. The model is based around another deceptively simple idea, namely that higher returns are possible only if you take on higher risks. In essence it looks at risk, the expected rate of return and the equivalent return from something called a risk-free asset, like cash or bonds.

An equation sits at the heart of this model which looks something like this:

$$E(R_i) = R_f + \beta_i(E(R_m) - R_f)$$

Where:

- $E(R_i)$ is the expected return on the share or security
- R_f is the risk-free rate of return from something like bonds or cash
- β_i is the beta
- $(E(R_m)$ is the expected return of the market
- $E(R_m) - R_f$ is sometimes known as the market premium or risk premium (the difference between the expected market rate of return and the risk-free rate of return).

The CAPM assumes that investors:

- will be rationally risk averse;
- intend to maximise their utility or benefit;
- are price takers and do not influence prices by themselves;
- can lend and borrow as much as they like using the risk-free rate of interest;
- trade with shares and securities that can be sub-divided into small pieces;
- will not incur any transaction or taxation costs.

With the CAPM in hand, investors should be able to work out whether any share or asset class sits sensibly in their portfolios given their appropriate level of risk. They should also be able to construct a graph called the efficient frontier, which shows the very best mix of assets for a given level of risk and reward, i.e. an optimal portfolio that gives the lowest possible level of risk for its level of return.

Clearly a great many analysts do not subscribe to this model – many analysts like James Montier at SocGen think that the assumption that investors will be rationally risk averse is ridiculous and ignores a large amount of evidence that suggests that investors are deeply behaviourally flawed and anything but rational. Many economists with a strong political economy bent also take issue with the idea that investors are simply price takers and do not influence prices by themselves, observing that any study of power in the market place would clearly reveal some substantial asymmetries.

A middle way – the reality of relatively efficient markets

Who are we to believe in this deeply charged debate? A strong case can be made for boiling down all this wealth of data and academic debate into six simple common-sense statements.

1. It's difficult to beat the market

You don't have to believe that all financial markets are completely 'perfect' to believe that most active fund management is a waste of money, most of the time. This is not to deny that some investors and some managers do not add value, some of the time. It is just a simple reality that most of the time, for most managers, you end up paying more for less. This fine balance should not also blind you to the reality that most investors – institutional and private – who use index-based strategies still make use of active fund managers for certain segments and markets.

2. Stock markets are mostly efficient but not always

Even within supposedly perfect markets there are imperfections. Buffett's observation is surely the important one, namely that while markets are mostly perfect, that is a long way from saying they are always perfect, all the time. Even the most ardent fans of perfect markets now accept that certain types of share – with certain risk profiles – can outperform the main market, much if not most of the time. This does not mean that this inefficiency and these market imperfections are easy to capture via some kind of index or fund or that in the future these imperfections will not correct themselves. Inefficiencies have a tendency to change over time and mutate and a rigid adherence to a fixed set of criteria in, say, a black box – an analytical computer-based system – full of variables might be a risky tactic if the markets do adapt and evolve.

3. It is possible to construct strategies that can deliver above-average returns ... some of the time

Equally if a group of professional investors is nimble and fast and able to look into the 'nooks and crannies' of the supposedly efficient markets, it might be able to construct strategies that do capture above-average returns, although those returns might be at the expense of higher potential risk. We will be returning to this idea in Chapter 6 when Rob Davies looks at how the fundamental indexers construct their investment strategies (also see box below on the new indexers).

4. Efficient stock markets do not necessarily behave rationally

The sensible investor recognises that in the debate between behavioural economists who use psychological insights and classical economists who have arrived at the Efficient Markets Hypothesis there is a sensible balance that needs to be struck – both are working towards the same goals from different directions. This is especially true at the macro level of national economies where it is clear that the behavioural insights of economists like Robert Shiller – his analysis of the pathology of booms and busts is deeply relevant – are hugely important in understanding why markets under- and overshoot in setting prices and valuations. It is clear that asset-backed markets like the stock market do not in the aggregate – in toto – behave that efficiently or even perfectly, thus requiring little or no regulation. To be fair to the EMH-based economists, they have never argued that efficient markets are 'perfect 'or that the markets ignore fundamentals-based valuation metrics, just that in aggregate the market is largely efficient. But investors ignore the wisdom of behavioural economists at their peril – their work may well give us causal explanations for market inefficiencies that might matter hugely in terms of our investment decisions.

5. For most investors copying an efficient market cheaply is a sensible long-term bet

The bigger the market, the more liquid it is, and the more liquid it is, the more likely it is to be relatively efficient. In these circumstances the key is to cut costs and be efficient when it comes to tracking these large, efficient markets – it means trying to copy the market most of the time, because most of the time the market is right, rather than trying to second guess it. The simplest way of doing this is to buy a fund that copies the market.

6. If you are going to copy the 'mind of the market', pick your index carefully

The best and most efficient way of copying 'the market' is to find an index that tells us the relative weights that the market attaches to its constituents, i.e. the shares in the market are weighted according to the price placed on those shares and then incorporated into an index. Crucially, not all market indices are created equally – some indices are based on very small and inefficient markets. By copying this kind of market you could be making a big mistake and opening yourself up to extra risk, whereas many markets are very large, very open and very transparent. These latter markets should be easier to track, replicate or copy using an index fund. The bottom line is that the best way to copy the 'mind of the market', as it is called, is to buy an index fund that tracks an index which in turns tracks the pricing decisions of the market.

Those myriad pricing decisions of the relatively efficient market translate through into a share, stock or security price and thus a market capitalisation (the value the market puts on the companies times the number of shares/stocks/securities issued). For most academic theorists the market capitalisation is the best measure of the market – this market cap figure isn't fair, or right, and it changes constantly, but it does represent the only true judgement of the market, namely the value placed on each and every company in the index. Add up all these market capitalisations and you have a total value for the market – an index simply takes this total market and then constructs a list of constituent shares where their percentage of the index is based on their market capitalisation. The key, then, is to buy this liquid and efficient market cheaply and efficiently. As we will discover in the next chapter, constructing an index is a deceptively simple idea, but the structures developed to capture those index returns have become increasingly complicated and varied over the last few decades.

Building the perfect index

In the next chapter we will explore how the rocket scientists and financial whiz-kids of Wall Street and now the City have taken on this challenge of building the perfect index fund. We will witness how a simple challenge from the big institutions – 'buy me the market' – has evolved into a wonderfully complex universe of new fund structures, strange acronyms and almost infinite choice.

Crucially, this explosion of innovation has brought markets ever closer to a vision of an ultimate diversified portfolio – if you want to track a major market or asset class, all you have to do is find an index that tracks that market efficiently and then track down an accompanying index fund. Suddenly the task of building a portfolio that comprises a diversified mix of assets becomes an awful lot easier. Also this profusion of new products and choice means that for those investors disenchanted with the traditional actively managed fund, a more efficient alternative is now on offer.

As we will discover in the next few chapters, though, there is still a big chasm between the theory we have discussed in this chapter and the reality on offer. Not all indices are created equally and investors need to be aware of the risks of investing in some types of index – they need to look in detail at the construction of the index and the risks involved. Crucially they might end up buying into an index tracking fund that apparently tracks an efficient market, efficiently, but in reality discover that tracking error, poor management, high costs and a multitude of other factors involved in the structure of the fund reduce efficiency and diminish returns. Over the next few chapters we will trace the evolution of the index tracking industry, look at the structures, warn about the pitfalls and then examine how you might start using these index funds in a diversified portfolio.

Do the right thing – track and diversify

'Tis the part of a wise man to keep himself today for tomorrow, and not venture all his eggs in one basket.'

Miguel de Cervantes, Don Quixote de la Mancha, 1605

'Behold, the fool saith, "Put not all thine eggs in the one basket" – which is but a manner of saying, "Scatter your money and attention"; but the wise man saith, "Put all your eggs in the one basket and – WATCH that basket".'

Mark Twain, *Pudd'nhead Wilson*, 1894

'A prominent magazine in 1926 recommended that a portfolio contain 25 per cent sound bonds, 25 per cent sound preferreds, 25 per cent sound common stocks, and 25 per cent speculative securities … Until recently [1994], asset allocation was a pedestrian affair. Many institutional investors were advised to allocate 60 per cent of their assets to stocks and 40 per cent to fixed-income.'[28]

Academic economists haven't spent all their time slamming active fund managers and constructing elegant efficient markets theories. They have also spent the last few decades building astonishingly sophisticated analytical frameworks about how to construct the perfect portfolio. At the heart of this work is a focus on diversification.

We have already mentioned this widely abused word when discussing Geoff Considine's portfolios – many investors already intrinsically understand the concept of not putting all your eggs in one basket and practise a primitive form of diversification when it comes to building their portfolios.

Academic economists have obviously taken the obvious and turned it into a much more noble form – modern portfolio theory. We are not going to bore you with a lengthy exposition of the ins and outs of this field, but suffice to say that most investors have three building blocks that comprise their total return:

- the risk-free return – this is usually the rate of return you get from cash, although economists like to use terms like 'the rate that best neutralises your risks';

- return from beta – technically speaking this is the return you get above the risk-free rate of return from holding an asset class like equities or a market. So if the risk-free rate of return is 2 per cent and you buy a tracker for the FTSE All Share index that gives you 8 per cent pa, your beta is 6 per cent;

- return from alpha – this is the tricky one as it is the value added by a manager which is derived by the manager moving away from the beta.

It is important to emphasise that even investors who concentrate on using tracking funds and thus cutting down on costs do make some use of actively managed funds – there are a great many specialised markets where trackers are of more dubious benefit compared with the diligent, research-focused active fund manager.

When investors do trust an active fund manager they want to get the most extra added value from that expertise and that 'extra' added value is called alpha.

The key to understanding diversification is that lots of different kinds of markets and assets – bonds mixed with equities and, say, an alternative asset such as commodities – can give you lots of different betas and if you are lucky those different betas do not move as one, i.e. they are not correlated. Thus if equities go down, bonds might rise in value along with, say, commodities like gold – the key is that mixing up different betas might give you added benefits and improve returns.

In fact, economists are so smitten with the idea of diversification – some call it the diversification premium – that they suggest it is the one free lunch left in investing, although in recent years even that looks like it might now come at a rather hefty price, as we will discover. The prime mover in this field of optimising portfolios through beta was economist Harry Markowitz, who showed how you could combine different asset classes and betas without increasing risk. But it is later economists and analysts who have taken Markowitz's ideas and fleshed them out – Yale's fund manager David Swensen, for instance, has spent decades running hugely diversified portfolios investing in everything from forests through to private equity funds and hedge funds.

The key is that you can now juggle all these different betas in an accessible manner via index tracking funds. Swensen in particular has gone on the record and said that his hugely diversified portfolio is expected to return about 10.1 per cent per year, with expected standard deviation of 11.8 per cent per year, and that for most private investors the only sensible way of achieving that diversification is through index tracking funds. In an interview in the March/April 2009 issue of the Yale Alumni magazine Swensen proclaims: 'With all assets, I recommend that people invest in index funds because they're transparent, understandable, and low-cost … Almost everybody belongs on the passive end of the continuum. A very few belong on the active end. But the unfortunate fact is that an overwhelming number of investors find themselves betwixt and between. In that in-between place, people end up paying high fees, whether to a mutual fund or a stockbroker or another agent. And they end up with disappointing net returns.'

The killer piece of research, though, came in 1991, when three academics looked at what really contributes towards the performance of a portfolio. Brinson, Singer and Beebower looked at a fund manager's market-timing skills, their ability to pick shares or their ability to diversify assets.[29] They studied the largest 91 pension plans in the US over a ten-year period, with portfolio sizes reaching to $3 billion. Yet again the virtues of traditional active fund management were found to be wanting – the academics calculated that only 6 per cent of total returns could be attributed to market timing and stock selection. A massive 94 per cent could be explained by the careful use of diversification and the use of varying asset classes and markets over time. In fact, the study found that traditional active fund management skills like timing and stock picking produced negative returns over time after they had been adjusted for risk. The bottom line? Don't bother picking shares or trying to time the market, just allocate across different asset classes in an intelligent, diversified manner.

Another study, this time by consultants at research firm Ibbotson Associates in Chicago, looked at how including 'alternative' assets like commodities in a well-balanced portfolio could improve returns. They discovered that the average improvement in returns from these uncorrelated assets was worth 133 basis points per annum (1.33 per cent per annum). They also found that 81.4 per cent of the monthly variation in balanced return funds could be accounted for by asset allocation and active diversification. This analysis was backed up by eponymous fund management group Vanguard – big passive investors in the US – who have also studied the importance of active diversification or asset allocation. They found that 76.6 per cent of the monthly variability of a fund's return around its average return depends on its asset-allocation policy.

By now you will be able to see that diversification can work wonders if done properly, especially if you are willing to stack up your portfolio with different types of asset classes. Geoff Considine has even gone so far as to put a number on the value of the diversification premium – between 2 per cent and 2.5 per cent per annum.

Traditionally, though, there has been a problem with trying to put this theory into everyday practice – although active fund managers have launched some funds that cover alternative asset classes, for instance, until recently there has not been an enormous diversity of asset classes with active fund managers. The analysis we have encountered above suggests a rather more exotic and rich diversity is needed – it is possible to do this with actively managed funds nowadays, but it is a lot easier to do with index tracker funds and especially easy if you are willing to use exchange-traded funds, index tracking funds listed on the stock market.

3

Structuring the revolution

Not long ago I spent an entertaining afternoon talking to a focus group on investing. It was one of those amusing sessions organised by publishing companies to find out why so few people in the UK invest in shares.

The publishing director was concerned that the 'pool' of relatively active investors in the UK probably numbered only 500,000 and that that figure had not changed much in a decade. The publisher wanted to know why so many people think that houses are such a good investment compared with shares.

Shares do indeed provide greater returns over the very long term, but they do so with great volatility. In addition, most people do not actually pay themselves for the housing assets they buy – they have a mortgage, which means that their investment in housing assets is geared or on margin. Also, they live in their houses, not in their shares.

The focus group was hugely diverse, made up of people who had either actively invested in funds or shares or were thinking about it. My first set of questions was fairly general and included one about housing (bad) versus equities (good). But then I decided to see whether this group could grasp the logic behind EMH.

To my amazement, most of them understood that you cannot beat the system. Although they aspired, like all natural-born gamblers, to taking a flutter and beating that system (they all loved the idea of tips, of course), they were sufficiently cynical to know it's a mug's game and that it was largely bound to fail. That did not stop them thinking they could do it nevertheless, but it did mean they were arch realists.

When a 45-year-old working mum asked how they were supposed to make money in these stock markets if most fund managers did not actually produce the goods, I replied: 'Buy the market. Simply buy a fund that tracks a big index, like the FTSE 100 I suppose,' trying not to offer any advice whilst also sounding knowledgeable.

I followed up with this group a few months later and to my huge surprise discovered that out of the 12 in the room, 8 had done nothing at all, 2 had ignored the entire discussion and bought some dodgy unit trust offered by a high-street bank, and just 2 had bought a FTSE 100 tracker.

My point in recounting this story is that a great many of the central contentions of the efficient markets hypothesis when applied to stock markets are common sense, based on a kind of cold realism that we British specialise in, a brooding cynicism against all experts and a willingness to work with the system if it makes us a bit wealthier. The group mostly understood the central charges laid against the active fund management industry – although a few had ignored this realism in the subsequent months – but they were all at a loss to understand how to take advantage of their newly acquired insight.

Which is where the crucial insight into the index comes in – they realise that the odds are stacked against you beating the market, which implies that you may as well buy the market, and what better market to buy than an index you hear every day on the news channels. Buy the index. Buy the FTSE 100.

Add up all the wisdom of the random walk of markets, all the discussion of efficient markets and potential inefficiencies – and in the end its central invitation is to simply buy the market. That concept of 'buying the market' means that you buy an index you understand and think will deliver the right mix of returns alongside risk.

Building the perfect index – the FTSE 100?

By now you will begin to understand that the index you track really matters to the efficient markets theorists – track an imperfect index which is weighted improperly or does not truly represent the aggregate pricing decisions of the market on a daily, even real-time, basis and you are potentially opening yourself up to extra risk as well as to a host of inefficiencies that could cost you lots of money over time.

Luckily investors have a huge range of major markets to copy or track, with many of the key markets featuring an index that has become a part of everyday language. In the US, for instance, the level of the Dow Jones Industrial Average or the Standard & Poor's (S&P) is the subject of intense daily discussion on any number of major news programmes, while in the UK, all the major news organisations talk hourly about the current level of the FTSE 100 index of major London-listed blue chip shares.

These indices are not real as such – unlike the major exchanges which do exist in an electronic form, even if their trading floors have largely been consigned to the dustbin of history. In essence they are mathematical constructs, which are then marketed as brands to both institutional and private investors – they are a short-hand way of 'capturing' the changes in major markets. The number of these index 'brands' has increased exponentially in recent years with major providers like Dow Jones, MSCI, S&P and even the FTSE turning into research houses sporting every kind of niche index imaginable – want an index that tracks Islamic-compliant emerging markets stocks, then why not look at a niche index supplied by the likes of the FTSE (originally set up as a partnership between the Financial Times and the London Stock Exchange) or Dow Jones? The FTSE Group, for instance, calculates over 120,000 indices covering more than 77 countries and all major asset classes.

These global index brands – tracked by every kind of imaginable fund, actively managed or passively via an index fund – are usually built around one of those famous core indices that track a main market. In the UK the actual market-making bit is provided by the London Stock Exchange and the key indices are the FTSE 100 (known as the Footsie) and its related sibling, the FTSE All Share index, which comprises around 98 per cent, by value, of all stocks listed on the London Stock Exchange. (Many very small listed companies based on market cap are not included in the FTSE All Share and thus this index is not one that features all listed companies and funds, despite the 'all' in its title.)

The FTSE 100 – some handy facts

■ The FTSE 100 is a market-capitalisation weighted index representing the performance of the 100 largest UK-listed large cap or blue chip companies.

■ All companies in the FTSE 100 must pass a test that looks at size in terms of market capitalisation and the availability or liquidity of their shares, i.e. only easy-to-purchase shares or investable shares are included. Constituents also need to have a full listing on the London Stock Exchange with a sterling or euro-dominated price on the SETS electronic trading system. Most constituents must by law include the abbreviation 'plc' at the end of their name, indicating their status as a publicly limited corporation.

■ The index represents just over 80 per cent of the entire market value of the various London-based stock exchanges.

■ The index began on 3 January 1984 with a base level of 1,000; the highest value reached to date is 6950.6, on 30 December 1999.

■ The FTSE 100 is calculated in real time and the level of the index is published every 15 seconds. Trading lasts from 08.00–16.29 (when the closing auction starts) and closing values are taken at 16.35.

■ The constituents of the index are determined quarterly – the larger companies in the adjacent index, the FTSE 250, are pushed up or promoted to the FTSE 100 index if they pass the tests above and their market cap goes above a certain level, which at the time of writing (February 2009) is about £1.7 billion in market cap.

■ The weighting of shares in the index is a relatively simple exercise – the index is built around the market capitalisation of the constituent companies (all 100) so that the larger companies have a disproportionate impact on the value of the index, compared with a smaller (by market cap) company. So if HSBC, the bank, for instance, comprises 10 per cent of the index and its shares rise by 10 per cent, all things being equal with the other constituent companies, the index should rise by 1 per cent. This 'methodology' is called the free-float methodology for constructing an index and the basic formula for any index is:

Index level = (Price of stock* Number of shares)*Free float factor/Index Divisor.

The **free float adjustment factor** represents the proportion of shares floated as a percentage of issued shares and then it is rounded up to the nearest multiple of 5 per cent for calculation purposes. To find the free-float capitalisation of a company, first find its market cap (number of outstanding shares × share price), then multiply its free-float factor. The free-float method, therefore, does not include restricted stocks, such as those held by company insiders.

At the back of this book we look at the 30 essential indices worth tracking, including the FTSE 100 and the FTSE All Share Index. In each page we analyse the index, looking at its composition, past returns and pitfalls. We also suggest a range of index tracking funds that track this investment space.

To better understand how an index fund might try to capture the major moves of a major, very efficient market, let's focus on the Footsie. Box 3.1 lists some of the key characteristics of this hugely popular index as of July 2009, but in simple language the FTSE 100 has a number of key attributes at the time of writing, including:

1 There are, it goes without saying, 100 stocks in the list.

2 These are valued at a total of £966 billion – that is £966,000 million.

3 The top 5 stocks are valued at a total of £320 billion.

4 The top 10 stocks are valued at £480bn.

5 The bottom 50 stocks are valued at £118bn.

6 Some companies in this list rose in value by more than 50 per cent in 2008 (a very bad year for shares), others dropped by more than 80 per cent in the same year.

7 The top stock – BP – comprises 8.9 per cent of the entire market cap while the bottom stock, industrials group Invensys, comprises just over 0.143 per cent of the entire market cap of the FTSE 100 – see Table 3.1

Table 3.1 **The FTSE constituents**

Name	EPIC	Share price	FTSE 100 Weighting	Capital (£m)
BP PLC	BP	4.61	8.93	86375.3
HSBC Holdings PLC	HSBA	4.1075	7.31	70668.8
Vodafone Group PLC	VOD	1.282	6.96	67284.3
GlaxoSmithKline PLC	GSK	10.725	5.76	55645.3
Royal Dutch Shell PLC	RDSB	15.02	4.19	40491
BG Group PLC	BG	10.84	3.76	36398.3
AstraZeneca PLC	AZN	24.25	3.63	35105.5
British American Tobacco PLC	BATS	16.07	3.32	32080.5
BHP Billiton PLC	BLT	13.71	3.13	30258.1
Tesco PLC	TSCO	3.333	2.72	26315.2
Rio Tinto PLC	RIO	23.48	2.43	23446.4
Diageo PLC	DGE	7.9	2.04	19746.4
Reckitt Benckiser Group PLC	RB	26.1	1.92	18532.6
Unilever PLC	ULVR	13.22	1.76	16967.3
Standard Chartered PLC	STAN	8.82	1.73	16735
SABMiller PLC	SAB	10.65	1.66	16060.1
Imperial Tobacco Group PLC	IMT	15.67	1.65	15928

Table 3.1 Continued

Name	EPIC	Share price	FTSE 100 weighting	Capital (£m)
Anglo American PLC	AAL	11.95	1.63	15732
Xstrata PLC	XTA	5.105	1.55	14973
National Grid PLC	NG	5.455	1.37	13249.3
Barclays PLC	BARC	1.57	1.36	13161.5
BAE SYSTEMS PLC	BA	3.3925	1.24	11970.5
Centrica PLC	CNA	2.3075	1.22	11786.7
Lloyds Banking Group PLC	LLOY	0.71	1.2	11605.1
Scottish & Southern Energy PLC	SSE	10.97	1.04	10097.2
Royal Bank of Scotland Group (The) PLC	RBS	0.251	1.02	9903.5
Prudential PLC	PRU	3.4225	0.88	8545.8
British Sky Broadcasting Group PLC	BSY	4.3275	0.78	7585.4
Cadbury PLC	CBRY	5.325	0.75	7262
Morrison (Wm) Supermarkets PLC	MRW	2.5425	0.69	6686.3
Tullow Oil PLC	TLW	7.95	0.66	6360.5
BT Group PLC	BT.A	0.798	0.64	6180.3
Aviva PLC	AV	2.2725	0.62	6039.6
Compass Group PLC	CPG	3.255	0.62	6010.7
Eurasian Natural Resources Corporation PLC	ENRC	4.485	0.6	5775.6
Pearson PLC	PSON	7.095	0.59	5745.8
Rolls-Royce Group PLC	RR	3.055	0.59	5658.5

Table 3.1 Continued

Name	EPIC	Share price	FTSE 100 weighting	Capital (£m)
Sainsbury (J) PLC	SBRY	3.15	0.57	5508.4
Reed Elsevier PLC	REL	4.91	0.56	5414.9
WPP Group PLC	WPP	4.0725	0.53	5102.5
Associated British Foods PLC	ABF	6.38	0.52	5050.9
Antofagasta PLC	ANTO	5.09	0.52	5018
Marks & Spencer Group PLC	MKS	3.0925	0.5	4879.3
Shire Ltd	SHP	8.335	0.48	4669.5
Experian PLC	EXPN	4.45	0.47	4562.8
RSA Insurance Group PLC	RSA	1.288	0.44	4290
Capita Group (The) PLC	CPI	6.775	0.44	4211.9
Smith & Nephew PLC	SN	4.4025	0.4	3891.9
Man Group PLC	EMG	2.1775	0.38	3718.9
Standard Life PLC	SL	1.703	0.38	3714
Kingfisher PLC	KGF	1.569	0.38	3704.1
Carnival PLC	CCL	16.37	0.36	3492.8
Cable and Wireless PLC	CW	1.369	0.36	3474.6
Land Securities Group PLC	LAND	4.485	0.35	3390.7
Fresnillo PLC	FRES	4.6525	0.35	3336.6
United Utilities Group PLC	UU	4.8275	0.34	3289.9
International Power PLC	IPR	2.125	0.33	3228
Autonomy Corporation PLC	AU	13.52	0.33	3223.8

Table 3.1 Continued

Name	EPIC	Share price	FTSE 100 weighting	Capital (£m)
British Land Co PLC	BLND	3.7675	0.33	3210.6
Randgold Resources Ltd	RRS	38.83	0.31	3015.6
Cairn Energy PLC	CNE	21.86	0.31	3009.6
Old Mutual PLC	OML	0.552	0.3	2912.7
Thomson Reuters PLC	TRIL	15.72	0.29	2848.9
Next PLC	NXT	14.1	0.29	2779.1
G4S PLC	GFS	1.953	0.28	2750.4
TUI Travel PLC	TT	2.395	0.28	2677.6
Legal & General Group PLC	LGEN	0.448	0.27	2626
Smiths Group PLC	SMIN	6.62	0.27	2575.3
Severn Trent PLC	SVT	9.99	0.24	2356.9
Admiral Group PLC	ADM	8.745	0.24	2316.9
Johnson Matthey PLC	JMAT	10.7	0.24	2297
Lonmin PLC	LMI	14.29	0.23	2255.2
Sage Group (The) PLC	SGE	1.705	0.23	2234.3
Inmarsat PLC	ISAT	4.76	0.23	2187.2
Home Retail Group PLC	HOME	2.4225	0.22	2125.6
Kazakhmys PLC	KAZ	3.915	0.22	2095.5
Cobham PLC	COB	1.775	0.21	2026.7
Thomas Cook Group PLC	TCG	2.355	0.21	2021.3
ICAP PLC	IAP	3.1075	0.21	2012.8
Vedanta Resources PLC	VED	6.925	0.2	1933.5
Petrofac Ltd	PFC	5.3	0.19	1830.8

Table 3.1 Continued

Name	EPIC	Share price	FTSE 100 weighting	Capital (£m)
Bunzl PLC	BNZL	5.56	0.19	1818.6
Hammerson PLC	HMSO	2.585	0.19	1798.3
AMEC PLC	AMEC	5.375	0.18	1787.9
Alliance Trust PLC	ATST	2.66	0.18	1787.3
Schroders PLC	SDR	7.91	0.18	1786.2
Serco Group PLC	SRP	3.6575	0.18	1780.5
Drax Group PLC	DRX	5.2	0.18	1764.9
REXAM PLC	REX	2.67	0.18	1716.6
British Airways PLC	BAY	1.47	0.18	1695.8
Friends Provident PLC	FP	0.723	0.17	1681.1
Amlin PLC	AML	3.5275	0.17	1658.2
Balfour Beatty PLC	BBY	3.4575	0.17	1652.8
InterContinental Hotels Group PLC	IHG	5.59	0.17	1596.5
Foreign & Colonial Investment Trust PLC	FRCL	2.19	0.15	1486.8
Pennon Group PLC	PNN	4.1225	0.15	1440.6
Liberty International PLC	LII	3.9275	0.15	1436.4
Whitbread PLC	WTB	8.19	0.15	1428.3
Intertek Group PLC	ITRK	8.995	0.15	1419.6
Invensys PLC	ISYS	1.73	0.14	1386.5
Total £m				966763.3

Putting it all together in an index fund

To replicate this index, any tracker fund must try to copy it perfectly using its own basket or portfolio of shares. That means it must make sure that BP comprises 8.9 per cent of the total value of the fund while the holding of Invensys shares should be around 0.1 per cent. Figure 3.1 shows the huge range of weightings necessary for such an index tracking fund.

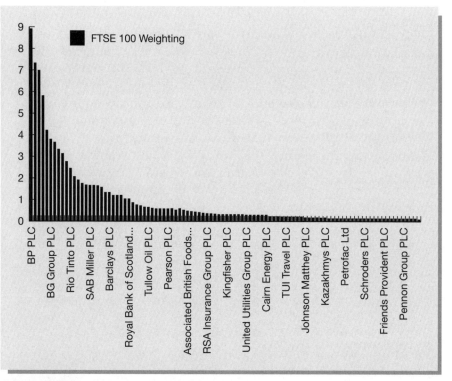

Figure 3.1   **FTSE 100 weighting**

This challenge of 'copying' the FTSE 100 introduces a number of hugely important issues:

- The composition of the fund – which in turn replicates the index – is **constantly changing**. Shares change in price on a daily basis and that change in relative weighting needs to be reflected in the index tracking fund if it is to faithfully replicate or copy the index.
- Some companies drop out of the index altogether every few months. That means not only that the weighting of stocks in the fund must be

adjusted but the actual list of company holdings will also alter dramatically. In recent years resource companies (miners and oil outfits) as well as the banks have dominated the FTSE 100 index, at times accounting for more than 60 per cent of the market capitalisation of the entire index. At the time of writing, these two sectors account for only less than 40 per cent of the FTSE 100.

■ With such a long list of possible constituents – 100 in this example – it is much easier if your index fund is very large. If you have an index fund that is worth £1000m (£1bn), then that implies buying £1.4m of shares in the smallest company in the list, Invensys (with 0.14 per cent). Dealing costs are likely to be very low as a proportion of that purchase cost and the market makers (the institutions which buy and sell shares) will probably offer the fund managers a tiny spread between the bid and offer price. If, however, your total fund is valued at just £1m, buying Invensys means buying £1,430 worth of shares. Proportionately that makes dealing costs much more expensive, and in addition you run the risk of getting caught out by high bid–offer spreads, i.e. the market makers might also add in a 1 per cent or even 2 per cent markup in the difference between the buying and selling price for relatively small deals.

The Vanguard definition of market cap-weighted indices

According to researchers at Vanguard:[1] *'Indices should reflect the market – or market portion – that they are intended to measure. They are therefore weighted according to market capitalization, where:*

Market cap = Price per share × Number of shares outstanding.

Market cap-weighted indices reflect the consensus estimate of each company's value at any given moment. In any efficient market, new information – economic, financial, or company specific – affects the price of one or more securities and is reflected instantaneously in the index via the change in its market capitalization. Thus, a continuously updated market index gives an indication of how well a market is performing, and of the market's structural and risk characteristics at any given point in time. Since, according to capital market theory – specifically, the Capital Asset Pricing Model – current prices (and, hence, company values) are set based on current and expected events, cap-weighted indices represent the expected ... portfolio of securities in a given asset class. In addition, market-cap-weighted indices are continuously reweighted, and turnover is limited to changes in the constituents or in their shares outstanding due to corporate events such as share buybacks or issuances.'

Capturing the index

So much for the idea of capturing the index, but how do you go about building an index fund that does the job cheaply and effectively? To understand the inner workings – the mechanics – of such a fund you first have to understand the journey that brought us to the perfectly formed index fund.

This journey started many decades ago in the US. Many market professionals worked together in different organisations and stock markets to develop the first index funds, but one name towers above everyone else, John Bogle. Founder of giant US fund management firm Vanguard, Bogle is rightly regarded as one of the wisest men on Wall Street, whose open letters end up as op-ed pages on *The Wall Street Journal*.

Bogle graduated from Princeton University in 1951, boasting a thesis entitled: 'Mutual Funds can make no claims to superiority over the Market Averages'. His painstaking research showed that three-quarters of fund managers would not have earned more than an investor who had managed to invest across the index of America's 500 largest companies.

Clearly Bogle was already no great fan of active fund management and he spent the subsequent decades perfecting his idea of the perfect index tracking fund. Then, in 1974, his ambitious ideas began to take shape as he founded his own investment company, The Vanguard Group, now the second largest mutual fund company in the US. Curiously, the debut of his new concern closely followed the 1973 publication of *A Random Walk Down Wall Street* in which the Princeton economist Burton Malkiel called for the establishment of a low-cost fund that reflected the market index.[2] Bizarrely – given the timing – John Bogle later admitted that he had not actually read the book at the time, only catching up with it many years later. One of his first funds was a rather innocuous little fund called the First Index Investment Trust, which was started on 31 December 1975. According to one account of the start of this fund it was 'labeled Bogle's follies and regarded as un-American, because it sought to achieve the averages rather than insisting that Americans had to play to win'. Another account of Vanguard's history noted the sour-puss reaction of one mutual fund executive who claimed that 'indexing is a sure path to mediocrity'.[3] By August 1976 this small fund had been relaunched with a snazzier name, the Vanguard 500 Index Fund, which in turn tracked a rather familiar index known as the Standard and Poor's 500 index (the S&P 500) – see Table 3.2.

The fund started with comparatively meagre assets of $11m but at the time of writing has assets totalling a huge $74bn. Even Bogle himself, now transformed into a titan of investing, seems to have been surprised by the success of the fund. Commenting on its success he noted, 'in the financial markets it is always wise to expect the unexpected' though it is very likely that few of his investors will be complaining about the returns from the fund. Annualised profits since inception have hit 9.70 per cent per annum.

Table 3.2 Performance of Vanguard 500 as of 31 January 2009 – average annual returns

	1 Year	3 Year	5 Year	10 Year	Since Inception 31/08/1976
500 Index Fund Inv	−38.63%	−11.85%	−4.34%	−2.73%	9.70%
S&P 500 Index*	−38.63%	−11.78%	−4.24%	−2.65%	–

It is important to say that Bogle was not the only person experimenting in the index tracking space. John McQuown and David Booth at Wells Fargo and Rex Sinquefield at American National Bank in Chicago were all toying with similar funds, and in 1971 Wells Fargo established the first Standard and Poor's Composite Index Fund, with a minimum investment of $100,000. With such a high initial investment level, this proto-index fund was clearly aimed at institutions and not the private investors Bogle wanted to serve. Wells Fargo started with $5m from its own pension fund, while Illinois Bell put in $5m of its pension funds at the American National Bank version of the index fund. Within 30 years these institutional-side outfits had developed and been bought out by a hitherto unknown player in this space, Barclays Bank. The British investment bank had big plans to develop a strong global investment fund management business and reckoned that selling specialist funds that tracked an index was a potentially brilliant business to be in. How right they were.

So although the genesis of the index fund is hotly contested and does not really belong to any one person or institution, Vanguard's John Bogle has certainly made the biggest success of it. To describe the Vanguard 500 fund as the grand-daddy of modern mass-market index funds is possibly under-estimating its impact – it is quite simply the biggest fund aimed at private investors in the US today. Tables 3.3 and 3.4 provide a quick snapshot of the fund as of the end of 2008.

Table 3.3 Equity characteristics of Vanguard fund as of 12/31/2008

	500 Index Fund Inv	*S&P 500 Index*
Number of stocks	510	500
Median market cap	$39.5 billion	$39.5 billion
Price/earnings ratio	11.3x	11.3x
Price/book ratio	1.8x	1.8x
Return on equity	22.1%	22.1%
Earnings growth rate	17.4%	17.4%
Foreign holdings	0.1%	–
Turnover rate (as of fiscal year end December)	5.6%	–
Short-term reserves	0.3%	–
Fund total net assets	$74.9 billion	–
Share class total net assets	$38.8 billion	–
Total expense ratio	0.15% pa	

Table 3.4 Equity sector diversification

	500 Index Fund Inv		*S&P 500 Index*
	as of 12/31/2008	*as of 12/31/2007*	*as of 12/31/2008*
Consumer discretionary	8.40%	8.50%	8.40%
Consumer staples	12.90%	10.20%	12.90%
Energy	13.30%	12.90%	13.30%
Financials	13.30%	17.70%	13.30%
Health care	14.80%	12.00%	14.80%
Industrials	11.10%	11.50%	11.10%
Information technology	15.20%	16.70%	15.30%
Materials	3.00%	3.30%	2.90%
Telecommunication services	3.80%	3.60%	3.80%
Utilities	4.20%	3.60%	4.20%

This Vanguard fund tells you everything you need to know about the structure of a great index fund. It is big, it is cheap and it works brilliantly. Crucially, the fund does an amazing job of replicating or copying the index that it tracks. Its returns do not perfectly match those of the S&P 500 but they are very close – see Tables 3.5 and 3.6. Oddly enough, the fund has 510 stocks while the S&P has, of course, 500 stocks. But the composition of holding in the portfolio absolutely matches those in the index and the median market capitalisation of each underlying share is exactly the same, at $39bn, with the average PE ratio being 11.3.

Table 3.5 Annualised returns from the Vanguard 500 Index fund vs the S&P 500 Index

Average annual performance of Vanguard 500 Index Fund as of 03/31/2009	1 Year	3 Year	5 Year	10 Year
08/31/1976				
500 Index Fund Inv	–38.09%	–13.13%	–4.86%	–3.08%
S&P 500 Index*	–38.09%	–13.06%	–4.76%	–3.00%

Table 3.6 Returns by year

Annual investment returns as of 12/31/2008		
Capital return	Total return of Vanguard 500 fund	S&P 500 Index
2008	–37.02%	–37.00%
2007	5.39%	5.49%
2006	15.64%	15.79%
2005	4.77%	4.91%
2004	10.74%	10.88%
2003	28.50%	28.68%
2002	–22.15%	–22.10%
2001	–12.02%	–11.89%
2000	–9.06%	–9.10%

Table 3.6 Continued

Annual investment returns as of 12/31/2008

Capital return	Total return of Vanguard 500 fund	S&P 500 Index
1999	21.07%	21.04%
1998	28.62%	28.58%
1997	33.19%	33.36%
1996	22.88%	22.96%
1995	37.45%	37.58%
1994	1.18%	1.32%

Source: Vanguard Group

You will also notice from Tables 3.4 and 3.5 – they both detail annual returns – that there is never more than a 0.2 per cent per annum difference in returns between the fund and the index it tracks, i.e. its tracking error is very low. Remember that the tracking error is always negative, i.e. the fund *underperforms* the underlying index and that is because the total expense ratio, which is the cost of managing the fund, is 0.15 per cent per annum. That cost is, in fact, the primary reason for the tracking error – every year the investor must bear the burden of paying that 0.15 per cent cost which in turn reduces fund returns. But that 0.15 per cent is also probably a tiny price to pay for the tracking expertise. Most actively managed funds in the US, by contrast, charge more than 1 per cent per annum and deliver poorer returns than the Vanguard fund.

The new indexers

The traditional model for index investing is based on holding a market cap or price value weighted portfolio of shares or stocks. The reality, even for big tracker funds, is that there are thousands of tiny stocks at the smaller end of the spectrum that are too costly to trade. Trackers tend to sample from these stocks, buying only some of the names until they have a portfolio that looks and hopefully behaves like that segment of the stock universe. This tiny 'long tail' of shares – lots of small companies, making up the list but not really mattering in terms of total market cap – can cause fund performance to deviate from the index, especially during small-stock-led bull markets. It also demonstrates that even pure indexers do not mimic the market exactly.

The new indexers, led by Eugene Fama, start from a different place. As we noted in our earlier chapter looking at the theory behind trackers and the critics who have lined up to attack the new orthodoxy in academia, economists like Fama reckon that there are, in fact, three distinct risk factors in stock investing. Small company stocks expose investors to a completely different form of volatility, for instance they have unique risk–return characteristics. Each of these risk 'flavours' is unrelated to the others. Small stocks can do well when the overall market does poorly and value stocks can have dreadful returns when small stocks do well, and so on. According to new indexers like Fama, each of these risk factors has as much potential for increasing investment returns as wider market returns.

Fama says: 'In the presence of more than one risk factor, the goal of indexing [now] switches from diversification across the available stocks to diversification across the available risk-return dimensions.'[4] To old-school indexers like John Bogle this all sounds a bit like taking a bet on sectors or themes – Bogle still believes that the overall market itself, what we call market risk, primarily determines performance and that small stocks and value stocks are not separate sources of risk and return.

An even brasher new school of critics has emerged in recent years. These critics believe investors should dump the whole market cap weighting methodology, not alter and tilt its composition using the factors favoured by Fama.

One school of radicals maintains that the best way to build an index is to equal weight every company in the index. In a paper entitled 'Are equal weighted indices better than market cap weighted indices?', Greg Burgess spells out this new line of thinking which has produced an entirely different form of index, something called the Equally Weighted S&P 500.[5] The key insight here is to challenge the standard index structure which is biased towards a small number of very large companies. According to Burgess, the S&P EWI (Equal Weight Index) is a more 'neutral' version of the S&P 500 in that it offers higher exposure to small cap companies (and conversely lower exposure to really large cap companies), although it also has a higher turnover as a result of its quarterly rebalancing, and very different risk and sector profiles.

This radically different return and risk profile is a direct result of the very different small vs large cap exposure – an equally weighted index is bound to be biased towards smaller cap companies in the index as it gives them the same weighting as the huge, mega-caps. To use the earlier example of the FTSE 100, the smallest company on the list – Invensys – would theoretically comprise 1 per cent of the total index weighting, as would the largest (by market cap), BP, which would also comprise just 1 per cent. The index developers reckon that this new style of index might produce better returns but with a lower level of risk – index managers S&P also observe that 'historically when large companies have done well the S&P 500 has outperformed, and when smaller companies have done well the S&P EWI has outperformed'.

Burgess also points out that this new type of index is a trickier beast to track – it is reset quarterly and funds that track it end up with higher trading turnover, and that higher turnover tends to result in higher costs, which eat into returns. 'This means that the index's performance is difficult, but not impossible, to replicate with a low degree of tracking error,' suggests Burgess. Exchange traded fund provider Rydex does have an index fund that tries to replicate the performance of the S&P 500 Equal Weight Index, but its turnover rate is high – at 40 per cent per annum.

But does this radical new way of constructing an index actually work, even if you can find a way to efficiently track it? Figure 3.2 looks at the price returns over the last five, turbulent years from the Rydex S&P Equal Weight Index fund compared with the standard S&P 500 index (^GSPC – the dotted line). In good years, i.e. bull markets, the Equal Weighted Index does seem to produce better returns than the standard index, if only because of its relative weight towards smaller cap stocks. In distressed markets the EWI does not seem to offer any great advantage, especially as investors flee smaller stocks for the safety of mega-caps.

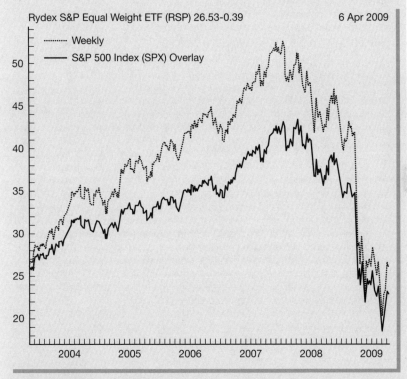

Rydex S&P Equal Weight ETF (RSP) 26.53-0.39   6 Apr 2009

Figure 3.2   **Price returns: Rydex S&P Equal Weight Index fund v. standard S&P 500 index**

Dark line = The Rydex ETF
Lighter line = The Mainstream S&P index

Even more radical ideas about how to build an index are emerging from the asset management companies. These new approaches use some very different ideas about how to construct an index – some private banks in Europe, for instance, are pioneering an index built around a concept called minimum variance. This weights an index of stocks not by its market cap or its value-based fundamental measures but by each stock's volatility, i.e. low volatility stocks get a higher weighting.

Yet another approach comes from a brash new fund company called TOBAM, which has emerged out of the ashes of Lehmans. Its principals have come up with a radical new concept called anti-benchmarking. The methodology behind this new approach to indexing was outlined in a paper called 'Towards Maximum Diversification' in the *Journal of Portfolio Management* in autumn 2008 and was devised by two French quantitatively trained investment analysts, Yves Choueifaty and Yves Coignard. They looked at the construction of traditional market cap weighted indices, such as the S&P 500, and questioned whether investors were taking on too much risk from lack of diversification and high levels of volatility. Their research acknowledged the reality that much of the S&P 500 or the FTSE 100 is closely correlated, thus providing low levels of diversification for those trying to build a balanced portfolio. For the TOBAM analysts, diversification is the crucial component of returns in a portfolio, so they set about finding a different way to construct an index of stocks. Their resulting anti-benchmark portfolios use an equation-based system to examine both correlation and volatility as the key components of any weighting system. In essence, their system looks for stocks with lower relative volatility and higher diversification.

Table 3.7, from a TOBAM publication in May 2008, shows what a typical basket of the top ten stocks in the FTSE might look like in one of its anti-benchmark portfolios versus a traditional market cap weighting (used by the FTSE 100 and most trackers), a fundamental indexing strategy (used by the likes of Eugene Fama), an equal weight portfolio and a minimum variance portfolio. The TOBAM approach is not to overinvest in volatile stocks (it has low holdings of very volatile stocks like Barclays and Anglo American) but to weight its holdings towards shares that provide extra diversification because of their low correlation to the other stocks within the list, i.e. pharma companies like GlaxoSmithKline tend to move in a different way to a gaggle of bank stocks, providing investors with some extra diversification. Add up the lower volatility and higher diversification, and the TOBAM analysts believe you have a more diversified portfolio. In practical terms the resulting portfolios from the TOBAM and minimum variance approach look very different from more traditional indices – the top five banks comprise just 18 per cent of this top ten as opposed to 45 per cent in a market cap weighted system, while Tesco is a staggering 27.90 per cent of total holdings (compared with just 5.80 per cent in a market weighted system).

Table 3.7 Example stock allocation system using TOBAM system

Company name	Stock volatility	Market cap portfolio	Fundamental indexing portfolio	Equal weight portfolio	Minimum variance portfolio	Anti benchmark portfolio
HSBC	13.48%	16.90%	19.36%	10%	25.90%	3.20%
RBS Group	17.42%	9.60%	12.05%	10%	0	1.90%
Barclays	22.24%	7.40%	8.04%	10%	0%	05%
HBOS	17.59%	6.40%	6.91%	10%	0%	2.60%
Lloyds TSB	16.13%	5.105	5.72%	10%	9.70%	10.30%
Tesco	15.73%	5.80%	4.50%	105	28.40%	27.90%
Anglo American	35.32%	65	5.08%	10%	0%	5.705
Royal Dutch Shell	16.04%	17.90%	17.47%	10%	20.50%	18.70%
GlaxoSmithKline	16.86%	13.10%	8.13%	105	15.50%	22.40%
Vodafone Group	22.18%	11.90%	12.75%	10%	0%	7.30%

The rise of ETFs

Vanguard may have been at the forefront of this indexing revolution in the 1970s and 1980s but by the 1990s a new type of fund structure had emerged. To all intents and purposes this new creature – called an exchange traded fund – was almost identical to the Vanguard range of index tracking mutual funds (Vanguard does not run index tracking funds only and has entered the ETF market aggressively in recent years). These new-fangled ETFs also track key markets via an index and they are cheap and easy to understand like the Vanguard 500 index fund, but there is one crucial difference – the ETFs are listed funds, bought and sold in real time, on the stock exchanges that they in turn track. The Vanguard funds by contrast are mutual funds, bought via an adviser with pricing based on an end-of-the-day review structure. While Vanguard funds may be loved by many American financial planners, ETFs are stock market creatures and it is no surprise that the creator of this fund structure was a stock market itself, namely the American Stock Exchange in New York.

The AMEX market had evolved from its origins quite literally on the kerb of Broad Street in New York. As it grew it became the home to the many smaller companies that were not quite big enough to get on the New York Stock Exchange (NYSE). But its very success in the small cap business soon caused it problems – rival markets started emerging that were much keener to let in even newer, even riskier, younger, untested, untried companies. In particular NASDAQ erupted on the scene and the love affair with tech start-ups blossomed with private investors. AMEX needed to innovate and stay ahead of the competition. By the late 1980s the gist of a new business idea began to take shape – why not combine AMEX's competitive edge with products like derivatives (options and other forms of futures) alongside more traditional closed-end funds? The initial idea was to get mutual funds to list or trade their shares on the exchange – the market even invited John Bogle to see whether his index fund could be traded like a share. Vanguard refused – the exchange traded platform would simply add to costs and Bogle's mission was to produce funds with the lowest cost possible.

Suddenly the clever futures-based rocket scientists working deep within the bowels of AMEX hit on an idea. Why not separate out the functions of fund management from the actual exchange trading – portfolios of stocks could be deposited with a trustee which could then be turned into a form of 'depositary receipt', an idea borrowed from the world of commodity trading where warehouse receipts were given to traders for hosting their products. That receipt, in turn, could be sub-divided into lots of little units that could then be traded on the exchange as 'equity securities'. These individual units would not be redeemable by the fund but could be reassembled into a full depositary receipt and redeemed by the trustee – a process of creation and redemption that was eventually to be turned into an art form.

The first of these new-style ETFs was born on 29 January 1993. It was called the Standard and Poor's depositary receipt – or SPDR for short, although an 'I' was soon added to the acronym to make SPIDER. This 'trust' tracked the popular S&P 500 index – also tracked by the Vanguard fund – and was built from scratch to appeal to institutional investors who wanted something cheap and easy to trade in.

American commentator Archie Richards notes that when the idea of the SPIDER was first presented to members of the Securities and Exchange Commission it was greeted with confusion and eventually took three years to get full approval.[6] The commissioners, Richards says, could not relate these new-fangled shares to anything else they had seen and eventually they classified these SPIDERs as something called a unit investment trust. These investment trusts were and are closed-end vehicles – a fixed amount is raised up front – and are listed on the exchange like any other share. But ETFs, unlike these traditional vehicles, changed in size and market capitalisation constantly via a creation and redemption process and were not managed on an active basis like most traditional investment trusts, i.e. they simply reflected the composition of the underlying index they tracked.

The structure used for the actual operation of the ETF was something called a depositary trust. The trustee of the SPIDER Trust ETF, for instance, is a bank called State Street, while the beneficial owners are the investors in the fund – both private and institutional. As Richards notes, this first ETF was as simple and effective as the first Vanguard fund: 'The trust, says the prospectus, is a pooled investment designed to closely track the price and yield performance of the S&P 500 Index. Tracking the S&P 500 worked for Vanguard, why not the SPIDERS.' Crucially, this depositary structure allows for something called an undivided interest – every share purchased in the trust represents an infinitesimal holding in the underlying companies which are, in turn, held in the fund. So, every time you buy a SPIDER share, you buy into a basket of actual shares that track the composition of the S&P 500 and in turn you end up owning a tiny, tiny holding in not only the largest share in the index but also the smallest, and everything in between. Crucially, each share of the SPIDER contains one-tenth of the S&P index and trades at roughly one-tenth of the dollar-value level of the S&P 500.

This depositary structure – familiar to the SEC commissioners who had authorised it – allows a number of key advantages for both the issuer of the shares and the investors. A crucial change in the investment rules governing the US stock markets in 1990 had allowed for the creation of what were called SuperTrusts – funds that could operate like any share but also permit constant creation and redemption of new shares. This process is crucial to the inner workings of an ETF, as we will discover a little later, but in essence this simple process means that the SuperTrusts do not have to go through the palaver of shares placings and rights issues to create new stock – they can just operate a constant process of creation and redemption to make sure that the quoted share price is as close as possible to the underlying value of assets in the fund.

An even bigger advantage was that the trust structure let the SEC allow the short selling of ETFs. This meant that the SPIDER rapidly turned into a simple and cost-effective shorting instrument for investors looking to sell the S&P 500. This rapidly became a key feature of all ETFs – during the market meltdown, assets under ETF management doubled in a few weeks as shorters used ETFs as an instrument for hedging. Also, the depositary trust company structure of the SPIDERS meant that the managers did not have to keep track of individual shareholders, they only had to keep a book entry form at the trustees, substantially cutting down on costs. The Vanguard funds, by contrast, cannot be used as vehicles to short the markets and involve the fund managers in some fairly laborious administration and client management – they need to keep meticulous records of who owns each of the units within the fund.

This trust structure also endowed ETFs – or at least what we might call classic ETFs – with one last crucial advantage, namely management and custodial control of the fund. This structure is detailed in Table 3.8. The manager of the fund, State Street, is separate from the actual trust which is owned by its investors. This separation is crucial – modern-day variants of this SPIDER exchange traded fund structure, managed by outfits like Barclays, have retained a separation between your (tiny) bit of the overall fund and the various service providers to the fund, such as the investment manager, index providers, custodians, etc. If your manager goes bust, that theoretically does not have any effect on your investment as hopefully another manager will simply take control and carry on with the task of replicating the index.

Table 3.8 Parties involved in running an ETF

Investment manager	Day-to-day management of the fund
Index provider	Determines the index that is tracked by the fund
Data provider	Provides daily pricing for securities
Authorised participant	Creation and redemption of shares at primary market level
Custodian	Safe keeping and accounting of fund assets
Administrator	Processing subscription and redemption requests and other elements of fund administration
Registrar and transfer agent	Responsible for carrying out transfer agency and paying agency functions

Source: Barclays iShares

The SPIDER fund went on to be a huge long-term success – at the time of writing it is still the largest ETF on the market and accounts for about 16 per cent of all assets in the ETF market – but for the first few years ETF trading was subdued as investors quietly came to terms with the new structure and the regulators grappled to understand the new product.

As the SPIDER ETFs slowly began to take off, rival forms (beset by a nasty case of acronymitis) also began to spring up. In Canada, for instance, the Toronto Stock Exchange had been trying out a similar structure called 'index participations' or TIPs, while in Philadelphia a short-lived variant of a futures contract emerged that allowed investors to track indices through something called index participation shares or IPS. In 1998 another variant called World Equity Benchmark Shares (WEBS) emerged, offering investors the chance to invest in single countries – Morgan Stanley's nation-specific indices were used as the index and the funds were managed by Barclays Global Investors, which had taken over Wells Fargo's fund management arm. By now the acronyms were exploding all over the place and another variant called DIAMONDS was launched – these were ETFs based on the Dow Jones index. The NASDAQ 100 Trust also emerged in 1999 – BNY's – and by 2000 ETFs were changing the face of modern investment. But despite the huge growth in both structures and dazzling acronyms, the basic idea that powers this innovation has remained relatively constant – buy the market efficiently and cheaply.

Defining ETFs

The American Stock Exchange defines an ETF as follows: '[They are] open-ended registered investment companies under the Investment Company Act of 1940, which have received certain exemptive relief from the SEC to allow secondary market trading in the ETF shares. ETFs are index-based products, in that each ETF holds a portfolio of securities that is intended to provide investment results that, before fees and expenses, generally correspond to the price and yield performance of the underlying benchmark index.'[7]

This long-winded and overly technical definition sums up ETFs very nicely. They are:

- an investment company
- that offers secondary market trading on the main exchanges, much like any other share;
- they are index based and are
- based on a portfolio of securities.

ETFs are in fact a mutant mix of the traditional investment trust – very familiar to British readers – and the open-ended mutual fund or unit trust. Like mutuals, ETFs represent a fractional ownership in an underlying portfolio of shares that tracks a specific index, but unlike mutual funds, individual investors do not purchase or redeem shares from the fund. Instead individuals buy and sell ETFs like ordinary shares on an exchange. Also, the price of the ETF varies on the basis of changes in the underlying portfolio *and* according to the changes in the market supply and demand for ETFs themselves.

How they work in detail

Let's assume that you are a large institution. You are managing a large pot of pension money for a local authority. This troublesome bunch of Northern municipal socialists has some rather old-fashioned ideas about keeping costs down and not trying anything too fancy by keeping it simple. They want a slice of the FTSE 100 – nice, boring companies paying a steady dividend.

In the 1980s, before the rise of ETFs, they could approach a big bank that operated something called portfolio trading to sell them a futures-based option that essentially gave them access to the FTSE 100 in one product. Alternatively they could, if they were large enough, just order their brokers to go out and buy all the constituents of the FTSE 100, in the right proportions. They would in essence have their own private ETF. But if they were really clever and were still doing this by the next decade, they could, in theory, take this ready-made basket of shares and pop along to a big ETF issuer like Barclays' iShares and swap that portfolio for a bunch of shares in the iShares FTSE 100 ETF. Barclays would then simply create more shares in its ETF and absorb the pension fund assets into its mutual fund.

Flash forward another year. The Northern pension fund types have noticed that their shares in the FTSE 100 ETF are behaving rather strangely. The year before they had swapped their basket of FTSE 100 shares for ETF shares, but they have now noticed that there is a difference between the market price of the ETF (for argument's sake, say £100) and the actual basket of assets in the fund (worth, say, £101). That discount to the underlying value or net asset value makes them a bit anxious, so they tell their City types to go to the ETF company and cash in their millions of shares for their 'bit' of the total fund, i.e. the basket of shares in the FTSE 100. Suddenly they have their old basket of FTSE 100 stocks back again and they have (hopefully) made a small profit because they have used their ETF shares (worth £100 per share) to buy £101 per share of assets.

Being really crafty types, this pension fund could carry on trading its assets back and forth with the ETF as the discount waxes and wanes, sometimes turning a discount into a premium – constantly making a bit of money on the side until the politicians in City Hall realise that the pension fund has in fact turned into what experts call an arb fund, making endless small profits from big trades. This rather ridiculous example – who would imagine boring pension funds involving themselves in risky activities normally reserved for hedge fund tyros? – demonstrates the very simple principles and processes that lurk in the engine room of an ETF.

The ETF manager or custodian decides that there is some money to be made setting up a fund that tracks a key index. They buy a basket of shares that tracks this index as faithfully as possible and then sell the shares to big institutions – and small investors alike – looking to buy exposure to that index. These shares have some important numbers pinned to them that indicate various levels of 'value':

1 The price to buy the shares – this is set by the market maker (a financial intermediary) and not the ETF manager.
2 The price to sell the shares – this is also set by the market maker, not the manager, and is usually less than the purchase price.

3 The net asset value (NAV) of the shares in the ETF. This is simply the total value of all the assets divided by the number of shares issued. This NAV should (hopefully) be very close to the market price above … but not always.

Sometimes a difference emerges between the NAV and the market price – in traditional investment trusts, the investors just have to put up with this discount and hope that somebody important shouts loudly and the fund's managers work out a way of buying back the shares. In ETFs, by contrast, some very smart market players called authorised participants – also known as arbitrageurs or arbs – can exploit this difference as long as they have got enough money to buy a minimum 50,000 shares per deal. They can, like our pension fund, simply buy the same basket of shares and then present them to the ETF issuer and demand some ETF shares in return. If the ETF shares are trading at a discount to the NAV, that exchange – real shares in the index companies for shares in the ETF – might make them a quick profit. That profit is rarely the 1 per cent difference experienced by our pension fund above – it is usually just a few basis points, but if you are dealing in millions of pounds of ETF shares, a few basis points every day can make your traders a lot of money.

The point of all this arbing and trading is that hopefully the efficient market in ETFs (remember that theoretical creature from the previous chapter) will constantly smooth out the premiums and discounts and keep the share price of the ETF close to the value of the underlying shares. That means when you buy your well-constructed, large FTSE 100 ETF you really are buying an almost perfect facsimile of the index, with no drag from any discounts to the NAV.

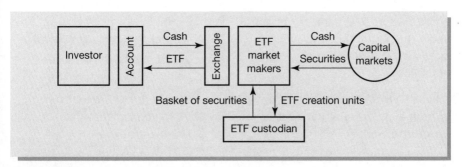

Figure 3.3   The creation/redemption process

Source: The London Stock Exchange

There is, of course, a more technical way of describing this chain of creation and redemption. Figure 3.3, from the Education service of the London Stock Exchange, demonstrates a process that goes something like this:

1 The market maker purchases a basket of shares, as specified by the ETF custodian, for cash.

2 This basket of securities is then exchanged with the ETF custodian for a set number of ETF units or shares (creation).

3 The market maker then has an inventory of ETF shares through which to satisfy market demand for buy/sell orders.

4 Redemption – this is simply the whole process in reverse, whereby a market maker will swap a defined number of ETF shares with the ETF custodian for the underlying basket of shares, which can then be sold for cash in the secondary market.

The key point is that the price of an ETF is not entirely determined by market supply and demand, but rather the creation/redemption process. This 'arb' business is graphically demonstrated in Figure 3.4, again from the London Stock Exchange. It effectively shows that if the share price is above the net asset value, an arbitrageur can buy the index portfolio and sell the ETF short, thus making an instant profit. If the market price is below the NAV, they simply do the reverse, namely buy the ETF, and sell the index portfolio short. The net effect? As we have already discussed, the market price should be very, very close to the underlying net asset value of the basket of underlying stocks.

An ETF in action

What does an ETF look like in action? Perhaps the best way of getting under the skin of these clever creatures is to look at one of the biggest and most successful funds in the UK, the iShares FTSE 100 index fund, with a ticker ISF.

Table 3.9 gives you a quick snapshot of the key facts of the ETF on one day in April 2009. Its total net assets amount to £2.782bn and comprise 99.07 per cent in equities (102 shares, not 100) and 0.93 per cent in cash, accumulated from dividends and merger and acquision (M&A) activity.

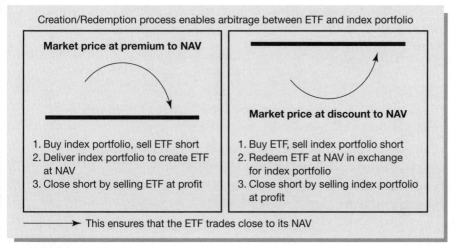

Creation/Redemption process enables arbitrage between ETF and index portfolio

Market price at premium to NAV

Market price at discount to NAV

1. Buy index portfolio, sell ETF short
2. Deliver index portfolio to create ETF at NAV
3. Close short by selling ETF at profit

1. Buy ETF, sell index portfolio short
2. Redeem ETF at NAV in exchange for index portfolio
3. Close short by selling index portfolio at profit

This ensures that the ETF trades close to its NAV

Figure 3.4   **Creation/redemption process enables arbitrage between ETF and index portfolio**

Source: The London Stock Exchange

Table 3.9 Snapshot of the ETF

Holdings summary 06/04/09	
Ticker	ISF
Total net assets £ (000)	2,781,919
Number of holdings	102
Currency	GBP
Percentage stocks	99.07
Percentage cash and other	0.93
Dividends	Paid quarterly
Total expense ratio	0.40%
Rebalance frequency	Quarterly for index
Dividend yield	5.39%

Drilling even deeper into this snapshot in time we can see that the ETF is priced at £3.91 on Tuesday 7 April 2009 (with the FTSE index at 3930), with a bid-offer spread of just 0.05 per cent (that is a half of one-tenth of a per cent).

Table 3.10 Top 20 holdings in iShares ETF vs the FTSE 100 Index

THE ETF		THE INDEX		
All holdings as 06/04/09		All holdings as 06/04/09		
% Weight	Security	Name	FTSE100 Weighting %	Capital (£m)
8.51	BP PLC	BP PLC	8.67	84923.2
7.73	HSBC HOLDINGS PLC	HSBC Holdings PLC	7.92	77550.7
6.6	VODAFONE GROUP PLC	Vodafone Group PLC	6.75	66053.3
5.4	GLAXOSMITHKLINE PLC	GlaxoSmithKline PLC	5.48	53699.7
5.38	ROYAL DUTCH SHELL PLC-A SHS	Royal Dutch Shell PLC	4.1	40140.6
4.03	ROYAL DUTCH SHELL PLC-B SHS	BG Group PLC	3.77	36880.3
3.69	BG GROUP PLC	AstraZeneca PLC	3.51	34381.7
3.45	ASTRAZENECA PLC	British American Tobacco PLC	3.17	31042.6
3.09	BRITISH AMERICAN TOBACCO PLC	BHP Billiton PLC	3.12	30567.1
3.05	BHP BILLITON PLC	Tesco PLC	2.64	25826.6
2.56	TESCO PLC	Rio Tinto PLC	2.25	22048.4
2.2	RIO TINTO PLC	Diageo PLC	2.02	19746.5
1.98	DIAGEO PLC	Standard Chartered PLC	1.86	18215
1.81	STANDARD CHARTERED PLC	Reckitt Benckiser Group PLC	1.84	18042.9
1.79	RECKITT BENCKISER GROUP PLC	Anglo American PLC	1.8	17601.5
1.77	ANGLO AMERICAN PLC	Unilever PLC	1.71	16749.1
1.67	UNILEVER PLC	SABMiller PLC	1.67	16346.7
1.53	IMPERIAL TOBACCO GROUP PLC	Imperial Tobacco Group PLC	1.57	15389.2
1.44	BARCLAYS PLC	Xstrata PLC	1.57	15339.7
1.28	NATIONAL GRID PLC	Barclays PLC	1.48	14469.2

The core holdings of the fund from the day before – we took this snapshot before the market closed and the composition of the fund was recalculated – are in Table 3.10, with the index holdings in the box to the right. As you can see there are some material differences in the holdings. BP, for instance, has a weighting of 8.67 per cent in the FTSE 100 index that day compared with the iShares fund which has 8.51 per cent – it is a tiny difference and in reality does not matter greatly, but it can add up over time.

In all there are 696,419,707 shares in issue with total net assets of £2,782,000,000, which equates to £3.994601 per share – the closing market value of the shares on 6 April was £4 a share. So there is also a tiny premium to the NAV.

And returns? In 2008, for instance, the underlying index returned –28.33 per cent while the ETF fund returned –28.59 per cent (see Table 3.11) – that tracking error of 0.26 per cent is accounted for by the total expense ratio, which was 0.40 per cent per annum.

Table 3.11 Performance difference

Period to	31/12/2007 31/12/2008
Annualised performance difference	0.26%
Performance difference is the difference between the fund and index returns	
Fund return	–28.59%
Index return	–28.33%

The bottom line? The iShares fund largely does what it says on the tin – it tracks the FTSE 100 cheaply (it is not the cheapest as Lyxor has an ETF that charges just 0.30 per cent but is considerably smaller, with less than £140m in funds), fairly accurately (the tracking error in a volatile 2008 was less than 0.30 per cent per annum) and with roughly the same holdings in proportion as the actual FTSE 100 Index.

ETFs – what to watch out for

In Chapter 5 Paul Amery from Index Universe – a web-based information resource on ETFs – will drill a little deeper into the intricacies of how funds are structured, their tax treatment and what private investors need to watch out for. But hopefully our brisk description of the development of index funds and their evolution into exchange traded funds should have alerted you to a number of likely problems.

Perhaps the most obvious is **tracking error**. When the ETF manager holds the basket of shares (or assets) that comprises the asset, notice that they do not promise to pay the actual return on the underlying index (although newer variations on the index tracking theme do in fact make this promise – look out for our description of exchange traded notes or ETNs below). They merely promise to try to track the index and sometimes a discrepancy opens up between the fund return and the index return, as we noticed with the Vanguard 500 fund where there has been a 0.2 per cent error some years. Most listed funds like ETFs manage to keep that tracking error to the absolute minimum, but be aware that some listed funds and many unit trust index trackers produce some hefty errors amounting to more than 1 per cent or even 2 per cent per annum. This tracking error is caused by a number of factors, including the following.

1 **Sampling error:** A fund may sample the universe tracked by the index rather than employ full replication. To understand this complex-sounding idea, compare an index tracking vehicle that tracks a big and easy-to-track market like the FTSE 100 with one that tracks the Chinese or Vietnamese markets, which both suffer from a number of regulatory 'issues' that include different classes of shares and government interference. It is incredibly simple to buy the basket of FTSE 100 shares cheaply and efficiently, whereas with some less efficient markets like these Asian ones errors can easily creep in. That forces index providers in these more 'difficult' markets to use a method called sampling, where they build a model that samples the spread of shares in a market but does not fully replicate it. This produces a portfolio that replicates the vast majority of the underlying index holdings, but sampling is simply never as strong as fully copying or replicating. What happens if your sampling model begins to produce errors?

2 **Regulatory requirements:** US investment company regulations state that a single company may account for no more than 25 per cent of a fund's total assets. Thus, if a company makes up more than 25 per cent of a market's index, that stock would be underweighted by the fund. To optimise a portfolio, the manager may increase weightings of other portfolio components or even go outside the index.

3 **Expenses:** Even if a fund identically weights all the stocks in its benchmark, performance will be reduced by the expense ratio (i.e. net return equals gross return of index less expenses). This is what is called the expenses drag and it is a major factor in explaining why more expensive unit trust-based trackers produce bigger tracking errors after fees.

4 Dividend payments. One other factor that can result in tracking errors for some ETFs is dividend payments. An exchange traded fund typically pays out dividends received from the underlying shares it holds on a quarterly basis, but the underlying stocks pay dividends throughout the quarter. Therefore, these funds may hold cash for various time periods throughout the quarter, even though the underlying benchmark index is not composed of cash.

Add up all these factors and it is easy to see how tiny tracking errors of, say, 0.2 per cent (typical of the Vanguard 500 index fund in the US) can turn into 2 per cent tracking errors per annum – over five or ten years that could produce some radically different returns compared with the underlying index.

Another factor to watch out for is **market risk** – the risk that the sector or the market the ETF is tracking may drop based on a variety of factors such as economic conditions and global events, investor sentiment and sector-specific factors. In a big sell-off, investors typically sell all shares regardless of structure – ETFs being very liquid may suffer disproportionately. Be honest, if you are panicking, what are you likely to sell first, an ETF share you can sell in real time via your broker or a unit trust fund where you have to wait until the end of the day to establish a proper pricing level?

Investors also need to be careful of **expensive ETFs and even more exotic indices**. The reality is that not all ETFs are created equal. Market-leading ETFs may quote wonderfully low expense ratios in their marketing blurb, but a more detailed analysis of the US market reveals huge variations in costs. A study by the US-based American Association of Individual Investors (AAII) organisation was able to identify expense ratios for 281 of the 299 funds in the US market in 2006. Of these 281 funds, 35 had an expense ratio of between 0 per cent and 0.22 per cent, 130 between 0.21 and 0.5 per cent and 96 between 0.51 per cent and 0.75 per cent. Rather more alarmingly, 14 funds had expense ratios above 0.75 per cent – that is an awfully high charge for what should be a simple exercise in tracking a major market.

Investors also need to be wary about the index that is being tracked – as competition in the sector intensifies, more suppliers are turning to highly specialised indices. In recent years, for instance, research firms have launched all manner of complex indexes that track hedge fund strategies – it is clever stuff but it is not really the same as tracking the 'bog standard' FTSE 100. If you are not careful you could end up tracking an index no one uses or cares about or which has no real economic value. Take a look at Table 3.12 for the advantages and disadvantages of ETFs.

Table 3.12 Advantages and disadvantages of ETFs

Advantages	Disadvantages
Cheap	Substantial trading costs, i.e. dealing charges and bid–offer spread. Bid–offer spread can sometimes be over 1%
Liquid and easy to trade – continuous pricing during the day	ETFs can trade at a discount or premium to net asset value
Can be shorted and leveraged to increase returns	Short track record of many funds
Huge choice and access to wide range of indices, i.e. you can broadly diversify	Unsuccessful ETFs can quickly shut down
Ability to invest in whole market through one fund	Not all ETFs are that cheap – some specialist ETFs charge close to 1%
	A tracking error can emerge, i.e. a difference between the change in the value of the fund and that of the index

Acronym city – ETFs and beyond

The basic ETF model has now been tinkered with and adapted to produce a number of structures, all built around the simple idea of index tracking via a fund.

ETFs are by far the most successful structure in the US and are currently taking Europe, and the UK in particular, by storm. The classic ETF outlined above is still pretty much the standard for the industry. This involves a process called **replicating** or copying the index using real shares held by the fund; these are also known as in-specie funds by the experts. As we have already seen this might involve a £1bn FTSE 100 ETF buying £1bn worth of FTSE 100 shares in the exact proportion as the index.

But in recent years two new variations have arrived on the same theme. One innovative model involves the provider abandoning physical replication altogether – a new structure emerges that involves a swaps-based contract worth up to 10 per cent of the value of the fund, which guarantees to generate the index payment, while the remaining 90 per cent (or more in some cases) consists of shares held as security or backup (known as collateral). Those shares may be those being tracked but may be completely different and are used only as collateral. These swaps, or IOUs, are effectively guarantees by another financial party to pay out the exact return from the underlying index – thus smoothing out any discrepancy between the index return and the fund return.

This swaps-based structure – using a combination of 'secured' assets (shares lodged as collateral) and a futures-based swaps contract – has already mutated as competition has intensified. Some issuers have developed fully synthetic-based funds, which consist only of swaps-based contracts (these are structurally very similar to what are called tracker certificates), while other issuers have stuck to the 90/10 collateral/swaps idea and offered gilts or even cash as the secure assets held in collateral overlaid by those swaps futures contracts. With all these structures it is important to realise that although you are buying a FTSE 100 tracker, for instance, you may not be holding any shares which actually constitute that index – the options purchased guarantee the index return but you are taking on some 'counterparty risk' because that payout is only as good as the bank or institution issuing the swap or the quality of assets held as collateral.

Exchange traded commodities (ETCs) do what they say on the tin – they track either a physical spot commodity market price or a composite commodity index. In effect they are close to the synthetic ETF structure noted above, in that the fund managers (ETF securities in the UK) buy swaps with a counterparty which in turn guarantees to pay out the returns of the underlying index. With many of these commodities-based funds the underlying index is also not comprised of shares but futures indices – we will examine the specifics of the commodity tracking sector in Chapter 4.

The more mass-market variation of the index fund is called the **mutual** or **unit trust**. This structure is based on the big daddy of index funds, the Vanguard 500 fund. It is an open-ended vehicle that is priced daily and which may issue new units on a daily basis if it so chooses as more and more investors buy in. These are typically run by large fund management groups like Vanguard in the US and Fidelity, Scottish Widows, Legal and General and HSBC in the UK. There should be no discrepancy between the underlying value of the units and the price quoted to your adviser or dealer and any dividends that come from holding the shares in the portfolio are distributed as a yield, paid on a regular interval, to unit holders.

Beware – not all trackers are cheap

It never ceases to amaze how brilliantly the UK-based financial services industry can take a simple concept like the tracker and then comprehensively foul it up. Trackers – whatever their structure – should be cheap, it is part of their USP (unique selling point). Yet in the UK some trackers are distinctly poor value. The horrible fact is that there is a 1.7 percentage point difference between the lowest and the highest tracker annual management charges in sectors like the FTSE All or the FTSE 100.

According to one respected adviser in the field, Patrick Connolly, research and investment manager at John Scott & Partners, that difference is inexcusable: 'We believe 0.5 per cent is absolutely the most you should be paying for a tracker fund.' Another analyst, from Hargreaves Landown, a stockbroker cum IFA, put it even more succinctly: 'Tracker funds charging 1 per cent are a rip-off in my view.'

Yet the list of high-charging tracker unit trusts in particular is lamentably long. Here is our roll call of dishonour: Axa UK Tracker, Credit Suisse FTSE 100 Tracker, DWS UK All-Share Equity Tracker, Eagle Star UK Index Tracker, Gartmore UK Tracker, Halifax's FTSE 100 and UK All-Share Trackers, Isis FTSE 100 Tracker, L&G UK Stock market, Marks & Spencer UK 100 Companies, Norwich Union's tracker range Sovereign FTSE 100, St James's Place Tracker and Virgin UK Index Tracking.

Charges vary even more significantly on indices outside the UK market. For example, Allianz Dresdner charges 0.25 per cent a year more for its Euro Index Tracker than it does for its UK offering. At the same time, HSBC has a range of fees going from 0.5 per cent for its UK and Japan trackers to 1 per cent for some of its other regional tracker funds. The bottom line is simple – never accept an index tracker costing more than 1 per cent per annum, especially when there are plenty of good funds (identified in this book) that charge 0.5 per cent p.a. or less.

This shocking state of affairs reflects rather badly on UK-based index fund providers. In the US, by contrast, market leaders like Vanguard have priced their funds aggressively to undercut even ETF providers. Leading Vanguard funds are frequently priced at less than 0.20 per cent per annum, and for major, large markets exchange traded funds are rarely cheaper than their mutual fund rivals. Vanguard is also quick to point out that its funds never trade at a discount (or premium) to net asset value and that its mutual funds are better suited to investors looking to make a regular (monthly) investment. 'Trading costs tend to make ETFs less suitable as investments for company-sponsored retirement plan accounts, because plan participants typically make frequent contributions. Unless the ETF's expense ratio advantage is substantial, transaction-oriented costs can quickly overwhelm the benefit of a lower expense.'[8] Just to confuse matters though, Vanguard has in recent years conceded that ETFs have some value and it now offers not only mutual funds but also ETFs.

Table 3.13 Vanguard mutual funds vs Vanguard ETFs

	Mutual index fund	Vanguard ETF
Total US Stock market Index	0.15%	0.07%
Total World Stock	0.25% plus 0.25% purchase fee	0.25%
Total US Bond Market	0.19%	0.11%

Table 3.14 Snapshot of conventional index fund shares versus ETFs

Conventional index funds in the US and the UK	ETF shares
Purchased and redeemed directly from fund company	Purchased and sold on secondary market through stock brokers
Provided once a day at 4pm at net asset value	Priced by market throughout the day and market price can differ moderately from net asset value
No brokerage fees but possibly up-front initial charge: low expense ratios outside the UK	Broking fees for every transaction; the vast majority of ETF shares have expense ratios lower than those for most mutual funds
Trading restrictions in order to curtail frequent trading	No restrictions
Cannot be sold short, on margin or using stop, limit or open orders	Can be sold short, margin trading possible, stop, limit or open orders possible

Source: Vanguard

Table 3.15 US costs – active mutual funds versus index mutual funds versus iShares ETFs

Fund category	Average active fund expense ratio %	Average index fund expense ratio %	iShares fund	The fund
US taxable bond	1.10%	0.39%	0.15%	Lehman 1–3-year Treasury and iBoxx $ Investment Grade Corporate
Large cap/blend	1.30%	0.62%	0.09%	S&P 500
Large cap value bias	1.40%	0.63%	0.20%	Russell 1000 Value and S&P 500 Value
Small cap	1.57%	0.74%	0.20%	Russell 2000 and S&P 500 Small Cap 600
Diversified foreign equity	1.74%	0.81%	0.75%	MSCI Emerging Markets
Specialist equity	1.73%	0.56%	0.48%	DJ US Sector Series

Yet another variation is the index tracker **investment trust**. There are a small number of index tracking funds in the UK listed as traditional investment trusts which also happen to track key UK and US indices. These investment trusts are like all their peers in that they issue a fixed number of shares, although they may also issue subsequent tranches of shares to raise additional capital. They may also boast fixed terms, i.e. they wind up after a specified date, and their institutional structure is like any other quoted company. They have a board, which reports interims and finals, and has shares that are quoted on a real-time basis, although the trust will typically issue a daily net asset value update, plus there is a management team hired by the board to run the fund. Like ETFs, a difference may emerge between the underlying net asset value and the market price and this is expressed as either a discount or premium to NAV, but there is no creation and redemption process to keep that difference in check. UK examples include the Edinburgh US and UK investment trust trackers.

You may increasingly encounter yet stranger creatures called **certificates and ETNs**. Certificates are a fairly new innovation in the investment market and are in fact a hybrid product and very popular on the European mainland. They were developed by traditional covered warrants issuers like SG, which wanted to move into the index tracking space. Investors typically buy a certificate that offers direct exposure to an index for either a fixed period of time or an open-ended commitment. Those funds are then used to purchase options that 'buy' that index with the counterparty – frequently the investment bank that issues the certificate – guaranteeing to pay the return on the index, thus eliminating any risk of tracking error or a discount/premium. In the US these certificates are also known as exchange traded notes or ETNs. These are virtually identical to European certificates in that the issuer effectively promises to pay the return on the index. No income is paid out via dividends and all the returns are rolled up into the fund return, thus triggering capital gains tax only at sale. The key issue for both certificates and ETNs is the counterparty risk – the promise to pay is worth anything only if you think that institution (usually a bank) is going to be in business in the future. If not, your ETN could be worthless. Paul Amery discusses counterparty risk in Chapter 5.

On a similar theme there are vehicles called **structured product investment trusts**, offering a very different tracking proposition. They are structured like an investment trust – they are closed end, typically with a finite life span, and they track a core index, frequently the FTSE 100. But they also offer some form of geared upside, typically more than 100 per cent of the increase of the underlying index, and also frequently offer some form of capital protection on the issue price provided the index does not fall too much in value. They do not pay out a dividend from holding the underlying basket of shares. They are similar in style to **investment notes**, which are the newest innovation in the market. Effectively they are a cross between a certificate and structured product investment trusts. They are issued by Barclays (not its iShares unit note) and traded on the secondary market like a structured investment trust.

Phenomenal growth worldwide

The ETF revolution is now truly global – in almost every part of the developed world new ETF providers are springing up and ETFs are even threatening to invade the developing world with new launches in places as varied as Botswana and Taiwan.

The guardian of all key ETF data is Deborah Fuhr, a managing director at the iShares ETF business. For the last few years she has been chronicling the remorseless rise of the ETF sector, starting from very small acorns in the early 1990s (with the launch of the SPIDER funds) through to today's vibrant marketplace where ETFs seem to be almost the only form of fund still growing in the midst of one of the worst bear markets on record.

The aggregate data from Fuhr's 2008 Year Preview sets this extraordinary growth in context. The key observation is the continued growth in funds under management. According to Fuhr's analysis, 'on a global basis ETF net sales were US$187.5bn while net sales of mutual funds were minus US$256.7bn through the end of October'. By iShares, reckoning at the end of 2008 the global ETF industry had 1,590 ETFs with assets of $711.0bn, from 85 providers on 42 exchanges around the world. Crucially, active traders seem to be embracing the ETF revolution – the iShares data suggests that in 2008 the average daily trading volume in US dollars increased by 32.5 per cent to $80.4bn. And that extraordinary decades-long growth shows no signs of abating – according to Fuhr there are plans to launch 604 new ETFs.

Much of the recent growth seems to have centred on Europe and especially the UK (see Table 3.17). At the end of 2008 the European ETF industry had 632 ETFs with 1,539 listings, assets of $142.82bn, from 29 providers on 19 exchanges, and in 2008 assets under management by the ETF companies had risen by 11.2 per cent, with the number of ETFs increasing by 49 per cent (219 new ETFs were launched in 2008 alone).

Table 3.16 Summary of structures

Structure	Listed on stock market, i.e. buy through a stockbroker	Full replication, i.e. full physical basket of underlying assets	Uses swaps (or other derivatives) to produce index return	Major counterparty risk	Could pay an income	Real-time dealing	Can a discount or premium emerge to NAV?	Any capital protection on offer?	Tax treatment	Stamp duty on purchase?
(Classic) exchange traded funds	Yes	Yes	No	No	Yes	Yes	Yes	No	CGT on capital gains income tax on income	No
Unit trust or mutual fund index fund	No	Yes	No	No	Yes	No – daily only	No	No	CGT on capital gains income tax on income	Yes
Investment trust tracker	Yes	Yes	No	No	Yes	Yes	Yes	No	CGT on capital gains income tax on income	Yes
Certificate	Yes	No	Yes	Yes	No	Yes	No	Yes – in some cases	Only CGT	No
Exchange traded note (US only)	Yes	No	Yes	Yes	No	Yes	No	No	Only CGT	No
Synthetic ETCs or ETFs	Yes	No	Yes	Yes	No	Yes	No	No	Only CGT	No
(Hybrid) European ETFs issued by Lyxor and Deutsche DBX	Yes	No	Yes	No	Yes	Yes	Yes	No	CGT on capital gains income tax on income	No
Listed structured products and investment trusts	Yes	No	Yes	Yes	No	Yes	No	Yes – in some cases	Only CGT	No

Table 3.17 Growth in global ETF market

	Global Dec 08	Global YTD change %	US Dec 08	US YTD change %	Europe Dec 08	Europe YTD change %	Japan Dec 08	Japan YTD change %	Asia ex Japan Dec 08	Asia ex Japan YTD change %
Assets under management $bn	711	-10.8%	497	-14%	142	11.2%	27.43	-19%	23	-12.7%
Number of ETFs	1590	35.8%	698	16.1%	632	49%	61	306%	95	37%
Number of providers	85	13.3%	18	5.9%	29	3.6%	5	25%	34	25.9%
Daily trading volumes US $m	80387	32.5%	77,028	32%	2025	21.69%	169	51%	527	85%

	1993	1994	1995	1996	1997	1998	1999	2000	2001	2002	2003	2004	2005	2006	2007	Dec 2008
ETF assets total	0.8	1.1	2.3	5.3	8.2	17.6	39.6	74.3	104.8	141.6	212	309	412	565	796	711
Commodity assets										0.1	0.3	0.5	1.2	3.4	5.3	9.9
Fixed-income assets								0.1	0.1	4	5.8	23.1	21.3	35.8	59.9	104
ETP assets													15.6	28.1	45.9	53.2
Number of ETFS	3	3	4	21	21	31	33	92	202	280	282	335	461	714	1171	1589

Source: iShares

The UK has not missed out on this exponential growth, although most of its increase has come only in the last few years. This late-adopter status is even more curious bearing in mind that the world's leading ETF issuer – with 45 per cent of the worldwide market for ETFs and the leading player in the US – is a British company. Step forward iShares. To describe it as a powerhouse of the ETF industry is to sell it short. One of its recent gushing PR releases states: 'iShares is the world's leading ETF brand, with 181 ETFs trading globally, registered in 10 countries and amounting to approximately US$272.2 billion in assets under management (as at 1 December 2006).' Yet despite its huge international market share, its UK presence has until recently been fairly subdued.

It waited until April 2000 to launch its first three ETFs, one based on the FTSE 100, one on the DJ STOXX 50 and one on the DJ EuroSTOXX 50. In December 2000 it launched just one more fund, this time based on the FTSEurofirst 80, followed by another two between 2001 and 2002. In 2003 there were three more funds and in 2004 the number swelled to another six. The biggest growth in the UK market was in 2007 and 2008 – it now has more than 60 funds on the London market. It is still the biggest provider in the tracker space by far. Every year iShares issues more and more funds – usually in two cycles, one around late spring and the other in late autumn – and investors should confidently expect it to add to its existing range. One note of caution about iShares – its focus until recently has been on serving the institutional market and it has not really bothered to develop products aimed exclusively at private investors, although that is changing fast.

As iShares has grown in confidence, so have its competitors. In the main market for general funds, French-owned Lyxor (part of SocGen), and Deutsche DBX (owned by Deutsche Bank) have emerged along with smaller niche players such as ETF Securities (a big player in commodities), Powershares (part of the wider Invesco Perpetual stable of funds) and SPA, a small, British-based US funds specialist sold under the MarketGrader platform.

This global growth has been accompanied by an increasing number of new exchange traded structures. Some of these structures are particularly useful for private investors, allowing them to combine asset classes in one ETF or gear up returns.

Leveraged exchange traded funds and ETNs have been growing fast in the US, led by small providers such as Direxion and Rydex. The first wave of funds offered investors *inverse* ETFs that made money from falling markets alongside geared ETFs that leveraged up returns in bull markets. Initially these were offered as simple 1:1 trackers, but as this niche has expanded fast that has quickly been extended to 2× bear (they go up when markets go down) and bull (they go up when markets go up) trackers. This market evolved again in 2009 with the launch by US provider Direxion of 3× bear and bull trackers on the major indices, including the Russell 1000 sub-index of energy companies and the MSCI Emerging Markets Index. The full list is in Table 3.18.

Table 3.18 List of US leveraged funds

Symbol	Fund	Index/Benchmark	Daily target	Bloomberg index symbol
Bull				
BGU	Large Cap Bull 3× Shares	Russell 1000	300%	RIY
TNA	Small Cap Bull 3× Shares	Russell 2000	300%	RTY
ERX	Energy Bull 3× Shares	Russell 1000 Energy	300%	RGUSEL
FAS	Financial Bull 3× Shares	Russell 1000 Financial Services	300%	RGUSFL
DZK	Developed Markets Bull 3× Shares	MSCI EAFE Index	300%	MXEA
EDC	Emerging Markets Bull 3× Shares	MSCI Emerging Markets Index	300%	MXEF
TYH	Technology Bull 3× Shares	Russell 1000 Technology Index	300%	RGUSTL
MWJ	Mid Cap Bull 3× Shares	Russell Midcap Index	300%	RMC
Bear				
BGZ	Large Cap Bear 3× Shares	Russell 1000	−300%	RIY
TZA	Small Cap Bear 3× Shares	Russell 2000	−300%	RTY
ERY	Energy Bear 3× Shares	Russell 1000 Energy	−300%	RGUSEL
FAZ	Financial Bear 3× Shares	Russell 1000 Financial Services	−300%	RGUSFL
DPK	Developed Markets Bear 3× Shares	MSCI EAFE Index	−300%	MXEA
EDZ	Emerging Markets Bear 3× Shares	MSCI Emerging Markets Index	−300%	MXEF
TYP	Technology Bear 3× Shares	Russell 1000 Technology Index	−300%	RGUSTL
MWN	Mid Cap Bear 3× Shares	Russell Midcap Index	−300%	RMC

These leveraged funds, currently at least, make their geared returns based on daily pricing – that means you should receive 3× the return of the underlying index on a daily basis. That gearing on both the downside and the upside means that these ETFs can become hugely volatile. It also means that they are not ideal for long-term investors looking to capture a major trend playing out on the markets. To see how this can happen in the table below we've looked at one of the sets of Direxion ETFs, the energy shares that track the Russell 1000 index of mega-cap energy companies. Tables 3.19 and 3.20 below detail the returns every day over March 2009 of the 3× bull and bear shares.

Over this one month the underlying index moved up by 11.3 per cent in total (between 2 March and 31 March), which was clearly good news if you held the bull shares, which aim to pay out 3× the daily returns of the index. You thus might have expected the bull shares to go up by 34 per cent, say, but in reality the bull shares went up only 29.87 per cent – that lower return was because the underlying index had some bad days where the index lost over 4 per cent, which in turn produced double-digit losses for the bull shares. Those losses eat into the capital sum and have a disproportionate effect on compound returns, yet on a daily basis the actual tracking error (the last column on the right) was remarkably low, at under 0.06 per cent per day including expenses. Clearly, you would also expect the bear shares to have done badly and they did in fact fall back by more than 3× the monthly return, dropping more than 36 per cent over the month, in part because of the compounding effect of big losses. The point here is that daily returns mean daily returns and these hugely volatile ETFs will deliver some unusual returns over a long period if markets are very volatile – do not expect an asset class that goes up over 50 per cent in a year to produce a straight 150 per cent gain in the bull shares if markets have yo-yo'd up and down over this year. Nevertheless the value of these products is obvious, especially for more active investors looking to gear up their returns from an asset class in either direction.

Unsurprisingly other ETF providers have jumped on board this broad trend. In the UK one of the major provider of bear trackers is Deutsche DBX with its popular FTSE 100 inverse tracker, while ETF Securities has quietly been building up its leveraged and inverse/short-commodity trackers structured as exchange traded certificates (ETCs are also known as ETPs or exchange traded products). The leveraged ETCs offer 2× the upside while the short ETCs offer 1× gains with every 1× move down in the index. The full list of ETF Securities, leveraged and short ETCs is given in Table 3.21.

Table 3.19 Direxion energy bear 3x shares

	Index return			Components of expected fund return				Fund return	
Date	RGUSEL	Index return	–3 return	Fees and expenses	Expected return	Expected NAV	ERY NAV	Daily return	Tracking difference
02-Mar-09	446.60	-6.686%	20.059%	-0.003%	20.056%	$60.83	$58.93	20.069%	0.013%
03-Mar-09	448.42	0.408%	-1.223%	-0.003%	-1.225%	$60.08	$58.21	-1.222%	0.003%
04-Mar-09	467.57	4.271%	-12.812%	-0.003%	-12.814%	$52.38	$50.74	-12.833%	-0.019%
05-Mar-09	445.30	-4.763%	14.289%	-0.003%	14.286%	$59.87	$57.98	14.269%	-0.017%
06-Mar-09	451.06	1.294%	-3.881%	-0.008%	-3.888%	$57.54	$55.68	-3.967%	-0.078%
09-Mar-09	453.37	0.512%	-1.536%	-0.003%	-1.539%	$56.65	$54.81	-1.563%	-0.023%
10-Mar-09	477.70	5.366%	-16.099%	-0.003%	-16.102%	$47.53	$45.99	-16.092%	0.010%
11-Mar-09	472.18	-1.156%	3.467%	-0.003%	3.464%	$49.18	$47.56	3.414%	-0.050%
12-Mar-09	486.17	2.963%	-8.889%	-0.003%	-8.891%	$44.81	$43.32	-8.915%	-0.024%
13-Mar-09	482.48	-0.759%	2.277%	-0.008%	2.269%	$45.82	$44.30	2.262%	-0.007%
16-Mar-09	486.32	0.796%	-2.388%	-0.003%	-2.390%	$44.73	$43.25	-2.370%	0.020%
17-Mar-09	503.14	3.459%	-10.376%	-0.003%	-10.379%	$40.09	$38.76	-10.382%	-0.003%
18-Mar-09	507.74	0.914%	-2.743%	-0.003%	-2.745%	$38.98	$37.70	-2.735%	0.011%
19-Mar-09	516.31	1.688%	-5.064%	-0.003%	-5.066%	$37.01	$35.79	-5.066%	0.000%
20-Mar-09	496.66	-3.806%	11.418%	-0.008%	11.410%	$41.23	$39.88	11.428%	0.018%
23-Mar-09	536.07	7.935%	-23.805%	-0.003%	-23.808%	$31.42	$30.39	-23.796%	0.011%
24-Mar-09	524.17	-2.220%	6.660%	-0.003%	6.657%	$33.51	$32.41	6.647%	-0.010%
25-Mar-09	526.88	0.517%	-1.551%	-0.003%	-1.554%	$32.99	$31.91	-1.543%	0.011%
26-Mar-09	532.41	1.050%	-3.149%	-0.003%	-3.151%	$31.95	$30.90	-3.165%	-0.014%
27-Mar-09	517.54	-2.793%	8.379%	-0.008%	8.371%	$34.62	$33.49	8.382%	0.011%
30-Mar-09	499.72	-3.443%	10.330%	-0.003%	10.327%	$38.20	$36.94	10.302%	-0.025%
31-Mar-09	**497.18**	-0.508%	1.525%	-0.003%	1.522%	**$38.78**	**$37.50**	1.516%	-0.006%
Change over month	11.33						-36.37		

Table 3.20 Direxion energy bull 3x shares

	Index return			Components of expected fund return				Fund return	
Date	RGUSEL	Index return	3 return	Fees and expenses	Expected return	Expected NAV	ERY NAV	Daily return	Tracking difference
02-Mar-09	446.60	-6.686%	-20.059%	-0.003%	-20.061%	$17.37	$17.71	-20.081%	-0.020%
03-Mar-09	448.42	0.408%	1.223%	-0.003%	1.220%	$17.58	$17.92	1.186%	-0.034%
04-Mar-09	467.57	4.271%	12.812%	-0.003%	12.809%	$19.83	$20.22	12.835%	0.026%
05-Mar-09	445.30	-4.763%	-14.289%	-0.003%	-14.291%	$17.00	$17.30	-14.441%	-0.150%
06-Mar-09	451.06	1.294%	3.881%	-0.008%	3.873%	$17.65	$17.98	3.931%	0.058%
09-Mar-09	453.37	0.512%	1.536%	-0.003%	1.534%	$17.92	$18.26	1.557%	0.023%
10-Mar-09	477.70	5.366%	16.099%	-0.003%	16.097%	$20.81	$21.20	16.101%	0.004%
11-Mar-09	472.18	-1.156%	-3.467%	-0.003%	-3.469%	$20.09	$20.47	-3.443%	0.026%
12-Mar-09	486.17	2.963%	8.889%	-0.003%	8.886%	$21.87	$22.30	8.940%	0.054%
13-Mar-09	482.48	-0.759%	-2.277%	-0.008%	-2.285%	$21.37	$21.79	-2.287%	-0.002%
16-Mar-09	486.32	0.796%	2.388%	-0.003%	2.385%	$21.88	$22.31	2.386%	0.001%
17-Mar-09	503.14	3.459%	10.376%	-0.003%	10.373%	$24.15	$24.62	10.354%	-0.019%
18-Mar-09	507.74	0.914%	2.743%	-0.003%	2.740%	$24.81	$25.30	2.762%	0.022%
19-Mar-09	516.31	1.688%	5.064%	-0.003%	5.061%	$26.07	$26.58	5.059%	-0.002%
20-Mar-09	496.66	-3.806%	-11.418%	-0.008%	-11.425%	$23.09	$23.54	-11.437%	-0.012%
23-Mar-09	536.07	7.935%	23.805%	-0.003%	23.802%	$28.59	$29.14	23.789%	-0.013%
24-Mar-09	524.17	-2.220%	-6.660%	-0.003%	-6.662%	$26.68	$27.14	-6.673%	-0.011%
25-Mar-09	526.88	0.517%	1.551%	-0.003%	1.548%	$27.10	$27.56	1.548%	-0.001%
26-Mar-09	532.41	1.050%	3.149%	-0.003%	3.146%	$27.95	$28.43	3.157%	0.011%
27-Mar-09	517.54	-2.793%	-8.379%	-0.008%	-8.387%	$25.61	$26.04	-8.407%	-0.020%
30-Mar-09	499.72	-3.443%	-10.330%	-0.003%	-10.332%	$22.96	$23.35	-10.330%	0.002%
31-Mar-09	497.18	-0.508%	-1.525%	-0.003%	-1.527%	$22.61	$23.00	-1.499%	0.028%
Change over month	11.32557						29.87013		

Table 3.21 ETF Securities' leveraged and share ETCs

Name	EPIC
LEVERAGED ETCs	
ETFS Leveraged Agriculture Dj-aigci	LAGR
ETFS Leveraged All Commodities Dj-aigci	LALL
ETFS Leveraged Aluminium	LALU
ETFS Leveraged Cocoa	LCOC
ETFS Leveraged Coffee	LCFE
ETFS Leveraged Copper	LCOP
ETFS Leveraged Corn	LCOR
ETFS Leveraged Cotton	LCTO
ETFS Leveraged Crude Oil	LOIL
ETFS Leveraged Energy Dj-aigci	LNRG
ETFS Leveraged Ex-energy Dj-aigci	LNEY
ETFS Leveraged Gasoline	LGAS
ETFS Leveraged Gold	LBUL
ETFS Leveraged Grains Dj-aigci	LGRA
ETFS Leveraged Heating Oil	LHEA
ETFS Leveraged Industrial Metal DJ-AIGCI	LIME
ETFS Leveraged Lead	LLEA
ETFS Leveraged Lean Hogs	LLHO
ETFS Leveraged Live Cattle	LLCT
ETFS Leveraged Livestock Dj-aigci	LLST
ETFS Leveraged Natural Gas	LNGA
ETFS Leveraged Nickel	LNIK
ETFS Leveraged Petroleum Dj-aigci	LPET
ETFS Leveraged Platinum	LPLA

Table 3.21 Continued

Name	EPIC
ETFS Leveraged Precious Metals DJ-AIGCI	LPMT
ETFS Leveraged Silver	LSIL
ETFS Leveraged Softs Dj-aigci	LSFT
ETFS Leveraged Soybean Oil	LSYO
ETFS Leveraged Soybeans	LSOB
ETFS Leveraged Sugar	LSUG
ETFS Leveraged Tin	LTIM
ETFS Leveraged Wheat	LWEA
ETFS Leveraged Zinc	LZIC
INVERSE ETCs	
ETFS Short Agriculture DJ-AIGCI	SAGR
ETFS Short All Commodities DJ-AIGCI	SALL
ETFS Short Aluminium	SALU
ETFS Short Cocoa	SCOC
ETFS Short Coffee	SCFE
ETFS Short Copper	SCOP
ETFS Short Corn	SCOR
ETFS Short Cotton	SCTO
ETFS Short Crude Oil	SOIL
ETFS Short Energy DJ-AIGCI	SNRG
ETFS Short Ex-energy DJ-AIGCI	SNEY
ETFS Short Gasoline	SGAS
ETFS Short Gold	SBUL
ETFS Short Grains DJ-AIGCI	SGRA
ETFS Short Heating Oil	SHEA

Table 3.21 Continued

Name	EPIC
ETFS Short Industrial Metals DJ-AIGCI	SIME
ETFS Short Lead	SLEA
ETFS Short Lean Hogs	SLHO
ETFS Short Live Cattle	SLCT
ETFS Short Livestock DJ-AIGCI	SLST
ETFS Short Natural Gas	SNGA
ETFS Short Nickel	SNIK
ETFS Short Petroleum DJ-AIGCI	SPET
ETFS Short Platinum	SPLA
ETFS Short Precious Metals DJ-AIGCI	SPMT
ETFS Short Silver	SSIL
ETFS Short Softs DJ-AIGCI	SSFT
ETFS Short Soybean Oil	SSYO
ETFS Short Soybeans	SSOB
ETFS Short Sugar	SSUG
ETFS Short Tin	STIM
ETFS Short Wheat	SWEA
ETFS Short Zinc	SZIC

iShares has not been left behind when it comes to new product ideas and has been developing a new platform consisting of **multi ETF portfolio funds**. These typically offer investors a portfolio of various asset classes comprised of iShare's own ETFs, all packaged into one fund appealing to everything from low-risk to high-risk investors. We will look at these funds in more detail at the end of this book when we examine how investors can use ETFs to build their own portfolio. iShare's competitors have also been developing their own takes on a one-size-fits-all approach, trying to develop a singular fund that could be used as the major building block of a portfolio, if not comprise the whole portfolio in one fund. US firm

Claymore, for instance, has licensed a small proprietary index (from Dorchester Capital Management) to offer a total market ETF that includes sub-indices that track everything from key US equity segments to bond markets. We will look at this new fund later in the book as well.

The greatest innovation has been felt in the commodity space. There were no ETFs tracking this huge and varied investment space until 2000 but since then the market has exploded, with new funds launching every month, tracking every conceivable part of the commodity business. There are now hundreds of funds on offer in the UK market and one firm in particular, ETF Securities, has carved out a reputation for daring and innovative funds. In the next chapter we will look at this specialist niche in greater detail, examine the rationale for investing in this alternative asset category and look at the structures used to track the major indices.

4

Investing in commodities using index funds

A funny thing happened in the early part of the first decade of the twenty-first century – investing in commodities suddenly became sexy.

Anyone who remembers the wonderful John Landis film *Trading Places*, starring Eddie Murphy and Dan Akroyd as the hapless victims of a giant bet placed by some Wall Street titans, will also remember their subsequent encounters with the peculiar but high-powered business of pork belly futures trading. Commodities, you could reasonably surmise from the film, was a slightly obscure, rather niche business that was best left to specialists. Gold has always had its admirers and oil has been gaining traction in investing circles, but most investors remain firmly wedded to the great bonds:equities face-off.

At the turn of the century barely any commodity-based index funds existed worldwide. Then the wider investing world started becoming interested in the peculiar business of commodities trading. It is impossible to pin any one factor on what prompted the change, but as interest increased, commodity prices started soaring. Whether it was a booming global economy or possibly China, something seemed to have permanently changed. The legendary biking billionaire Jim Rogers caught the wave of euphoria perfectly in *Hot Commodities: How Anyone Can Invest Profitably in the World's Best Market*, a best-seller that clearly laid out the argument for a commodity super-cycle to beat all others, driven by a booming global population, China's industrialisation and a global economy operating at full capacity drawing down on limited reserves of key resources such as oil and coal.[1]

Small British exchange traded fund firm ETF Securities came to typify this incredible wave of investment euphoria. The management behind the small asset management firm launched the world's first listed index tracking fund called Gold Bullion Securities in Australia, followed in 2004 by a London-based sibling of the same name. In July 2005 it stepped up a gear and launched the world's first oil index tracking fund, ETFS Brent Oil, and by 2006 it had $2bn in assets under management on the London Stock Exchange. By 2008 inflows into ETF Securities funds were totalling more than $170m a week and the firm had over 50 different funds on five different exchanges. Flash forward yet another year, to the beginning of 2009, and the firm had over $9bn under management in an astonishing 130 different index tracking funds. Suddenly mainstream British and American newspapers were writing about exchange traded commodities almost as much as mainstream bond ETFs – if not more.

A visitor from Mars might be tempted to ask at this point what was behind this huge success. Cynics were and are tempted to point to those rising prices – are commodities the classic momentum play involving shallow investors chasing the booming sectors until they crest, then fall, taking private investors' money with them? The statistics suggest otherwise. A wide range of commodities hit a peak in the early part of 2008 – oil crashed past $145 a barrel, for instance – yet by the end of the year most were on their back up as the global depression set in. Yet inflows into ETF Securities index funds have continued to grow – investment in gold exchange traded commodity funds set new records in the first part of 2009.

A more subtle process seems to be at work – the mainstreaming in portfolio terms of commodities. You did not have to buy all the arguments surrounding a commodity super bull cycle to accept that resources have a role in a portfolio. Even hard-bitten, research-led outfits, like Ibbotson Associates, one of the world's leading consultancy firms, had concluded that commodities provided valuable diversification for investors of all shapes and sizes. In March 2006 the US bond giant Pimco commissioned the firm's researchers to look at commodities as part of a wider portfolio planning process. This research commission itself deserves some note. Pimco is a dedicated bonds house and for it to ask the world's leading investment research consultancy to look into the value of commodities in a portfolio is itself a testament to commodities mainstreaming.

But it was Ibbotson's conclusions that were even more revealing. The researchers discovered that magically adding some commodity index fund exposure to your portfolio appeared to add real diversification and spiced up returns. Looking at the period 1970–2004 the researchers found that this extra spice could be worth as much as an extra 133 basis points per annum to total returns. They concluded: 'We believe that commodities offer an inherent or natural return that is not conditional on skill.' The causes of this extra performance bonus were legion but none seemed to really matter. The researchers decided that commodities nearly always seemed to improve the risk/return characteristics of a portfolio, especially in inflationary times.

The Ibbotson research drew on an earlier, much more important paper that deserves a quick mention, 'Facts and Fantasies about Commodity Futures'. This 2005 paper by Gorton and Rouwenhorst looked at returns from commodities over the 45 years to 2005 and concluded that 'the average annualized return to a collateralized investment in commodity futures has been comparable to the return on the SP500 ... [and] ... outperformed corporate bonds'. These equity-like returns had been achieved with higher volatility, the authors concluded, and decade-long returns varied greatly (1970s great versus stocks, 1990s bad versus stocks), but crucially they discovered that 'over all horizons – except monthly – the equally-weighted commodity futures total return is negatively correlated with the return on the SP500 and long-term bonds. ... These findings suggest that Commodity Futures are effective in diversifying equity and bond portfolios'. Even more importantly, the longer the holding period of the commodity index, the bigger the diversification benefit. They also investigated what provided this diversification and suggested two factors. 'First, commodity futures perform better in periods of unexpected inflation, when stock and bond returns generally disappoint. Second, commodity futures diversify the cyclical variation in stock and bond returns.' See Table 4.1.

Table 4.1 risk premium of commodity futures, stocks and bonds –
annualised monthly returns 1959 to end 2004

	Commodity futures	Stocks	Bonds
Average	5.23	5.65	2.22
Standard deviation	12.10	14.85	8.47
Sharpe ratio	0.43	0.38	.26
% returns above 0%	55	57	54

Research findings from Gorton and Rouwenhorst on volatility in commodities and equities include the following:

■ During the 5 per cent of the months of worst performance of equity markets, when stocks fell on average by 8.98 per cent per month, commodity futures experienced a positive return of 1.03 per cent, which is slightly above the full sample average return of 0.89 per cent per month.

■ During the 1 per cent of months of lowest performance of equity markets, when equities fell on average by 13.87 per cent per month, commodity futures returned an average of 2.36 per cent.

Commodities, the academics finished, provided one last supreme advantage: inflation proofing. They noted that commodity futures had 'outpaced local CPI inflation in the UK and Japan'. With conclusions like these, it is little surprise that both private and institutional investors have suddenly decided to jump on board the commodities super-cycle, pouring money into index tracking funds provided by ETF Securities.

How to invest using index tracking funds

This London-based asset management firm is far from being the only provider of index tracking commodity funds. In the US Powershares is very active, as is the ELEMENTS ETN platform, while in London Lyxor has its own small range of broad commodity index ETFs, but it offers by far the biggest choice through its exchange traded commodities platform. Structures include:

■ classic ETCs based on a major family of futures indices developed by Dow Jones and AIG;

■ leveraged or geared upside ETCs based on the same index family but gearing up the upside;

■ short or inverse ETCs that make money for investors even as a commodity falls in value;

■ physical ETCs which are not based on an index as such but physically hold a commodity on behalf of an investor. They track the spot price of a commodity rather than the futures price of an index;

■ Futures ETCs which allow investors to track the 3- and 12-month futures price of a commodity.

This fearsome list of structures (each family of funds has dozens of specific commodities) should immediately alert investors to one crucial distinction: what exactly is it that you are tracking? Are you tracking the spot price or the futures price of an index? This distinction is hugely important – many investors make no distinction between these two sets of prices, overlaying their judgements about the spot price (gold going up, oil going down) into the futures markets, which boast very different dynamics.

Spot prices v the futures index

When most ordinary investors think of commodities they think of the spot price that is quoted in the media, but in reality most professionals tend to ignore this as an investable idea except as the core component of something much more important – most commodity investors tend to use an index of some sort as the basis of their investment process and that index usually incorporates some form of futures contract.

Before diving into the slightly murky world of futures-based commodity indices it is worth mentioning that there are a small number of vehicles that do track actual spot commodity prices, in a fashion. On the London stock market both Close and BNP Paribas offer investment trusts (with tickers of EMB and CEO respectively) that structure a long-term investment (five years or more) around the final total returns of a combination of spot prices. These 'basket funds' usually mix and match energy-based commodities with hard commodities like metals and some agricultural prices also known as softs. The resulting basket is then offered to investors with a geared upside that ranges between 200 per cent and 350 per cent of any gains in the combination of spot prices.

This makes for easy-to-understand vehicles – which also offer some capital protection – but these structured investment trusts are not really representative of the mainstream of commodity investing. The ETCs and ETFs offered by ETF Securities (and Lyxor) tend to be based on broader indices that base their returns on futures-based contracts. In technical language this means that these commodity indices represent the total return of something called a non-leveraged (no loans involved) futures portfolio. Simply put, that means the full contract value of a futures contract – not just the margin requirement – nominally secures each position in the index. To understand how this might work, imagine a futures index for gold. Imagine that the spot price of each ounce is $900. Many producers of gold may want to make sure they have a good idea of the price their future production of gold will fetch and maybe even sell the rights to future production now in order to lock in prices. On the other side of this futures trade, buyers of gold like Indian jewellers might want to lock in a decent price in three months' time now. Thus you have two parties to a futures contract, namely the producer and the buyer. They might agree a price for 3 months in the future or even 12 months, or anything in between. To secure the purchase the gold buyer might pay an option price – they are, after all, simply buying a futures-based option on a commodity – and then deposit the rest of the final payment as a deposit in the form of Treasury Bills. This way the buyer locks in the price and the seller receives their payment. Add up all these non-leveraged futures contracts and you have a futures index.

The returns from these futures-based commodity indices come in three different ways: the interest earned on that collateral deposited to secure the futures positions (typically you pay an advance as a deposit, based on collateralised Treasury Bills on which you earn income), the return obtained from holding and trading futures themselves (based on moves in the underlying spot price) and something called the roll yield. To understand this crucial last term, let's go back to that example of gold with a spot price for delivery today of $900 per ounce. Let's assume that the supply of gold is low because stocks are down. Futures contracts might start trading at $895 a few weeks out and then fall to, say, $890 for two months. A smart investor could decide to buy these futures contracts and then sit around and wait for the due delivery date on the future. If nothing happens to the spot price, you would expect the futures price to move towards the spot price as delivery date approaches. This means you sell your fast-maturing futures contract (bought for $895) closer to $900 and then buy another futures contract for the $895 again. Over time this constant action of buying the cheaper short-term futures contract and rolling it as delivery approaches can produce a handy profit.

This roll yield is a crucial part of total index returns. These futures indices capture the 'roll' from one contract to another, selling the expiring contract and buying the new one. The next month's/quarter's contract frequently changes in price – if it costs more the market is in 'contango' and you lose out, while if it costs less the market is 'backwardated' and you make more money. The existence of contango indicates, among other things, that there are adequate supplies to be carried into future months. This roll yield is hugely important long-term and probably accounts for a large component of total long-term returns. To understand just how important the roll yield is, go to a US-based website and resource called HardAssetsInvestor.com. This is full of great comment and insight, but its research clearly shows up why that roll yield is so crucial. Table 4.2 shows a snapshot from the middle of 2008 of annualised roll yield looking one month out. The differences can be immense – lean hogs' annualised returns were –94 per cent while heating oil was 44.6 per cent. Get this roll yield wrong and you could end up destroying your investment.

Table 4.2 Annualised roll return from 2008 – based on next available month

Commodity	Annualised roll return %
Lean hogs	−94.52%
Feeder cattle	−30.63%
Cotton	−24%
Sugar	−14.9%
Corn	−12%
Gold	−1.94%
Natural gas	2.86%
Copper	3.50%
WTI crude oil	4.54%
Gas oil	16.4%
Heating oil	44.96%

Source: HardAssets.com

HardAssets has also done the long-term maths on which bit of the return profile really matters. According to data from the GSCI index series (more on that index below), the roll yield killed investors in the 2000s while in the 1980s the cash or interest income element was the biggest component of total returns (see Table 4.3).

Table 4.3 Annualised returns 1970–2005

Annualised	1970s	1980s	1990s	2000s*	2005
GSCI Spot Return	9.05%	−1.37%	−0.63%	12.39%	39.05%
GSCI Roll Yield	4.24%	2.44%	−0.53%	−3.45%	−12.55%
GSCI Cash Yield	6.67%	9.52%	5.11%	3.05%	3.24%

* January 1, 2000, through September 30, 2006
  ** Through September 30, 2006
  >GSCI Excess Return = Spot Return + Roll Yield
  >>GSCI Total Return = Spot Return + Roll Yield + Cash Yield

Source: Van Eck Global Research, Bloomberg

So, all in all, it's a bit confusing. Quite how you make your profit from investing in commodities varies over time and between these different components, but there is one crucial last point to understand – these three components of return all add up to the total return or TR. You will see this term bandied about a fair amount in the world of ETFs and ETCs and it means that all the income from holding the underlying index is rolled up into the total return and is *not* paid out separately to the investor, i.e. you do not receive that interest income from holding the T Bills as a collateral.

The main commodity index providers

If all these different and varying components to total returns from investing in futures indices have not completely foxed you, you are ready to face the next big challenge – which index to track. Sadly, there is no straightforward answer as there are a number of different index families that track a range of commodities in completely different ways (though they all track futures prices). Your exchange traded fund could track a number of futures indices, including the following.

The **S&P Goldman Sachs Commodity Index** is perhaps the most widely used index in the US and is what's called a 'production-weighted benchmark' of two-dozen commodities adjusted for liquidity. It is currently heavily weighted in energy products; 40 per cent of the index's weight comprises crude oil futures. Agricultural and soft commodities, such as wheat and sugar, make up 11 per cent, metals 6 per cent and livestock 2.86 per cent. Because the GSCI index is based around this notion of 'world production', the constituents can vary widely – the dominant energy sector, for instance, has varied over time from 44 per cent through to 78 per cent, making it very volatile indeed. This also makes SP/GSCI most susceptible to the effect of rotation between contango and backwardation in crude oil prices.

The **Dow Jones-AIG Commodity Index** is an equally popular series of indices and sits at the core of the ETF Securities range of funds. It is made up of 19 commodities weighted primarily for trading volume and secondarily based on global production, with index rules 'designed to dampen volatility' by setting floors and caps on component weights. Crucially the index has been set up so that no single commodity can comprise more than 15 per cent of the index and no single sector can make up more than one-third of the benchmark's weight. By sectors, energy now carries the biggest weight of 33 per cent, followed by industrial metals at 20 per cent, precious metals at 10 per cent, softs at 8.7 per cent and grains at 18 per cent. This index series is used by ETF Securities in the UK and the iPath range of ETNs in the US. DJ-AIGCI is the most evenly balanced across all five sectors, which means it captures much of the contango in livestock, agriculture and precious metals, without the luxury of having a larger presence in the energy sector where the backwardation is rife.

The **Deutsche Bank Liquid Commodity Index** consists of only six commodities, based around the most liquid (in trading terms) commodities in each sector. These are heating oil, light crude oil, wheat, aluminium, gold and corn. The index company claims that this narrow range of underlying commodities reduces the actual cost of roll and rebalancing. In practical terms it means that energy makes up 55 per cent of DBLCI; agriculturals and metals equally split the remaining 45 per cent. There is no exposure to livestock or softs in this index family. Crucially, the designers of this index – and the Powershares range of ETFs that tracks it – claim a unique 'roll strategy'. Rather than simply rolling expiring contracts to the next available month, DBC looks out as far as 13 months for the contract with the highest roll yield. Theoretically, the index developers claim, this should improve roll yields in both backwardated and contango-ed markets.

Lyxor, the UK ETF provider, has a small family of index funds that tracks a venerable and widely followed index called the **CRB Commodity Index**, started by the Commodity Research Bureau in 1981. This index is made up of 22 futures contracts combined into an 'All Commodities' grouping, with two major sub-divisions: raw industrials and foodstuffs. Metals make up 20 per cent, energy carries a weight of 39 per cent and soft commodities 39 per cent.

Last but by no means least, many commodity purists rather like something called the **Rogers International Commodity Index**, which is by far and away the broadest and most international of all the indices. The RICI consists of 35 commodities, including such exotics as azuki beans, silk, rubber and wool. Energy comprises 44 per cent of the index, agriculturals and softs 32 per cent, metals 21 per cent and livestock 3 per cent. See Table 4.4.

Table 4.4 Commodity index comparison

Commodity	Measure	S&P GSCI	DJ AIG Commodity index	Reuters Jefferies CRB	Rogers International Commodities Index (RICI)
ENERGY		74.28	35.1	39	44
WTI Crude Oil	$ barrel	39	14.6	23	21
Brent Crude Oil	$ barrel	14.02	0	0	14
RBOB Gasoline	$ cents/gallon	4.06	3.95	5	3
Heating Oil	$ cents/gallon	5.22	4.47	6	1.8
Gasoil	$ metric ton	5.34	0	0	1.2
Natural Gas	$mmBtu	6.64	12.08	6	3
LIVESTOCK		4.16	8.5	7	3
Live Cattle	$ cents pound	2.49	5.43	6	2
Feeder Cattle	$ cents pound	0.44	0	0	0
Lean Hogs	$ cents pound	1.23	3.07	1	1
PRECIOUS METALS		2.58	10.2	7	7.1
Gold	$ troy oz	2.36	7.91	6	3
Silver	$ troy oz	0.22	2.29	1	2
Palladium	$ troy oz	0	0	0	0.3
Platinum	$ troy oz	0	0	0	1.8
INDUSTRIAL METALS		6.39	17.78	13	14
Aluminium	$ metric ton	2.59	7.27	6	4
Copper	$ metric ton	2.5	6.75	6	4
Lead	$ metric ton	0.34	0	0	2
Nickel	$ metric ton	0.49	1.63	1	1
Tin	$ metric ton	0	0	0	1
Zinc	$ metric ton	0.47	2.13	0	2

Table 4.4 Continued

Commodity	Measure	S&P GSCI	DJ AIG	Reuters	Rogers International
AGRICULTURE		12.58	28.43	34	31.9
Wheat	$ cents bushels	3.35	3.71	1	7
Kansas Wheat	$ cents bushels	0.82	0	0	0
Corn	$ cents bushels	3.45	6.2	6	4.75
Soybeans	$ cents bushels	2.09	6.67	6	3
Soybean Oil	$ cents pound	0	2.68	0	2
Soybean Meal	$ short ton	0	0	0	0.75
Cotton	$ cents pound	0.76	2.15	5	4.05
Sugar	$ cents pound	1.22	4	5	2
Coffee	$ cents pound	0.64	3.12	5	2
Cocoa	$ metric ton	0.26		5	1
Orange Juice	$ cents pound			1	0.66
Rubber	JPY kilogram				1
Lumber	$ 1k board fleet			1	
Canola	CAD metric ton			0.67	
Rice	$ cwt				0.5
Oats	$ cents bushels			0.5	
Azuki Beans	JPY bag				0.5
Barley	CAD metric ton			0.27	
Greasy Wool	AUD kilogram				0.25
Data	1	10-Oct-08	30-Sep-08	31-Aug-08	12-Dec-07

Source: iShares

Composite or not?

If you are determined enough to have made your way through this maze of index families, you have probably ended up using the DJ-AIG group tracked by ETF Securities if you are based in the UK. You are now faced with one last choice, namely which bit of the index to track.

Many non-specialist investors look to commodities and ETCs in particular as a way to add a broad swathe of diversification to their equity- and bond-dominated portfolios. In reality they are not that bothered about which commodities they want to track, rather they want a 'composite' return. This composite idea is crucial to most private investors – they want to invest in a broad composite index that tracks all the commodities in a diversified manner, rather than pick out a favourite few.

But many specialist investors are suspicious of this broad-brush approach – they are aware that indices like the GSCI, for instance, are heavily biased towards energy-based products. This energy effect has been very significant over the last few years as the price of crude oil has doubled, dragging up heating oil and gas prices in its wake. But it makes many investors nervous about effectively betting their investment on geo-political risk, the proclivities of the Saudis and the huge debate raging over whether there is such a thing as peak oil. Some investors may want to buy exposure to commodities but want to exclude energy-related commodities – the index developers have anticipated this and developed a layering of sub-indices that groups, commodities into energy and non-energy components. But composite indices drill down into even greater detail if you choose – some investors want to buy only hard commodities outside energy (say metals) while others want to invest in agricultural but not include wheat. These baskets tend to break down into four main sub-groups:

■ energy commodities;
■ agriculturals broken into softs and hards plus livestock;
■ industrial metals including copper and nickel;
■ precious metals.

Beyond these baskets of commodities you are into individual indices that track a specific commodity. These tend to be the territory of professional investors with specialist knowledge and are best avoided by most private investors.

The different types of returns on offer from ETCs

There is, sadly, one last important choice to make when it comes to finding the right commodity-based ETF and ETC for your portfolio: which fund structure do you want? In the early days of ETFs, investors were faced with a simple classic tracking proposition – a 1:1 return structure that made you money if the underlying futures index went up in value. Now you have much, much greater choice – you can, for instance, juice up returns by using short and leveraged ETCs.

These leveraged index funds, for instance, pay out two times the *daily* returns on the underlying futures index (before fees and adjustments) while short ETCs provide an exposure equal to minus one times (–1x) the daily percentage change in the 'Index'. Here's how these work: if the index falls by –1 per cent in a day, a short ETC will hopefully increase by +1 per cent in that day. If, by contrast, the index increases by 2 per cent, the leveraged ETC makes a 4 per cent gain (and vice versa if the index drops).

ETF Securities also offers yet another variation on the idea of tracking futures contracts – investors can specifically choose whether or not they want to track the 3-month and 12-month forward-based futures price of particular commodities. According to ETF Securities, these forward ETCs were launched because they 'have historically shown lower volatility, while the effects of contango and backwardation also vary between the existing Classic and Forward ETCs. The Forward ETCs provide investors with the opportunity to optimise returns by increasing exposure to back-wardation or decreasing exposure to contango'.

Just to completely confuse private investors, they can also avoid the whole futures index-based business altogether and invest in the actual spot prices of precious metals like gold and platinum via a physical ETC. These give investors an actual share in a physical stockpile of precious metals (held in a bank deposit vault, of course) with the price based on the spot price, not the forward futures price.

The risks of investing in commodities

All these different fund structures, composite indices and varying compo-nents to total returns should alert private investors to one of the biggest risks of investing in commodities – the sheer variety of index and fund structures could end up confusing private investors and encourage them to invest in the wrong index and fund. You might, for instance, want to build some exposure to oil prices into your portfolio – each of the different composite indices offers very different levels of exposure to this commodity class and even within the broad sector of oil there are different sub-indices for West Texas and Brent Crude plus separate markets for heating and gas oil. These futures-based markets are also hugely affected by backwardation or contango and different ETC fund structures will also deliver different return profiles.

Investors also need to be aware of a much broader issue, namely that commodities as an asset class can be, like many equities, risky and volatile. To understand just how volatile these markets can be, look at Table 4.5 which shows performance from a broad range of commodities before 2007 via the Dow Jones AIG Commodity Index. The overall picture is one of steady gains but with some very big exceptions. Notice how energy-based ETCs had performed spectacularly well but with huge volatility. By contrast many agricultural commodities over those five years had performed spectacularly badly, with cotton, for instance, falling in price in four of the last five years.

Table 4.5 Commodities perormance before 2007 via the Dow Jones AIG Commodity Index

Index/Index history	2006	2005	2004	2003	2002
DJ/AIG AGT Index	17%	22%	13%	21%	−23%
DJ/AIG CI Energy Index	2%	21%	9%	24%	26%
DJ/AIG CI Ex-Energy index	−41%	42%	19%	32%	55%
DJ/AIG CI Industrial Metals index	28%	12%	5%	20%	11%
DJ/AIG CI Precious Metals (SM)	72%	33%	25%	44%	3%
DJ/AIG CI Grains index	27%	20%	7%	20%	19%
DJ/AIG CI Livestock (SM)	24%	−3%	−24%	22%	17%
Individual Commodities	−6%	0%	27%	−4%	−11%
DJ/AIG HG Copper Total Return Index					
DJ/AIG Coffee Total Return Index	52%	61%	44%	46%	3%
DJ/AIG Corn Total Return Index	6%	−9%	35%	−12%	0%
DJ/AIG Cotton Total Return Index	47%	−16%	−28%	−3%	−2%
DJ/AIG Gold Total Return Index	−15%	2%	−43%	20%	16%
DJ/AIG Natural Gas Total Return Index	22%	18%	5%	19%	25%
DJ/AIG Silver Total Return	−10%	33%	56%	36%	62%
DJ/AIG Sugar Beat Total Return Index	45%	29%	14%	23%	4%
DJ/AIG Wheat Total Return Index	−25%	49%	24%	-20%	35%
Brent Oil Spot Price	26%	−6%	−29%	5%	2%

Table 4.5 Continued

Index/Index history	2006	2005	2004	2003	2002
West Texas Spot Price	–7%	32%	45%	17%	53%
FTSE All Share	–10%	33%	56%	36%	62%
	17%	22%	13%	21%	–23%

Looking even further back in time, it is worth taking in the cautious prog-
nostications of stock market historian William Bernstein, one of America's
best investment thinkers. He looked closely at long-term commodity
returns and did not like what he saw. You can read his analysis at
www.efficientfrontier.com and see Table 4.6. His headlines included
the following:

■ Gold and silver 'both did exceptionally well in the high-inflation '70s
when other traditional investments suffered, but have performed mis-
erably during other market environments.' But the average annual
return for gold since 1970 has been 'a modest 7.7 per cent, below long-
term government bonds and only modestly above the long-term
inflation rate of 5.3 per cent'. 'Silver hasn't even managed to outpace
inflation, with an average annual return of only 4.3 per cent.' 'These
modest returns have been at the expense of massive volatility.' The best
return for gold was a whopping 126.5 per cent in 1979, while silver's
return was even more glittering at 267.4 per cent. However, the worst
returns came just two years later in 1981 – a loss of 31.6 per cent for
gold and a loss of 46.4 per cent for silver.

■ Bernstein also looked at commodity spot prices for 23 different commodities, including cattle, pork bellies, cocoa, heating oil, gold, copper,
orange juice, lumber and sugar. His conclusion? 'They haven't really
performed as advertised: although their best years were in the '70s, the
returns for the decade were only a few percentage points above inflation, and the long-term average has been considerably below inflation
– the worst performer of all asset classes!'

Table 4.6 Long-term commodity returns

Annual returns	1970s	1980s	1990s	Average	Best	Worst
Gold	30.6	−2.4	−4.1	7.7	126.5 (1979)	−31.6 (1981)
Silver	28.3	−13.4	1.7	4.3	267.4 (1979)	−46.4 (1981)
REITs – NAREIT Index	4.8	12.5	14.1	10.5	48.9 (1976)	−31.6 (1981)
Commodities Spot Index	9.6	−1	0.5	3.1	57.7 (1973)	−46.4 (1981)
S&P 500	5.9	17.5	16.6	13	37.4 (1995)	−26.5 (1974)
Small Cap Stocks	11.5	15.8	16.5	14.4	57.4 (1976)	−31.9 (1973)
Long Term Govt Bonds	5.5	12.6	10.7	9.5	40.4 (1982)	−7.8 (1994)
Treasury Bills	6.3	8.9	4.9	6.8	14.7 (1981)	2.9 (1993)
Inflation	7.4	5.1	3.3	5.3	na	na

Source: William Bernstein, www.efficientfrontier.com

Table 4.7 tells another story. It shows summarised long-term returns from the broad CRB index dating back to the 1950s, compared with the FTSE 100 and the S&P 500. Between 1956 and the beginning of June 2008, the total return from the CRB TR index was 399 per cent, compared with 2680 per cent from the S&P 500 (in nominal terms). By comparison the FTSE has returned a total of 374 per cent since 1984. And within these returns, some commodities have clearly performed badly over the very long-term – the CRB Metals Index over the entire period has returned only a total of 150 per cent.

Table 4.7 Summarised long-term returns from the broad CRB index

Summary	Correlation to CPI	Correlation to FTSE 100	Total return	Annualised average return
FTSE 100			%	% pa
S&P 500				
Reuters CRB Index (CCI)	0.781250713	0.386970964	399.95	6.96
CRB Spot Index	0.84	0.33	321.83	8.44
CRB Livestock Sub-index	0.85	0.31	351.40	7.35
CRB Fats & Oils Sub-index	0.66	0.22	306.41	6.87

Table 4.7 Continued

Summary	Correlation to CPI	Correlation to FTSE 100	Total return	Annualised average return
CRB Foodstuffs Sub-index	0.74	0.19	306.41	6.87
CRB Raw Industrials Sub-index	0.87	0.37	286.24	8.44
CRB Textiles Sub-index	0.87	0.19	351.43	3.62
CRB Metals Sub-index	0.73	0.42	150.96	16.08

To be fair, this table also reminds us of two of the positives of investing in commodities – they are a great **inflation hedge** and they are also **relatively lowly correlated** with equities, thus offering investors some diversification within their portfolios. First, that inflation point – the telling number is the one which compares correlations between the CRB index and the US Consumer Prices Index (the CPI) – 0.78 per cent for the broad index, which is statistically very significant, rising to 0.85 for livestock. These figures suggest that commodities could work wonders in stagflationary markets, with gold likely to do especially well. Investors also love the diversification benefits of commodities. Table 4.8 below is from Blue Sky Asset Management and compares a number of equity markets with key commodity classes. The statistics suggest that the diversification story is compelling, with wheat, oil and gold being particularly lowly correlated with the FTSE, for instance. But a slightly more disturbing picture emerges for other commodities – copper's correlation with the FTSE 100, for instance, has risen to 0.47 in recent years as more and more mining companies come to dominate the London Stock Exchange.

Blue Sky's research also points out that the three-month price relationship of wheat and gold as measured by something called the R^2 factor is 0.26, a near doubling in recent years. The researchers conclude that 'this is also seen in the wheat/copper correlation (from 0.09 to 0.46) and the wheat/oil correlation (from 0.10 to 0.57). This highlights the recent investment trend of lumping commodity markets into one basket – they all go up and they all go down in tandem'.

It is also worth pointing out that as investor interest in the whole broad investment space snowballs, individual indices for specific commodities are beginning to move broadly in line with each other, even though they

Table 4.8 Equity markets v key commodity classes

90 day/ 365 day	S&P 500	FTSE 100	Gold	Copper	CRB	Wheat	WTI oil	USD/JPY	EUR/CHF	VIX
S&P 500	1.00	0.62	-0.25	0.32	0.49	0.35	0.39	0.30	0.62	-0.80
FTSE 100	0.57	1.00	-0.26	0.50	0.57	0.47	0.41	0.34	0.33	-0.45
Gold	-0.02	0.03	1.00	-0.08	-0.03	-0.20	-0.12	-0.38	-0.22	0.25
Copper	0.27	0.55	0.27	1.00	0.62	0.34	0.38	0.32	0.08	-0.23
CRB	0.36	0.54	0.39	0.73	1.00	0.66	0.83	0.35	0.38	-0.40
Wheat	0.22	0.37	0.26	0.46	0.63	1.00	0.57	0.28	0.40	-0.23
WTI oil	0.30	0.42	0.29	0.53	0.82	0.45	1.00	0.35	0.39	-0.37
USD/JPY	0.60	0.39	-0.13	0.21	0.23	0.09	0.24	1.00	0.16	-0.27
EUR/CHF	0.60	0.37	0.03	0.16	0.27	0.14	0.27	0.52	1.00	-0.54
VIX	-0.83	-0.54	0.07	-0.25	-0.31	-0.23	-0.26	-0.56	-0.53	1.00

Source: Blue Sky Asset Management, 2008

contain a very different mix of underlying constituents. According to 15-year data (to March 2008) from Barclays and 10-year data from Deutsche Bank, the three main broad 'composite' commodity indices tracked by index funds have an approximate 0.80 to 0.90 correlation based on their returns in the long run.

Another big concern for analysts and advisers alike is that the commodity markets may have fundamentally changed in the last decade as invest-ment levels have increased. Hedge funds and big fund management institutions have piled into the commodity markets, fundamentally changing them in quite possibly unknown ways. This evolution opens up some potentially very worrying issues about scale – take gold and the huge success of just one US-based ETF, the Street Tracks Gold Trust (GLD in the US). Launched just a few years ago it is already worth a staggering $20 bil-lion and sits on 659 metric tons of the stuff, which is more than held by the Bank of England and most other central banks. According to one report this one fund is buying up every year between 13 per cent and 14 per cent of annual mine supply and has more assets than the next five largest gold mutual funds combined. Such a huge concentration of physi-cal ownership, especially by a legion of private investors through a fund, raises the possibility that a sudden loss of confidence in gold could spark a run, with the ETF selling huge quantities of gold overnight, causing prices to plummet even further.

Yet another concern raised by many portfolio managers is that commodi-ties as a whole have become too dependent on that roll yield we encountered earlier on. Recent academic studies of long-term commodity returns by big commodity funds have shown that between 1959 and 2004 the annual return from changes in spot prices averaged just 3.47 per cent. What happens if this one-way road to future profits suddenly switches and the futures markets turn back to contango? As William Bernstein points out, this new world could spell disaster for investors in ETCs and ETFs as the producers of commodities turn the tables and stop paying for this pro-tection against inflation, i.e. stop using forward futures contracts. 'In a market whose major propelling force is the demand for insurance against inflation, those who supply it will demand a premium. Goodbye Keynesian normal backwardation, hello … forwardation?'

The ETC and why commodities make sense for private investors
An Interview with Nicholas Brooks, Head of Research at ETF Securities

Q: What do you think has powered the growth of ETCs? Is it still largely institutional?

I think the main reason there has been such strong demand for ETCs is that they have opened commodity investing to mainstream investors. Before ETCs were created, commodity investing was mostly dominated by a relatively small group of specialist investors. Because ETCs are listed on major stock exchanges, trade and settle like stocks and are highly liquid, they provide traditional fund managers, pension funds, private wealth managers and retail investors simple and direct access to an asset class previously difficult for them to gain exposure to. The bulk of the funds invested in ETCs are institutional, but there are signs of increasing retail activity as awareness of ETCs among the public has increased. Investors use ETCs for a variety of investment objectives. The largest flows tend to be long-term buy-and-hold investments by investors seeking to benefit from the diversification properties of commodities and to play long-term growth themes. Some are investing to hedge against inflation and currency risks and some are tactical investors using long, short, leveraged and different maturity ETCs to implement a variety of strategies.

Q: How do you actually structure your mainstream, classic ETCs?

We have three main types of ETCs. We have physically backed precious metal ETCs – gold, silver, platinum and palladium. These ETCs are 100 per cent backed by physical bullion in vaults held by a custodian bank. We also have ETCs that track commodity indices based on commodity futures returns ranging from individual commodities such as sugar and copper to baskets tracking industrial metals, agriculture and other commodity sectors. These ETCs provide investors with long, short and leveraged exposures. All of these ETCs are 100 per cent backed by collateral. The third group are our oil ETCs which track oil prices through different maturity oil futures contracts such as Brent 1mth, 1yr, 2yr, 3yr and similar for WTI oil futures. These ETCs are 100 per cent backed by commodity contracts purchased from Shell.

Q: Why did you introduce later variants such as the forward ETCs and the physical ETCs?

The physically backed gold ETC was the first of the ETCs (and, incidentally, the world's first gold ETF) and silver, platinum and palladium naturally followed. Because most other commodities are difficult to invest in physically as they are difficult to store, are heterogeneous and decay, they are generally priced off commodities futures. ETF Securities therefore created the first exchange traded commodities to track futures returns, making it possible for investors to access commodity returns through securities traded on stock exchanges. Following the launch of the 'classic' ETCs that track near-dated commodity futures, forward ETCs were the next logical extension. Forward ETCs were created to provide a wider choice of investment options, giving investors the ability to gain exposure to either shorter-maturity or longer-maturity futures returns, depending on their views on the outlook for the shape of the futures curve.

Q: Back in the dark days of late 2008, you ran into controversy because of the implosion of American financial giant AIG. What happened and how did you react?

Because our ETCs based on the DJ-AIG index (not the physically backed or oil securities) were backed by swaps guaranteed by AIG, during the short period between AIG looking as if it might go bust and the US government stepping in to bail it out, many market makers were reluctant to take AIG risk on their books and there was a temporary reduction in liquidity in these ETCs. Recognising that the problem went well beyond AIG and was related to a general freezing up of financial markets globally as credit risk moved to centre stage for most investors, a decision was made to 100 per cent back these ETCs with collateral (marked to market daily and held by a ring-fenced custodian) to ensure this liquidity problem would not occur again. Since then the ETCs have traded normally and volumes in a number of them are amongst the highest in Europe. The silver lining of this event is that these ETCs are now backed by one of the most robust structures in the industry. [Author note: AIG is now owned by the US government.]

Q: Do you think that commodities ETCs should sit in private investors' portfolios? Aren't they just too specialised, volatile and risky?

It depends very much on the investor's asset mix and investment goals. It is difficult to generalise about ETCs as there are ETCs that track broad commodity indices such as ETFS All Commodities or ETFS Precious Metals, which over the past ten years have had lower volatilities (and higher returns) than the S&P 500. There are other ETCs such as ETFS Copper or ETFS Wheat which historically have been more volatile in the same way that individual stock volatility is often more volatile than broader equity indices. Most studies indicate that adding the returns of a broad commodity index to a diversified portfolio of equities and bonds has improved the long-term risk-return profile of the portfolio. The main reason is that commodities have tended to have a low – even negative for some – correlation with equities and bonds, providing diversification benefits difficult to find in any other asset class. A number of endowments and large institutional investors have recognised and taken advantage of these characteristics, but until ETCs were created a few years ago, these strategies were not easily available to private investors. In addition, in the same way that private investors are able to take a view on a stock or equity sector, now they are able to implement strategic or tactical views on gold, oil, agriculture and nearly all key individual commodities and sectors.

Q: Do you think the commodities super-cycle, so beloved of Jim Rogers, is dead?

Commodity markets, like all financial markets, will always be affected by the cyclical swings of supply and demand. However, unlike other financial assets, supplies of commodities are finite and in some cases – such as oil – are in rapid structural decline. Extraction costs are rising, new discoveries are falling and existing fields and mines are being depleted. Technological innovation may be able to improve the efficiency of use of commodities and perhaps slow the rise in the cost of extraction, but ultimately commodities are finite in supply. Until the world's population stops growing and global per capita incomes stop rising, structural demand for commodities will continue to rise. Although the current economic slowdown is likely to be the largest since the Great Depression, structural demand from rapidly industrialising economies such as China and India is likely to remain extremely strong on at least a 10- to 20-year view. Given the size of their populations, the impact on final demand for commodities is likely to be extremely large. Because of natural supply constraints, higher commodity prices will likely be the key adjusting factor – both to force increased efficiency of their use and to stimulate new innovations to boost the productivity of their supply.

5

The fiddly detail – risks, caveats and the indices

Not all index tracking funds are created equally. Investors need to understand the nitty gritty of how index funds are actually constructed and then managed on a day-to-day basis – pick the wrong fund, with the wrong structure, high fees and little disclosure and you could be buying into trouble. Paul Amery is editor of www.indexuniverse.eu, the leading source of independent information and analysis for the European exchange traded and index funds market. Paul is one of the leading experts on exchange traded funds in the UK – ETFs are much the biggest part of the index tracking space – and is the ideal person to outline what investors need to watch out for when it comes to buying an index tracking ETF.

Exchange traded funds have seen huge growth since their introduction in Europe in 2000. ETF assets under management across the region had risen to over €100bn by the end of March 2009, according to the research team at Barclays Global Investors. Assets continued to pour into the sector throughout the 2007–2009 credit crunch, as investors fled expensive, illiquid and opaque savings products in favour of the cost-effectiveness, transparency and ease of use of ETFs.

Nevertheless, not all tracker products are created equal, and it pays investors to be aware of some hidden costs, which can end up as a multiple of a fund's advertised total expense ratio. These costs can result from a number of sources, from the product structure itself, to the design of the index, from poor secondary market liquidity, unamortised fund expenses and differences in tax status. Accordingly, different ETFs can have subtly different risk profiles, not all of which are immediately apparent. For the uninformed, choosing the wrong ETF might land you with an unexpected and unwanted surprise, just when you thought you had escaped the commission and fee-hungry world of financial advisers and active fund managers.

So what are the key details in fund and index design that investors should be focused on when choosing their ETF?

Fund structure

Almost all European ETFs are structured as Undertakings for Collective Investments in Transferable Securities (UCITS) funds under a key set of regulations – the EU directives, now heading towards their fourth revision, setting out how collective investment schemes can operate across the member states. Once authorised in one country, a UCITS fund can be sold in other EU member states.

The few non-UCITS ETFs in Europe are those employing non-conventional structures (for example, with high leverage) or managed from a country outside the EU (for example, Switzerland). Also, since UCITS rules for financial indices require a minimum level of diversification, investment products tracking one asset (for example, a single commodity) or a limited number of assets cannot be structured as UCITS. That does not mean that these are bad investment products, but if it is not a UCITS, check why.

The UCITS stamp has gained broad acceptance as an assurance that basic regulatory standards are met, to the extent that many investors outside Europe have become familiar with it. But for European ETFs in particular, one important result of UCITS has been that it allows 'synthetic index replication', a method followed by an increasing number of European tracker funds. Synthetic replication is possible under UCITS because of the flexibility that the 2001 revision of the rules (UCITS III) introduced regarding financial derivatives.

The result has been that European ETFs tend to fall into one of two broad categories.

The first category includes those funds using 'physical' or 'in specie' replication to track indices. Under this methodology, the ETF's manager will purchase all the stocks, or a representative or optimised sample of the stocks in the index, and hold them. This was the original ETF structure, as pioneered in the US, and this type of fund represents the majority of ETFs run by Europe's largest manager, iShares. Other European ETF managers, such as Stockholm-based XACT and German firm ETFlab, follow this method of fund construction.

The other broad category is the funds using the 'synthetic' or 'swap-based' index replication technique. Here, the ETF achieves its index return through a derivative contract (a swap) written by a counterparty, usually a bank and often the parent bank of the ETF issuer. In effect, the swap counterparty guarantees to pay to the ETF the return on the index.

Since UCITS rules do not allow exposure to a derivatives counterparty to exceed 10 per cent of the net asset value of the fund, the cash that comes into the ETF as the result of an investor subscription is used to buy a 'basket' of stocks or bonds, which is then held by the fund as collateral for the swap. So a UCITS ETF using synthetic replication will own a basket of securities that is typically unrelated to the actual index being tracked (though it may well come from the same asset class), plus a promise from the swap counterparty to pay the return on that index to the fund.

As a result the websites of ETF issuers using the synthetic replication technique will often refer to the stocks in the index being tracked as the 'perfect basket' or 'implied fund constituents'. The actual securities owned by the funds in the collateral basket can be found in the balance sheet of the ETFs' semi-annual and annual accounts and may be disclosed more frequently by the issuer.

Most European ETFs now follow the swap-based route, including the funds offered by Lyxor and db x-trackers, the second and third largest European issuers in early 2009.

What are the pros and cons of the two different replication methodologies? Swap-based ETF proponents argue that their funds have the advantage of eliminating the tracking problems that can occur in in specie or physically replicated ETFs as the result of index turnover costs, the tax treatment of dividends and the timing of dividend payments. The only tracking error for swap-based ETFs would therefore be the fund fee. Since the swap counterparty guarantees the index return, the risk of imperfect tracking is transferred from the ETF to the bank that writes the swap.

But this promise of perfect tracking does not come for free. Since the index swap is an over-the-counter (OTC) financial derivative, this type of ETF carries some counterparty risk to the bank that writes the swap. While UCITS rules specify that this risk should not exceed 10 per cent of the fund's net asset value, and the issuers of swap-based ETFs have in place mechanisms that ensure that collateral is moved on a daily basis so that the limit is not breached, the real increase in bank default risk since the start of the credit crunch has meant that some investors have been wary of any uncollateralised counterparty exposure. Certain swap-based ETF issuers have responded to these concerns by managing counterparty exposures to well below the 10 per cent limit, mitigating such risks.

Counterparty risk exposures are not confined to swap-based ETFs either. Those ETFs using in specie replication as their tracking technique often lend out the underlying securities to third parties, usually sharing the revenues from such activities with fund investors. While the lending of such securities is done on a collateralised basis (the borrower typically offers cash, money market instruments or bonds as backing for the loan), in the case of a borrower default and a large market movement there could be losses incurred by the fund.

Ultimately, both types of ETF structure have a role to play and so far the two replication methods seem to have coexisted fairly happily. Synthetic replication may be a more cost-effective method of tracking where indices consist of a large number of securities, or where some of the underlying index components are less liquid. Physical replication is unlikely to go away, as it is the original method of indexing and the easiest to understand.

In any case, it is worth pointing out that either type of ETF compares well to many types of investment vehicle which give full counterparty exposure to the issuing bank. This applies to many bank structured products and some trackers also. For example, most exchange-traded notes (ETNs) have no collateral backing, meaning that in the case of an issuer bankruptcy, the investor will have to line up with other creditors in the bankruptcy courts. In the case of Lehman Brothers, ETN holders will probably recover only a few cents for each dollar invested.

Other tracking vehicles – ETCs, for example – may or may not have collateral backing, depending on the commodity or commodity index tracked.

So, from the point of view of the investment vehicle's structure, it can be a confusing world for investors in exchange traded products. Whether it is a swap-based or physically replicated ETF, ETN or ETC, each vehicle carries its own risks and its own merits. But with many financial institutions still in intensive care, it is very important to be aware of what counterparty exposure you face as an investor. Do your homework and read the 'risk factors' in the fund or note prospectus.

Index structure

How the index your ETF tracks is constructed is a secondary consideration, at best, for many investors, but it can play a key role in determining your investment outcome.

Most investors will be familiar with the names of key share indices in different countries – the Dow Jones Industrial Average and S&P 500 in the US, the FTSE 100 in the UK, the CAC 40 in France, the German DAX and the Japanese Nikkei 225, to give a few examples.

Relatively few will know that there are major differences in the index compilation technique used to calculate these benchmarks. While the S&P 500, the FTSE 100, CAC 40 and DAX are based on capitalisation weighting, the Dow Jones Industrial Average and the Nikkei 225 indices are price-weighted. Capitalisation weighting means that each constituent company's importance in the index is determined by the market size of the company. The larger the company (calculated as the number of shares in issue multiplied by the share price), the larger the index weighting it gets. The Dow and the Nikkei, by contrast, are price-weighted, so that the index allocates greater importance to companies whose share prices are higher in absolute terms, regardless of the actual economic importance of the companies concerned. A company with a share price of £10 automatically gets ten times the weight of a company with a £1 share price.

There are many more index compilation techniques than just these two. Indices tracked by ETFs often weight their components equally; they can be dividend-weighted or compiled according to some quantitative model. Such models may be more or less transparent to the investor.

Since indices were developed as a means of measuring the performance of financial markets, using a variety of methodologies, it was a natural extension of their role to act as the basis for index funds and, later, for exchange traded funds. However, the indices' suitability as the basis for investment portfolios was little discussed at the outset. When ETFs first came on the scene, issuers tended to colonise all the major index names available, in a bid for 'first-mover advantage'.

More recently, however, a vigorous debate between the proponents of different types of indices has emerged, with some claiming that certain index construction techniques are better than others when used as the basis for an investment portfolio. A key argument in this debate has been the one between the supporters and the opponents of capitalisation weighting.

Since this methodology allocates each company a share in the index in accordance with its market 'footprint', critics say that company and sector weightings can be thrown out of line with economic reality by the impact of the market bubbles and busts. This becomes easier to understand if one looks at some examples from history. When Japanese stocks hit their peak in 1989/1990, Japan represented over 40 per cent of the MSCI world index, and anyone buying an index fund based on that benchmark then would have had to devote nearly half their portfolio to Japanese shares at the time of the country's peak valuation. More recently, the internet bubble of 1999/2000 and the financial sector overvaluation in 2007 would have caused investors to allocate a large part of their assets to those sectors if investing according to a capitalisation-weighted index, such as the S&P 500.

This criticism is rejected by many indexing specialists, who maintain that markets are broadly efficient and they are merely replicating the 'market portfolio' when using capitalisation-weighting. Nonetheless, much research effort has recently gone into different methods of index construction. California-based firm Research Affiliates has patented a series of 'fundamental indices', weighting component companies according to four fundamental factors (dividends, cash flow, sales, book value), and has produced back-tested results showing that the 'fundamental' index versions can outperform their capitalisation-weighted counterparts by a percent or two a year, in many cases – Rob Davies explores this fast-growing space later in this book.

In fact, there is now a wide choice of ETFs tracking non-capitalisation-weighted benchmarks. From Research Affiliates' 'RAFI' index ETFs, to funds based on other model-driven, equally weighted or dividend-weighted indices, there is a huge and constantly growing variety of index construction techniques in use.

It is also worth considering the reality that many of these newer indices necessarily result in higher turnover when tracking portfolios are set up. While market capitalisation-weighted index portfolios need to adjust their weightings only when constituent companies fall out of the relevant size bracket, to be replaced by others, the model-driven portfolios rebalance their portfolios more frequently, incurring greater costs. This can have more or less of an effect on the tracker funds and their end-investors, depending on the secondary market trading liquidity for shares in the market being tracked. ETFs tracking non-traditional indices typically also come at a significant premium in fees to the established index ETFs, something investors also need to take into consideration.

As a response to some of the perceived drawbacks of 'pure' capitalisation weighting, many index compilers have introduced modifications to remove some of the potential concentrations of risk that the pure method can introduce – many, for instance, operate something called a cap, which is typically applied to a portfolio to limit an individual component's index weight.

An index construction drawback that few non-specialist investors are aware of relates to the tracking of commodities. Since commodities usually incur substantial storage costs, the future or forward price of a given raw material may differ substantially from the price (spot price) for immediate delivery. If prices for forward or future delivery of the commodity are higher than the spot price, the commodity price structure is said to be in contango and any index that follows a passive strategy of reinvesting from one contract into the next, as each approaches expiry, can incur substantial costs. This is known as a negative roll yield and is effectively a headwind that the commodity investor must overcome. It is not always blowing against you, but anyone considering an investment in commodity ETFs should understand how this operates.

Finally, it is worth knowing about the potential distortions that can be introduced in an index offering leveraged exposure to a market. While leveraged ETFs (offering two or even three times an index's return) are much less popular in Europe than in the US, some buyers are still unaware that the leverage is applied to the daily return of the index. Over time, the daily resetting of the leverage factor can lead to very large divergences from the equivalent multiple of the whole period's index return.

In summary, the index construction technique used for an ETF or other tracker product can make a big difference to your investment outcome. Be aware of it and understand the technique's advantages and potential drawbacks.

Trading and other costs

When looking at a potential ETF investment many investors will start by looking up the fund's TER, understandably so since one of the key attractions of ETFs is their low cost, especially when compared with actively managed mutual funds, with their 1.5–2 per cent annual management fees and initial charges of up to 6 per cent of the invested amount.

Of course, since ETFs are traded like shares, an investor will need to pay a stockbroker's commission on any purchase or sale. Fortunately, since the arrival of internet-based discount brokers, such costs are pretty modest. It is worth ensuring that the broker you use operates a segregated custodial account for client securities, since this will ring-fence your assets in the case of the failure of the institution concerned.

In addition to the TER, the investor should consider the likely bid–offer spread that the ETF commands in the secondary market. The spread – the difference between the buying and the selling price – can be minimal in the most liquid ETFs, around a few basis points (hundredths of a percentage), but in the less liquid ETFs it can easily jump to a percent or more. There is no free lunch here – bid–offer spreads generally represent the real trading costs of the securities underlying the ETF, so if you are investing in an emerging market small cap fund or a corporate bond ETF, expect to pay more in percentage terms as spread than in a large benchmark ETF, such as one of the DJ Euro Stoxx 50 eurozone equity funds, or in one of the money market ETFs that have become very popular in Europe as an alternative to bank deposits.

However, there may be structural problems underlying high bid–offer spreads. The larger the number of market makers trading in a particular ETF, the greater the chance that the arbitrage mechanism which underlies the ETF's creation and redemption process (where market makers, acting as 'authorised participants', exchange ETF units for the underlying securities, and vice versa) will work efficiently. If there is only one market maker, perhaps part of the bank that owns the company promoting the ETF, the arbitrage mechanism may not work so well. This information should be available on the issuer's website. If it isn't, ask.

If you look up the actual trading volumes for European ETFs on the issuers' or exchanges' websites, you'll find that while some funds are very actively traded, there is a long tail of funds in which activity is pretty low. ETF issuers often point out that reported trading statistics ('on-exchange volumes') are not entirely representative of the real liquidity of their funds, since in Europe a lot of institutional trading in ETFs takes place over the counter, that is, away from the official exchanges. Therefore, the true liquidity is probably greater than the reported figures suggest and, as issuers like to say, 'an ETF is as liquid as its underlying components'.

Nevertheless, the reported trading volumes and bid–offer spreads are likely to give you a good feel for the trading liquidity of a particular fund. Spread information can be found on the websites of the German XETRA exchange, the Borsa Italiana in Milan and the NYSE Euronext exchange in Paris, which all publish monthly or quarterly reviews of ETF secondary market liquidity, and it is certainly a good idea to look up the trading costs for any fund you are considering buying. As European ETFs tend to be cross-listed in different countries, such data should be broadly applicable across the region for particular funds, in case your local exchange does not publish the data.

Finally, the recent closure of ETFs run by SPA ETF plc was accompanied by the charging of unamortised marketing and establishment costs to the remaining investors, a cost that exceeded 10 per cent of net asset value for some of the funds. ETF issuers differ in the way that they amortise or absorb establishment expenses and other fixed costs, so it is worth checking the prospectus to see whether there might be unpleasant surprises if a fund needs to be wound up.

Tax questions

For a UK investor, there are a few important tax rules to be aware of. Tax, as always, can be a complicated subject and investors should check with their own advisers to be absolutely sure of their tax position.

Since most ETFs sold in the UK are domiciled in established overseas fund jurisdictions such as Dublin or Luxembourg, where the funds pay little or no tax, distributions to UK residents will be considered to be foreign dividends and subject to dividend tax rates, which are currently 32.5 per cent for higher-rate taxpayers and 10 per cent for basic-rate taxpayers.

When listed for trading in the UK, most of these foreign-domiciled ETFs have 'distributor' status, meaning that gains made on ETFs for taxable investors are subject to capital gains tax (CGT), rather than income tax. Since the CGT rate is currently 18 per cent and income is taxed at rates up to 40 per cent, ETFs with distributor status are clearly preferable for a tax-paying UK investor.

European-domiciled ETFs are generally eligible for inclusion within tax-protected savings accounts such as ISAs, PEPs and SIPPs. ETF issuers' websites should confirm whether a particular fund has distributor status and whether a fund is ISA-, PEP- and SIPP-eligible.

A big obstacle to the popularity of ETFs in the UK was removed in 2007 when stamp duty on secondary market trading was removed. This has led to a big increase in the number of ETFs listed for trading on the London Stock Exchange, giving UK-based investors a much greater variety of choice.

If you are UK-based and investing in a taxable account, the decision on whether to invest in bond ETFs or direct bond holdings is a tricky one.

While capital gains on direct bond holdings are not taxable, gains on bond funds such as ETFs are liable to CGT. However, investing in bonds via an ETF gives you immediate diversification and may be the only practicable route for an investor with a few thousand pounds to devote to the sector.

A final checklist

Here is a summary of useful checks to perform when selecting a particular ETF or other tracker product:

1   Is it UCITS-compliant?
2   What is the ETF structure and replication method, and do I understand what counterparty risks the product carries?
3   How is the index constructed and could there be any drawbacks in the construction method (excessive concentrations, index turnover, roll costs, tracking error over time)?
4   What is the secondary market liquidity like? How large are bid–offer spreads for the ETF I am considering buying?
5   Is the fund company or fund likely to close, and if so, what costs might arise?
6   Is the ETF's tax status suitable for me?

6

The new fundamental indexing revolution

Like all great revolutionary movements, the adherents of an indexing approach to investment have multiplied exponentially in numbers over recent years and that growth has been accompanied by an inevitable splintering into smaller groups with ever more detailed and considered doctrines. A vocal and hugely sophisticated group of analysts and fund managers has coalesced around a simple idea – that the traditional index is flawed in its design and that it needs to be rethought and linked back to a much older idea that suggests the only sensible investment idea is one that is based around the concept of good 'value'. Fund manager Rob Davies, from Fundamental Tracker Investment Management (FT/M), based in Glasgow, is one of these new-style indexers trying to combine the best of 'value' investing with the transparency and efficiency of index fund investing. He is in the front line of a new movement of 'fundamentalists' who think that simply following a traditional index like the S&P 500 or the FTSE 100 is a deeply flawed exercise.

What is wrong with conventional indexing?

Accepting the logic of index investing is a big step, but it is only the first one. The next step is to understand what you are actually tracking in an index. For most people that will amount to a choice between segments of the market usually based on size, such as the FTSE 100, the 250, or an all-encompassing single index such as the FTSE All Share, which captures nearly all the UK listed market. All these popular indices use a similar methodology and, until just a few years ago, there was no choice, as every index was based on capitalisation. That meant the weight of each stock in the fund was determined by its market capitalisation, with its total value determined by multiplying the share price by the number of shares outstanding.

For many academics this methodology for constructing an index simply reflects the underlying ideas of the EMH, namely that the share price of a company captures everything that is known about the business. That includes its balance sheet, business prospects and the quality of the management. The theory is that modern capital markets are so efficient that it is impossible for any individual to secure a sustainable, legal information advantage over their competitors. The fact that 80 per cent of the market is still managed on an active basis by people who do not believe markets are efficient does not compromise the theory in the eyes of its academic adherents.

An equally important reason for using capitalisation as the mechanism for constructing a fund is that most, but not all, major stock exchange indices are based on the sum total of the value of the constituents. Basing a fund on the same principle as the index is a neat way of ensuring that the performance of the fund will never deviate too far from that of the index. There are exceptions however. Both the Dow Jones Industrial Average and the S&P 500 are determined by a committee and can best be viewed as 'active' indices in contrast to the rules-based indices like the FTSE and the Russell. The old FT30 used a similar, committee-based, subjective approach.

Whatever the process, both rules-based and subjective indices have a growth bias. At first pass this looks illogical: why does a market cap-based index have a growth bias? The reason for this comes back to the issue of market capitalisation. Any company on the threshold of accession to the FTSE 100 will, by definition, be doing better than its peers. That means its valuation will be at a premium to its near neighbours, in other words valued as a growth share. In contrast, the company that is about to be ejected will have fallen on hard times and its value will be discounted relative to its comparable companies. So companies joining an index will always be expensive and those leaving will always be cheap. The largest 100 companies in the FTSE All Share will not necessarily be the largest 100 by profits, book value, dividends or revenue, just price.

A real-life example of how this works in practice can be found in the March 2009 changes for the FTSE 100. Out went Tate and Lyle with a price to book value of 1.37 and a PE ratio of 7.4. It was replaced by Fresnillo, trading at a price to book ratio of 5.1 and a PE ratio of 25. The fact that the Tate share price had slid from 400p to 250p while Fresnillo had soared from 100p to 434p in the few months prior to these changes confirms the view that indices overpay for growth.

But there is a problem with using just share prices to create a portfolio – they do not have a direct correlation to the value of the underlying asset, namely the company that the market is valuing. Instead they represent the opinions and views of all the market participants and that means they are subject to all the manias and fashions that dominate financial affairs. In the last few decades, those fashions have included technology, commodities, property and biotechnology. In previous centuries they have included railways, tulip bulbs and South Sea bubbles. Conversely, at the same time as one sector is fashionable, another one is out of favour. At some point or other these have included commodities, utilities and banks. What this means is that an investor buying into a conventional index fund will always have a larger position in sectors that are popular and a smaller position in unpopular sectors, irrespective of the relative valuation of those sectors. In practical terms this means that any capitalisation-weighted index is always overweight expensive shares and underweight cheap shares, as this little exercise will demonstrate.

Assume the components of a stock index have aggregate earnings of £100m and the whole market is valued on a PE ratio of 10. Therefore the total market is valued at £1000m. Assume also that half the stocks have an above-average valuation of 11 so the other half must be valued at 9 times earnings. It follows, therefore, that the expensive half of the market is valued at £550m and the cheap half at £450m. Consequently any index tracker fund will have 55 per cent of its assets in the expensive stocks and only 45 per cent in the cheap stocks. We might not know which of the stocks are cheap and which are expensive, but we do know that cheap stocks outperform expensive stocks over time, yet the index fund is underweight in them. However, the situation is worse than that. Because the fund is overweight expensive shares it has a higher PE ratio than the market. In our example it actually has a PE ratio of 10.1, 1 per cent more than the index itself. You might be buying £100m worth of earnings, but doing it this way you are paying 1 per cent more than the average. That is not good for long-term returns. The situation is even less attractive if there is a bigger discrepancy between the high and low valuations. If the market values the most expensive shares at 15 times earnings and the cheapest at 5 times, the average PE for the index fund becomes 12.5.

If that seems counter-intuitive this analogy might help. Imagine going shopping for apples and oranges. The apples are priced at 5p a pound and the oranges at 15p. A buyer, using the logic of a tracker, wanting equal amounts of the different fruits would buy one pound of apples for 5p and three pounds of oranges for 45p. He buys three times as many oranges because they are three times as valuable. So the shopper has spent 50p for four pounds of fruit at an average cost of 12.5p a pound. A more rational shopper would buy a pound of each for an average cost of 10p a pound.

Of course, no one really knows which shares are expensive and which are cheap at any given time. However, we do know two things:

- First, the market always overpays for growth. That is why value stocks outperform.
- Second, valuations always revert to the mean. Expensive earnings, like those of Vodafone in 2000, eventually become earnings that are priced in line with the market. That erodes returns for the investor.

Over time the index components will change as the popularity of a stock or sector waxes and wanes, yet starting a portfolio with an overweight position in an expensive sector and an underweight position in a cheap one is almost inevitably going to have a negative impact on returns in the long run. One of the oldest, and best, clichés in the money management business is that in the short term markets are voting machines in the long run they are weighing machines. Conventional index funds are great at capturing the voting element of the stock market, yet what is needed is a way of weighing the market.

Is there a better way to index?

It is clear from this discussion that there is a potentially fundamental flaw in creating a portfolio based solely on capitalisation, i.e. share price alone. After all, in what other walk of life do we make purchase decisions solely on the basis of price? We do not, for instance, choose our mix of vegetables at the supermarket by buying most of whichever is the highest price on that day. Indeed, we do the opposite. Any special offers are snapped up, reducing our average cost per pound of vegetable. Cars are purchased on the basis of their size, reliability and performance, not just on price. Indeed, in every other avenue of commercial life we prefer to pay less for more. Supermarkets do not make buy-one-get-one-free offers without knowing what the reaction of shoppers is likely to be. Normally, when we spend our money we want some measure of what we are buying other than price. It might be the weight of a cauliflower, the top speed of a car or the number of springs in a bed. Why should we not do something similar when we buy shares? What we need is some fundamental measure of the value of a company.

A far-sighted investment manager called Robert Jones at Goldman Sachs is credited as being the first to ponder these issues back in 1990. He designed and ran a fund based around earnings, but the fund was closed down after it failed to beat the-inhouse enhanced index fund. Since then the main proponents have been Rob Arnott of California-based Research Affiliates, (also known as RAFI) and Jeremy Siegel of Wisdom Tree. The main issue these two US-based analysts have had to address is which measure, or measures, they should use, as well as working out more mundane issues such as the frequency of rebalancing and whether to use historic or forecast data.

The attraction of a tracker fund is that it buys all the shares in a particular index. That reduces risks by ensuring that the fund holds all shares that might do well. Equally, it will hold ones that might do badly, thus dragging down the whole portfolio. So if we are going to design a mechanism that can be used across all stocks in the market we have to use some measure that is appropriate to a wide variety of companies and industries. Fortunately, there is no shortage of measures that can be used and ways in which they can be applied, though each has advantages and disadvantages.

One point to note is that all fundamental funds are blind to the data they use. This is in sharp contrast to active fund managers, who categorise companies by the sector they are in. Each sector will have its own valuation range to reflect the underlying nature of the business. That is why, for example, yields from utilities are always expected to be higher than yields from tech companies. The market is saying that dividends from tech companies are worth more than dividends from water or power companies. Fundamental funds say all dividends, book values, revenues and profits are equal. All index funds treat data in this agnostic way. But which measures should we focus on?

Book value

One traditional measure of value is the book value of the company, also sometimes known as net asset value. This is a pure accounting measure of the capital subscribed to create the company, the initial equity, less any debt, but including the profits it has retained over its life and minus the dividends paid out. This narrow definition can work for some industries such as those that develop a product or service over time and sell those profitably, but there are a number of necessary caveats. The financial accounts can become quite distorted where companies have made a lot of acquisitions as goodwill and write-offs have become significant. Periods of high inflation also have an impact by eroding the real value of debt and increasing the nominal value of tangible assets such as property or inventory. Companies working in natural resources that have made large discoveries of oil or other commodities are not able to include that additional value in the books. All they can do is record the cost of finding the deposits. Equally, a pharmaceutical company that develops a new drug can only charge the cost of discovery and development to its profit and loss account. As far as its book value is concerned, inventing a drug is just research and development expenditure. Other companies may have established important brand names, but it is hard to quantify their value and even harder to find a way to give that a value in the accounts. Without advertising, many brand names fall by the wayside. Finally, markets and tastes change so that what was valuable several years ago may be worthless now. Records and cassettes, for example, are no longer so much in demand when music can be digitally downloaded. Book value then has some merits as a measure, but it also has many drawbacks. Book value is usually seen as a key factor in selecting value stocks, so it is no surprise that it figures strongly in the approach used by leading US fund management firm Dimensional (DFA). Research Affiliates also uses it as one of its four measures.

Profit and loss

The profit and loss (P&L) account is the traditional source of data for determining value. Starting at the top of the P & L statement many are attracted to the idea of using revenue as a measure because there is less scope for distortion. After all, it makes sense to assess a business on how much it sells. There is a problem with that though, and it is summed up in this little ditty:

Revenue is vanity

Profit is reality

Cash is sanity

Quite often companies will chase business and then fail to make any money from it because the margins are too low. Unprofitable business has no value and giving it a weighting will lead to an index with a bias that does not reflect the real source of profits. In some industries even defining revenue is very difficult in a classic profit and loss sense, i.e. the banks spring to mind as an example. Other businesses are agency businesses, such as advertising where the scope for gaming the numbers can be considerable – they can move booked sales back and forth between accounting periods, especially if the contract is over a long period of time. It is also fair to say that some industries, such as retailing, will always have large revenue numbers relative to the size of the business in comparison to, say, a drug company. Commodity companies such as miners and the oil majors are particularly susceptible to wild gyrations in their top line as prices change. Finally, currency volatility can make a big impact on sales. Depending on whether the costs that are associated with those sales are in the same currency can make a huge difference to whether that volatility is beneficial or not. Notwithstanding these concerns, revenue is one of the four measures used by Research Affiliates as it is a very simple measure of a company's economic footprint.

Profits are a logical measure to base an index on – they could be the operating profit, profit before tax or net profit. The problem is that whichever level is chosen there is a high degree of subjectivity as to which items are included and which are excluded. A particular problem is the issue of exceptional items that can affect one year but reflect the accumulation of many years of business success or problems. In essence, the uncertainty here is that a great deal of the profit and loss statement has a large discretionary element to it and that makes comparisons between companies difficult. The last decade has seen an unusually large number of seemingly profitable companies suddenly collapse, either through fraud or dramatic changes in their business conditions. In sum, profits have not always been what they seemed.

Many would argue that the cash flow statement is a better basis for comparison but again the issue of different standards is a key problem – what one company counts as capital expenditure another might include as operating costs. On top of that there are great differences in the nature of the cash flow between industries. A retailer, for example, will have a very different structure to its cash flow than, say, an oil company. Cash flow from a retailer may vary hugely over the course of the year as seasons change, but an oil company might be faced with years of exploration before it receives any cash. Moreover, cash flows for financial companies such as banks and insurance companies have a completely different nature to what might be called conventional companies. Using their data would distort any index based around them to a significant extent.

Dividends

There is, however, one measure that can be used across companies and has the great virtue of being independently verifiable. Dividends are the cash paid out by a company to its owners – the shareholders. That means it is a real transaction and can be confirmed by the recipients. Moreover, a dividend cheque from an oil company is just the same as a dividend cheque from a retailer, although usually larger! Nevertheless, there are cultural differences to the way companies view dividends. These are mostly between countries and usually derive from their tax treatment. Until quite recently the tax treatment of dividends in the US was quite adverse compared with stock options, so it therefore suited companies to issue fresh stock rather than cash, especially as issuing new stock diluted shareholders but did not impact the cash in the company. That was one reason why many US companies did not pay dividends. The other was a rather machismo reasoning that only mature companies paid them. It was argued that true growth companies reinvested cash to build the business. The tech bubble showed the fallacy of that argument.

The most important point about dividends is that in reality they account for virtually all the returns from equity investing. Active investors desperately seek capital gains, but study after study by the likes of Barclays, Credit Suisse and Société Générale on both sides of the Atlantic show the importance of reinvested dividend income and the growth of the dividend. Even over a short period of five years Société Générale showed that these two factors accounted for 80 per cent of the return. Jeremy Siegel has calculated that the figure rises to 96 per cent for US stocks over the 80 years from 1926 to 2006.[1] You ignore dividends at your peril. For these reasons all three fundamental fund processes use dividends either on their own or as part of a blend of measures.

A key argument of Rob Arnott at indexing firm RAFI is that he aims to measure the economic footprint of a company rather than its financial one – that means key indicators such as number of employees, square footage of factory or retail space are all valid because they give an assessment of how significant a company is to the community. The problem is that comparing people on the sandwich production line at Compass with advertising executives at WPP will necessarily give a distorted comparison.

Single-measure or blended, historic or forecast data

With all these different measures the would-be fundamental tracker or index builder now has to make two decisions:

- ◼ Should you use a single measure in isolation or blend several of them?
- ◼ Are historic data the best to use or should you rely on future estimates or forecast data?

Using one fundamental measure like profits or earnings per share is obviously simpler and easier to comprehend, yet that measure may be unfavourable for some companies, or even exclude whole sub-sectors of the market. If, by contrast, a blend of measures is chosen, what proportion of each valuation metric for instance should be used? Would equal weighting be valid? Blending has the obvious advantage of not giving preference to any one particular measure that might favour, or disadvantage, one particular company or sector, but it does not avoid that second, equally daunting challenge, namely whether a series of blended measures is backward looking or forward facing in its use of data.

This second challenge – whether to use forward- or backward-looking data – is based on the reality that companies report full accounts twice a year, usually two or three months after the period end. That is the most accurate picture we are ever going to get of a company. Sadly, even when the companies report, we will be faced with the challenge of working out what some of those numbers actually mean. Terry Smith in his famous book *Accounting for Growth* pinpointed the many ways that companies can flatter the way they present themselves to the investing public.[2] Remember, too, that companies have a habit of restating figures when it suits them, so we should not treat everything in the accounts as gospel. Nevertheless, published accounts are the best we have to go on. But accounts published in, say, February tell us what happened to the company as far back as the January of the previous year. In stock market terms that is ancient history. These historic data are obviously going to be the most accurate but, in a rapidly changing world, how much value is there in knowing the precise amounts for a company from as much as 14 months ago? To get the hard data we really need we have to wait in effect for a whole 12 months, with an update every 6 months. That suggests the data in the index could be quite stale.

Would the fund not be better using forward-looking estimated data rather than accurate but historic data? Is it better to be roughly right about the future than precisely wrong about the past? Markets change and what was a market-leading product last year might be obsolete today. Having a factory geared up to produce CDs is not much use if everyone is downloading music from the internet. That plant may have cost £10m to build, but it may not be worth that to a buyer today. Forecast data though is not without its problems, the key one being there is not much of it. Analysts tend to focus on only a few key measures like earnings and dividends. Not all will have reliable estimates for book value, or maybe even revenue. There is also the small matter of the reliability of those forecasts. That said, forecasts of fundamental measures do have the unique benefit of being able to incorporate expectations of the future on a real-time basis. Steadfastly holding to the historic book value of a company as a fundamental measure when its credit rating has changed from AAA to junk is clearly not satisfactory.

There are obvious attractions in using a blend of measures, namely that it smoothes out the numbers. Equally, there are some significant drawbacks, the most important being which ones do you use and how do you weight each parameter? The more subjectivity that is added by decisions such as these, the further the process moves away from being strictly fundamental. Research Affiliates is the only one to use a blended approach, while Wisdom Tree and Fundamental Tracker (my company) use single measures. Fundamental Tracker is the only one to use forecast data.

Having set out some of the issues related to data, we now need to consider the different research-based approaches to fundamental indexing offered by the big asset management firms.

The runners and riders

One of the first advocates of fundamental indices was Rob Arnott. He and his team at Research Affiliates use a blend of historic data to construct their indices. On the east coast of America the boffins at Wisdom Tree, by contrast, have opted to use two measures, dividends and earnings, but not in the same funds. In the UK there is only one fund using the fundamental tracker concept, the Munro Fund (which I manage), and it uses forecast gross cash dividends – this approach uses dividend payouts, weighted by volume not price as they would in a conventional index yield fund like the FTSE Dividend Plus.

Table 6.1 details the unique approaches of the key fundamental tracker/index managers. Although they all use different measures and processes, not one of them has any use for the traditional share price way of constructing an index.

Table 6.1 Fundamental approaches

	Wisdom Tree	RAFI	FTIM
Measures	Cash dividends, earnings	Blend of revenue, earnings, dividends and book value	Gross cash dividends
Time	Current annualised	Five-year historic smoothed	One-year ahead
Rebalancing frequency	Annually	Annually	Monthly
Vehicle	ETF	ETF	OEIC

A proper analysis of these different approaches is a long and detailed exercise and is beyond the scope of this chapter. Probably the most important factor to be considered is the benchmark the funds are compared with. ETFs are typically compared to the indices that were created for them so they can appear to be less risky, as measured by tracking error, than they are when measured against more familiar indices. A fund may appear to be doing very well against its own benchmark, but when compared with a traditional index it may appear as having a higher risk and a lower return. Ultimately, the test of any investment process must be whether it delivers better returns at lower risk than a conventional passive tracker.

Analysis of the data is also complicated somewhat by the profusion of funds that many of the fund providers have created, making it hard to choose one fund that is truly representative of each process. In the next section we take a brief look at each of the different index construction processes.

Dimensional Fund Advisers

One fund manager that does not quite fit into any conventional definition of fundamental indexing but is worth considering first is US firm Dimensional Fund Advisers (DFA). It does not describe itself as either a passive or an active fund manager – like some of the fundamental fund managers it has a clear and strong investment process but, unlike most of them, it has an overlay of subjectivity that makes it more akin to an active fund. Its aim is to outperform the index it is benchmarked against by taking positions that are biased to small-cap and value stocks. Its logic is based on the ground-breaking work by economists Eugene Fama and Kenneth French discussed in Chapter 2 – that small-cap and value stocks have an historic record of outperformance. DFA applies its process on a continuous basis so is not subject to the tyranny of being tied to only rebalancing a fund once a year. As we saw earlier, even when an index is rules-based, such as the FTSE 100, it still has an inherent growth bias, so any process that promotes value will have a built-in advantage over an index that has an inherent growth bias.

DFA's unique approach is very different from that of the three main fundamental indexing outfits.

Wisdom Tree

Wisdom Tree builds indices based on earnings and dividends using the latest trailing 12-month data while rebalancing its run on an annual basis, on 30 November. That passive approach can have its flaws, as Chief Investment

Officer Jeremy Schwarz admits. In 2008, for instance, Wisdom Tree was hostage to stale and out-of-date data, centred on rapidly changing dividend payouts and suffered dreadfully, as all value-biased funds did, when formerly reliable dividend payers cut payouts in response to extreme market conditions. Wisdom Tree is the brainchild of Jonathan Steinberg and started out as an indexing as opposed to fund management company. Steinberg kicked off with the concept of creating a blended index using market capitalisation and dividends and approached Professor Jeremy Siegel of Wharton to validate the exercise. Siegel, like many others, had realised the inherent flaws of cap-weighted indices during the dot-com bubble at the turn of the millennium. His regular surveys of long-term returns demonstrated the problems caused by cap weighting and in his 1994 publication reviewing capital market returns he acknowledged that other measures might be preferable.[3] That started him on the road towards the concept of using dividends to create an index. The triangle was closed when hedge fund manager Michael Steinberg joined and provided the financial backing to enable Wisdom Tree to launch its range of funds in June 2006.

Wisdom Tree creates indices for a very wide range of markets and sub-sectors. Some are based totally on dividends while some are based on earnings – in both cases annualised data is used. Its main funds are benchmarked against the S&P 500 index which, oddly, is a subjective index. This does present a slight inequality if only because a rules-based portfolio (Wisdom Tree's) is being measured against a subjective index like the S&P 500, whose composition is determined by a committee. In total Wisdom Tree runs 42 separate funds on fundamental indexing principles to track a variety of indices in and outside the US. All its funds are ETFs and in March 2009 it managed about $3.6bn. Like many value-orientated strategies, it suffered in the 2008 bear market relative to the main indices, but the lags were not large. To address the issue of a value bias, Wisdom Tree has launched an earnings-weighted fund based on NASDAQ stocks which uses a more complex blend of measures.

Research Affiliates

Rob Arnott of Research Affiliates is probably the most high-profile advocate of fundamental indexing and his seminal 2005 paper, simply called 'Fundamental Indexation', co-authored with Jason Hsu and Philip Moore, sets out the arguments very clearly. He uses an equally weighted blend of four measures to create the index. These measures are the trailing five-year smoothed data for revenue, book value, earnings and dividends. As with

DFA and Wisdom Tree, the danger here is that the data can become very stale as the annual rebalancing approaches. Like many observers he watched the turn of the millennium tech bubble with alarm and resolved to find a better way to construct an index. He assembled a vast array of data stretching back to 1957 when the S&P 500 index was created. From this mass of data he and his team deduced that the most efficient construction – the process that gave the best return for the lowest risk – was an equally weighted blend of the revenue, profits, book value and dividends. His back-tested time series starts in 1962, the first year on which five-year trailing (data from five years previous) can be assembled. This huge backtest showed clearly that Arnott's version of an index generated better returns than the S&P 500 index, with lower risk – although part of the reason for this relative success has, in my opinion, more to do with the construction of the S&P 500 index, which is subjective, than Amott's fundamental index.

Arnott delves into even greater detail in his 2008 book, *The Fundamental Index: A Better Way to Invest* co-written with Jason Hsu and John West.[4] In it he explores in the growth bias of traditional market capitalisation-weighted indices and details the extensive back-testing work he and his team have done to prove that their fundamental indexation produces better returns with lower levels of risk. He also argues that the EMH is still a hugely important concept, but one that does not actually work in the real world any more.

Fundamental Tracker Investment Management

FTIM it is the only UK-based firm to offer a fund-based fundamental indexing approach through its Munro Fund, which uses forecast gross cash dividends to create a portfolio benchmarked to the FTSE 350 index. It differs from the Wisdom Tree and RAFI approach in using forecast, not historic, data on the basis that it is better to be roughly right than precisely wrong – it uses the consensus forecasts from all the analysts sourced by Bloomberg for the financial year beyond the current one and then adjusts for share buybacks. Like its two US peers, FTIM uses the gross dividend the company will distribute, not the more commonly used per share figure – it weights dividends by volume not price as a conventional yield-based index fund would do. By rebalancing the model portfolio every month it is also able to continually adjust to the small changes that are made by analysts on an almost daily basis. Last but by no means least it assumes its key measure (the dividend) is all equal – in other words, the pound of dividend from an oil company is worth the same as a pound of dividend from a retailer. In conventional active management this is not the case.

The Munro Fund OEIC was launched in September 2007, just at the start of one of the worst bear markets in recent years and in absolute terms the initial performance was poor as the stock market collapsed under the weight of the credit crunch. In relative terms – and that is what really counts for an index fund – it has delivered on its promise, namely better returns in its asset class relative to conventional index tracking funds.

Fund management in detail

As this fund is run by the writer it might be fruitful to describe the mechanics of the process in detail. Each month we run the following process at the Munro Fund:

- The consensus forecast dividends per share, for one year ahead, for all the companies in the FTSE 350 are downloaded together with the issued share capital.

- Adjustments are made where appropriate for changes in share capital for such things as rights issues or share buybacks.

- The forecast dividend for each company is then multiplied by the expected number of shares to calculate the forecast gross cash payment, converted to sterling if needed. For a company such as Vodafone this can be as much as £4.5bn while Marks and Spencer might be only £213m. Individual contributions are then aggregated to get a total for the FTSE 350. In March 2009 this figure was £63bn.

- Finally, each company's contribution to the total is calculated as a percentage. So in one month, for instance, Vodafone's weight in the model portfolio might be 6.8 per cent while Marks and Spencer's is 0.33 per cent. These new weights are then applied to the portfolio. Normally this is done by using uninvested cash to top up underweight holdings to keep trading to a minimum.

- Occasionally, where positions have become substantially overweight, the holding is trimmed back to bring it in line with the model. In essence the process keeps the fund aligned to the largest flows of cash, from dividends, into the market.

Wegelin & Co

It is worth mentioning one last fund manager that has its own very unique process. It is not a pure fundamental index provider or tracker fund manager, although it does follow a strict rules-based procedure for its investment process. Swiss private bank Wegelin & Co operates what it calls an 'active indexing' process to manage its SFR3bn portfolio of pension and private money.

The bank has based its approach to markets on the simple concept that markets eventually revert to mean over the long-term, especially at the national level – it does not buy individual stocks but looks to invest in national markets that represent good value. Central to this approach is that it has no exposure to markets viewed as expensive – the secret sauce in its process is its proprietary process for determining the value of stocks relative to cash that underlies the methodology. This calculation uses a variety of measures such as leading indicators, risk premiums, credit spreads and investment behaviour that are blended (with equal weights) to give a measure relative to the global market. Once it has determined which national markets have good prospects, and which do not, it aligns its portfolio accordingly, with the overall universe of stocks (the potential markets to invest in) based on the MSCI World index, which contains 22 countries including Japan, the US and the UK. This wide 'opportunity set' does not mean it will have a position in every nation; if the measure or indicator is negative it might have no position or even go short. One of the authors of the process is Dr Magne Orgland, who says one of the great virtues of the process is that they no longer have interminable investment committee meetings – they simply rely on their process as they have found it throws up better results than the consensus of experts. This simple statement is actually one of the most important aspects of any rules- or fundamentals-based investment process – if done properly, fundamentals-based investing saves an enormous amount of time in decision-making, with investment committees suddenly redundant because of the quantitative-based processes. While that may be disturbing to those who enjoy the cut and thrust of debating business models, valuation metrics, demographics and money supply, there is a great deal of evidence that decisions made by such groups are rarely consistently good. Anyone with experience of investment clubs will quickly realise that democracy and investing are not compatible.

As with many rules-based investment processes much of the value derives from rebalancing to bring the actual portfolio back into line with the model – Wegelin rebalances its funds every month, which it claims is a major reason for its low tracking error.

Why fundamental funds?

So, to conclude, the advantages of fundamental tracking/indexing over mainstream actively managed funds are numerous and easy to understand and include the following:

1 Defined process that eliminates subjectivity and human emotion.
2 That elimination of subjectivity reduces manpower, reducing costs and time to action changes.
3 Lower management fees improve returns to investors.

4 The defined process improves transparency for investors.

5 Most fundamental processes focus on dividends, the largest source of wealth creation in equity investing.

6 The process will not change even if the fund manager does – active fund managers suffer from high turnover so you never know who will be managing your money in five or ten years' time.

Fundamental funds also offer some substantial advantages over conventional index-based funds:

1 They remove the growth bias – eliminating price from the construction process provides a better way of tracking the underlying earnings because it eliminates the popularity measure inherent in share prices.

2 Fundamental index funds generally offer higher yields.

3 Some fundamental fund managers offer more frequent rebalancing.

No one should expect any index fund to shoot the lights out – these funds are designed to give the returns of the index they are benchmarked to – but because they are process driven they are (hopefully) cheap to run and have lower management fees. Reducing costs has the same effect on the investor as higher returns, but without the risk. Most importantly, with index funds you are only paying for what is called beta – the returns of the market. With active funds you pay more for the pursuit of alpha (the ability of a manager or process to deliver more than the returns of the market) but often fail to get even that beta. Conventional index funds will never beat the index, indeed many lag the index by a considerable amount because of fees and the factors mentioned above. The advantage that fundamental funds offer is the ability to close the gap between the return of the fund and the return of the index.

Perhaps the most profound thought on the logic behind using fundamental indexing comes from Rob Arnott, who claims that the returns of fundamental funds are proportional to the square of the pricing errors of shares, i.e. the more active investors try to beat the market by taking bigger and bigger bets, the easier it is for fundamental funds to beat the market.

7

On portfolios

James Norton is the Head of Investment at one of the most progressive financial planners in the UK, Evolve Financial Planning. A former stockbroker, like many he had an epiphany – he realised that endlessly chasing after hot tips and the next big small-cap was an exercise in grand futility. Arguably it helped destroy his clients' wealth and encouraged investors to take a short-term view of financial planning and it was not making him a happy man. So he changed his entire way of working. He quit his job with a prestigious London-based stockbroker and the stockbroking game in general and decided to take a more holistic approach to money, investment and personal financial planning.

Two simple concepts sit at the core of his new approach. The first is to look at the individual and what they want out of their finances, especially via their portfolio or pension pot, which involves asking some tough questions about the purpose of investment and a client's needs for the future.

The other idea is to take these planning ideas and then work them into a winning portfolio that makes extensive use of passive investment funds, bought at the lowest cost, with the greatest efficiency. To understand how this approach might work we asked James to outline in this chapter how he would go about building such a portfolio after asking some searching personal questions about why we invest.

James will then venture into the thorny issue of how to construct a portfolio – a diversified portfolio – where both risk and return are sensibly balanced. Along this journey we will encounter the tricky issue of market timing (a subject we will return to later in this book) and hold the fund management industry to account for its rampant abuse of marketing to sell us the latest hit thing. Not everyone in the investment business will agree with James's views, but his belief in passive investing is slowly gaining traction among an elite band of financial planners.

Introduction

Car A has 5 doors, a 2-litre petrol engine, a top speed of 140 miles per hour and goes from 0–60 in 7 seconds. It has a history of reliability.

Car B has 5 doors, a 2-litre petrol engine, a top speed of 160 miles per hour and goes from 0–60 in 6 seconds. It has a few more 'bells and whistles' than Car A and is seen as a more sporty/fashionable car. The make in question has a poor record of reliability.

Car B costs three times more than Car A. Which one would you buy?

This simple analogy reflects the fund management industry in the UK today. A typical investor can invest in a UK all-share index fund with no up-front charge and an annual management charge (AMC) of 0.5 per cent, while if they used fee-based financial planners that charge could be as little as 0.2 per cent pa. Most actively managed funds, meanwhile, charge either 1.5 per cent or 1.75 per cent pa. and depending on how you access them, often carry a hefty initial charge, generally up to 5 per cent. It is no surprise, therefore, that active funds have a history of underperformance and it is easy to see why so many fee-based advisers are recommending an index tracking approach to their clients.

What's the meaning of life?

Evolve Financial Planning makes extensive use of index funds in its approach to investment – index funds very much sit at the core of the process of building a client portfolio. But before we explore exactly how it goes about constructing such a portfolio using index funds, put this book down for one moment and ask yourself the following question: 'What is important to me about money?'

If you cannot give a good answer to this simple question, then getting the right mix of investments is pure guesswork.

I have seen many clients in their late 50s and early 60s who have been working hard in jobs they do not like in the belief that in order to enjoy their retirement they need a pot of money far larger than they actually require. Sitting down and doing some simple financial planning, modelling income and expenditure, stress testing for inflation and investment 'shocks', many people are often surprised by how little money they need. Although it is never advisable to reach your 'actuarial deadline' (a politically correct term for death!) with an empty wallet, most people have an unrealistic desire to reach this time with as much in the pot when they retire. It is human nature to want more than we need.

So, if you can help clients to understand how much they actually need as well as to question what their money is for, I contend that it follows that their chances of financial success will be greatly improved. For many, the goal is to achieve what we call 'financial independence', i.e. to make enough money so they do not have to continue working. It may not actually mean they are going to retire, but they want the option of retirement. For others, who have already achieved this goal, capital protection or maintenance of financial independence is often more important. Nearly everyone will have secondary goals, such as funding school or university costs for children, mitigating inheritance tax or increasing charitable giving. As financial planners, once we understand these goals we can help quantify them and really 'flesh out' the implications.

Take a couple in their mid 30s with a high income who are conscientious savers into their ISAs and pensions. They own their home but have a sizeable mortgage. They have two children aged five and seven. What might be important to them about money?

- Financial security in the event of illness/death/redundancy.
- Paying off their mortgage.
- Buying a larger house.
- Providing for their children's education.
- Helping their children financially after university.
- Making the most of their current investments.
- Making the most of excess income.
- Providing for a secure (early) retirement.

The death/illness scenarios could be addressed quickly and cheaply through insurance, allowing them to focus on other goals. If they want a bigger house and a private education for their children, unless their income is significant there is a distinct possibility that they will need to take a reasonably high degree of investment risk to have any chance of achieving early retirement. Perhaps the bigger house is not so important if it means working for an extra 5–10 years? As they are young they may be comfortable taking a relatively adventurous approach to investment.

Move this same couple forward 20 years to their mid 50s. What might be important to them about money now?

- Financial security in the event of illness/death/redundancy.
- Helping their children financially after university.
- Making the most of their current investments.
- Making the most of excess income.
- Providing for a secure retirement.

The couple are now much closer to retirement. Their earnings potential is therefore greatly diminished. There is no turning back. Because of this they would probably be wise to reduce investment risk, particularly on pensions if they plan to convert their funds into an annuity. If they plan to use some form of income drawdown arrangement from their pensions, the fund choice decision will be different as the money will be invested for longer. By now the couple will have built up a sizeable ISA and collective fund portfolio in the knowledge that this will supplement their retirement income. The amount of risk they need to take on this portfolio will depend quite heavily on what sort of income they will draw from their pensions. It may be that the job of the investment portfolio is to provide protection in the event of high inflation and therefore a reasonable allocation to asset-backed investments such as equity and property funds might still be appropriate.

Now let's move them forward a further 20 years, to their mid 70s. What might be important to them about money now?

- Capital preservation.
- Passing money to the next generation.
- Reducing inheritance tax.

In their mid 70s the couple might be looking to downsize their home. They may find themselves in the fortunate position that they will never run out of money. The question they now need to ask themselves is whether there is really any point in investing for growth when any growth, and much of their capital, will get clobbered by 40 per cent inheritance tax on their deaths. Given that one of their aims is to pass money to the next generation, they might consider gifts, whether as outright gifts or via a trust. If gifts are via a trust, they may retain control over how the investments are managed. This then raises a question over what investment risk to take. The couple could decide that the investment really belongs to their children and grandchildren and therefore timescales for investment are much greater, meaning more scope for investment risk.

The process I am trying to highlight here is what is called a lifecycle approach to investing, namely that the opportunities and threats change significantly at different stages of our lives and it is up to us to adapt our investment strategy accordingly.

Why invest?

This is really the most important question and one that is often forgotten. Although many people think that investing is exciting, this is just down to clever marketing by fund groups. The reality is that if a portfolio is doing its job properly, it should be boring. Surprises are not good. So if you are not investing for excitement – and I would certainly recommend that you get your kicks elsewhere – why invest in the beginning?

Most people are not able to control their income completely. They work as hard as they can, fight for promotions and earn as much as possible. To some degree they may be able to control expenditure by eating out less, going on less expensive holidays and cutting back where possible. However, these simple tools may not be enough to achieve financial independence.

For many people, investing is therefore a necessity. If we put all of our excess income under a mattress, it would lose its real value year on year due to inflation. People often talk of wanting their money to 'work harder for them'. This is why we invest. Most people understand the concept that risk and reward go hand in hand and therefore in the long run if we take some risk we should be rewarded.

The figures in Table 7.1 are from the Barclays Equity Gilt Study and show simply why we invest in equities. The numbers speak for themselves. Equity returns have trounced those of cash and bonds over time.

Table 7.1 The value of £100 invested at the end of 1899 without reinvesting income (1899–2000)

Asset class	Nominal (without taking account of inflation)	Real (taking account of inflation)
Equities	£9,129	£139
Gilts (government bonds)	£49	£1

Source: Barclays Capital

Despite the fact that equity returns have been so poor for the last ten years, equities still come out on top by a substantial margin over the very long-term. It is this additional return over cash and bonds that is the reason we invest and for many it will help fund the shortfall between earned income and lifetime expenditure. Without investment returns many of us would die in debt. The financial planning exercise helps us to understand the scale of this shortfall, if any, and can therefore assist us in determining an appropriate level of risk.

Good investing should be goals based and built around clear objectives. This is why investment advice must be personalised, not through standardised portfolios built by big investment houses with names like 'LOW RISK', 'MEDIUM RISK' and 'HIGH RISK' or 'INCOME', 'BALANCED' and 'GROWTH'.

A passive portfolio – why it matters

Financial planning is about making the best use of money. Tax optimisation is a key part of this and can offer guaranteed returns or savings. The investment element is the big unknown, but one thing we do know is that costs damage returns. Although much has been said about costs in this book already, it is worth reiterating it briefly at this point.

When we were experiencing high, double-digit equity returns in the 1980s and early 1990s, few people questioned costs. When the stock market returned 10–20 per cent a year, 1.5 per cent pa. in costs seemed immaterial. But with much more pedestrian returns, costs have taken on a new significance. Again, it is important to look back and ask why we invest when we all know it carries additional risk. What we are trying to capture is the equity risk premium. This is calculated as the difference in the expected return of the stock market and the risk-free rate of return (this is usually taken as the return on government bonds). In other words, it is the additional return that investors seek for taking the additional risk. The equity risk premium changes over time, but a reasonable long-term estimate is 4 per cent pa.

So with an equity risk premium of 4 per cent pa. and the average active fund charging in excess of 1.5 per cent pa., 37.5 per cent of the potential reward for investing in equities is being taken by the fund manager. This simply does not make sense.

Looking at it in pure monetary terms the impact of charges is staggering. Taking a 45-year period, which is a reasonable investment time horizon for most people (who might start saving at 20 and retire at 65), the charging structure has a huge impact. Assuming an index (or market) return of 7 per cent pa, £10,000 will be turned into £210,025 (before inflation). Using a portfolio of index trackers with annual charges of 0.5 per cent this will reduce the return to £170,111 – so even using trackers a large part of the index return is eroded. However, taking the average AMC of an actively managed fund, the return would fall to £111,266. Finally, taking an annual charge of 2.5 per cent, which is not uncommon for many 'fund of fund' structures, the return would be £72,482, with about 65 per cent of the return eroded by charges. This is clearly illustrated in Figure 7.1.

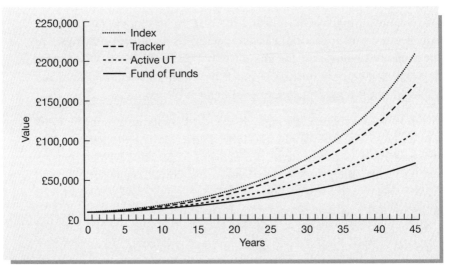

Figure 7.1   Impact of investment costs – gross of tax and inflation

Evolve sees fund management as a commodity service. Fund managers would raise their arms in horror at this as they try to justify their 'value add', but the fact is that more than half are likely to underperform the index in any one year. It is mathematically impossible for all funds to beat their benchmark, even though that is what all active funds aim to do.

Although the index approach will not deliver outperformance of an index, it should produce outperformance over the average actively managed fund.

Many people who adopt the passive route to investing have gone through some sort of conversion to get there, having invested actively for many years and realised that it was not working. This is certainly the case for most of the contributors to this book. Stockbrokers, private bankers and fund managers by their nature must believe that they can do better than their peers and competitors. As a species, many behavioural physiologists have proved that by nature we all think we are better than average. However, we all know that in reality this cannot be the case.

Believing that active management does not work is not a reflection that we think analysts, brokers and fund managers are stupid. The reality is that a great many truly sophisticated brains work in 'the markets', so many in fact that achieving a competitive edge is nigh on impossible. If you accept that insider dealing rules are effective then all the market participants gain information at the same time. The next news that comes out must by definition be random. After all, that's what news is.

This is important to understand because when you accept that many of the brightest brains rarely beat the index with any consistency, it is easier to accept that you will not. This helps with the discipline.

The aim of the rest of this chapter is therefore to look at the practicalities of running a portfolio using index funds. This ultimately comes down to two factors – investing with *a clear set of objectives* and above all *discipline*. Using index funds, in my opinion, requires the investor to understand the science behind this strategy and accept it is not an art form – it does not require constant fine tuning and matures best when it is left to do its own thing, which is to capture the market return. The temptation to make changes to a passive portfolio will generally be the result of external influences. Remember that changes increase cost, seldom add value and usually result in poor market timing decisions.

Risk

By now it should be clear that investing should *not* be about trying to get rich quick. It is seldom that easy. It is about knowing your objectives and building a portfolio that has the greatest chance of meeting returns consistent with those objectives. Assuming you have decided that some sort of investment is appropriate, where do you start with such a strategy?

At the very end of Chapter 2, we looked at the benefits of diversification, noting the research of Brinson, Singer and Beebower and the more recent research of Ibbotson. In this chapter we are going to take some of these basics and use them to look at the principles involved with constructing a portfolio.

The one decision that will have the greatest impact on portfolio returns for any individual is their allocation between fixed income and equities. Both in my previous role as a stockbroker (yes – in a former life I worked on the dark side!) and now as a financial planner, the common response when I tell investors they are going to hold a sizeable allocation of fixed interest is that it is boring and adds no value to a portfolio. The first part of this statement is largely correct as fixed income should be boring, but it certainly adds value.

To understand this it is important to revisit the relationship between risk and return. As those figures from the Barclays Equity Gilt Study show, equities have trounced fixed interest over the last 100 or more years. Equities are the engine of long-term growth of any portfolio. They are the risk assets that are funding the large corporations to invest and grow. The equity holders of a company are the owners of the company – they are the ones who have put up the capital and are taking the risk.

However, this is not a free ride. Intuitively, we all know that investing in the stock market involves risk. Most of the time the stock market just does its job, but it does sometimes make it to the front page of the newspapers. In early 2000 everyone was talking about how much they were making in tech stocks and how good they were at stock selection. With hindsight it is clear that the levels of euphoria were too high and it would all end in tears. Sadly, at the time of writing, 18 months into the credit crunch, the stock market is once again making the headlines, this time because it is making new lows.

Figure 7.2 shows the returns of the FTSE All Share from January 1956 to the end of 2008 – £1 invested at the start of this period was worth £362.74 by the end of the period. Importantly it shows the best return and worst return of the index over various timeframes. This is shown on a total return basis and so includes the very important dividend income that delivers a crucial part of the return.

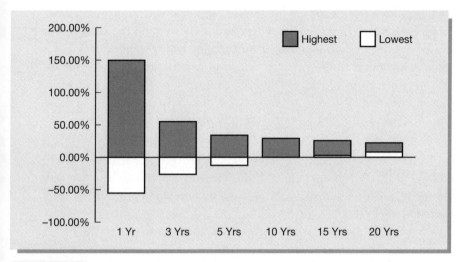

Best and worst returns FTSE All Share January 1956 to December 2008

Table 7.2 Annualised average rolling return using monthly data

	1 Yr	3 Yrs	5 Yrs	10 Yrs	15 Yrs	20 Yrs
Average	14.75%	13.69%	13.17%	13.47%	14.01%	14.53%
Highest	151.41%	56.52%	36.06%	31.62%	27.71%	23.02%
Lowest	−55.84%	−26.21%	−10.58%	0.53%	1.25%	8.02%

Source: FTSE, analysis by Evolve Financial Planning

The worst 12-month period for the FTSE All Share was a negative return of almost 56 per cent in 1973. This was followed a couple of years later by the best one-year return of 151 per cent in 1975 (see Table 7.2). In other words, volatility is enormous, with a difference between the best and worst return of over 200 per cent. However, when the timeframe of invest-ment is extended to ten years the worst annual return is positive at 0.53 per cent pa. and the best is 13.47 per cent pa. The range has narrowed enormously – taking the analysis further to a 20-year period, the difference between best and worst narrows even further.

This is absolutely crucial as it illustrates the fact that not only are risk and reward correlated, but that the longer one invests, the lower the risk of loss. Given that investing is for the long-term this is a significant advantage.

So what about fixed interest? Investing in fixed interest is a very different beast. Fixed-interest securities is a term we use to describe government bonds or gilts and corporate bonds, which are the borrowings of a company. It is simply a different way for a company to raise finance. A bond will usually have a fixed term and pay out interest over this term at a pre-agreed rate. The owners of a fixed-interest instrument do not own part of the company, but their bonds will often be secured over some of its assets. If the company fails, then bondholders are paid out as well as ordinary shareholders. This is important to understand as it helps define the main characteristics of fixed-interest holdings.

Figure 7.3 analyses the returns of one-year UK Treasury bills over the same period as the FTSE All Share in Figure 7.2. The difference is striking. First, £1 invested in 1956 grew to only £52.06. Not bad, I hear you say, but after inflation is taken into account, it is worth only £2.76. Crucially, however, the fixed-interest element has not lost money in any period and the volatility in returns is much lower. Over one year the worst return was a perfectly acceptable 3.38 per cent compared with the best year of 16.83 per cent. When the timeframe is extended to the best and worst 10-year rolling period, the picture is not much different and for a 20 year rolling period the worst return was 6.23 per cent pa and the best was 11.67 per cent pa.

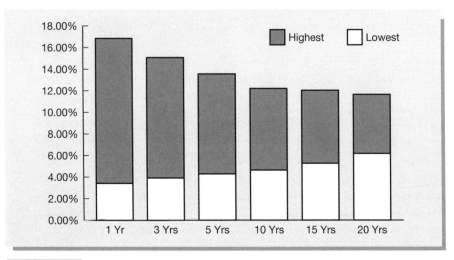

Figure 7.3   Best and worst returns UK T-bills January 1956 to December 2008

Table 7.3 Annualised average rolling return using monthly data

	1 Yr	*3 Yrs*	*5 Yrs*	*10 Yrs*	*15 Yrs*	*20 Yrs*
Average	7.86%	7.96%	8.09%	8.49%	8.88%	9.23%
Highest	16.83%	15.09%	13.56%	12.27%	12.14%	11.67%
Lowest	3.38%	3.97%	4.30%	4.73%	5.36%	6.23%

Source: Datastream, analysis by Evolve Financial Planning

These figures help show that it is simply not right to say that equities are high risk and bonds low risk. While in essence this is true, time can change everything. In some respects, over the long run when the volatility of equities is greatly reduced, bonds are actually a potentially higher-risk asset class as they have less chance of protecting a portfolio against inflation.

Asset allocation

A portfolio invested entirely in the FTSE All Share is going to be suitable for very few individuals due to the risk profile highlighted above, so it is the combination of the different asset classes that counts – balancing some of the higher- and lower-risk assets. This is very simply demonstrated in Table 7.4.

This shows the performance of five portfolios of differing risk. The first portfolio holds only one-year Treasury bills. In other words it is the ultra-low-risk portfolio. Each portfolio thereafter picks up equity exposure (FTSE All Share) in increments of 25 per cent until the final portfolio is invested entirely in equities.

Table 7.4 Portfolio returns and risk 1956 to 2008 – FTSE All Share and Treasury bills

Portfolio mix	*Annualised return %*	*Growth of wealth*	*Annualised standard deviation %*
0 : 100 (only bonds)	7.74	52.06	0.96
25 : 75	9.13	102.36	4.66
50 : 50 (mixed bonds and equities)	10.25	176.43	9.21
75 : 25	11.13	268.72	13.94
100 : 0 (only equities)	11.76	362.74	19.17

Source: Datastream and FTSE

As you would expect, as the equity exposure is increased so the average annual return increases. At the same time, so does risk. In this table risk is shown as something called the standard deviation – this is a statistical measurement for how returns have varied over a given period. Simply put, a low standard deviation indicates a high consistency of returns and a high standard deviation indicates that returns are spread out over a large range of values – in other words, higher risk.

As the equity weighting in the portfolio falls from 100 per cent to 75 per cent, the return falls only slightly from 11.76 per cent to 11.13 per cent pa, but there is a disproportionate fall in risk, with standard deviation falling from 19.17 per cent to 13.94 per cent pa. This is more clearly illustrated in Figure 7.4. Each of the portfolios is shown with risk along the X axis and return on the Y axis. As the equity component of the portfolio increases, so does the return, resulting in a shift from bottom left to top right with an increase in risk. More importantly, the figure clearly shows that the correlation between risk and reward is not a straight line; there is a bulge in the line to the left. If the correlation was on a straight-line basis one would expect the return of Portfolio 2 to be nearer 8.6 per cent than the 9.1 per cent that is actually the case. What this is showing is the free lunch in investment. Diversification has rewarded the investor with an increased return that is not proportionate with the increase in risk.

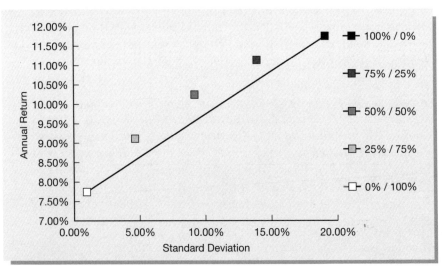

Figure 7.4   Returns and standard deviation of portfolios January 1956 to December 2008

Source: DataStream and FTSE

When deciding on the most suitable mix of fixed interest and equities, it is therefore important to consider the time horizon, the average return that such a portfolio may deliver and also the best and worst returns you may experience.

More on fixed interest

Since equities – stocks and shares – are generally regarded as the main building blocks of a portfolio it is worth focusing on the chief alternative – fixed-income securities or bonds. Most investors have a good knowledge of equity markets, but many would admit that they are on weaker ground when it comes to fixed-interest stock.

By now it is relatively obvious that fixed-interest stocks play a valuable role in reducing risk. It can also enhance yield for those looking for an income. But how do investors go about investing in fixed-income securities like gilts (government bonds)? Fixed-income securities and especially corporate bonds display a huge diversity of risk profiles, just as in equities. There are investment-grade bonds, which are issued by large, reliable companies like McDonald's (the fast-food chain), that bizarrely have lower risk ratings than some government bonds. By complete contrast, there are also much riskier bonds issued by sub-prime entities – private equity deals, for instance, or small African countries – where the debt is regarded as very, very risky and each $100 of face value is actually priced at below $50 on the open market. Such bonds behave more like equities than gilts.

Unsurprisingly, the higher the risk profile, the higher the likely interest rate or yield. Traditionally that credit risk spread has also been true for time spans – if a government issues a 30-year gilt, it is likely that it will have to pay for the privilege of borrowing for a very long time as opposed to a two-year gilt. This last statement needs a qualification though – in some unusual periods, that yield spread inverts and we are presented with the odd spectacle of very long-dated gilts paying less than very short-dated gilts. Nevertheless the general principle holds true over the longer term – the riskier and longer dated the debt or bond, the higher the yield and the greater the spread between short-dated/low risk and long-dated/high risk.

As you have probably already guessed, two concepts are crucial to understanding this spread of yields – default risk and duration. It is pretty obvious by now that the lower the quality of the bond (in terms of risk), the greater the chance of default – the lowest risk comes from developed world sovereign debt with US government T-bills regarded as essentially risk free.

The concept of duration is also easy to grasp – as we have already noted, the greater the length of time that a bond is in issue, the greater the risk. Table 7.5 shows the returns of different maturity US bonds from 1964 to 2008 – as the maturity of the fixed-interest instrument increases, so does the return. The increased return between one- and five-year notes is modest but meaningful, but there is also a significant increase in risk. However, when the maturity of bonds is extended to 20 years, not only is there another jump in risk but the increase in return is only marginal.

Table 7.5 Returns and standard deviation of different fixed interest maturities 1964–2008

	One-month Treasury bills	Six-month Treasury bills	One-year Treasury notes	Five-year Treasury notes	20-year government bonds
Annualised compound returns %	5.69	6.46	6.66	7.50	7.87
Annualised standard deviation %	1.34	1.71	2.32	6.24	11.1

Sources: Merrill Lynch and CRSP (Centre for Research in Security Prices, University of Chicago)

Some investors may be tempted to think that bonds are still risky (to a limited degree) and thus they may be tempted to invest more in the 'riskier' gilts for instance. The problem is that this probably will not work as Table 7.5 clearly tells us that additional risk (extra years for instance) does not appear to be proportionately rewarded. Remember that fixed interest is included in a portfolio in order to reduce volatility and risk, not to increase it. The real risk element should be taken in equities and those seeking extra thrills should spend some of their budget on smaller companies and value stocks. The bottom line – fixed-interest exposure should be concentrated in short-term, high-quality bonds. If they are globally diversified, that is even better.

What about equity diversification?

Once the split between the main building blocks of fixed income and equities has been decided, the next job is to think about the equity diversification. That aim is the same here, in other words to try to get the win–win of disproportionately increasing return compared with risk.

The example below shows the building blocks of a simple portfolio and how some basic diversification can be of benefit to all investors. All of the data for these portfolios is for the 21-year period 1988 to 2008 and it is designed to represent an 'average' risk portfolio with 40 per cent in fixed income and 60 per cent in equities.

The first portfolio is a plain vanilla portfolio. All the equities are in the FTSE All Share and the fixed interest is in a well-respected high-quality bond index.

Portfolio 1

Citigroup UK govt. bond index 1–30 years unhedged	40%
FTSE All Share	60%

This portfolio produces a respectable annualised return of 8.83 per cent with a standard deviation of 9.58 per cent.

The first change (which is not actually to do with equities at all) is to switch the Citigroup UK government bond index for a globally diversified, short-dated bond strategy, but keeping the equity/bond split exactly the same.

Portfolio 2

Global short-dated bond strategy	40%
FTSE All Share	60%

As we would expect, the element of 'risk' actually falls as a consequence of this small change – risk as measured by standard deviation falls to 8.97 per cent and the return shows a marginal increase to 9.20 per cent. Making this sort of change is an absolute no-brainer!

The next change to look at is the impact of international diversification. We live in an increasingly globalised economy, but not all regions have the same growth rates or prospects. In this portfolio the UK equity exposure is reduced to allow exposure to international equities and more specialist emerging markets equities.

Portfolio 3

Global short-dated bond strategy	40%
FTSE All Share	25%
International companies	25%
Emerging markets	10%

The effect of this diversification is to increase the annualised compound return to 9.50 per cent with an increase in risk to 9.41 per cent. This is not such a no-brainer as the first change, because although the return has increased, risk has risen as well.

The final stage of building a portfolio is to further diversify some of the equity exposure to capture some of the small-cap and value premium. To do this we need to look at some of the long-term sources of equity returns. A wealth of academic research from Fama and French has highlighted the fact that the long-term returns of smaller company shares and value companies have been much greater than the market as a whole.

A simple reminder, via some statistics, should remind the reader of what this shift towards small-cap and value stocks can produce. From January 1956 £1 invested in the FTSE All Share index grew to £363 by the end of 2008. However, £1 invested in UK smaller companies grew to £1,664 and £1 invested in value companies ended up as £2,183. What is interesting is that research shows that these effects of small-cap and value companies are repeated around the world. Although the risk/volatility of these asset classes is higher, the potential benefits of investing are obvious. So what is the effect of adding these to the portfolio? In the table below we have spread the UK equity exposure equally between the FTSE All Share and value and smaller company strategies.

Portfolio 4

Global short-dated bond strategy	40%
FTSE All Share	10%
MSCI World ex UK index	10%
Emerging markets	10%
UK value companies	7.5%
UK small companies	7.5%
International value companies	7.5%
International small-cap companies	7.5%

The effect of this diversification is to increase the annual return of the portfolio to 9.91 per cent per annum, with a modest increase in risk to 9.69 per cent.

The results of these changes in the portfolio are summarised below.

	Annualised compound return %	Annualised standard deviation %
Portfolio 1	8.83	9.58
Portfolio 2	9.20	8.97
Portfolio 3	9.50	9.41
Portfolio 4	9.91	9.69

What this example has shown is that two basic portfolios with the same weighting in equities and fixed interest can have very different returns. By taking some simple measures, the annual return of Portfolio 4 was 1.08 per cent higher than Portfolio 1 with almost no additional risk (only 0.11 per cent). This may not sound like much, but over the 21-year period £100 invested in Portfolio 1 would be worth £591 compared with £727 for Portfolio 4. This is a difference in return of just under 25 per cent and it was achieved through very basic diversification, the three main components of which were:

■ globally diversified, short-dated bonds;
■ international and emerging markets exposure;
■ smaller companies and value companies.

This chapter only has the space to look at some of the basics of diversification. The portfolio above is not recommended for anyone in particular, but is merely designed to illustrate some of the benefits of investing in these different asset classes. It is also worth noting the value and small-cap stocks are international in nature and cross all major equity markets and would also argue for the potential benefits of investing in areas such as private equity, hedge funds, commercial property and commodities, all of which may have diversification benefits. However, the simple conclusion still stands – the more you diversify, the better your returns, with less risk.

Timing your investment in the markets

In the last two chapters we will return to the hugely thorny issue of how to construct a disciplined investing process and whether you should even attempt to 'time' your investments into the market. Should you simply invest a regular lump sum every month and then leave the investment alone or should you attempt to increase or decrease the amount you invest, based on varying market conditions?

One way of looking at this hugely important issue is to consider what the industry likes to call 'money-weighted returns'. When looking at, say, an individual unit trust, the money-weighted return looks at when money is invested and withdrawn from the fund and therefore shows the fuller picture of investor returns. This is different to the more commonly used 'time-weighted returns' which simply calculate the difference in fund value between the start and end of a period without weighting those money flows – you will only ever see time-weighted returns in marketing literature for funds, not money-weighted returns.

To illustrate this simple distinction, consider a fund that returns 80 per cent in year one and loses 40 per cent in year two. The time-weighted return of this fund is 3.92 per cent per annum. This simply gives equal weighting to each year's return. In other words, a capital sum of £100,000 would be worth £180,000 at the end of year one and £108,000 at the end of year two, resulting in a compound return of 3.92 per cent.

However, now look at the money-weighted return of two different investors. First, let's look at Tom, who is saving for retirement and has accumulated £150,000 in this fund. He is a long-term investor and is not making any additional investments or withdrawals. At the end of this two-year period his investment would be worth £162,000, representing a return of 3.92 per cent per annum, which is the time-weighted or 'buy-and-hold' return.

Our second investor, Katie, is also saving for her retirement. However, she does not want to invest all of her money at once because she thinks that good investment opportunities will emerge over time – she wants to time her entry into and exit from the markets. Therefore she invests only £100,000 at the beginning of the investment period. After she sees that the fund has done really well she decides to make an additional contribution of £50,000 to her account. At the end of the period, her portfolio would be worth £138,000, representing a loss of –4.90 per cent. The performance gap between the time-weighted return and the money-weighted return is –8.82 per cent (–4.90 per cent to 3.92 per cent).

Although both Tom and Katie have invested the same amount of £150,000 over the entire time period, Tom has achieved a superior investment outcome. This is due to the fact that Katie made her additional investment when the fund was at its peak value and just before the negative returns. This is something that happens all too often to investors, both professional and retail, good examples being the dot-com bubble of the late 1990s or the more recent property and commodities boom.

As far back as 1996, John Bogle, the founder of Vanguard, started lobbying fund companies to report money-weighted returns. This finally started in 2006 when Morningstar took up the mantle in the US. Sadly, we still seem to be far from this in the UK.

So what do the real numbers tell us? Russel Kinnel, a director at Morningstar in the US, conducted research into the difference between funds' official returns and the returns earned by the typical investor – in other words, the difference between time- and money-weighted returns. As Bogle had been arguing for ten years, Kinnel states: 'The best measure of a fund's quality (i.e. how much it makes for the typical investor) is actual money-weighted returns.'

The results of this research were staggering. The data showed that across the board the returns earned by investors were worse than officially stated returns. This was particularly noticeable in growth funds where average ten-year annualised money-weighted returns were 3.4 per cent below the stated return. In many sectors, such as technology, the figures were much, much worse.

Until recently, there has been no significant research into money-weighted returns in the UK, but that changed with a recent paper – actually a thesis – called 'Are UK fund investors achieving fund rates of return?' by Lukas Schneider of Dimensional Fund Adviser. His conclusions are equally as damning as those of Morningstar. The data suggested that from 1992–2003 the annual return of the FTSE All Share was 8.99 per cent. Looking at 266 funds which were active in this sector over the period, the average fund returned 6.93 per cent. To those who buy index trackers this result may not be surprising – this difference is presumably largely due to costs. Estimating the total expense ratios of funds conservatively at around 1.6 per cent, the difference is easily accounted for.

However, when money-weighted returns are looked at, the picture gets even worse. The average fund investor received only 4.91 per cent over the same period. To put this into context, if an individual invested £100,000 at the start of the period, the actual return of the index would have resulted in a sum of approximately £281,000 compared with only £178,000 from the money-weighted average of the funds examined. Remember, it is the latter figure that most investors are actually getting.

Schneider's research goes much deeper than simply looking at the overall market. He also splits the funds into categories for growth, value and smaller companies. This research showed that the performance gap was as much as 2.43 per cent pa for smaller companies compared with 2.06 per cent for growth stocks and a relatively modest 1.00 per cent pa for the equity income sector. This suggests that investors may actually be better off capturing market returns in less aggressive sectors such as equity income.

These studies suggest that the niggling feeling many investors have that their returns are not as good as the marketing material tells them is correct. The reason? Poor market timing – investors have put too much money into funds at the wrong time. It is easy to understand when one looks at the advertising of the fund management houses. Most fund adverts detailing returns cover short periods – some as little as one month when performance may have been particularly impressive. Truth be told, even periods of say three or five years are not especially revealing in a true statistical sense – the manager might have done well but it is not really that meaningful, thus the fund managers' constant qualification that 'past performance is no guarantee of future performance'.

There is also a trend among fund managers to launch and promote 'hot' funds. There are no prizes for guessing which sector saw the most fund launches and largest fund flows in 1999 – technology – and which sector crashed in 2000 – technology. But fund houses and investors do not learn. Since then we have seen a boom and bust in both commercial property and commodities. It is important to remember that fund houses are remunerated on funds under management and therefore if they can gain critical mass for a fund in a very short timeframe, that is going to be very attractive to them. Investors must take responsibility for this, but the 'noise' created by the fund management industry does not help.

So what relevance does this discussion of market-weighted returns and hot funds have for anyone trying to build a portfolio? We simply do not think it makes sense to dip in and out of different sectors trying to time markets, whether to increase exposure to commodities, property, infrastructure or indeed any other market sector. Some decisions will be right, some will be wrong, but each of them will have a cost.

In fact, we see this as one of the great problems of ETFs. There is so much choice and therefore the ability to slice and dice a portfolio – gaining exposure to the most minute market sectors – if not used wisely, can do more harm than good. The temptation is to listen to the noise – you have just read an article on private equity offering great returns so you call your stockbroker and pick up an ETF that specialises in this sector, or your partner on the golf course has just told you that Japanese small-caps are the place to be, so you log on to your online share-dealing account and pick up an ETF. Noise acts as a temptation and it is there all the time. We cannot escape from it. The money and business sections of the newspapers are full of insightful articles recommending all sorts of investments. This 'helpful' advice is best avoided. It removes the focus from the long-term investment programme.

So if we are not going to listen to the noise created by the media and the financial services industry, what should we listen to? Many passive managers opt for an alternative called regular rebalancing.

Rebalancing

Remember that word discipline? A large part of the discipline of the investment process is not twisting and turning with the prevailing opinion but an equally large element consists of realising that portfolios need some care and maintenance via a periodic rebalancing. The process behind this concept is best understood with an example.

Assume you have a £100,000 portfolio nominally split with 50 per cent invested in global short-dated bonds and 50 per cent in global equities. After a year, if equities have risen by 20 per cent and the fixed interest by 5 per cent, then the equity component would have risen to £60,000 and the fixed interest to £52,500 for a total of £112,500. The equities now make up a little over 53.3 per cent of the portfolio and the fixed interest 46.7 per cent. Now there is no real harm in that, but if returns continue in that manner then after five years the equities would be worth two thirds of the overall portfolio. Again, you may think that is fine – the portfolio is growing well and providing excellent returns.

However, think back to earlier in this chapter. Investing is not simply about making money – it is about achieving goals. While letting a 50:50 portfolio simply run is likely to deliver the best long-run returns (as equities should outperform the volatility reducing fixed interest), this is not what we think the investment and planning process is about. Investing must be about managing risk. When the stock market suddenly falls by 25 per cent in one year, the unbalanced portfolio is clearly going to suffer much more. Although it may still be worth more, the journey getting there has been much more volatile.

While there has been much academic research on the subject of rebalancing there seems to be little consensus as to the best way to do it. At the one extreme David Swensen, the legendary manager of the Yale endowment fund, rebalances on a daily basis. He argues that frequent rebalancing activity allows investors to maintain a consistent risk profile. Others argue that portfolios should be allowed to run for two or three years before rebalancing, citing the often-quoted 'the trend is your friend' argument. In other words, whatever direction the market is moving in at any time, it seems to have some momentum. Another solution is rebalancing on the basis of pre-defined tolerances, i.e. when a particular asset class moves more than a pre-set amount then it is rebalanced back. In the penultimate chapter of this book, we will look in detail at each of these strategies, plus a few novel ideas. However, a simple compromise which works for most people is to review the portfolio annually and if the portfolio has not moved sufficiently, do not make any changes. Where movements are more material, then go ahead and make the changes.

Conclusion

We all like to make money, but unless it has some sort of context it is meaningless. While it is wise for all of us to have a decent buffer to fall back on when times are tough, what is the point in having £1,000,000 if you actually require only £750,000? Would it not be better to take less investment risk or even stop working a few years earlier rather than build up excess, unnecessary capital? In other words, investing should have a purpose and a clear set of objectives. Once that is done, a suitable investment strategy can be designed and implemented.

Hopefully this chapter will have helped demonstrate that investing is something for the long-term and that there are some clear and logical rules that should be followed. This does not guarantee riches (because it will deliver only the market return), but it does help to avoid many of the pitfalls that both private and professional investors face. The marketing of active fund management is extremely good and investors are lured in by high potential returns. But it seldom delivers satisfaction to the end-user in the long run. Remember that the more times your money is 'touched', the more the resulting charges will sap long-term returns.

My message is simply to build a sensible, long-term portfolio and stay disciplined. Concentrate on the aspects that you have control over, such as tax, costs, the right level of risk and reward and the overall suitability of a portfolio to your circumstances. Do not get sucked in by clever marketing of active funds. Remember, it is ultimately the fund's investors who are paying for that marketing. Do not let it be you!

8

Big theme investing and index funds

The enthusiasm surrounding the development of index tracking funds should not blind us to the fact they are not an end in themselves – they are simply tools, cheap, efficient tools nevertheless, that aid us in building better portfolios.

The huge choice of index funds does provide us with one unique advantage however – pretty much every big idea or theme that is prevalent in investment can be accessed by investing in some sort of index tracker, be it an ETF, an ETC or a structured product with a tracker in-built.

We should, rightly, be concerned with how index funds are constructed and why they might be a better structure, but a detailed examination of index funds should not ignore much more important debates about where growth will come from in the future and how and where are we going to make our positive returns. What are those big themes that will be reflected in our choice of index funds?

Dr Stephen Barber, Head of Research at Selftrade, one of the UK's biggest stockbroking firms, is ideally suited to help us answer these weighty questions. His focus is on providing ordinary private investors with reasoned investment ideas based on wider macro-economic and political trends. He is not really concerned with pinpointing any one ETF but with providing the 'brain food' that might prompt a closer examination of the range of emerging markets ETFs, for instance.

It is all very easy to get bogged down in the detail of individual investments. Just how far the Aroon Oscillator has moved or calculating the unlevered beta is all very interesting and should not be ignored. But it is not the little details that move markets or create trends. Investing historically is all about the big themes: political and economic change, industrial sector renewal, the rise and fall of national power and the like. It is about adjusting strategies to meet market conditions and not missing out on new growth areas. We all like themes, whether it is the property market or the dot coms, to name two that have raged and burned and could rage again.

Investors need to ask the questions: which companies are prospering? What links their prospects? What developments across the world are affecting markets? Which are the sectors that will dominate the next decade?

Index tracking funds such as ETFs are ideal for big-theme investing. Low cost, accessible and transparent, they allow you to get in and out of regional and industrial sectors at the click of a mouse. And with such a wide range of underlyings, it is possible to build a portfolio of trends from the four corners of the world.

That is true for bull *and* bear markets – even in bull markets, a thriving sector will often be off-set by the downturn in another. Likewise, even in downturns, there will be countries and industries which catch the wave of the next big thing. Using index funds is the simplest way of buying exposure to these trends.

This chapter will look at how investors can profit from the big themes. It will look at a number of big questions – the business cycle, big themes of years gone by, advice on avoiding bubbles, the advantages of momentum investing, the importance of diversification, the impact of globalisation and the big investment trends of this young century.

The business cycle

The first port of call for the big-theme investor is the business cycle. Cycles mean that there are identifiable trends and in the economy that suggests that different sectors prosper and decline as the economy grows or contracts.

The pattern of growth, prosperity, contraction, recession and back to growth reflects the behaviour of actors in the economy and participants in the market. Think of the over-optimism as economies peak and the over-pessimism of the trough. The market cycle tends to run ahead of the business cycle, declining and recovering earlier. And within the market different sectors prosper and decline at different times, with financials associated with the growth phase and utilities doing better (relative at least) during contraction. Here we see the difference between cyclicals and non-cyclicals: the former produce products and services which are in demand when people feel financially comfortable (leisure, consumer electronics and the like), while the latter produce the necessities of life and include heating, food and healthcare. But the big investment themes are not about simply cyclical markets, they are about structural changes in the economy. The economic cycle is important in identifying environments most attractive to potential business growth, but it will not show the new trends that will outperform the herd. For that you need to look beyond the market and to what is going on in the world.

As themes go by ...

The big themes of the past are part of the fabric of our history, from the 'never had it so good' 1950s, to the flower power 1960s, the industrial strife of the 1970s, Thatcherism of the 1980s, dot-com mania of the 1990s and the globalisation of the new millennium.

In a broad sense, each decade tells a big-theme investment story and those who identified the story early enough have been able to profit by weighting their portfolios in favour of these trends. As the tectonic plates of state and economy shift, new sectors emerge as the pioneers of their age, forging ahead in profits and influence.

In the post-war 1950s, it was industry, the age of the car and consumer goods. In 1946 there were a mere 17,000 televisions in the United States; by 1953 two thirds of US households owned a set. But it was car manufacturing that could be said to have driven the 1950s' Western economy as the middle classes burgeoned – real weekly earnings of US factory workers, for instance, increased by 50 per cent during the decade and car ownership exploded. Reconstruction in Europe and mass affluence in the United States drove the growth of technologies, automation, engineering and construction.

By the time The Beatles had their first number one, gross domestic product, trade and real incomes were higher than ever. The world yearned for the raw materials to fuel this affluence and the big theme was to be metals and other commodities. The oil crisis of the 1970s brought world growth to a shuddering halt and the big-theme investor of this sideburn-wearing decade would have been following oil. Black gold and its associated industry was one of the best-performing sectors as economies slowed. It was an asset class which responded well to rising inflation and crisis. So, too, did real gold, which as a store of wealth always prospers in economic downturn.

The 1980s were years of deregulation, laissez faire and privatisation. Thatcherism and Reaganomics meant that ordinary people invested in shares for the first time and good profits were to be made from the British government's sale of the 'family silver': utilities, telecoms and oil companies, once nationalised industries. Remember to Tell Sid … (the privatisation of British Gas).

The dot-com rise of the 1990s lasted until 2001, resulting in a multitude of reckless investors eventually investing billions in internet companies based on a speculative whim. While many technology companies were solid, long-term, innovative businesses, the dot-com era was sustained by speculation which eventually spiralled downwards to bust. Like bubbles before it and since, the good companies were outnumbered by those which would never make the profits their multiples suggested. One US grocery company, Webvan, gained and lost $1.2bn within 18 months. In order to make it to the top, companies had abandoned previous business plans and plunged all efforts and exceptional sums of money into creating brand awareness. Such was the dot-com euphoria, people were even reported to have quit their jobs with the intention of becoming full-time day traders. Wise hands with experience in the markets were already nodding their heads sagely and warning of the repeated existence of investment bubbles.

Waves not bubbles

A note of caution for big-theme investors is to ride the investment waves and not to get sucked into the bubbles. To explain how stock markets work, the great economist John Maynard Keynes developed what he called his *beauty contest* concept. Here he described a fictional newspaper competition whereby entrants had to pick the six most beautiful women from a page of photographs. Those who picked the six most popular would win a prize. 'Easy,' you say. So what would your strategy be? The more naïve (but well adjusted) might spend a pleasant afternoon selecting what they consider to be the prettiest faces. But the shrewd entrant would be more interested in what he thinks the majority think is pretty and would make a selection based on that view. And it doesn't end there. As Keynes puts it: 'We have reached the third degree where we devote our intelligences to anticipating what average opinion expects the average opinion to be.'[1]

What Keynes means is that, perhaps too often, investment decisions are not made dispassionately, based on the real merits of the instrument, but rather on what we think other people are doing. This creates bubbles: as a share or asset class does well, it attracts investors, which in turn pushes up the price. As investors pour funds into the stocks, even more investors sniff potential profits and buy into the ideas of their fellow investors, increasing confidence and valuations.

Economist Hyman Minsky had the idea that 'stability is unstable' and he had a point, even though many of his mainstream contemporaries take a different view. Minsky believed that during periods of economic stability investors increasingly take on more risk. As a result, we see an increase in debt and a willingness to buy increasingly expensive assets. Eventually investors rely on the value of their assets to finance their debt. And because of continued economic stability, these assets, on which debt is secured, become increasingly overpriced. The longer the period of stability, the easier the credit and the more overpriced the assets. As debts exceed investors' ability to repay from their revenues, this eventually causes a financial crisis. The bubble bursts. This will all sound very familiar to students of the 2008 sub-prime crisis in the United States which led to a world banking crisis.

But don't think it is only the inexperienced that get sucked into these bubbles – professionals are just as vulnerable. Think of the fund manager who, fearful of underperforming, buys into the concept and sets up a voguish fund to tap the private investor markets with sexy billboard advertising. While history is littered with examples of bubbles, rarely do we notice when we are in one. There is always a reason that makes things 'different this time' and investors buy and buy more. The stock becomes more and more expensive until eventually someone blinks. With asset bubbles, someone always blinks eventually and then the bubble bursts.

Put another way, we might call it the *greater fool* theory of investing – the idea that you buy a financial instrument not because of a belief in its merits but rather because you think there is a greater fool than you who will buy it at a higher price. This, in a rather cynical view, is how markets can sometimes work. But big-theme investors can select sectors with real momentum – the key is to know the difference between a long-term trend and a short-term bubble.

'It's better to travel than arrive': momentum investing works

It is stating the obvious, but avoiding dangerous asset bubbles is easier said than done. However, momentum investing is one approach that has been shown to be hugely effective. Eschewing fundamental analysis, momentum investors not only identify sectors which have performed well but also identify durable trends. Although requiring steady nerves, in essence the process could not be simpler.

Examine the market for sectors which have performed badly over, say, a 12-month period and ignore them; instead look for those sectors which have performed well in price terms and start buying into them in a systematic way. Naturally, it is crucial to identify these trends towards the beginning of their run and then get out as they show signs of waning, always shifting funds into sectors of new momentum potential. It is a strategy that comes with great risks, both in terms of correctly identifying the trend and, just as crucially, timing investment and exit. There is also a broader market risk that a big drop in the stock markets might well cause chaos in popular, market-leading sectors.

The onset of a bear market can be particularly detrimental to momentum strategies which worked in nice, comfortable bull markets. But you don't have to focus just on price momentum – look at earnings momentum and revenue growth as well as relative strength. Using these measures, momentum investors can profit from big themes, especially in strong markets. But it is important to be disciplined and sell on any alert such as bad news.

The point about momentum investing is that not only can it work but focusing on the big themes gives the strategy added drive. This works both ways, helping to select the big trend but also as a way of running a portfolio where these themes can be identified independent of the screening. By analysing the market for new themes for inclusion in your portfolio, combined with this disciplined methodology, you can make investments work harder and deliver greater profits.

Mark Glowrey and Tarquin Coe from research firm StockCube look at this momentum-based approach in the next chapter. They will examine some key signals-based approaches to running a momentum-based portfolio.

Diversify

For those with weaker constitutions, building a diversified portfolio which gives exposure to the big themes could be a sensible strategy, as James Norton discussed in the previous chapter.

All investing is about the trade-off between risk and reward; you need to accept enough risk to achieve your desired returns but not so much that you stay awake at night worrying. Diversification is key to managing risk and it also means that you can gain access to numerous investment themes. Build a portfolio of diversified asset classes, allocating portions as you see fit.

One drawback of trend-picking is ensuring you do not pick the right theme but fail to select an instrument which benefits from this trend. Buying into an index or sector can help here, ensuring your portfolio has exposure to big themes without the need to pick the specific shares that might do well. This is a particularly useful tactic when investing beyond your home markets where specific research is more difficult to obtain.

Also be careful of fads – remember, at one point someone was telling investors that tulips were the future. Ask yourself why this is a big theme, where are future revenues coming from and what are the actual profits? Even if you can answer these questions, be careful not to pick the last trend, look to the next. Always relate these secular trends back to much bigger global shifts: does the theme work inside a broader narrative of globalisation? Themes that clash with these broader, almost 'tectonic' shifts are unlikely to have much shelf life.

Globalisation

Understanding this globalisation shift is a crucial part of understanding the success of any big themes-led strategy; understanding what makes globalisation tick is the easy part, the more difficult challenge centres on building it into your investment process.

As the world has grown smaller and communications have become faster, the interdependence between countries has meant big changes for business, governments and investors – cross-border capital flows are more frequent, plentiful and easier than ever before. Funds can move around the world at the push of a button, seeking the best available returns. Stock markets in one corner of the world react rapidly to market or economic changes happening in other countries as speedily as they react to more local events.

But these broad changes do not always develop in quite the way that most analysts first think. Take the once-fashionable notion of decoupling. This is, or should we say was, the belief that the economies and markets of the US-led West were becoming uncorrelated with those of the China-led East. As a consequence, we were once told, diversifying between these geographic sectors could protect against weakness in one or the other. The global economic downturn which began in 2008 put paid to that idea as markets around the world declined together – the bear market and subsequent recession showed just how interdependent and indeed synchronised economies and markets have become. But that does not mean that investors should avoid international investment.

International diversification works, too

Diversifying into overseas markets means that a portfolio can take advantage of the best the world has to offer and gain exposure to the growth stories being written every day in these disparate and exciting economies.

Bear in mind that the MSCI world index of developed markets weights the United Kingdom at under 10 per cent, which means that a portfolio comprised only of FTSE securities is not properly diversified. Over recent years, the big growth areas of the world have been in China and other emerging markets. Portfolios exposed only to Britain would have missed out on these exciting prospects. While it is true that these markets have tended to be more volatile, this risk can be mitigated by drawing the asset classes into a diversified portfolio.

Effective diversification means building a portfolio of securities which is not positively correlated. While not always the case (as was evidenced following the 2008 credit crunch), one of the easiest ways to achieve this is by buying into the lower correlation existing between assets of different countries. Add to this mix hard assets such as commodities and property and over the long term the portfolio should not only perform as required but do so having managed risk effectively. Over the longer term, there will be times when equities and bonds underperform, but it is usually these periods that see a boom in real assets of oil, gold, land and metals. And such commodities are usually located in economies from across the globe.

Gone are the days when a portfolio would contain only stocks from home, but gone too are the days when gaining access to international markets was difficult and expensive. One of the great attractions of ETF is the ability to buy into these markets, easily and cheaply. Building a globally diversified portfolio has never been simpler.

By building a portfolio of ETFs rather than using, say, traditional open-ended funds such as unit trusts and OEICs, investors are exchanging one type of diversification for another. Those who buy unit trusts are buying a readily diversified fund and paying for a fund manager to make investment decisions. But the ETF investor turns that logic on its head. First decide on your asset allocation and design this to meet your investment objectives and attitude to risk. Decide how much international and commodity exposure you want alongside bonds and domestic market. Draw up a simple pie chart where these asset classes are allocated in broad percentage terms. Then all you need to do is buy ETFs which track these markets in the appropriate quantity. You can adjust the allocation at any point and introduce new asset classes as you see fit. A big-theme investor would weight the portfolio toward the trends which embody the major stories of our time.

The big themes of the next decades?

It is all very well to have identified the big themes of the past, but just what are the big themes of the second decade of the 21st century? After all, investors want to be able to profit from the next big story, the next industry to boom, the consequences of economic change. Picking the next big theme is perhaps not as easy as it might seem, but there are some interesting candidates. For once the business pages of the newspaper are not necessarily the best place to look to find these themes. Take a look at international and domestic news for stories which represent changes in the way things are being done. Which new economies are emerging as the major players of the future? Which industries are they beginning to dominate? What are the major international institutions talking about? What are the trends in academic research? You could think about the businesses in which you, your friends and family work. What are the big changes that are affecting the business, from outsourcing to new customers to new products? Pretty soon you will get an idea of the big themes of our time. Here are a few thoughts.

Farmland and agriculture

The world population is not only growing but it is getting hungrier. It is estimated that the world's inhabitants will increase from 6bn today to more than 8bn by 2030. Over the same period it is anticipated that 3050 kilocalories will be available per person per day compared with 2800 today. This has already grown from 2360 kilocalories back in the 1960s and can be attributed partly to rising consumption in developing countries. Asia, for instance, now consumes far more protein from livestock than it did a generation ago.

Statistics produced by the United Nations' Food and Agriculture Organisation show just how much meat consumption has increased over the past 25 years, in virtually every comparable country. The average American consumes around 130kg of meat each year, compared with around 115kg in 1980. But the comparison is starker in China with its population of 1.2bn. In 1980 the average Chinese person ate around 15kg of meat per year; today it is almost three times that amount and growing annually. Meanwhile, if one were to examine world agricultural area per person, in 1960 it was almost two and a half times the size it is today – populations may be growing fast but the pool of useful land is not growing at anywhere near the same rate.

We also have to factor in climate change, which is making its impact felt on crop yields. It is also fuelling diversification into ethanol as a clean fuel, which means more land is required for growing crops. This rush to biofuels is one of the biggest pressures on farmland in the United States and one of the biggest drivers of grain prices. One only has to look to Iowa, the country's biggest producer of ethanol, to see how demand has forced pasture values to rise. It is projected that in the next few years as much as a third of corn crops will be used to produce ethanol, even though it will account for less than 8 per cent of annual US gasoline use.

Add to these trends both increasing urbanisation in the developing world and exurban sprawls in the developed world and one can begin to understand why so many analysts are bullish on land values.

Infrastructure

Every decade or so a whole new asset class emerges out of nowhere. Hedge funds, for instance, first hit the investment landscape in the 1990s, prompting a massive scramble into new funds by the first decade of the 21st century. Not long after, another innovative, headline-grabbing asset class emerged into investors' consciousness, namely infrastructure funds. These were built on the idea of investing in utility companies (long quoted on the markets) and new public–private partnerships and ventures to build roads or airports – all these 'secure' assets were and are regulated by the state and provided solid, dependable cash flow streams. Those secure income streams are crucial to anyone looking to protect their portfolios against the ravages of inflation and provide defence from volatile equity markets. Offering solid, durable and predictable returns, combining capital growth and reasonable income over the longer term, infrastructure can seem like the perfect investment sector. Remember that even in a recession infrastructure reaps returns from its underlying projects because children still drag themselves to school, the police still try to catch baddies, aircraft still need somewhere to land and we still fill up the roads with traffic. And these returns bear little relation to what is going on in the stock market.

Crucially, these projects can be found right across the world, in Europe and North America as well as the emerging economies of Brazil, China, India and elsewhere. Take China as one example. It is spending 10 per cent of its gross domestic product on these infrastructure projects over the next decade. Elsewhere, it is estimated that a staggering $20,000bn will be spent on infrastructure worldwide during the next decade. The Organisation of Economic Cooperation and Development (OECD) believes some $53tn of infrastructure spending is needed by 2030 simply to meet development goals. By any estimation, that is a massive pot of spending and, for big-theme investors, it represents plenty of solid, foreseeable returns. There are, of course, some inevitable caveats – we need a balanced picture. Infrastructure funds will usually suffer from underperformance during the early stages for the practical reason that funds take time to be invested into projects. Also, given the popularity of the sector, investors will rarely find a bargain. Its defensive nature can also be a drawback since it can result in more cash being raised than can find its way into viable road or rail projects, forcing the state to step in later to guarantee income streams. You can have too many roads and railways and power stations and they can lose money in certain circumstances – Victorian investors in the UK lost millions on rail projects and new canals.

Water

Old-fashioned H_2O may seem like an innocuous and rather dull theme for investing but that is perhaps because most people reading this book have constant access to a clean supply from the tap. We cannot, of course, live without water and it must therefore be considered as precious as any commodity. As a global sector it is already worth $400bn a year in revenues. With wars already fought over natural resources, especially oil, it is not inconceivable that we will have wars fought over water in the next few decades.

The very same demographic factors affecting farmland are hitting water supplies. A growing population, many of whom lack access to safe drinking water, is increasing demand and global warming and environmental damage are reducing supply. It is this that is driving vast investment in water engineering projects across the world. Water is a big theme that is here to stay, not least because farmers use so much water in the production of cereal crops.

New energy and green investing

A fad it may well be but renewable energy is one of the big themes of our age and if ever there were a global sector that seemed to represent the future then it is surely this. The harsh realities of today's world should be foremost in investors' minds: peak oil, global warming, population growth and emerging economies mean that there is an increasing demand for carbon alternatives. And it is big business. Around $30bn a year is being spent on developing renewables, representing something like a quarter of all investment in the energy industry.

Longer-term answers to reduced carbon emissions will lie in technology. We now know that companies which invest in technological alternatives and improvements are the companies which weather economic storms better. A lesson from the beleaguered Detroit car industry during the last economic downturn is that businesses which failed to invest in making their motors cleaner suffered the worst as demand fell off. In this new era of state intervention, funds provided by governments in Europe as well as the US have been linked to green technologies.

Nevertheless, investors should be balanced in their approach to this sector. It remains notoriously difficult to pick individual stocks and there remains the 'Betamax' risk – a new technology like Betamax tapes may be the best, most rational answer, but that doesn't mean that a rival technology with better resources and marketing might not win out in the end.

Going nuclear

For those not so socially conscious, nuclear power is seen as a realistic carbon alternative of the future, not least in Britain where the government has firmly thrown its lot behind it as the solution to the country's and the world's energy needs. For proponents of nuclear, it is a clean, plentiful alternative to carbon. But its detractors worry about massive expense, gallons of toxic waste and catastrophe.

Whatever the rights and wrongs of the debate, it is undeniable that it is going to be increasing demand for alternative power sources that will cater for a growing and more prosperous world population. It is the developing countries playing catch-up to the West which represent a major driver of energy demand. According to ETF Securities, it is the non-OECD countries which are experiencing the strongest energy demand growth, with these countries and China projected to represent the largest source of demand in absolute terms within a few years. There is considerable scope for change in the world's energy mix as coal and gas remain the most significant fuels for electricity generation, with nuclear representing around 16 per cent.

Observers of the world today will find 439 operating nuclear reactors. A new nuclear programme in the United States will see a further 32 reactors added to its current 104. Seven reactors are under construction in China and a five-fold increase is planned over the next decade. India is building six, Russia is building seven to add to the 32 it already operates, and four reactors are under construction in Europe, bringing the total to 154.

Nuclear energy will always be contentious and there are plenty of reasons for opposing its growth. But its progress appears somewhat unstoppable, playing a significant part in the energy mix for years to come, not to mention the billions of dollars being poured into its development across the world.

Create your own themes

If you are in search of the big themes, why not create your own? This is not as strange as it might sound. It is about searching for innovation and creating baskets of sectors which combined represent a trend. New brands could be one such talisman, bringing together globalisation, the growth of emerging markets and consumer behaviour. Brand trends from fashion to food are no longer localised in the metropolis of a single country but form part of the aspirations of the growing middle classes from Europe to India to China and the United States. Successful brands are increasingly global, appealing to mass markets across the world.

A quite different consideration in today's brave new world is security. We have looked at how globalisation has meant interdependence between countries, greater communication between companies and more movement of people and goods across borders. As a big theme, this might include macro-level defence of countries, traditional aerospace and arms. But business also needs improved technology security against viruses and attack. It needs security against political instability and with pirates in the news, theft and hostage taking need to be tackled.

The perennial alternative asset class is commodities, seen time and time again as a theme of an era. They support other themes and trends, supplying industry with the necessary raw materials. Investors such as Jim Rogers believe that a commodities bull market is under way and will continue for years. While many disagree with the legendary investor, balanced portfolios can create commodity themes of these hard assets, raw material-rich economies and companies which invest in and produce such assets.

For those with a really creative eye, themes might be created around alternative assets such as rare coins, art, collectable wine, boats, stamps and the like. Alternative assets have their attractions in that they are fairly uncorrelated to equities (although demand is linked to prosperity), but the major drawback is that they produce no income. Creating alternative asset themes can be both profitable and fun. But if you are investing directly, it is probably important to buy things you like too because if you judge the market wrong, you're stuck with them. So you may as well own a painting you would hang on your wall. For the ETF investor, buy into sectors exposed to these asset classes. The theme could range from the assets themselves through to the storage, sale and dealing.

Exchange traded funds have opened up a world of big-theme investing for the ordinary investor. Building a thriving portfolio is about more than the technicalities of stock market movement. It is about viewing the world and creating investments which reflect the successes across the globe. With some creativity, the big themes can be rewarding and profitable.

9

Active portfolios using ETFs

Most investors who use ETFs are happy to stick with a buy-and-hold philosophy – they are using ETFs to access certain asset classes over the long term. But a sizeable minority of investors also use ETFs in a much more active sense – they invest in a particular asset class to take a short-term view on its direction. That decision to actively time the direction of a market or sector forces them to use some form of defined methodology – many use the direction of a share's market price in an attempt to gauge the 'momentum' of that stock. This methodology is commonly called technical analysis and is used by a great many investors to manage their ETF portfolios over the short term. Tarquin Coe and Mark Glowrey are analysts at Investors Intelligence, a research firm that specialises in using technical analysis as an aid to building a better ETF-based portfolio.

Technical analysis and ETFs

The beauty of technical analysis is that the discipline is applicable to all asset classes. Providing a liquid market exists and price data history can be obtained, technical analysis (TA) can be applied to identify the trend and extrapolate trading and investment strategies.

From the point of view of a technical analyst, ETFs are no different from any other tradable instrument. However, the variety of ETF issues available, particularly in the well-developed US market, opens up the possibility to trade indices, sectors, baskets, spreads and other activities previously accessible only by professional fund managers or proprietary traders.

Before we look at some of the applications of TA to ETFs, we should address the key tenets of this approach. The most important concept in technical analysis is that of objectivity. Charts have to be analysed in isolation, with no input from outside events such as fundamental news flow, as well as personal emotions.

Technical analysis itself is the study of past price and volume behaviour through charts to forecast future direction. A huge range of tools is available to the technical analyst, but even the simplest concepts can enhance the investor's judgement considerably. Indeed, it is fair to say that technical analysis, if done well, with discipline, is simple and straightforward.

In any trade, the three most important attributes are *entry*, *exit* and a *stoploss*. Over the next few pages we will outline some simple TA tools that can be used to identify these points, including:

- using TA to determine price entry
  - support and resistance
  - momentum indicators
  - breadth indicators
  - industry analysis
  - relative strength;
- using TA to determine stops;
- using TA to determine price targets;
- using TA for currency, bond and commodity ETFs;
- six golden rules for trading with TA.

Using technical analysis to determine price entry

Support and resistance

The first step in analysing a chart is to study the long-term picture and identify major support and resistance levels. These levels reflect the battle-grounds between buyers and sellers. Although trendlines certainly exist, it is the horizontal levels that are more important as they are more readily identifiable and persist for many years.

It is good practice to limit the chart to two support levels and two levels of resistance. Each level should be based on a different timeframe, such as medium term and long term. Looking at the US-listed SPY (an S&P 500 index tracker) ETF chart in Figure 9.1, we can see long-term resistance at 153 formed off the 2000 highs. Long-term support sits at 80, formed off the 2003 lows.

Tests of support and resistance are rarely perfect and often a lot of noise occurs in and around these levels as bulls and bears battle for control. Note the behaviour at the 2007 high and at the test of support in 2008/2009.

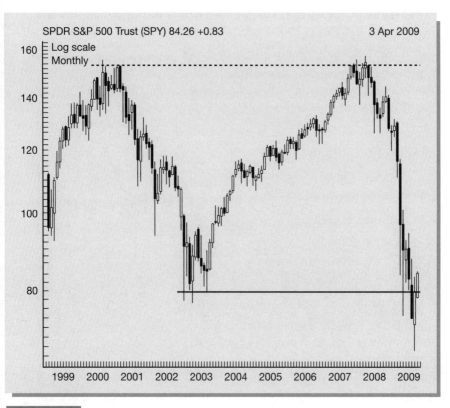

Figure 9.1

With support and resistance identified, the next step is to look at what we call the 'market internals' to determine whether a support level, or a break-through resistance, will hold.

Momentum indicators

One measure of the internals of the market can be gauged through momentum. A popular measure of momentum is the Relative Strength Index (RSI).

RSI was developed by a technical analyst by the name of J. Welles Wilder and this indicator is detailed in many technical analysis books. One of the indicator's greatest strengths is its ability to highlight divergences – situations where uptrends and downtrends start to lose momentum.

Divergences are either bullish (at bottoms) or bearish (at tops). The SPDR Trust chart for the SPY in Figure 9.2 shows an example of bearish divergence. The 14-day RSI made a high in April 2007, followed by a lower high in October 2007. That lower high by the indicator was a sign of waning momentum and was a warning sign that SPY was vulnerable to a downturn.

Other useful behaviour to watch for is oversold and overbought, indicated by below 20 and above 80 respectively.

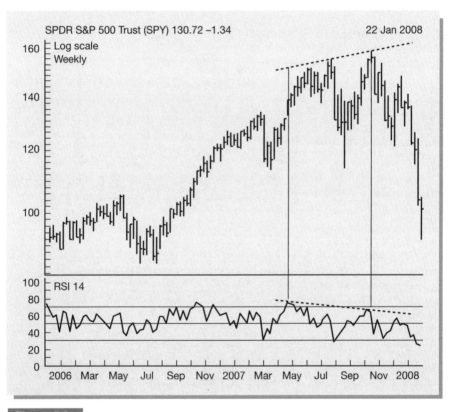

Figure 9.2

Breadth indicators

Breadth is a measure of participation and is another valuable tool for measuring the internal health of the market. For instance, it may be common knowledge that a major index is moving up (or down), but what is behind this? Is the move caused by just a few stocks, or is participation being seen across the index's constituents? Breadth is a measure of this participation. For instance, an index showing a 60 per cent breadth reading will have 60 per cent of the constituent stocks displaying uptrends.

Investors Intelligence favours the bullish percentage technique for establishing the breadth of a sector or market index. This technique, which classifies stocks as 'bull' or 'bear' based on the trend displayed on their point and figure chart, was introduced in the 1960s.

Investors Intelligence uses many other breadth measures, such as per cent 10-week moving average (stocks trading above the 10-week moving average), per cent 30-week moving average (stocks trading above the 30-week moving average) and per cent relative strength (stocks with outperforming trends). These breadth studies are applied by Investors Intelligence to the major indices across the world, from the NYSE to the FTSE.

The key point to consider when applying breadth studies is this: sustainable bull markets can be supported only by firm or rising breadth data. That means a healthy bull market will need to see breadth of support from constituent stocks in the 40–80 per cent range. Weak or falling breadth, by contrast, will not support a rising market. Consider also extremes of breadth will indicate oversold/overbought conditions – often major turning points.

The same principles used for RSI studies can be used for breadth, namely bullish and bearish divergences and overbought/oversold readings. Note the bearish breadth divergence on the SPY chart in Figure 9.3 at the bull market top in October 2007.

Industry analysis

The principles outlined above are equally as effective when applied to the charts of industry groups/sectors and their corresponding ETFs. US investors are fortunate in this aspect, in as much that a wide range of sector-tracking ETFs is on offer. At present, the selection in the UK, and indeed Europe, is limited but rising fast.

For instance, the SPDR Energy (XLE) chart in Figure 9.4 shows breadth for the S&P Energy sector measured by the percentage of stocks in P&F bull

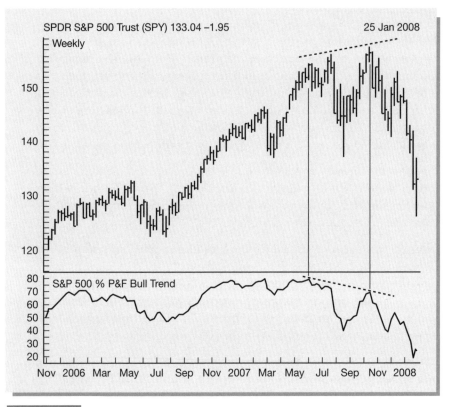

SPDR S&P 500 Trust (SPY) 133.04 −1.95   25 Jan 2008
Weekly

Figure 9.3

trends. Extremes in the breadth are useful in timing tops and bottoms in the Energy ETF. Where over 90 per cent of the constituents are in P&F up trends, the sector, and thus the related ETFs, is overbought, such as in May 2008. Likewise, when the reading is below 10 per cent, the Energy ETF is oversold, as illustrated in October and November 2008.

Divergences in breadth indicators relative to the price chart can also provide great timing signals. On the chart, note the bullish divergence evident on the breadth indicator as the Energy ETF broke below the October 2008 low. That divergence occurred ahead of a 20 per cent rally in the ETF.

In the deep US market, all the major sector ETFs can be analysed in this way and any moves in the underlying sector captured by the wide range of sector-specific ETFs available. This gives investors and traders an excellent opportunity to trade the powerful intra-market sector rotations that are so often seen in the financial markets.

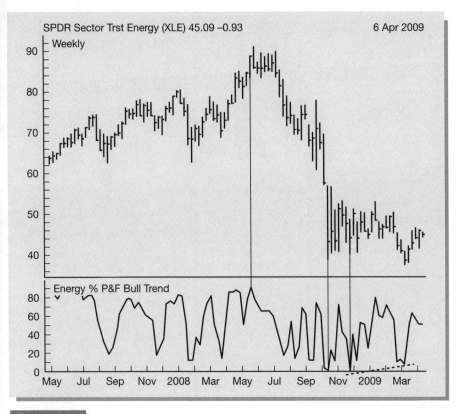

SPDR Sector Trst Energy (XLE) 45.09 –0.93   6 Apr 2009

Figure 9.4

The reason that these sector rotations are so important is this: profession-ally managed money rarely leaves the market. Instead, fund managers attempt to improve the performance of their funds by switching to higher beta sectors in upturns and back into defensive sectors (utilities, etc.) in market downturns.

For instance, at the time of writing this chapter (April 2009), the recovering US stock market has a fairly conventional distribution of sector strength, with the largest number of industry groups positioned within the neutral 40–60 per cent area (see Table 9.1). However, we note that the defensive Electric Utilities (UTEL), Pharmaceuticals (DRUG), Food Beverages and Soaps (FOOD) have lagged. The recovering consumer cyclicals such as Restaurants (REST) have surged ahead and are now arguably overbought. This is a classic rally pattern.

Table 9.1 The US industry bell curve

			−BANK	+LEIS					
			+BUSI	+MEDI					
			+COMP	+OIL&					
			+ELEC	+POLL	+AERO	+OILS			
			+ENER	−PREC	+CHEM	+REAL	+AUTO	+LATI	
			+HOUS	+PROT	+FINA	+SEMI	+BUL	+META	
			−INSU	+SAVI	+FORE	+SOFT	+GAMI	+RETA	
		+FOOD	+JAPA	+TELE	+EURO	+TEXT	+ASIA	+STEE	
+BIOM	+UTEL	+DRUG +HEAL	+INET	+UTGA	−MACH	−WALL	+CHIN	+TRAN	+REST
10 %	20 %	30 %	40 %	50 %	60 %	70 %	80 %		

Oversold – below 32%   Above 68% – Overbought </DIV< td>

Updated through Apr 21, 2009

Groups marked with a + are in an up column.
Groups marked with a – are in a down column.

Thus, the market is setting itself up for a defensive rotation. At present, the level of 'skewness' is fairly restrained, but the potential is certainly there. This potential is visible on the price charts of the SPDR Consumer Discretionary ETF (XLY) in Figure 9.5, looking overbought and up against the sideways resistance seen at $22–23.

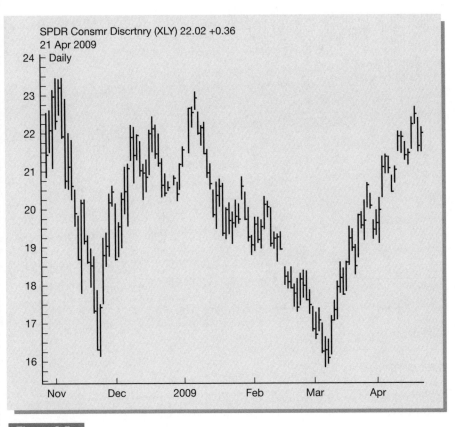

SPDR Consmr Discrtnry (XLY) 22.02 +0.36
21 Apr 2009
Daily

Figure 9.5

By comparison, the rally in the Utilities sector looks much more restrained (see Figure 9.6). Similar chart patterns can be seen in the laggardly Biomedics and Pharmaceuticals sectors.

At times, these sector divergences can get quite extreme. As a rule of thumb, we would look to play divergences on the short side where the sector breadth has peaked and rolled over back through 80 per cent. Conversely, rallies up through 30 per cent on the BP chart should be viewed as a sign of interest moving back into the sector.

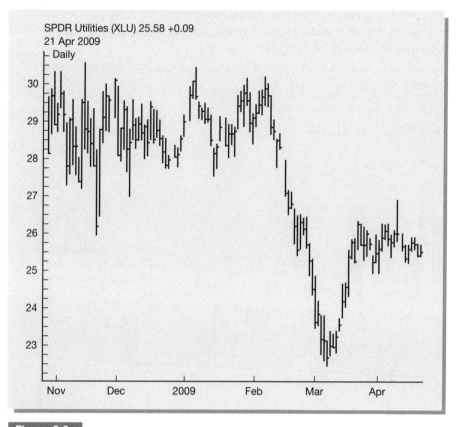

Figure 9.6

Relative strength

When using ETFs it is important to be invested in the areas that are out-performing. This can be achieved through analysing relative charts.

Relative charts typically come in two forms, P&F and line charts. Line charts offer more analytical scope, in that momentum and breadth studies can be applied. Support and resistance can be applied to both chart types. Some prefer one over the other, though it is largely down to personal preference and experimentation by the investor to see what they feel more comfortable with.

Figure 9.7 illustrates the relative performance of the SPDR Materials ETF against a broad benchmark, the S&P 500 equity index, plotted on a P&F chart. Observe how the chart bottomed in late 2000 (the S&P 500 did not bottom until 2002). The base was confirmed with a P&F breakout in

February 2001. That relative buy signal lasted until September 2008 and if you had followed this chart, you would have outperformed the market substantially during that bull run.

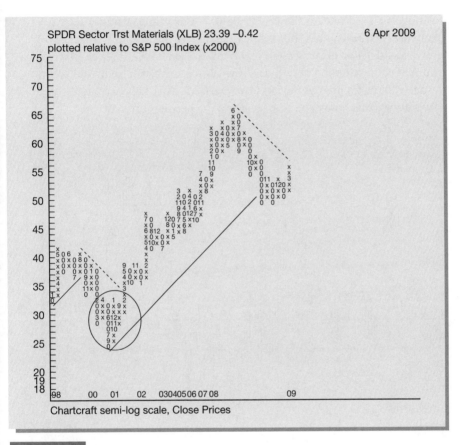

Figure 9.7

Using technical analysis to determine stops

Just as much importance should be placed on the positioning of stops as determining a good entry price. Support and resistance levels, for longs and shorts respectively, are central to identifying a good stop loss. However, volatile trading often occurs in and around support and resistance levels for ETFs, so stops need to be flexible.

Flexibility can be gained through using stops where trading has to fall below or above a stop level for a number of sessions. A strategy used at Investors Intelligence is to use a setup where a position is closed out only following three consecutive end-of-day closes above or beneath a level (if triggered the position is closed out on the fourth day). For example, a trader sells the Diamond Trust Dow Jones Industrials ETF (DIA) at the start of October 2007 following the failed break above the July high (Figure 9.8). He then places a stop based on three consecutive closes above that July high (red line). Despite volatile trading for the next two weeks, the ETF fails to achieve three consecutive closes above the stop level and the position survives.

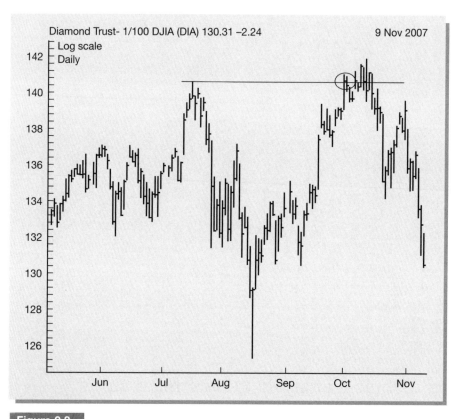

Figure 9.8

Using technical analysis to determine price targets

A number of methods are available to the ETF investor to determine price targets. More complex target determination can be calculated using something called Fibonacci extensions, but a very simple method called the 'measure rule' is just as effective. This technique is straightforward and involves taking the depth of a trading range and adding that to the point from where a breakout would occur (the support or resistance of a range). For example, using the 'measure rule' for the Currency Shares British Pound Sterling Trust (FXB) for the trading range of August through November 2006 (Figure 9.9), a price target was determined and then met in late January 2007.

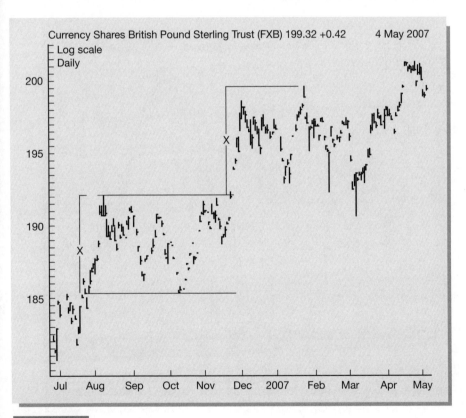

Figure 9.9

Using technical analysis for currency, bond and commodity ETFs

The introduction of ETFs for commodities, fixed income, currencies and other non-equity asset classes has greatly increased the scope of investment possibilities for the man on the street. Technical analysis can be applied to all ETF areas and not just be limited to equity ETFs. The principles of charting are exactly the same.

Figure 9.10 illustrates the Deutsche Bank Liquid Commodity index tracking fund (DBC). The writing was on the wall regarding the bubble in the first half of 2008. As the fund marched higher, the 14-day RSI was exhibiting bearish momentum divergence.

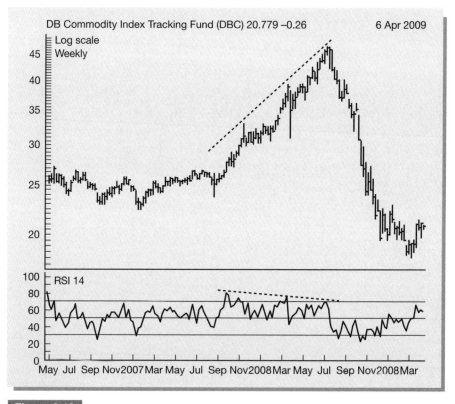

Figure 9.10

Six golden rules

We believe that technical analysis should be part of every investor's toolkit. Certainly, we would not dismiss the excellent work performed by many fundamental analysts, but in trading, as in life, timing is everything. TA is more likely to provide this timing input and is infinitely more useful in managing the subsequent trade in terms of fixed and trailing stops.

Hopefully, you will start applying some of the techniques we have summarised in this chapter to your own trading or portfolio management techniques. If so, the list below may help – these are our six golden rules for trading with TA.

1 *Trade the trend not the countertrend* – look at the long-term chart first to identify this long-term trend.

2 *Consider commonality and underlying index direction* – do not attempt to buck the general trend. The majority of your trades should be with-trend, not countertrend.

3 *Let the chart determine the tactics* – direction, time, expectations. Examine the instrument's historic price action.

4 *Consider volatility to determine trade size* – high volatility, smaller position, a similar point to (3) above. The market dictates the style and size of trade. This technique will allow you to use wider stop levels on more volatile instruments, helping the position to ride out the 'noise'.

5 *Protect unrealised gains with trailing technical stops* – avoid 'meaningless' financial stops (5 per cent, 10 per cent, etc.). Use identifiable technical levels such as prior support, etc.

6 *Have goals/targets – but never get too greedy or too fearful by taking profits early.*

10

Putting it all together

'I can calculate the motions of the heavenly bodies but not the movements of the stock market.'

Isaac Newton in the 1600s after he had been wiped out in a stock market crash

'Usually, you know a hot sector after the fact, not before.'

Marshall Blume, Finance Professor at the University of Pennsylvania's Wharton School

Portfolios, like stock markets, are very strange creatures indeed.

I constantly fret over the health of mine – it is my other child, that constantly causes me limitless grief and anxiety, interspersed with the odd moment of euphoria. What makes my behaviour towards my portfolio even more inexcusable is that I also constantly break all the rules advanced by behavioural investment gurus like James Montier at SocGen, and constantly monitor my ragbag of investments. Montier claims this constant fussing over my pension pot is perhaps the greatest sin of modern portfolio management (and trust me when I say there are many, many other sins which he identifies). He contends that a smart investor structures their portfolio intelligently and then leaves it alone for weeks or even months on end, without constantly checking to see whether it is going up, down or sideways.

To be fair Montier does not suggest that you hide away, ignoring all that goes on around you, only that you intervene when it is obvious that significant events are occurring which have a direct effect on 'the life plan', i.e. global depressions, rampant inflation, government defaults.

If this all sounds a bit too good to be true, it's because it is. Montier is by background a value investor with a strong contrarian streak and like many of this creed he is used to taking a stand – based on many well-thought-through principles, it must be said – and then steadfastly sticking to this analysis through thick and thin. He is also benefiting from the mountain of research (courtesy of his leading position in the City) that suggests that certain approaches work over the long term and that most of the time markets revert to the mean – or mean reversion, as it is called.

For the rest of us life is considerably tougher, especially if we do not have access to Montier's constant stream of institutional information. Truth be told, we have probably not thought through the principles underlying our portfolios – they are largely opportunistic, built through bolt-on acquisitions and desperate forced sales – and we do not really look in detail at the very long-term evidence that suggests an alternative approach.

James Norton may well be right in his clarion call to diversification, outlined in Chapter 7, but for most of us managing a portfolio is about rather more mundane issues, including our tolerance of risk (which, of course, changes as we grow older), our individual financial goals (plentiful but not always realistic), our time horizon (are we saving for a specific point in the future?) and the growth (or otherwise) of our non-financial wealth. Any change in these very individual variables can have a major impact on our investing habits and no amount of academic evidence of what constitutes 'best practice' is likely to force us to change tack.

But once you have accepted that long-term saving through investment is a personal and idiosyncratic business, you can at least recognise that certain aspects of investing behaviour are dangerous and counterproductive and need to be understood and, hopefully, improved upon.

At this early stage in our discussion of portfolios it is probably worth reminding readers of the biggest and most dangerous behavioural bias – it is an absolute, incontrovertible truth that sits above and beyond all the other slightly murky debates that ooze around the tricky business of running a portfolio, and it is incredibly simple, namely that too many of us overtrade.

We have already made this point earlier in the book, but it is worth repeating yet again the sad reality that the more you trade in your portfolio, the lower your returns. And just in case you desired any more evidence for this, it is probably worth citing the work of behavioural finance professors at the University of California, Terry Odean and Brad M. Barber, who researched the portfolios of 66,400 investors at Merrill Lynch between 1991 and 1997.

The good professors concluded there were two very specific factors that reduced returns: lousy stock picking and transaction costs. In fact, the most active traders averaged 258 per cent portfolio turnover annually and earned 7 per cent less annually than buy-and-hold investors, who averaged 2 per cent turnover. To keep repeating what should by now at least be an obvious truth, costs add up and eventually destroy your wealth. Assume you have a £50,000 savings pot (your portfolio) and that you expected an annual return of 8 per cent. The results in Table 10.1 detail the cost of a seemingly small difference in the annual management charge of a fund. The data suggest that the difference of just 1 per cent per annum in charges over 30 years results in a reduction of more than £100,000 in final returns.

Table 10.1 Annual management charge of a fund

Fees	5 years	10 years	20 years	30 years
0.5%	71,781	103,052	212,393	437,738
1%	70.128	98,358	193,484	380,613
1.5%	68,504	93,857	176,182	330,718

But although pretty much everyone in the world of investment accepts that overtrading and high costs kill long-term returns, the debate about many other aspects of running a portfolio is much murkier. Should you, for instance, constantly rebalance your portfolio to make sure it is not being pulled in different directions by varying returns from stock sectors and asset classes? If you do then decide to rebalance, how often should you do it, and how?

And what about trying to time the market? Is it an obviously daft idea that is bound to end in ruin or could you operate a simple system that saves you from much of the pain of bear markets? Should you just use index funds in a portfolio or should you instead use some active managed funds to add a little oomph to returns? Crucially, aren't index funds potentially vulnerable to big momentum-based moves in the market? If you invest in a FTSE 100 index fund, won't you simply become a victim of over-reliance on sexy sectors like technology or banks which come crashing back down to earth as markets eventually wake up to the risks? Once all these really rather tricky questions have been answered, one last crucial issue remains: how do you actually go about building that perfect portfolio? Should it be complicated and full of lots of different, diversified index funds or should it be incredibly simple and easy to run? What would a model, diversified portfolio actually look like?

In this chapter we are going to build on the analysis first outlined by James Norton in Chapter 7 and try to guide you through the maze of port-folio construction and maintenance obstacles with the help of five simple questions, the answers to which should make your life considerably easier.

Q1: To rebalance or not to rebalance? Should I constantly rebalance my portfolio?

Many leading investment thinkers, including the eponymous John Bogle, reckon that the best way to survive turbulent markets is to adopt an almost Zen-like calm and never cut losses, and never rebalance. Mainstream experts take a middle course and suggest a limited form of (annual) rebal-ancing, while a few hardy radicals suggest a much more active approach. Who's right? Sadly, there is no definitively right or wrong answer, as we will discover – it all depends on your attitude to risk and how confident you feel about managing your portfolio.

To understand the challenge involved, let's imagine the portfolio of my good old Uncle Fred with his simple holding of three index funds tracking UK equities, UK bonds and gold (he's a cautious type). He invests £100 in each fund and within six months his equity investment has doubled, whereas his bonds have gone down by 5 per cent and his gold holdings have dropped by 20 per cent.

At the end of six months – an eventful six months it must be said – his portfolio looks something like this:

- UK equities £150.
- Bonds £95.
- Gold £80.

In total his portfolio is now worth £325, but equities account for 46 per cent of total holdings against the original 33 per cent allocation whereas gold has sunk to just under 25 per cent. What should he do? Should he take his prof-its on equities and then reinvest in gold or stick with the asset mix?

Uncle Fred decides not to do anything until the end of this first year. By that point his equities have come down a little to £130, his bonds are back at £100 and his gold has rallied to £90, implying a total portfolio that is worth £320. Equities are still worth 40 per cent of his portfolio but at least gold is back up to 28 per cent of total holdings. Uncle Fred decides that he is now going to rebalance and sells some of his equity holdings (just over £23) and invests just over £16 back in gold and another £6 in bonds.

According to advisers Paul Merriman and Richard Buck, Uncle Fred was spot on – he managed his returns to control his risks. In a paper entitled 'One portfolio for life?', the US-based advisers suggest that although 'annual rebalancing is not absolutely necessary, if it's neglected, the portfolio's risk can start creeping up. To maintain the proper amount of risk, you should keep the portfolio within reasonable distance of its . . . target allocation. When the stock market is hot, as it was in the 1990s, the equity part of a balanced portfolio can quickly creep up'.[1]

To back up their conclusions the authors studied a hypothetical portfolio, without rebalancing, that began with a 60 per cent holding in US equities and 40 per cent in bonds at the start of 1990 through to 2005. By the end of 1999, 78 per cent of the portfolio was in equities and only 22 per cent in bonds. Investors may have been very satisfied with the total returns, but Merriman and Buck remind us that 'that was just in time for the bear market of 2000 through 2002 to come along and teach unwary investors about the dangers of being over-exposed to equities. The portfolio that had never been rebalanced lost 22.2 per cent of its value from the end of 1999 through 2002. But if that portfolio had been rebalanced every year, the loss was only 12.6 per cent'.

Merriman and Buck adhere strongly to the view that rebalancing on an annual basis is the right thing to do if only because it is so counterintuitive, forcing you to punish the winners to reward the losers. 'A more productive attitude is to think of rebalancing as a mechanical way to require investors to buy low and sell high,' suggest the authors.

Merriman and Buck are not the only advocates of a regular rebalance. A recent study from US brokers Smith Barney concluded: 'Rebalancing also tends to reinforce one of the main benefits of portfolio diversification: the tendency of returns on different assets to offset each other over time. By remaining close to their target allocations, investors should be able to reduce portfolio volatility. This allows the magic of compound growth to work more quickly, boosting long-term returns.'[2]

Vanguard has also weighed into this debate, looking at returns from both a rebalanced portfolio and one that is unbalanced. The conclusion: 'If a portfolio is never rebalanced, it will gradually drift from its target asset allocation to higher-return, higher-risk assets. Compared with the target allocation, the portfolio's expected return increases, as does its vulnerability to deviations from the return of the target asset allocation.'[3] The Vanguard bottom line? If you do not rebalance, you open yourself up to greater risk by becoming over-exposed to the fastest-growing, most risky asset classes.

To demonstrate what can happen if you ignore 'best practice', the Vanguard researchers looked at a very boring and standard split of 60 per cent stocks and 40 per cent bonds that was never rebalanced. According to the Vanguard study: 'Because stocks have historically outperformed bonds, the portfolio's asset allocation gradually drifts towards 90 per cent stocks and 10 per cent bonds', i.e. your portfolio becomes too risky because the allocation of risky equities becomes dominant.

But not everyone in academia and commentator land agrees with this conventional annual rebalancing wisdom. David Jackson, author of the excellent online *ETF Investing Guide*[4] suggests that although annual rebalancing is a sensible risk-control mechanism, there may be a better alternative. 'Think about the multi-year outperformance of US technology stocks until 2000, for example,' he says. 'Imagine that you had divided your portfolio between only two asset classes – tech growth stocks and non-tech value stocks – and you frequently rebalanced the portfolio to maintain an equal weighting between the two. In that case, you would have limited your upside from the run-up in technology stocks, because you'd be constantly selling tech stocks too early to maintain your asset allocation. Instead, you should have rebalanced your portfolio only when it became heavily misaligned. That way, you would have benefited from the momentum run-up in technology stocks, but would have periodically corrected your portfolio to avoid a situation where 80 per cent of your portfolio was in tech stocks that subsequently collapsed. For this reason, the correct question may not be 'How often should I rebalance?' but rather 'How far should I allow my asset classes to stray from their target allocations before I rebalance?'. Rebalancing only when an asset class reaches 150 per cent of the target allocation, for example, will perhaps result in a more tax efficient and more profitable portfolio.'

US-based financial commentators Phil DeMuth and Ben Stein agree with Jackson's preference to use percentage-based tolerance limits, i.e. sell only when an asset reaches 150 per cent of total holdings. DeMuth and Stein suggest that the rival idea of annual rebalancing is in fact a mug's game. They argue that the 'financial services industry loves to tout portfolio rebalancing as a value-adding strategy. The idea is that every year we should sell a little of that 12 months' winners and use them to buy the current losers so that we bring our portfolios back into alignment with their original specs. Although it can incur tax and transaction costs, rebalancing is promoted on the idea that it gets us into a righteous "sell high, buy low" discipline.'[5]

Rather than accept the conventional wisdom Stein and DeMuth put it to the test. They used a fairly standard 60/40 equities/bond split of assets in a port-folio and then looked at 10,000 (Monte Carlo) simulations involving complex, seven-asset-class portfolios. They 'experimented with several calen-dar-based strategies, rebalancing the portfolios monthly, annually, or never. We also looked at tolerance-based rebalancing approaches: rebalancing when the portfolio wandered 10, 15, and 20 per cent from its original allocations'.

The results of their simulations are shown in Figure 10.1, but the bottom line is simple to understand: although never rebalancing is hugely risky, annual rebalancing is also risky compared with an alternative strategy sug-gested by the authors.

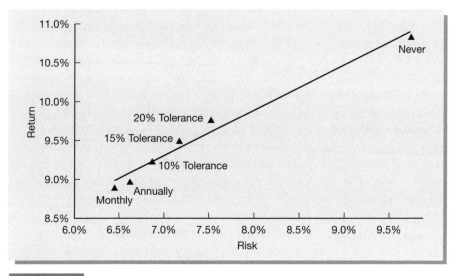

Figure 10.1   Results of Stein and DeMuth's simulations

'The first thing that stands out,' they conclude, 'is that the more frequently we rebalance, the worse our returns. The next obvious point is that, as is commonly observed, rebalancing cuts our risks. What we'd hasten to add, however, is that it doesn't cut our risks efficiently. Specifically, the most fre-quently recommended ritual – annual rebalancing – puts our portfolio's returns risk profile below the efficient frontier.'

The authors suggest an alternative approach, called a tolerance-based approach. This involves setting a barrier or tolerance level above which you force a rebalancing – in their analysis a 20 per cent tolerance-based approach is suggested as the best compromise. How would this work for Uncle Fred and his portfolio? Suppose an asset class is 20 per cent of his portfolio and it has a 20 per cent rebalance band. Tolerance-based types like Stein and DeMuth would suggest rebalancing back to the original 20 per cent mix only when the portfolio strays outside of a range of 16–24 per cent, i.e. 20 per cent of the original 20 per cent allocation.

Academic turned portfolio software guru Gobind Daryanani, creator of the rules-based rebalancing software iRebal used by many US-based financial advisers, takes a similar view to Stein and DeMuth. He thinks it is wise to 'look frequently' for rebalancing opportunities by setting a tolerance band. He suggests that the problem with 'traditional' annual rebalancing ideas is that 'the dates chosen for rebalancing are arbitrary, and thus we cannot possibly expect to catch the juiciest buy-low/sell-high opportunities'. Daryanani spells out what he thinks we should all do.[6] We should:

- use wider rebalance bands [around 20 per cent];
- evaluate portfolios biweekly;
- only rebalance asset classes that are out of balance – not classes that are in balance;
- and increase the number of uncorrelated classes used in portfolios.

He suggests that a 20 per cent threshold monitored every second week is the optimal rebalancing strategy, producing a 'rebalancing benefit' of 55bps, or half a per cent per annum. According to Daryanani, this kind of tolerance-based rebalancing is particularly important in volatile markets, otherwise 'you are likely to miss the rebalancing benefits during periods of short-term fluctuations'.

Is there a widely accepted, undisputed bottom line? Should you rebalance annually or use tolerance limits? Or should you perhaps never rebalance at all? If anyone deserves the last word on this subject, it is probably John Bogle. He recently completed an analysis for *The New York Times* on the subject of rebalancing. Controversially, he is not convinced by most forms of rebalancing, annual or otherwise. According to a report on Bogle's blog: 'Fact: a 48 per cent S&P 500, 16 per cent small cap, 16 per cent international, and 20 per cent bond index, over the past 20 years, earned a 9.49 per cent annual return without rebalancing and a 9.71 per cent return if rebalanced annually. That's worth describing as "noise" and suggests that formulaic rebalancing with precision is not necessary. We also did an earlier study of all 25-year periods beginning in 1826 (!), using a 50/50 US stock/bond portfolio, and found that annual rebalancing won in 52 per cent of the 179 periods. Also, it seems to me, noise. Interestingly, failing to rebalance never cost more than

202 The Financial Times Guide to Exchange Traded Funds

about 50 basis points, but when that failure added return, the gains were often in the 200–300 basis point range; i.e., doing nothing has lost small but it has won big.' Bogle's conclusion? 'Rebalancing is a personal choice, not a choice that statistics can validate. There's certainly nothing the matter with doing it (although I don't do it myself), but also no reason to slavishly worry about small changes in the equity ratio … I should add that I see no circumstance under which rebalancing through an adviser charging 1 per cent could possibly add value.'

Q2: The consensus seems to be to buy and hold over the long term. Does that mean I should never attempt to time the market?

The standard long-term advice from most equity enthusiasts, as well as nearly every fan of the EMH, is to run a buy-and-hold strategy, i.e. stick with shares through thick and thin and do not try to change your buying and selling behaviour based on market conditions. A host of both academic and broker research suggests that trying to work out the best time to 'buy the market' is difficult at best and disastrous at worst. For buy-and-hold enthusiasts the idea that private investors sitting at home watching their computer screens can somehow judge the direction of sophisticated global markets is frankly delusional. Researchers at the Schwab Center for Investment Research in the US has put some hard numbers on the cost of this curious behavioural vice of overconfidence.[7] It looked at three buy-and-hold investors who each received $2000 annually for 20 years to invest in the markets, a grand total of $40,000. Two decades later here were the results:

- The Perfect Timer – $387,120. Strategy? The money is put into the market at the monthly low point every year.
- Treasury Bill (government gilt) Investor – $76,558. Strategy? Terrified of shares, the investor puts their money only into Treasury bills.
- Autopilot Investor – $362,185. Strategy? This investor automatically invests the money on the day received and then leaves it alone.

The Schwab study is just the tip of the research-based iceberg that suggests that poor market timing is incredibly costly. In 1998, academics at the University of Utah and Duke University reviewed 132 investment newsletter portfolios involving some form of market timing, over a period between 1983 and 1995.[8] The average return from these 'timed' portfolios was 12 per cent with 11.9 per cent volatility. An S&P portfolio with the same volatility returned 16.8 per cent for the same period.

Embarrassingly the researchers suggested that the more famous the market timer, the worse the results. A newsletter called Granville Traders Portfolio lost 2.2 per cent annually and the Elliot Wave Theorist Traders Newsletter portfolio was down 10.1 per cent. The academics' withering analysis was backed up by investment research outfit the Hulbert Financial Digest, which also reviewed 25 newsletters with 32 portfolios and found that none of the newsletter timers beat the market. With a ten-year study ending 31 December 1997, market timers averaged from 5.84 per cent to 16.9 per cent, the average being 11.06 per cent. However, the S&P 500 index earned 18.06 per cent and the Wilshire 5000 value-weighted total return index returned 17.57 per cent. Another ten-year study showed averages from 4.4 per cent to 16.9 per cent a year, with the average of 24 market timers at 10.9 per cent. Even when adjusting for something called the risk–return average, these expert 'market timers' were still far below the average of the buy and hold.

US research firm Morningstar took a slightly different angle, looking at how investment risk declines as stocks and funds are held for longer periods of time, suggesting that buy and long-term hold is the only solution. The Morningstar researchers found that the best return on stocks for one year was +53.9 per cent while the worst return was –43.3 per cent. However, the best and worst returns over a 25-year period were less variable at +14.7 per cent and +5.9 per cent, i.e. the longer you decide to stay in the market, the lower your potential risk.[9]

Morningstar fund analyst Peter Di Teresa then grouped 4,880 domestic equity funds by turnover ratio and examined their performance over one year. These funds were, by and large, run by active fund managers who included market timing as one of their skill sets. 'In a bear market, the feeling is that the pros should at least be able to avoid the big disasters through trading,' said Di Teresa. First, he compared the performance of funds in the top third in terms of turnover ratio against the bottom third. The trigger-happy funds in the top third (1,626 funds) lost 10.5 per cent over the year as of 2/28/2002, while the lowest third shed 6.3 per cent. 'The effect of high turnover gets even more pronounced when you break things down further,' said Di Teresa. This time, he took the same group of domestic stock funds and broke them up evenly by turnover into five groups. Over the same time period, the highest turnover fund group (976 funds) finished down 11.5 per cent for the year, while the lowest turnover group lost 5.8 per cent. The presumption against attempting to time the market seems to hold true even for professional fund managers – the less you time your buys and sells, the less you trade and the higher the returns.

Just in case you thought it was only academics who suggest that market timing is for mugs, it is worth listening to the man who mightily influenced the great Sage of Omaha on the subject of market timing. Warren Buffett's great hero Benjamin Graham was one of the most famous timing sceptics, declaring in his book *The Intelligent Investor* that: 'We are sure that if [the investor] places his emphasis on timing, in the sense of forecasting, he will end up as a speculator and with a speculator's financial results.'[10]

But as is often the way with presumed investment orthodoxy, many investors beg to differ. The key to successful investing, these enthusiasts maintain, is not to keep moving in and out of the market but to work very irregular intervals when timing a big purchase or sell makes absolute sense. To use the jargon, this is not tactical market timing (constantly buying and selling to try to catch the high) but strategic market timing (timing the one key move every year, for instance).

Consider a report from US magazine *Business Week* in 2002. An MIT economist had calculated that someone who invested $1,000 in the S&P 500 or Treasury bills and correctly selected the right month to buy on a month-by-month basis since 1926 would have earned $14tn by 2002.

A rather more realistic analysis came from technical analysts at Birinyi Associates of Westport, Connecticut. They looked at market data and showed that investors who were out of the market during the five worst days each year do astronomically better than those who hold their stocks throughout each year. For example, in 2000, the S&P 500 stock index dropped 10 per cent (not including dividends), but an investor who invested in the S&P on every day but the five worst days of 2000 made a profit of 9 per cent. In 1998, being out of the market during the five worst days would have given you a return of 56 per cent instead of 27 per cent. Overall, a dollar invested in the S&P stocks in 1966 became $12 for the buy-and-hold investor (again, without dividends) but an incredible $987 for the investor who missed the five worst days each year. The only problem with these genius schemes is that it is relatively easy to spot the worst days with the benefit of hindsight but considerably more difficult on the day. A more sensible middle path lies in simply avoiding the excesses of the market, i.e. sell your stocks to control potential risks when valuations are too high or economic indicators suggest a recession.

Even a small but hardy band of academics has suggested that this strategic form of market timing might have some validity. Professors Hashem Pesaran and Allan Timmermann looked at simple systems to market time in a paper for the *Economic Journal*.[11] Using data sets from 1970 to 1993 their work suggested that without the benefit of hindsight, an investor could have correctly predicted the direction of the UK stock market roughly 60 per cent of the time on a monthly basis. They suggested that when exploited in a market timing investment strategy, investors could have more than doubled their returns per unit of risk, even after accounting for transaction costs. The academics reckoned that using publicly available information, such as interest rates, money growth, oil prices and growth in industrial production, small degrees of predictability still remain and these could have been exploited by developing a relatively simple forecasting model that was incredibly simple to use.

In fact, a market timing strategy is conceptually fairly easy to understand. One strategy could be to stay invested when the market is up or flat and avoid the downturns. The strategic market timer develops signals to identify what condition a market is in. An overvalued market is called 'expensive', 'overbought' or 'overextended'. A normal market is 'fairly valued'. An undervalued market is 'cheap'. Timers use some form of mechanical model, using computer software to crunch numbers such as interest rates and investor sentiment – the timers are looking for signals that indicate a reversal of trend, overpriced markets or an early warning signal to switch from buy to sell or vice versa. Some will act immediately on that signal, while others will wait to see whether it is confirmed by subsequent trading days or weeks. Bizarrely, a huge number of private investors, who think they are buy-and-holders, are in fact using the most basic and least successful method of market timing, otherwise known as ICSIA or 'I can't stand it any more'. The markets are grim, so sell everything indiscriminately!

Hedge fund manager Hugh Hendry of hedge fund Eclectica is one of those who sides with the view that investors need to operate some form of simple market timing and dump the mantra of long-term buy-and-hold investing – simply sitting tight and waiting is going to make investors very poor over the next few decades in his view. He is one of the most successful hedge fund managers in the UK and even in the rough markets of 2008 had a good year – rather annoyingly for all those keen to predict the demise of hedge funds. In fact, his Eclectica fund registered a 49.8 per cent return in October of 2008 alone while other active or hedge fund managers were bemoaning huge losses. His view is that markets are fundamentally too volatile to stick to buy-and-hold investing. 'The stock market could oscillate or go sideways for a period as long as 25 years', suggests Hendry 'We've got another 15 years of markets rising, falling and going sideways.'[12]

His pessimism on future returns is shared by a quick perusal of investment history. According to data from Chicago-based Ibbotson Associates, from 1926 to 1999, 90 per cent of five-year periods were positive for stocks. That's the good news. The bad news is that those figures do not reveal long periods of pain in the stock market. After the 1929 crash, the Dow Jones Industrial Average took 25 years to regain its pre-crash levels. The Dow traded above 1000 in 1968, but failed to close above that level again until 1984.

The key is the mismatch between long series data which suggest huge compound returns and shorter period data which suggest the potential for sustained low or even negative growth. Various studies of long-term data for the last hundred years suggest that shares do return a simple average gain of 7.2 per cent pa but that is the *very* long term (100 years plus) and it is only an average. Most of us have to cope with finite life spans where we face a crucial 20-year window of opportunity to accumulate capital. Get the wrong 20 years and your buy-and-hold strategy is not such a winner. The evidence comes from the redoubtable US analyst and adviser John Mauldin (in a letter called 'While Rome Burns'),[13] who looked at 88 20-year periods and discovered that although most periods generated positive returns before dividends and transaction costs, half produced compounded returns of less than 4 per cent, while less than 10 per cent generated gains of more than 10 per cent. Plenty generated negative long-term annualised returns!

If you want to understand this huge variance go to yahoo.com, where you can download the full data set of price returns for the Dow Jones Industrial Average since inception at the end of the 1890s. Take these data and then chart them, and you will see long periods of dreadful price returns. The trend overall is clear – up – but there is a huge amount of variation on the way. For example, if you invested in December 1905, you would have bought in at around 96 index points, but fast-forward 17 years to 1922 and the index is still at 98.17, having traded in a range between 55 and 118. Similarly, take the Wall Street crash. At the beginning of April 1929, the Dow was at 333.79, but it did not hit that level again until April 1954. More recently, the returns from 1965 to 1980 were equally dismal. Admittedly, these indices are stated on a price-return basis and do not incorporate dividends reinvested, but in reality, most of us do not actually reinvest our dividends.

Mauldin maintains that most of us are victims of our own 'glide path', i.e. we have to pick a 20-year buy-and-hold investment window. When we are young, we do not really save much (or at least I didn't), so when we start saving in earnest, it is probably around our late 20s or early 30s. We therefore accept that we have 20–25 years in which we need to spice up our returns by investing in risky assets before we hit our 50s. Then we start winding back into safer assets such as bonds. However, if we pick the wrong 20–25-year glide path, we are in trouble unless we have been reinvesting those dividends diligently.

Mauldin, like Hendry, suggests that a simple buy and hold through thick and thin might be potentially calamitous. He suggests that investors need some form of signal that activates a switch from one asset class (defensive/aggressive) to another. Such a strategic 'switching rule' was in fact advocated early on by John Maynard Keynes, who combined investment in real assets with switching between short-dated and long-dated securities based on movements in interest rates.

Is there a simple signal system that investors could operate without constantly moving back in and out of the market, incurring huge trading costs along the way? That is the question posed by Mebane Faber in the *Journal of Wealth Management*.[14] It is a compelling piece of analysis and suggests a system that is incredibly easy to implement. Faber is a wealth manager (and prolific contributor to the excellent seekingalpha.com website) and he has been trying to work out a simple way of protecting wealth by timing his equity investments. What he aspires to is a system that is simple to administer and clearly tells you when to buy and when to sell. His solution is the 200-day simple moving average, one of the most basic technical analysis indicators. It is worked out by adding up all the closing prices for the past 200 market days and dividing by 200.

According to Faber, the rule is to buy when the asset price or market shows a monthly price above the 200-day moving average and sell when it moves below. It is not really more complicated than that, although one implication is obvious: you will be spending a fair amount of time holding large parts of your portfolio in cash. To test his idea, Faber has run the data over the entire last century.

Faber's system does not really add much to total, accumulated returns – in fact, it underperforms the index marginally in roughly 40 per cent of the years since 1900. But it massively cuts down on risk, the maximum loss and volatility. On average, Faber finds that you get roughly the same returns as the index but with less risk. You get Faber's paper online at http://papers.ssrn.com/sol3/papers.cfm?abstract_id=962461.

The bottom line? If you are willing to be bothered with rebalancing either annually or using a threshold, the evidence seems to suggest some advantage even if it only gives you some peace of mind that you are actively controlling risk. But equally, do not over-estimate your capabilities in this regard and constantly time the markets. The odds are that frequent market timers will mostly fail.

Q3: I'm worried by the volatility of equities. Are shares really worth the extra risk?

Talk to most investment analysts and they advance the view that for most portfolios equities should sit at the core because they produce higher returns than bonds. But does the evidence actually support this broad, sweeping conclusion? Luckily the answer seems to be – yes – equities are worth the extra risk because they produce extra returns over the very long term. The key piece of evidence comes from a long-term study by Tim Bond, head of asset allocation at Barclays Capital investment bank.[15] His analysis suggests that over the 80 years from 1926 to 2005, the compound annual growth rate of return was 11.77 per cent for the Small Cap Index of shares, 10.36 per cent for the Large Cap Index, 5.50 per cent for the Long-Term Government Bonds Index, and just 3.70 per cent for holding government bonds or T-bills. $1 invested in 1926 would have produced $18 if it had been invested in US Treasury bills and $2,661 if it had been invested in an equity-based large-cap index (and more than $7300 with a small-cap index).

Part of the explanation for these stellar long-term returns is that equities are much, much riskier than other asset classes. Figure 10.2 shows the annual real returns of the S&P 500 Index from 1872 to 2000. It clearly shows that although shares have produced some amazing returns, it is at the expense of very high volatility.

Q4: Should I only use index tracking funds to build my portfolio?

It's fairly obvious that we think that index funds should sit at the heart of any modern portfolio, but note the use of that term 'sit at the heart' – a sound portfolio is probably one that uses a core of well-diversified index funds around which circles a 'satellite' of slightly more unusual funds and shares that may involve some active fund management. That activity in the core may involve very inefficient markets where index trackers can be weak in both theory and practicality, i.e. the markets may be relatively inefficient and the resulting index funds could produce large tracking errors because of the difficulty of tracking these inefficient markets.

That acceptance of some role for actively managed funds, especially in imperfect markets, is in part motivated by the recognition that there are successful fund managers who do indisputably add value some of the time – they frequently work in those more inefficient bits of the market and

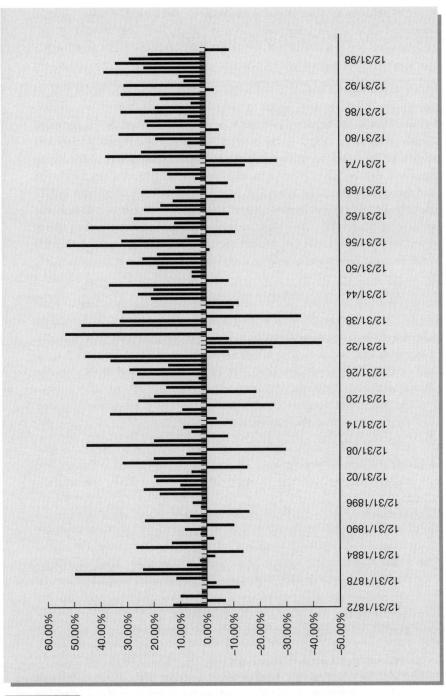

Figure 10.2 S&P 500 Composite Total Returns Index 1872 to 2000

they can produce excellent returns for a substantial period of time. US fund manager Bill Miller of Legg Mason, for instance, beat the S&P 500 for 15 straight years using a distinctive, value-influenced strategy. But even he has had some terrible recent years, which we think proves the broader point that even the best and most successful can lose their touch (their alpha).

Our general concern with active fund management is that most investors do not actually use the very best managers – they use below-average managers suggested to them by fund-wrap platforms and financial advisers motivated by news stories and commission kickbacks rather than true long-term excellence. If you had some magic ability to spot the successful managers, time and time again, we might concede that active fund management might be worth the greater risk most of the time. That is the promise of a band of experts called fund-of-fund managers – they claim that their constant focus on researching the best managers and switching between them produces huge long-term outperformance.

These fund-of-fund managers reckon that their risk-control mechanisms in picking the best fund managers more than make up for their higher fund charges. But their criticism of index funds goes even further – they think that index funds are fundamentally flawed in volatile and bear markets. They claim that index funds simply leave investors open to market risks. One of the most articulate critics is Jason Britton of T Bailey in the Midlands, a specialist fund-of-fund company. At the end of 2008 he produced research that suggested that sticking with index funds was 'crackers' in a bear market – or in fact any market.

The cornerstone of his highly critical analysis is a piece of research that looked at the average performance of FTSE All Share trackers in the UK and active fund managers over the 15 years between 1993 and the end of 2008. His conclusion? 'During this time, FTSE All-Share Index tracker funds have underperformed the Index by 24.7 per cent on average, equivalent to 1.9 per cent per annum. People investing for the long term (and after all, investment in equities should be for the long term) are being sold short here; having decided to replicate the market they would, on average, have found 24.7 per cent of their returns missing over the last 15 years.'[16]

Britton's argument then turns to specifics and to one of the most successful (in funds under management at least) UK index trackers, marketed by Virgin Money – the Virgin UK Index Tracking Trust, launched in March 1995. According to Britton this fund has underperformed the FTSE All Share Index by an average 2.4 per cent per annum. This accumulates to a total underperformance of 28.6 per cent by the Virgin UK Index Tracking Trust since its launch,' he says.

The cause of this underperformance by the Virgin fund is, Britton alleges, a high tracking error and a relatively high cost of 1 per cent per annum in management charges. Britton is spot on in his analysis of the Virgin fund, which is indeed expensive and not terrifically efficient at tracking the underlying index.

There are, by contrast, many other index tracking funds that do a similar job at half the cost and almost non-existent tracking error, a point that Britton glosses over. Britton then goes on to concede one key argument – that during the 2007 and 2008 bear market index trackers have actually caught up relative to the active fund managers. Britton suggests that the causes of this 'have included the very volatile markets (up or down by as much as 8 per cent in a day) and the desperate selling of good stocks (which are more likely to be held by active managers) at any price by hedge funds in the face of their huge redemptions'.

Britton's honesty is admirable because many active fund managers have over the last decade suggested the exact opposite – that index trackers do worse in a bad market because index trackers cannot make decisions about getting into and out of momentum-based sectors that are inherently risky. These critics maintain that by tracking popular indices like the FTSE 100, index tracking investors open themselves up to the peculiar biases that emerge in big markets. This extra risk can be better controlled by active fund managers who, allegedly, know a bubble when they see one and can avoid it by active stock selection.

The context to this broad charge that index trackers fail in bear markets is contained in a small paper from stockbrokers The Share Centre entitled 'The changing face of the FTSE', published at the back end of 2007.[17] This paper examined the composition of the hugely popular FTSE 100 Index and how it changed over time – see Table 10.2. It is a remarkable table and demonstrates how the composition of the FTSE 100 has changed over the period from 1984, when the index kicked off, through to the middle of 2007, just before the markets crashed. The holding in banks tripled in size, as a percentage of total holdings, followed closely by investment in the giant pharmaceutical companies, which more than doubled as a holding. Utilities came from no holdings to 6 per cent and retailers dropped back from 11 per cent to 6 per cent.

Table 10.2 The FTSE 100 Index over time

% share of the FTSE 100 Index as at:

Top sectors	01/01/1984	05/04/2007
Banking	6	22.8
Insurance	5.80	5.70
Mining	2	10.10
Oil and gas	15	17
Pharmaceuticals	4	9.7
Retailers	11	6
Technology	3	0.25
Telecoms	7	7.80
Tobacco	2.60	2.20
Travel and Leisure	6	2.2
Utilities	0	6

Source: The Share Centre

If we flash forward to the beginning of 2009, these figures would look very, very different. Financials – banks and insurance companies – have collapsed back to just 13 per cent of holdings, oil and gas companies are up at 23 per cent and the big drug companies, aka big pharma, have continued their remorseless rise to over 10.7 per cent of the total FTSE 100 index.[18]

What is extraordinary is that if you had bought the FTSE 100 tracker in spring 2008, you might not have thought there was anything wrong with having over 28 per cent of your fund in financials. Sadly, the catastrophic demise of the British quoted banking sector would have crushed your portfolio, losing you over 40 per cent in one year. The big problem, the critics maintain, is that big indices like the FTSE 100 become victims of style and fashion – they become weighted towards hugely risky sectors that shoot up in value and then shoot down again. One oft-repeated statistic is that at the height of the dot-com boom Cisco, the US networking company, comprised over 6 per cent of the total value of the S&P 500. Now it is less than 1 per cent. Successful share prices attract other investors to buy the shares, chasing up prices and making the successful companies a larger component of market-weighted indices. But that success is risky and investors in index tracking funds end up in effect buying momentum funds that chase the most dangerous stocks in an index. Introduce bear markets and momentum as a strategy collapses, taking your index trackers and your portfolio down with the market.

There is no particular way of denying this charge – market-cap indices obviously focus on the most successful companies. There are alternative ways of building indices that do not rely on market caps as a weighting system – we explored ideas like equally weighting an index in our section on alternative indices earlier in this book – but these are not regarded as mainstream by most analysts and are shunned by most investors. The reality is that if you accept that big markets are mostly efficient, then you must also accept the risk that goes with them.

More to the point, can active fund managers do a better job of controlling this style drift into momentum and thus control risk? Research from Vanguard in the US suggests otherwise. In a paper entitled 'The active passive debate: bear market performance', analyst Christopher Philips looks at how active fund managers performed in bear markets using the Morningstar Direct database of equity mutual funds in the US and Europe.[19] His results fit in with the general rule that active fund managers tend to underperform, even in bear markets. 'We observe that a majority of active managers outperformed the market in just 3 of 6 US bear markets and in 2 of 5 European bear markets. To be sure, in each bear market, funds existed that successfully outperformed the broad market. However, these results clearly indicate a lack of consistency with respect to the success of active funds in general.'

Philips looked in particular at the 2000–2003 bear market and found that although 60 per cent of all active funds outperformed the US stock market, only 23 per cent of active funds outperformed the European stock market over the same period. His conclusion? Although some fund managers can outperform in a bear market, there is no real consistency overall – in some bear markets they do, but for most of the time, most managers don't. 'As a result, it should not be assumed that an indexed investor is at an immediate disadvantage during a bear market relative to an actively managed fund, despite the opportunity for the manager to add value,' says Philips.

Table 10.3 Performance of active funds during bear markets

US funds versus Dow Jones Wilshire 5000 Index		
Bear market – years of low or negative returns	Number of funds	% outperforming market benchmark
1973/1974	110	43
1980/1982	167	78
1987	291	57
1990	405	44
1998	1082	39
200/2003	1405	60
European and offshore funds versus MSCI Europe		
1990	37	57
1992	81	33
1994	128	66
1998	378	39
2000/2003	796	23

Source: Vanguard

But look closely enough at the Vanguard data in Table 10.3 and you will see two interesting themes – first, that in Europe as the number of funds grows, their success in beating the markets falls; in the US, by contrast, active fund managers seem to have been more successful and to have worked their way through the bear markets moderately successfully.

Is there any bottom line? Some active fund managers indisputably do add value some of the time and there is evidence to suggest that active fund managers in inefficient markets can add value for certain periods of time. Also if you find a good fund-of-fund manager who is talented at consistently picking the good managers of the future, stick with them. Their skill and clairvoyance will deliver you above-average returns, but ask yourself how they spot these funds in advance. And even if they have been successful in the past, will that winning streak/consistent analysis and research hold for the future as well? More to the point, if most active fund managers fail to beat the index, why should most active fund-of-fund managers do any better? Last but by no means least, be aware of the index you are tracking and understand the risks you are taking – many big indices can perform truly badly in a bear market as momentum-based stocks take a hit. Do not blithely assume that the bigger the index, the less risky it is. Use our Essential 25 section at the back of this book and look at what you might be tracking when you buy an index fund – when you understand those risks, make sure you find an index fund with a low tracking error and minimal charges. Remember that the average fund-of-fund manager charges more than 2.3 per cent in costs for their expertise whereas most ETFs charge around 0.5 per cent pa. A superb fund-of-fund manager might deliver some extra value, but that extra 1.8 per cent per annum in lower fees via an ETF, for instance, adds up to a lot of money over the very long term.

Q5: How do I actually build a portfolio? Should I keep it simple?

To understand how you might go about building your own portfolio, it is probably a good time to mention the slightly odd world of portfolio theory. This hugely extensive and influential body of work was pioneered by economist Harry Markowitz. It isolates all the key elements of a well-diversified portfolio and then guides investors through an optimum portfolio construction process and how to build an efficient frontier. It is a hugely technical analysis which we are largely going to avoid in this chapter; instead we will simply repeat the following story. Professor Markowitz was asked at a conference in Chicago what he invested in. 'I should have computed co-variances of the asset classes and drawn an efficient frontier – instead I split my contributions 50/50 between bonds and equities,' he said. Just to ram the point home, it is also worth quoting the father of modern risk analysis in economics, Bill Sharpe, on the subject of how he builds his portfolio. 'I invest in various funds, large stocks, small stocks and international stocks.' Or Eugene Fama, the father of the index funds movement, asked by a publication called *Investment News* what he invested in, who replied by detailing a mixture of funds that invested in a very broad-based US index called the Wilshire 5000, plus a little in small-cap and international index funds and a little over a third in value-oriented stock indices and short-term bond funds. That's it.

Professor Fama, along with Professors Markowitz and Sharpe, did what so many people have done in the past, namely mix and match a small number of key asset classes, cheaply and efficiently. They could have made the exercise enormously efficient and endlessly optimised the mix of asset classes to build their own efficient frontier (which in turn defines the optimum efficient frontier), but they kept it simple and intuitive and mixed and matched a bit of equity and a bit of bonds. This consensus in favour of simple diversification is also in evidence when talking portfolios with most British investment academics. Most of these 'experts' personally stick to a simple, classic split, namely 60 per cent equities (broad equity market indices)/40 per cent in government bonds.

Keeping it really, really simple and lazy

In America the idea of keeping it simple has been adopted by a school of commentators which demands that we slow down our investment process, get simple, even lazy, and stick with simple long-term buy-and-hold portfolios made up of a small number of simple index funds.

These lazy portfolios are hugely popular in the US, especially with economists and market commentators like Paul Farrell, who has written a book on lazy investing and is a highly regarded commentator for the MarketWatch website.[20] Like many in the US, he is convinced that constantly buying into the latest hot funds is a complete waste of time for private investors. 'Unless you're working full-time in the financial world,' Farrell suggests, 'you don't have the skills, tools, information, time or interest in playing the market, especially the bond market. And even if you do play the market, the odds are you'll lose because the more you trade, the less you earn; transaction costs and taxes kill returns.'

You will probably recognise the principles embedded within his argument – simplicity and low cost. Farrell's answer is what he calls the lazy portfolio. Crucially, there is not just one portfolio. Farrell has asked a multitude of leading analysts and investment writers to build and then test their own simple, lazy portfolios.

Farrell's lazy portfolio proposition is built on four simple principles:

1   Use funds to capture the market not individual shares.
2   Use index tracking funds to track the market efficiently and cheaply.

3 Keep it simple, with most portfolios never comprising more than ten individual funds.

4 Buy and hold – do not overtrade and overcomplicate. Stick with the portfolio for the very long term.

One of the most compelling lazy portfolios was developed by William Bernstein, author of a seminal book called *The Four Pillars of Investing*.[21] Bernstein is a physician, neurologist and financial adviser to high-net-worth individuals as well as a commentator for the US magazine *Smart Money*. He is a big fan of two very simple portfolios – his No-Brainer Basic portfolio of just four funds (built using cheap unit trust trackers from Vanguard) and his slightly more complicated No-Brainer Coward's portfolio (also built using cheap Vanguard funds).

William Bernstein's Basic No-Brainer Portfolio

–25% in the main S& P 500 index (Vanguard 500 Index (VFINX))

–25% in the main US Small Cap index (Vanguard Small Cap (NAESX) or (VTMSX))

–25% in a diversified international index (Vanguard Total International (VGTSX) or (VTMGX))

–25% in a US bond fund (Vanguard Total Bond (VBMFX) or (VBISX))

William Bernstein's No-Brainer Coward's Portfolio

–40% in Short Term Investment Grade funds (VFSTX)

–15% in Total Stock Market (VTSMX)

–10% in (US) Small Cap Value (VISVX)

–10% in a Value Index (VIVAX)

–5% in Emerging Markets Stocks (VEIEX)

–5% in European Stocks (VEURX)

–5% in Pacific Stocks (VPACX)

–5% in real estate trusts or a REIT Index (VGSIX)

–5% in Small Cap Value (NAESX) or (VTMSX)

Bernstein has been running the Coward's portfolio since February 2002 and it has produced an annualised return of 9.37 per cent per annum (compared with 6.19 per cent for the benchmark S&P index – see Table 10.4) and 11.35 per cent over the past year (compared with 10.44 per cent for the S&P 500), all via simple tracker funds that in total cost less than 0.4 per cent per annum in management fees.

Table 10.4 The Coward's portfolio v the SSP 500 Index

Fund	1-year return	3-year annualised return	5-year annualised return
Coward's portfolio	14.70	11.35	9.37
S&P 500 Index	15.79	10.44	6.19

Another compelling lazy portfolio comes from David Swensen, Chief Investment Officer of Yale University's endowment fund, which boasts a two-decade investment record of +16.1 per cent per year returns, a track record that easily places him as one of the best managers of institutional money in the United States. Here is his portfolio, again built using ultra-cheap tracker funds from Vanguard.

David Swensen's Lazy Portfolio

–30% in Total Stock Market Index (VTSMX)

–20% in REIT Index (VGSIX)

–20% in Total International Stock (VGTSX) or (15% in VDMIX and 5% in VEIEX)

–15% in Inflation Protected Securities (VIPSX)

–15% in Short Term Treasury/Gilt Index (VFISX)

As with Bernstein, this simplicity does not come at a cost in terms of returns – it beat the S&P 500 17.6 per cent to 15.8 per cent in 2008 and on a three-and five-year basis – see Table 10.5.

Table 10.5 Swensen's portfolio v the SSP 500 Index

Fund	1-year return	3-year annualised return	5-year annualised return
Swensen portfolio	17.62%	13.55%	11.54%
S&P 500 Index	15.79%	10.44%	6.19%

Farrell, Swensen and Bernstein are just three of the more famous exponents of the lazy portfolio – a US website called the Kirk Report at www.thekirkreport.com has dedicated a whole section to this brilliantly simple idea, publishing a much longer list of simple, buy-and-hold portfolios. Some of the highlighted lazy portfolios on the Kirk Report site include the following:

▨ **American financial commentator and planner Paul Merriman's suggested portfolios** – see Table 10.6. Paul's website at **www.fundadvice.com** is a great source of simple, easy-to-understand research – we will look at his analysis of rebalancing later in this chapter. His model portfolios are built around a much larger number of components than Farrell's – his risk-based portfolios include as many as 14 different index funds or ETFs. This more diversified approach is essential according to Merriman because building a lazy portfolio with just four indices is not enough – his research suggests that owning ten asset classes increases your total return.

Table 10.6 Merriman model portfolios

Overall structure

	Aggressive	Moderate	Conservative
Equity	100%	60%	40%
Bond	0%	40%	60%

Individual portfolios

Fund name	Symbol	Aggressive	Moderate	Conservative
S&P Depositary Receipts (SPDR) S&P 500	(SPY)	11.25%	6.75%	4.50%
Vanguard Value VIPERs	(VTV)	11.25%	6.75%	4.50%
i-Shares Russell Micro Cap Index	(IWC)	11.25%	6.75%	4.50%
Vanguard Small Cap Value VIPERs	(VBR)	11.25%	6.75%	4.50%
Vanguard REIT Index ETF	(VNQ)	5.00%	3.00%	2.00%
i-Shares MSCI EAFE	(EFA)	9.00%	5.40%	3.60%
i-Shares MSCI EAFE Value Index	(EFV)	9.00%	5.40%	3.60%
i-Shares MSCI EAFE Small Cap	(SCZ)	9.00%	5.40%	3.60%
WisdomTree Int'l Small Cap Div Fund	(DLS)	9.00%	5.40%	3.60%
Vanguard Emerging Markets VIPERs	(VWO)	9.00%	5.40%	3.60%
i-Shares S&P World ex-US Property Index	(WPS)	5.00%	3.00%	2.00%
i-Shares Lehman 1–3 yr	(SHY)	0.00%	12.00%	18.00%
i-Shares Lehman 7–10 yr	(IEF)	0.00%	20.00%	30.00%
i-Shares Lehman Treasury Inflation linked	(TIP)	0.00%	8.00%	12.00%

Ben Stein is another hugely successful US commentator and adviser, whose colourful career has included being a speechwriter to Richard Nixon and a *Wall Street Journal* commentator. According to Charles Kirk (of the Kirk Report), 'Ben is in favour of indexed-focused long-term investing and believes that you should focus your investments on dominant big picture themes to produce even greater returns. For example, Ben has made it clear that he thinks Americans would be smart to have exposure to the world's emerging markets.' Stein also suggests a portfolio for those in or approaching retirement, called his 2 ETF retirement portfolio. Kirk reports that according to Stein's research, 'this portfolio presents no risk and plenty of upside potential for those who live 30 years after retirement who withdraw 5 per cent annually'.

Ben Stein's Long-Term Portfolio

–30% in Fidelity Spartan Total Market Index (FSTMX) or Total Stock Market ETF (VTI)

–15% to 20% in iShares MSCI EAFE Index (EFA)

–10% in iShares MSCI Emerging Markets Index (EEM) or Emerging Markets 50 ADR (ADRE)

–10% in iShares Cohen & Steers Realty Majors (ICF)

–10% in iShares Russell 2000 Value Index (IWN)

–15% in Cash

Ben Stein's Retirement Portfolio

–50% in StreetTracks Dow Jones Wilshire REIT ETF (RWR)

–50% in iShares Dow Jones Select Dividend (DVY)

Kirk is also a fan of Jim Lowell's Sower's Growth Portfolio. Harvard-educated Lowell is editor of a number of US newsletters (Fidelity Investor and The ETF Trader at Marketwatch), author of investment books including *What Every Fidelity Investor Needs to Know*[22] and a partner at investment advisery firm Adviser Investments, a private money management firm advising on more than $1bn, based in Newton, Massachusetts.

The Sower's Growth Portfolio

–25% in iShares MSCI EAFE (EFA)

–15% in iShares DJ US Total Market (IYY)

–15% in Mid Cap SPDR Trust (MDY)

–10% in Diamonds Trust (DIA)

–10% in iShares Russell 2000 (IWM)

–10% in iShares MSCI Emerging Markets (EEM)

–7.5% in Fidelity NASDAQ Composite (ONEQ)

–7.5% in Power Shares Dynamic Market (PWC)

The list of lazy portfolios could go on and on, and there are dozens of variations, many of them forming the centrepiece of hugely successful get-rich-quick finance books, so popular in the US. But it is worth mentioning just three more quick examples. The first of these alternative approaches is perhaps the very simplest. It is called the Couch Potato Portfolio, designed by Scott Burns, a financial columnist on the *Dallas Morning News*. Just two funds feature in his ultimate lazy portfolio:

1 50% Vanguard 500 Index – tracks the S&P 500.

2 50% Vanguard Total Bond Market Index Fund – tracks the Lehman Brothers Aggregate Bond Index.

Burns launched his Couch Potato Portfolio in 1991 but has back-tested it to 1973 – according to Burns returns have averaged over 10 per cent per annum. A slightly more complex variation sits at the centre of something called The Coffeehouse Portfolio, devised by Bill Schultheis, a former Saloman Smith Barney broker turned financial adviser. The portfolio sits at the heart of a hugely successful investing book stateside – called, unsurprisingly, *The Coffeehouse Investor*[23] – and is built around Schultheis's elegantly simple investing credo, which consists of the following rules:

- Diversify across different asset classes.
- Capture the entire return of each asset class – use index funds.
- Develop a long-term financial plan and start saving early.

As for the portfolio, Schultheis's advice is to keep it simple. Just six Vanguard funds should do the job long term:

- Vanguard S&P 500
- Vanguard Large Cap Value
- Vanguard Small Cap Index
- Vanguard Small Cap Value
- Vanguard International
- Vanguard REIT Stock Index.

According to Schultheis his Coffeehouse portfolio has averaged a 11.42 per cent annual return.

Last but by no means least, it is worth mentioning one worthy contender for the Keep It Simple Lazy Portfolio Challenge – it comes from US savings and investment magazine *Kiplinger*. The Kiplinger Keep It Simple Portfolio features just four investing ideas based on major indices:

1   25 per cent large-cap stocks.

2   25 per cent foreign stock funds – in particular the Vanguard European Stock Market Index or the Vanguard Total International Stock Market Index.

3   25 per cent small-cap funds. Russell 2000 or the S&P 600 BARRA Small Cap Value Index.

4   25 per cent domestic bond.

How's your lifecycle?

A growing number of asset management houses in the UK and the US take a slightly different tack to the challenge of building a one-size-fits-all simple portfolio. Clearly the concept of designing a simple two- or four-fund structure made up of cheap underlying funds is probably beyond the ken of most expense-heavy marketing departments (with the obvious exception of Vanguard) – most big fund managers are instinctively much happier selling a highly skilled fund manager with their higher expense structure. But more than a few innovative fund managers have started to roll out an easy-to-understand investment idea built around an eminently simple idea – it is called lifecycle investing and it is the institutional equivalent to lazy portfolios.

Imagine you are 25 years old. You have just landed a job managing the night shift at a Sainsbury's superstore in south London and the world is your oyster. You are earning just enough money to put aside say £100 a month in a fund that you will stick with for the next 40 years of your working life, but for now you want lots and lots of growth in your underlying investments. That means you are willing to take on some risk – now – and the long-term data on returns suggest that the riskiest, most rewarding of the major asset classes are equities. Bonds, by contrast, are a bit boring and safe and although you are probably never going to lose more than 20 per cent in any one year (that is called your maximum drawdown in the trade), equally you are never going to bag any huge tenbaggers that make your fortune. In summary, our 25-year-old thrusting young buck quite sensibly tells his adviser that his risk tolerance is high and that he wants to stack up on equity exposure and 'go for it' in terms of risk.

Flash forward 30 years. Our young buck is now a considerably older 55 year old who is just ten years away from retirement (still with Sainsbury's, now owned by a Mongolian coal conglomerate!), working in Department 23 at Head Office examining Sigma Six Efficiency. He can just about put up with the boredom of the job because he knows that retirement is only ten years away (although he has heard rumours that the retirement age might increase to 85 soon). That means capital preservation is all important. He absolutely cannot afford a 'drawdown' of something like 20 per cent in one year – that means he takes a very negative view of equities and he is a big fan of bonds.

This transition I have described in both tolerance of risk and awareness of potential returns sits at the heart of lifecycle analysis. Over those 30 years (from 25 to 55), our private investor changes – both physically and in his tolerance of risk – and over time that translates into a big change in their choice of assets. Early on he is sensibly interested in equities and probably no bonds, in his mid 40s he is probably making the shift away from equities into some bonds and by his mid 50 he is probably biased towards bonds. Curiously, once he gets to retirement at 65, the consensus on the 'correct' balance becomes a little muddier. On paper, retirees should be ultra cautious – they have to preserve their pension pot for a retirement that could last 30 or more years. But they also require an income to live on and the assets with the safest profile: bonds and especially government bonds or gilts – tend to pay the lowest yield. Also pensioners have to be cautious about another major risk – inflation. Sticking all your money in conventional bonds in high inflationary times might mean you preserve your nominal (before inflation) returns, but the real value after inflation could be diminishing rapidly. Some academics and economists maintain that pensioners should be willing to take on extra risk, to grow their income and to grow their capital sum in inflationary times. Investors Chronicle economist Chris Dillow has suggested that pensioners should not really be paranoid about preserving all their capital until death primarily because they cannot benefit from that wealth when they are six feet under. His strategy? Possibly consider taking on extra risk via equities, and especially those equities that pay a dividend, and reducing your bond exposure.

Regardless of this post-retirement debate, the simple process of constructing a mix of assets that can be used as the building blocks of a single portfolio and can change over time, has evolved into a complex research literature at whose heart sits something called the glidepath. Figure 10.3 is from one of the largest investment research organisations, Ibbotson Associates in Chicago, but most other outfits' glidepaths look pretty similar. This glidepath starts with high-risk assets, transitions through a balanced approach in mid life and ends with a mixture of assets with a bias towards bonds later in life.

Every provider and analyst will have their own starting and ending points and relative combinations, but they all feature the exact same blended glidepath. The only substantive debate seems to be whether a very young person has some limited bond exposure and whether a retired person should have some equity exposure and at what level.

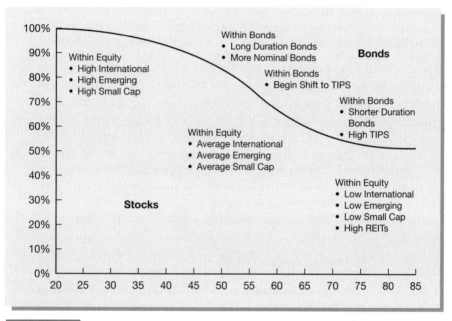

Figure 10.3 Generalised Ibbotson target maturity glide path

Source: www.morningstar.com

This blindingly simple analysis has evolved into something called a target date fund. This involves you sitting down, working out your planned retirement age (which will nearly always be massively wide of the mark, given changing longevity patterns) and then finding a fund that has the closest equivalent to that year, called a target date. Given that it is 2009 as this book is being written, if you are 30 now, you will probably be looking at retiring in 35 years' time, in which case your 'target date' is probably around 2045.

The Ibbotson Associates research notes: 'Target maturity investment solutions should help investors through the investment phases of accumulation, transition, and retirement.'[24] A second variation on the same model can also be found, called target risk funds, which do not specify an actual year but take a measured risk approach, suggesting a transition from ultra high risk to ultra low risk and all shades of risk control in between. This new niche is growing fast – according to Ibbotson's research, at the end of 2007 there were approximately 38 registered target maturity fund families in the US representing 256 individual target maturity funds with assets under management of $178bn. In 2008 two major UK providers, Fidelity and ABN Amro, also launched their own versions of the lifecycle approach and over the next few years investors can expect a plethora of new launches as asset managers wake up to the huge marketing opportunity.

Obviously this approach is not restricted to just index fund providers (although Vanguard is a major player in the US) and active fund managers have been positively salivating at the prospect of tying their customers into a savings scheme for life. But the index funds approach is uniquely well suited to supply the funds that sit at the core of such an approach, if only because of the low cost of their products and their refusal to keep taking a chance on an active fund manager's luck or skill over many decades.

ETF providers have moved fairly aggressively into this space and one of the pioneers is US stockbroking firm TD Waterhouse, which has teamed up with ETF provider XShares to run a range of target-date lifecycle funds. The composition of each of the funds in its target-date ETFs is detailed in Table 10.7.

Table 10.7 XShares TD Waterhouse Lifecycle Funds

	Before retirement							Retirement	After retirement			
Years	35	30	25	20	15	10	5	0	5	10	15	20
Equity (%)	100	100	100	90	82.5	75	60	50	37.5	30	25	20
Fixed Income (%)	0	0	0	4	8.5	14	29	40	63.75	62	67.5	73
Real Estate (%)	0	0	0	6	9	11	11	10	8.75	8	7.5	7
Age	30	35	40	45	50	55	60	65	70	75	80	85
Portfolio	2040		2030	2025	2020	2015	2010	2005				

A slightly different approach to the same target-date concept has also been launched by the giant ETF provider iShares, which has brought out its own lifecycle ETFs. These index tracking funds are based on an underlying target-date index independently provided by Standard and Poor's and featuring very low expense ratios that range around 0.30 per cent after fee waivers.

iShares has also brought out another variation on the same theme, not based on a target date but instead looking to tiered risk profiles or target risks, in this case ranging from aggressive (high risk) through to conservative (low risk), in all cases based around an S&P target risk approach with roughly the same fee structure. See Table 10.8.

Table 10.8 iShares asset class breakdown

Moderate

iShares asset class breakdown as of 2/13/2009

Asset class	% of Fund
Domestic Fixed Income	62.55
Barclays Aggregate Bond Fund	**26.25**
Barclays Short Treasury Bond Fund	24.07
Barclays TIPS Bond Fund	12.24
Domestic Equity	22.86
S&P 500 Index Fund	**17.87**
S&P MidCap 400 Index Fund	3.02
S&P SmallCap 600 Index Fund	1.98
International Equity	11.93
MSCI EAFE Index Fund	**10.86**
MSCI Emerging Markets Index Fund	1.07
Domestic Real Estate	**2.56**
Cohen & Steers Realty Majors Index Fund	2.56
Individual Securities	0.11

Growth

iShares asset class breakdown as of 2/13/2009

Asset class	% of Fund
Domestic Fixed Income	**44.3**
Barclays Aggregate Bond Fund	23.13
Barclays Short Treasury Bond Fund	11
Barclays TIPS Bond Fund	10.17
Domestic Equity	**34.9**
S&P 500 Index Fund	20.94
S&P MidCap 400 Index Fund	9.03
S&P SmallCap 600 Index Fund	4.94
International Equity	**19.77**
MSCI EAFE Index Fund	17.63
MSCI Emerging Markets Index Fund	**2.13**
Domestic Real Estate	0.85
Cohen & Steers Realty Majors Index Fund	**0.85**
Individual Securities	0.2

2010 Fund

iShares asset class breakdown as of 2/13/2009

Asset class	% of Fund
Domestic Fixed Income	**61.9**
Barclays Aggregate Bond Fund	44.77
Barclays Short Treasury Bond Fund	11.93
Barclays TIPS Bond Fund	5.21
Domestic Equity	**29.72**
S&P 500 Index Fund	25.51
S&P MidCap 400 Index Fund	2.6
S&P SmallCap 600 Index Fund	1.61
International Equity	**7.52**
MSCI EAFE Index Fund	6.36
MSCI Emerging Markets Index Fund	1.17
Domestic Real Estate	**0.76**
Cohen & Steers Realty Majors Index Fund	0.76
Individual Securities	**0.11**

Conservative Fund

iShares asset class breakdown as of 2/13/2009

Asset class	% of Fund
Domestic Fixed Income	**79.79**
Barclays Short Treasury Bond Fund	29.99
Barclays Aggregate Bond Fund	27.42
Barclays TIPS Bond Fund	22.37
Domestic Equity	**12.89**
S&P 500 Index Fund	8.9
S&P MidCap 400 Index Fund	3.01
S&P SmallCap 600 Index Fund	0.99
International Equity	**4.67**
MSCI EAFE Index Fund	4.67
Domestic Real Estate	**2.55**
Cohen & Steers Realty Majors Index Fund	2.55
Individual Securities	**0.04**

The all-in-one fund

Yet another take on the idea that simplicity – and low cost – is the best way forward for sinning, overtrading, overconfident investors comes in the novel idea that you might only ever need to buy *one* fund that tracks all the major moves in the market. This idea received its biggest boost in 2008 with the launch of a new index by small Texas-based company Dorchester Fund Management. According to the firm its 'CPMKTS' index or The Capital Markets Index 'views the capital markets on a broader basis and therefore includes stocks, bonds and money market instruments'.[25] So instead of just one big major index for bonds, another for money market funds and yet another for shares, you can invest in a fund that tracks all these major markets via one index.

According to Dorchester: 'The index was created over the past nine years, with more than four terabytes of compressed historical data – including government statistics and market changes – collected over the past three years. An additional 530 million pieces of new information are integrated into the CPMKTS database each day… The data is organized and processed using our patent-pending, rules-based methods, to formulate the index. This selection process removes the subjectivity associated with some other indices and more accurately reflects the capital markets environment. It is designed to track the weighted average of more than 1 million securities.'

This is clearly an ambitious project – it is one index that captures the vast majority of the investable (US) universe, with everything from inflation-linked Treasury (government) bonds through to dodgy tech companies. As its developer (a University of Chicago alumni) Warren Schmalenberger puts it, with one index you can 'cover the entire efficient frontier' of all asset classes. Schmalenberger started work on his all-encompassing index in 1995. 'For the next 3.5 years, I devoted myself to building a construct for a true capital markets index.' The end result is an index that is built around four separate computer systems in Chicago and Houston, processing a total of about 3.5bn different pieces of market information crunched every day in a single index that covers the 2000 largest US stocks, over 2000 short-term fixed-income instruments as well as 5600 investment-grade bonds. Its entire market cap at the end of 2008 was a staggering $31tn and covered 80 per cent of all the value of the US capital markets, although it did not include municipal bonds, junk bonds and convertibles.

Schmalenberger's hard work has found its way into index tracking land via a newish ETF from Claymore, the Claymore US-1 Capital Markets Index ETF (AMEX: *UEM*). Sitting besides this uber ETF are two variants based on sub-indices – the Claymore US Capital Markets Bond ETF (AMEX: *UBD*) and the Claymore US Capital Markets Micro-Term Fixed Income ETF (AMEX: *ULQ*). One is focusing on micro-term fixed-income markets, the other is just the master index's bond side.

Dorchester Capital's new index is an extreme variant on a rather more popular pursuit – to design a single exchange traded fund that captures *most* of the market. Yet again fund management group Vanguard has been most assiduous in this pursuit. One of its most successful ETFs is the Total US Stock market fund, which tracks an index from MSCI called the US Broad Market Index which is itself an aggregation of the MSCI US Large Cap 300, Mid Cap 450, Small Cap 1,750 and Micro Cap indices. According to the index designers at MSCI, 'this index represents approximately 99.5 per cent of the capitalization of the US equity market and includes approximately 3,900 companies'.[26] So when you buy the Vanguard ETF you are effectively buying the 'mind of the US market' at an extraordinarily low tracking charge of just 0.7 per cent.

Table 10.9 Vanguard Total US market index fund

TER		
Total US stock market	0.07%	MSCI US Broad Market Index
Total bond market	0.11%	Barclays US Aggregate Bond Index
FTSE world exc UK	0.25%	FTSE World exc USA

Table 10.10 Vanguard Total bond market fund

Total stock market fund			
Ticker	Description	Shares	Weighting
XOM	EXXON MOBIL	2,426	4.35%
JNJ	JOHNSON&JOHNSON	1,300	1.79%
MSFT	MICROSOFT CP	3,820	1.77%
PG	PROCTER & GAMBLE	1,385	1.70%
CVX	CHEVRON	962	1.65%
T	AT&T	2,740	1.61%
IBM	INTL BUS MACHINE	630	1.44%
GE	GENERAL ELEC CO	4,912	1.41%
WMT	WAL-MART STORES	1,115	1.29%
PFE	PFIZER INC	3,165	1.09%

Table 10.10 Continued

Total stock market fund

Ticker	Description	Shares	Weighting
JPM	JPMORGAN CHASE	1,732	1.09%
CSCO	CISCO SYSTEMS	2,750	1.07%
HPQ	HEWLETT-PACKARD	1,158	0.98%
KO	COCA-COLA CO	977	0.97%

Table 10.11 Composition of the two Vanguard funds

Total bond market
Distribution by issuer (% of fund) as of 01/31/2009

	Total bond market ETF
Asset-backed	0.80%
Commercial mortgage-backed	3.60%
Finance	7.00%
Foreign	3.30%
Government mortgage-backed	40.50%
Industrial	9.00%
Other	0.20%
Treasury/Agency	33.60%
Utilities	2.00%
Total	100.00%

Distribution by maturity (% of fund) as of 01/31/2009

	Total bond market ETF
Under 1 yr	1.30%
1–3 yrs	43.00%
3–5 yrs	27.30%
5–10 yrs	17.00%
10–20 yrs	5.30%
20–30 yrs	5.90%
Over 30 years	0.20%
Total	100.00%

Table 10.11 Continued

Distribution by credit quality* (% of fund) as of 01/31/2009

	Total bond market ETF
Aaa	80.90%
Aa	3.10%
A	9.00%
Baa	7.00%
< Baa	0.00%
Total	100.00%

Table 10.12 Vanguard FTSE All-World ex-US ETF (VEU)

Month end 10 largest holdings as of 01/31/2009

Rank	Holding
1	Nestle SA (Registered)
2	BP PLC
3	Total SA
4	Roche Holdings AG
5	Vodafone Group PLC
6	HSBC Holdings PLC
7	Novartis AG (Registered)
8	GlaxoSmithKline PLC
9	Royal Dutch Shell PLC Class A
10	Telefonica SA

Ten largest holdings = 10.8% of total net assets

Country diversification (% of common stock) as of 01/31/2009

Table 10.12 Continued

	FTSE All-World ex-US ETF 01/31/2008	FTSE All-World ex-US ETF 01/31/2009
Japan	14.60%	18.30%
United Kingdom	15.60%	15.10%
France	8.10%	8.10%
Switzerland	5.10%	6.00%
Germany	6.60%	5.90%
Canada	5.40%	5.80%
Australia	5.00%	4.30%
Spain	3.40%	3.60%
Hong Kong	2.40%	3.10%
Brazll	3.00%	2.80%
Italy	3.20%	2.80%
Korea	2.90%	2.70%
Taiwan	2.10%	2.20%
China	2.30%	2.00%

How much is enough? What does good diversification look like?

All these elegantly simple lazy portfolios may make some readers deeply nervous – simplicity may sound like an admirable principle but surely a common-sense definition of diversification suggests that we should use more than just a couple of funds to spread risk? Surely the Couch Potato approach of just two index tracking funds, for instance, is dangerously undiversified. In defence of Scott Burns and his Couch Potatoes he would argue that his chosen indices – the S&P 500, for instance – are already hugely diversified, containing the vast majority of the US equity market assets.

In Chapter 7 James Norton outlined how increasing the diversity of holdings within a portfolio can bring tangible benefits in both returns and the control of risk. An even more detailed analysis of what actually constitutes a diversified portfolio was attempted in the US by analysts Paul Merriman and colleague Richard Buck in September 2005 when they tried to resolve the struggle of how to go about building 'one portfolio for life'.[27] Using the database of Dimensional Fund Advisers, their research department looked at returns between 1955 and 2004, a 50-year period that included lots of bear, bull and sideways tracking markets.

They looked at three potential portfolios:

■ S&P 500 tracker.

■ Another variant invested 60 per cent in the S&P 500 Index and 40 per cent in five-year Treasury notes. This is very easy for any investor to replicate.

■ Another 60/40 split made up of 40 per cent Treasury bills and 60 per cent equity but this time the equity was split four ways between US-based large-cap stocks, large-cap value stocks, small-cap stocks and small-cap value stocks.

According to Merriman and Bucks's analysis, the 'all-equity S&P 500 Index portfolio had an annualized return of 10.9 per cent over that 50-year period' while the '60/40 version's annualized return was 9.6 per cent'. Surely the average private investor would have always plumped for this all-equity version? Merriman and Buck are not so sure – though the 60/40 equities/bond mix returned less than the pure equities approach, it did so with a much lower level of risk. 'Statistically, you could say the 60/40 portfolio reduced return by 12 per cent while reducing risk by 42 per cent,' say Merriman and Buck. 'Or you could say the 60/40 portfolio provided 88 per cent of the return with only 58 per cent of the risk.'

The best performer by far, though, came in the shape of the third mixture, the 60/40 portfolio with greater equity diversification. 'Over the 50 years in our study,' Merriman and Buck report, 'this diversified 60/40 portfolio produced a return of 11.4 per cent, with a maximum drawdown of 25 per cent. Compared with the all-equity portfolio, this diversified mix raised the return by an extra 0.5 percentage point while it reduced the risk by 44 per cent.' That 0.5 per cent per annum difference may not seem so great, but the authors remind us that over 50 years $100 invested at 10.9 per cent would grow to $17,643. The same $100 invested at 11.4 per cent would grow to $22,093, a difference of $4,450, or an increase of 25 per cent! 'In dollar terms,' they add, 'that difference alone is equal to more than 44 times the entire original investment of $100.'

But what about going global? Merriman and Bucks's original analysis looked only at US investments, but surely there must be some benefit from investing internationally as well? The authors agreed and subsequently looked at year-by-year returns from 1970 through to 2004 if an investor had stuck with the diversified option number three from earlier (no international stocks) or invested in an alternative strategy which consisted of a 60/40 per cent equity split but with that equity portion split 50 per cent into US-based stocks of varying sizes (large-cap stocks, large-cap value stocks, small-cap stocks and small-cap value stocks) and 50 per cent international (split five ways this time to include large-cap stocks, large-cap value stocks, small-cap stocks, small-cap value stocks and stocks in emerging markets). The returns increased by more than forty fold! The bottom line? The more you diversify internationally, the greater your potential returns.

11

The master portfolios

The rapid development of ETFs ready made for a diversified portfolio – detailed in the last chapter – is an almost exclusively American phenomenon. The mainstream investment industry in the UK by contrast is built around trying to get you to buy the latest 'best idea', be it a fund, an investment strategy or a new business concept that can be floated on the stock market. The idea that investors might crave a one-size-fits-all portfolio approach – with low costs to boot – has so far largely translated itself into expensive and largely failing absolute returns funds or slightly more successful balanced/managed equity funds that might, if you're lucky, include some form of bond exposure. It seems that here in the UK, although the idea of diversification has started to take root – more and more fund managers are offering diversified, actively managed multi-asset funds – no one has yet launched a cheap one-size-fits-all tracker portfolio available to the mass market.

This rather sorry state of affairs leaves you with a rather ambitious DIY project: build your own multi-asset index fund portfolio. The obvious answer to this conundrum is to consult a professional adviser – with luck they will have enough knowledge of the market and some understanding of the academic debates about sensible portfolio construction to develop a risk-adjusted personal approach. Sadly, most private investors are not quite so lucky – many IFAs (although not all) are happier dealing with mainstream insurance-based financial products and farm out their asset-allocation analysis (the term used in the trade to describe portfolio construction) to bigger firms that rely on black-box software systems to produce 'model portfolios'. These portfolios may well do the job, but the principles behind them are rarely spelled out and openly debated.

Which is where this last chapter comes in – working with *Investors Chronicle* magazine, we have developed a series of master portfolios which you can easily construct using ETFs and tracker index funds. These simple, easy-to-understand portfolios (first published in the magazine at the beginning of 2009) are built around a set of open principles – some of them uncontroversial, others highly debatable, but all detailed and discussed in detail.

Before we look at these 'portfolio principles' it is important to underline one crucial point – these model portfolios are exactly what they say they are, only models, and need to be adapted to suit your own principles and risk tolerance. If you accept that this 'model'-based approach has some validity, it is worth detailing some of the portfolio principles involved in building them.

It is asset class investing – the portfolios are based on asset classes and key markets, not individual shares or managers. This is an absolutely crucial first principle. Investors become obsessed by star managers, sexy sectors or cheap shares. They fixate very early on on identifying a hot share that might double, or a star manager who has a great winning streak. There is some validity to both exercises – there are good managers and some individual shares can make a great investment – but investors need to refocus much, if not most, of their attention on working out the broad asset classes and markets they want to be invested in. Do they want to focus exclusively on UK-based equities, probably with a blue-chip bias – the default position for most UK equity investors? Or do they want some foreign exposure or a small investment in bonds? The challenge is to work out the broad categories that will achieve your diversified return, not the much riskier reliance on individual fund managers or particular stocks and shares.

The portfolios are simple – they never comprise more than 15 and never fewer than 3 asset classes or markets. Remember Paul Merriman's analysis of what constitutes the optimum number of categories for true diversification? The consensus seems to be that at least three or four different broad asset classes is a minimum, with more asset classes generally regarded as a good thing. But there is also a sensible upper limit – you could end up having literally dozens of different asset classes, making your life virtually impossible as a result of all the portfolio monitoring and constant rejigging. For these *Investors Chronicle* model portfolios we have tried to cap the number of different asset classes at 15.

In an ideal world you would make the portfolios easy to operate on a day-to-day basis using ETFs. In the *Investors Chronicle* articles accompanying these portfolios we have been careful not to spell out any particular funds or managers – in this book we will be far more frank on whether an active fund manager or an ETF is a better idea. We would not entirely rule out actively managed funds in specialist sectors – private equity or emerging markets, for instance – but for very developed markets we would suggest buying the asset class exposure cheaply and efficiently through an index fund of some sort. The decision about which index to buy into is entirely dependent on the choice available, the expenses charged, the tracking error and the financial strength of the company running the fund.

The portfolios are based on a risk profile and/or stage in a lifecycle, i.e. low to high risk. There are five portfolios in all and they have been constructed using a very simple gradient, starting with low risk and ending up at global growth for equity investors. You could swap the risk-based titles around and use a target date approach and you would have the same portfolios. Lower risk are more likely to be useful for older investors keen to preserve capital while the higher risk portfolios are more likely to appeal to younger investors determined to shoot the lights out with potential rewards achieved through higher potential risk.

They are not optimised. Modern portfolio theory, and its application within large fund management firms and big investment banks, has spawned an alarmingly complex netherworld of fiendishly complex, dynamically allocated, multi-asset portfolios built by very clever people willing and able to crunch the data until it confesses. Every once in a while, a portfolio manager comes up with an alarmingly good mix of assets that could produce future bumper returns. This approach, usually involving some form of clever black-box analytics, is called the optimised approach and is great for building portfolios that are finely calibrated to balance risk and reward. Sadly, it is a far from ideal approach for ordinary private investors, who will probably have no idea what is going on inside the black-box quantitative model.

Our approach is to try to build something that is a 'best fit', is simple and can be easily understood. We have not built the mix of assets in each portfolio using backtesting; rather the starting point for this analysis was to analyse dozens of notional and actual portfolios published from around the world, including those from big British financial advisory firms, the *Financial Times's* own survey of wealth advisers plus academic analysis of big pension funds. In detail, this process involved the following steps:

1 The *Investors Chronicle* analysed lifecycle and glidepath studies as well as adviser-based, multi-asset class portfolios.

2 We analysed the mix of assets based on the criteria specified below and looked for average variables as well as median (most common) compositions.

3 We then applied the *Investors Chronicle's* own asset-allocation principles to alter the mix – detailed in the box below.

4 Finally, we looked at historic performance to understand past returns – but no alteration was made to the portfolio composition.

Armed with the aggregate data derived from this vast range of model portfolios, the *Investors Chronicle* then structured the actual building of each portfolio by a process of questions which produced trade-offs or ratios. This trade-off process consisted of a number of key questions:

- The first big question is exactly which risk profile you subscribe to – this suggests one of our five core portfolios.

- Based on this answer we then structure the first *layer* of components based on a trade-off between bonds and equities and what we call alternative assets, i.e. foreign exchange funds (forex), hedge funds, commodities. This established an overall balance between three very broad investment categories.

- We then focus on the equity index component of that three-fold structure and distinguish between *mainstream equities* (which is all developed and emerging markets stocks) and what we like to call '*equities – the rest*' which we define as real estate investment trusts (REITs), utilities and infrastructure funds. This latter group consists of actual equities – quoted on major exchanges – but they are tracking more unconventional markets.

- Within the first *mainstream equity* we then differentiate based on *region*, looking at the ratio between UK holdings and international holdings expressed as a ratio.

- Looking at the UK holdings, we then distinguish between a bias to the FTSE All Index (the main UK index) or whether we differentiate markets based on the size of the company, i.e. small vs mid vs large cap.

- Within the international equities component we distinguish between developed world and emerging markets.

- After this equities-based layer we then move on to *bonds*. Within bonds we distinguish between government *all* – both index linked and conventional – and corporate bonds (only ever sterling based).

- Within government bonds we differentiate between conventional and index-linked gilts or government bonds.

- We finally move to the major category of investments called alternative assets and distinguish two separate investment niches, namely *commodities*, broadly defined using the Dow Jones AIG index (now owned by UBS), and what we call *other* alternative assets, such as hedge funds and forex.

This process – a series of questions which involves a trade-off that results in a ratio of different assets – is summarised in the box below.

The trade-offs or ratios

Bonds vs equities vs Alt Assets

Equities: Mainstream vs Rest ratio

Equities: UK vs International ratio

Int Equity: Dev vs EM

UK Equity: ALL vs Size bias

Bonds: Corps vs Govt

Gilts: Conv vs Index L

Alt Assets: Commodit vs Other Alts

Clearly this process is far from being neutral or judgement free. It is based on some key asset allocation principles. We have broken down these principles into two distinct categories – the blindingly obvious motherhood and apple pie observations followed by the more debatable loaded principles.

First, though, those motherhood and apple pie concepts. These are fairly widely agreed ideas that should not spark too much debate. The most obvious example is that all portfolios are a trade-off of risk and return. Essential to this is the concept of the glidepath over time (when it comes to pensions) where the balance between risky assets and less risky assets changes over time. Our overall view is that the better risky assets are equities rather than bonds, although it is also true to say that over certain periods of time bonds can actually produce higher returns. Nevertheless, it is still largely true that equities are higher-return, riskier assets than bonds, which by contrast are less risky but tend over the very long term to produce lower returns.

The next key concept (familiar from previous chapters) is that based on the mountain of academic evidence (Ibbotson et al.) a diversified portfolio is better than an undiversified portfolio, and that optimal diversification is probably achieved with a minimum of five to six asset classes. Crucially, the data also suggest that developed world markets are increasingly correlated and that no great advantage is gained most of the time by choosing to diversify within developed world markets, unless there is a convincing rationale that says otherwise, i.e. to target small caps or value stocks based on portfolio assumptions. This means that wherever possible it is probably best to look for the broadest index that captures developed markets, i.e. MSCI World for developed world and FTSE ALL for UK.

Last but by no means least, international diversification is crucial. Most UK investors are too focused on purely UK-based stocks and shares and funds. The reality of global capital markets suggests that investors seriously consider the importance of international diversification, particularly with reference to emerging and frontier markets.

Not many investors or analysts would disagree with most of these conclusions, but the next set of arguments is much more contentious. Below, we have listed our top ten loaded principles – a great many analysts would probably radically disagree with each and every one of them, but these principles were outlined in the *Investors Chronicle* articles which kicked off this series. You may choose to disagree with them yourself, but if you do accept the logic, we have detailed the inevitable investment idea that results from this principle, i.e. an overweight position in an asset class or market or an underweight position (less than the market would suggest.)

1 Emerging markets will continue to power ahead and investors should have some bias if they are growth orientated. OVERWEIGHT emerging markets for mid and high-risk portfolios.

2 Although inflation will be a short-term issue, there are heightened risks over the very long term. UNDERWEIGHT index-linked gilts near-term portfolios OVERWEIGHT over a longer time horizon.

3 Be cautious towards commodities. They are too volatile and frankly underanalysed in portfolio terms. UNDERWEIGHT commodities for mid to low risk.

4 There is too much UK equity bias among British investors and not enough developed world focus, i.e. not great enough understanding of the importance of indices like the MSCI World Index. OVER-WEIGHT international developed equity markets for long-term or horizon portfolios.

5 Be very cautious when examining corporate bonds in the near term. They are much riskier than many advisers. UNDERWEIGHT all portfolios.

6 We generally like the investment space we have called equities rest – utilities, infrastructure and REITs. OVERWEIGHT equities rest for most portfolios.

7 Fundamental indexation is an interesting idea but for the vast majority of investors it is still a little risky if they do not fully understand what is actually involved with the stock-selection process. UNDER-WEIGHT fundamental index for all but adventurous portfolio.

8 Although there is a strong argument for equity income bias within developed world equities, we have chosen not to favour this over a straight UK FTSE All bias. UNDERWEIGHT UK equity income.

9 Within bonds it is probably not that good an idea to seek international diversification within either government or corporate themes. This view is largely based on accessibility – it is very difficult to find funds that track global bonds – and exchange rate risk, although more sophisticated investors might want to explore this as an option as new global bond ETFs launch. No international bond diversification currently.

10 Last but by no means least, none of these portfolios has any allocation for cash – these are invested portfolios, not portfolios based on market timing. Again this is a thorny issue, sure to generate much disagreement, but the question of market timing is crucial here. Our view is that for most investors, market timing is impossible to get right, so investors should not attempt it unless they work with a well-thought-through strategic valuation-based system or using a signal like the 200 Day Moving Average as a buy/sell signal. Market timing can and does work for some investors – it requires the use of relatively sophisticated ideas, which we explored in the last chapter.

With these asset-allocation principles explained, let's understand how they translate into an actual portfolio. Let's look at the most adventurous master portfolio of all, the Global Growth Portfolio, which is aimed at equity investors looking for some racy returns built around investing globally.

1 The Global Growth Portfolio

Target Date:		2045
Asset Class	Target Index	
Devel Equity: UK (FTSE 100)	FTSE 100	9
Devel Equity: UK (FTSE ALL)	FTSE ALL	0
Devel Equity: World exc UK	MSCI WORLD exc UK	27
Devel Equity: Value Stocks UK	FTSE Div Plus or equity income fund	0
Devel Equity: Value Stocks Global	DJ Global Select Divid	0
Devel Equity: Mid Caps	FTSE 250	4.5
Devel Equity: small Cap	FTSE Small Cap	4.5

Emerging Markets	MSCI EM	27
Global Infrastructure and Utilities	FTSE Util/S&P Glob Infra	9
REITS	EPRA/NAREIT Global	9
Corporate Bonds: Sterling	iBoxx Sterling Corporates	0
Government Bonds: Conventional	FTSE All Stocks Gilt	0
Government Bonds: Index Linked	Barclays UK Index Linked	0
Alts: Commodities	DJ-AIG Composite	6.5
Other Alts	Credit Suisse Tremont Hedge	3.5
Total		100

As the title says, this is very much a global equities-based portfolio, with a large percentage of its assets invested abroad, with nine different asset classes in all. Is it riskier than our low-risk portfolio for example? Absolutely, yes, but in the past this extra risk from investing in global equities would have produced extra returns for those willing to hold over the very long term and ride out any volatility. It boasts 9 per cent in the UK large-cap market – via a FTSE 100 tracker – plus another 4.5 per cent in mid caps and small caps. You will also see a chunky 27 per cent in a global developed markets index – the entire world's leading markets excluding the UK – so that we can capture the big European, US and Japanese markets. The other big idea is the emerging markets investment space which comprises another 27 per cent of assets. This is an unashamedly risky category that involves investing in countries like Brazil, Russia, India and China (collectively known as the BRIC countries) as well as the Gulf states and places like Vietnam.

Finally, you will see two groups of what are called alternative assets. The first is the 'equity rest', or the rest of the equity class outside mainstream companies. This rather strange moniker is meant to apply to things like real estate investment trusts in the commercial property sector and utilities and infrastructure companies. We have separated these off from core equity assets because they behave in a slightly different way, and in the case of utilities at least are viewed as slightly less risky.

The other big group of alternatives comprises a 6.5 per cent investment in a commodity index fund, broadly defined into one big index (the Dow Jones AIG composite index) and not broken down into individual commodities, plus a small 3.5 per cent investment in hedge funds.

In the box below you will see all these biases and weightings broken down into a simple form, with the actual trade-off percentages between different assets in the blue sub-box.

Portfolio Name: GLOBAL GROWTH

Lifecycle Target Date: 2040 (probably in their thirties with 30 years or less to retirement)

Global equity bias

No bonds at all

OVERWEIGHT Emerging Markets

International bias vs UK

OVERWEIGHT EQUITIES REST i.e. equities, infrastructure and REITs

BIAS towards size bias within equities i.e. focus on small caps – Size Bias in UK

	Glob Grwth
Bonds vs equities vis Alt Assets	90/10
Equities: Mainstream vs Rest ratio	1:4
Equities : UK vs International ratio	1:3
Int Equity : Dev vs EM	1:1 Size Bias SC in UK
UK Equity : ALL vs Size bias Bonds : Govt vs Corp	No Bonds
Gilts : Conv vs Index L	No Bonds
Alt Assets : Commodit vs Other Alts	2:1
Bonds : Int vs UK	No Bonds
Equities : Value Bias	No

More detailed look at assumptions for the Global Growth Portfolio

GLOBAL GROWTH ANALYSIS

1. 90% equities, 10% alternative assets

Equities	90%
Alt Assets	10%

2. Within Alt assets use 2:1 commodities over other assets

Commodities	
Others	

3. Within Equities

Mainstream	80%	
The Rest	20%	including REITs and Infrastructure
of which : REITS	50%	
Utilities and Infra	50%	

4. Within mainstream equities

UK	25%
International	75%

5. Within International

Emerging Markets	50%
Global Developed	50%

6. Within UK

FTSE 100	50%
FTSE 250	25%
FTSE Small Cap	25%

One final point: this portfolio is above all else a strongly equity-biased one and there are absolutely no bonds. If an investor has chosen this approach they are probably looking exclusively for higher-risk, higher-potential returns via equities and not for the safer and potentially boring qualities on offer from bonds.

James Norton's view on the Global Growth Portfolio

'It is a matter of buying into global capitalism and letting the markets do the work. Sit back and watch (not too often) and consider occasional rebalancing to realign the asset allocation. Anyone with a spare five minutes to check the websites of a few of the main providers of index funds could put this portfolio together. Some of my preferred funds would be the Lyxor FTSE 100 and 250 funds, the DBX Emerging Markets fund and iShares Infrastructure and REITs funds. For global developed market exposure I would consider either the iShares or Lyxor fund.'

2 The Low Risk Portfolio

This next portfolio is a complete contrast to its cosmopolitan sibling. It avoids much riskier equity-based assets, focusing instead on developed world equities, involving markets such as the FTSE All Share Index (which represents getting on for 98 per cent of the entire market capitalisation of the London Stock Exchange) or the much broader global benchmark index (again easily tracked by any number of funds and ETFs), the MSCI World excluding UK index. The beauty of a huge, global composite index like the MSCI World index is that it captures the vast majority of the total developed world large-cap companies, including those in the US and Japanese markets.

Target Date:		2020
		Low
Devel Equity: UK (FTSE 100)	FTSE 100	0
Devel Equity: UK (FTSE ALL)	FTSE ALL	16
Devel Equity: World exc UK	MSCI WORLD exc Uk	8
Devel Equity: Value Stocks UK	FTSE Div Plus or equity income fund	0
Devel Equity: Value Stocks Global	DJ Global Select Divid	0
Devel Equity: Mid Caps	FTSE 250	0
Devel Equity: small Cap	FTSE Small Cap	0
Emerging Markets	MSCI EM	0
Global Infrastructure and Utlities	FTSE Util/S&P Glob Infra	5
REITS	EPRA/NAREIT Global	4.5
Corporate Bonds: Sterling	iBoxx Sterlign Corporates	5
Government Bonds: Conventional	FTSE All Stocks Gilt	30
Government Bonds: Index Linked	Barclays UK Index Linked	25
Alts: Commodities	DJ-AIG Composite	4
Other Alts	Credit Suisse Tremont Hedge	2.5
Total		100

Portfolio Name: LOW RISK

Lifecycle Target Date: 2020 (closing in on retirement, probably in their fifties)

Bond bias

Capital Preservation

UK FTSE All Bias – avoid unnecessary currency risk from international diversification

Bias towards equity rest, i.e. utilities and infrastructure

Reliability of returns from government bonds versus heightened risk from corporate bonds

Some income

	Low
Bonds vs equities vis Alt Assets	60/33.5/6.5
Equities: Mainstream vs Rest ratio	72/28
Equities: UK vs Global Developeds ratio	66/33
Int Equity: Dev vs EM	ALL DEV, NO EM
UK Equity: ALL vs Size bias	FTSE ALL only
Bonds: Corps vs Govt	10/90
Gilts: Conv vs Index L	60/40
Alt Assets: Commodit vs Other Alts	66/33
Bonds: Int vs UK	UK only
Equities: Value Bias	No
Other alts (exc commodities) as %	2.5

What this portfolio avoids is any investment in emerging markets – these are much riskier than developed world markets, although potentially much more rewarding. We considered this deliberate omission very carefully and some experts may argue that emerging markets (EM) do have some small place even in low-risk portfolios (maybe 2–5 per cent) to spruce up potential returns, but recent evidence suggests that the risk of really big drawdowns (more than 50–60 per cent losses in one year) is just too great.

Stepping back from the equities component, this portfolio is heavily biased towards more cautious bonds, and in particular government bonds, although many experts would challenge our heavy bias against corporate bonds. At the time of writing – March 2009 – many analysts reckon that corporate

bonds are a great investment, especially with the most conservative companies called investment grade. This may be true, but there is no denying that
corporate bonds are much more vulnerable when equity markets are distressed; in fact, the main reason that corporate bonds may be such good
value in 2009 is partly because they have fallen so much in the collapses of
2008 as equities have sold off. Investors need to remember that the outfits
paying the coupons on these bonds are listed, quoted companies with ordinary shares and if the market thinks these companies will go bust, they will
also punish the corporate bonds. The correlation (positive and above 0.4)
between corporate bonds and equities is just too high for cautious investors,
although the yields on offer are, not unnaturally given the higher risk, much
higher. If you want to secure a higher income then you might want to consider increasing your corporate bond holding from 5 per cent to maybe 10
per cent or even 15 per cent, but only at investment-grade level of risk.

Within government bonds or gilts the holdings are weighted towards what
are called conventional gilts, as opposed to index-linked gilts that protect
investors against inflation. If you think that inflation over the very long
term of more than 2–3 per cent per annum is a real likelihood, you might
want to consider buying more index-linked gilts (also called linkers). These
portfolios are not meant as exercises in market timing – they are meant for
long-term buy-and-hold investors –although if inflation was to shoot up,
the composition of the portfolios might well be altered in the *Investors
Chronicle* regular updates. One last point on bonds: as we have already
noted, sophisticated investors may want to consider some exposure to
global gilts or bonds partly to protect sterling-based assets against any
sudden FX changes, but there are very few ETFs that offer this exposure – if
you can find such a fund or ETF, you might consider a 60 per cent UK bias
and 40 per cent in global gilts or bonds overall.

Last but by no means least, you may notice that category called alternative
assets – these could be everything from forex and hedge funds through to
commodities. We have included some commodity exposure, through the
DJ AIG composite index, partly because over the long term commodities
are fairly uncorrelated with equities and bonds (they move in different
ways at different times) and partly because commodities are usually a good
store of value in inflationary times. Some hedge fund exposure (very small
at 2.5 per cent) has also been included, mainly because the general commitment to what are called absolute returns in the sector is a valuable exercise
for cautious investors. It is worth noting that most hedge fund indices have
fallen sharply over the last year, but not by as much as most equity and
commodity indices. The key is to try lots of different assets in moderation.

Stephen Barber's take on the Low Risk Portfolio

'Low risk does not mean "no risk". Investors who are prepared to accept some risk in their portfolios can expect longer-term returns to be better than deposits or cash-based products. This portfolio reflects the trade-off between accepting sufficient risk to deliver desired returns but not so much that low-risk investors will have trouble sleeping at night. When thinking about this sort of strategy, our approach should be one of planning for the longer term, riding out short-term volatility and perhaps drip-feeding funds into the market to take advantage of pound/cost averaging.

This low-risk portfolio has been built to achieve relatively safe, dependable returns and that leads to a bias towards capital protection. Here it hits the nail firmly on the head by being overweight in fixed interest, primarily government bonds. And when selecting equities, it does so from the more reliable sectors such as the defensive utilities and dependable infrastructure. This sector, in particular, offers relatively safe and consistent returns from both capital and income over the longer term as \$20tn is spent on building roads, rail, hospitals and the like around the world over the next decade. This being said, the portfolio is careful to select assets which avoid the volatility associated with currency risk. So the objective is to minimise the potential downside while seeking good capital growth and yield. All portfolios should be diversified as this is a prime method of managing risk, but it also means that a list can have a spread of asset classes, some of which can be more adventurous. Such portfolios might also consider gaining equity exposure from using capital-protected products which give exposure to market growth but preserve capital or even cautious managed funds where fund managers select the best lower-risk multi-asset returns by mixing bonds, equities, commodities and the like.'

3 The Income Portfolio

The first decade of the twenty-first century has not been very kind to income investors. Those who chose to focus on equities via their dividend payouts had an awful few years around 2007 and 2008 as the global stock markets wilted, virtually all the major UK banks stopped paying dividends and the recession cut into companies' ability to afford to make dividend payouts.

Lifecycle target date for retirement:		2010
INVESTMENT SPACE	INDEX	Income
Devel Equity: UK (FTSE 100)	FTSE 100	0
Devel Equity: UK (FTSE ALL)	FTSE ALL	5
Devel Equity: World exc UK	MSCI WORLD exc Uk	2
Devel Equity: Value Stocks UK	FTSE Div Plus or equity income fund	6.5
Devel Equity: Value Stocks Global	DJ Global Select Divid	6
Devel Equity: Mid Caps	FTSE 250	0
Devel Equity: small Cap	FTSE Small Cap	0

Emerging Markets	MSCI EM	0
Global Infrastructure and Utlities	FTSE Util/S&P Glob Infra	12.5
REITS	EPRA/NAREIT Global	3
Corporate Bonds: Sterling	iBoxx Sterling Corporates	5
Government Bonds: Conventional	FTSE All Stocks Gilt	40
Government Bonds: Index Linked	Barclays UK Index Linked	20
Alts : Commodities	DJ-AIG Composite	0
Other Alts	Credit Suisse Tremont Hedge	0
Total		100

Portfolio Name: INCOME

Lifecycle Target Date: 2010 (close to retirement)

Could also be used for those already in retirement

Income and bond bias

Capital preservation

UK bias – avoid unnecessary currency risk

Equity income and value bias to generate income with blue chip focus

Reliability of returns from government bonds versus heightened risk from corporate bonds

	Income
Bonds vs equities vis Alt Assets	65/35
Equities: Mainstream vs Rest ratio	60/40
Equities: UK vs Global Developeds ratio	50/50
Int Equity: Dev vs EM	ALL DEV/NO EM
UK Equity: ALL vs Size bias	FTSE ALL only
Bonds: Corps vs Govt	10/90
Gilts: Conv vs Index L	66/33
Alt Assets: Commodit vs Other Alts	Only commod
Bonds: Int vs UK	UK only
Equities: Value Bias	yes
Other alts (exc commodities) as %	0%

For bond investors those terrible few years were a great deal less choppy – nominal capital prices shot up as investors fled risk – but yields crashed, especially as inflation plummeted, forcing radical cuts in interest rates. If you have to depend on safe government bonds or gilts as a source of income, your woes would have increased in almost every month of 2008 and 2009. The flat yield on the benchmark FTSE All Stocks Gilts index, for instance, was still paying around 4.3 per cent in the middle of 2009, but that was only something called a flat yield – the actual payout versus the current index level. If a different measure was used, namely the 'gross yield to redemption' – the income payout as a percentage of the value of the gilts on redemption, i.e. what you will get back when the gilt is redeemed – that return on UK gilts dropped to 2.95 per cent. For many US Treasury bills' short-term yields, the equivalent yields collapsed below 1 per cent on a redemption basis, while in the UK inflation-linked gilts (their payout is linked to inflation rates) were paying out just over 1 per cent.

These declining yields forced income investors to rethink everything. Although a focus on bonds – gilts or corporate bonds – is probably still the safest bet for a reliable yield, some exposure to other asset classes is also probably a good idea. Many 'alternative' equity assets, for instance, such as infrastructure shares – utilities and public–private partnership funds – pay out chunky, well-backed yields.

In this model we have tried to reflect these cross currents and very different views on risk. Overall the portfolio is weighted 65 per cent towards safer bonds and 35 per cent towards riskier assets. If you were to invest in ETFs – index tracking funds – that followed the main indices used in our model portfolio, you would be receiving a total portfolio return of 5.27 per cent at the time of writing (March 2009), with much the largest component of income coming from the biggest holding in the main conventional gilts index, the FTSE All Stock Gilt. Another 20 per cent of the portfolio is invested in those index-linked gilts we mentioned earlier, as a safety policy – if inflation were to start shooting up towards 4 per cent per annum, investors might want to consider switching around the 40 per cent conventional gilts/20 per cent index-linked ratio. The allocation of just 5 per cent to corporate bonds is probably the most controversial idea – many, many advisers think that corporate bonds with their current high yields are the best place to derive an income. One major benchmark index, the iBoxx Sterling Liquid Corporate Long-Dated Bond index, yields a very high 8 per cent flat yield and 9.5 per cent yield to redemption, as of March 2009. These are indeed very high rates and if the economy was bottoming out, they would be an obvious buy. But – and this is the really big but – if your view is still bearish and you believe the world is only beginning to work its way through a severe recession or even a depression, corporate defaults will shoot up and the yield will go even higher.

In the equity portion of the portfolio the holdings are deliberately weighted towards infrastructure assets, which are producing historically high and relatively safe yields, plus high-yielding equity indices. Tracking an index like the Dow Jones Global Select Dividend may well be a good idea – it follows the world's largest companies which pay out an above-average dividend yield.

Perhaps the most contentious idea in this portfolio is the 6.5 per cent in high-yielding UK stocks, either via an index like the UK Dividend Plus or through an established equity income fund. These kind of stocks suffered badly in the bear markets of 2008 and 2009, and the UK Dividend Plus index (a major dividend-based index) turned in some dreadful results, but if markets do recover some of their poise these cautious, value-based assets may stage a rally.

The other master portfolios

Lifecycle target date for retirement: 2030		2040 Absolute Returns (medium risk)	Adventurous
INVESTMENT SPACE	INDEX		
Devel Equity: UK (FTSE 100)	FTSE 100	0	12.5
Devel Equity: UK (FTSE ALL)	FTSE ALL	25.38	0
Devel Equity: World exc UK	MSCI WORLD exc Uk	19	8
Devel Equity: Value Stocks UK	FTSE Div Plus or equity income fund	0	15.5
Devel Equity: Value Stocks Global	DJ Global Select Divid	0	8
Devel Equity: Mid Caps	FTSE 250	0	2
Devel Equity: small Cap	FTSE Small Cap	0	1.5
Emerging Markets	MSCI EM	6.38	5
Global Infrastructure and Utlities	FTSE Util/S&P Glob Infra	5	8.75
REITS	EPRA/NAREIT Global	4.25	8.75
Corporate Bonds: Sterling	iBoxx Sterlign Corporates	10.83	4
Government Bonds: Conventional	FTSE All Stocks Gilt	10.83	8
Government Bonds: Index Linked	Barclays UK Index Linked	10.83	8
Alts: Commodities	DJ-AIG Composite	5	6.5
Other Alts	Credit Suisse Tremont Hedge	2.5	3.5
Total		100	100

4 The Mid Risk Portfolio

Portfolio Name: MIDDLE OF THE ROAD MID RISK PORTFOLIO

Lifecycle Target Date: 2030 (probably in their forties with 20 years or less to retirement)

Overall equity bias

Mainstream equity bias, i.e. underweight utilities and infrastructure

Balance between growth and capital preservation

Balance between conventional gilts and index linked gilts i.e. probably
OVERWEIGHT index linked gilts because of long term inflation risk

OVERWEIGHT corporate bonds

UNDERWEIGHT emerging markets vs international equity markets

	Mid Risk
Bonds vs equities vis Alt Assets	32.5/60/7.5
Equities: Mainstream vs Rest ratio	85/15
Equities: UK vs Global Developeds ratio	50/50
Int Equity: Dev vs EM	75/25
UK Equity: ALL vs Size bias	FTSE ALL only
Bonds: Corps vs Govt	33/66
Gilts: Conv vs Index L	50/50
Alt Assets: Commodit vs Other Alts	66/33
Bonds: Int vs UK	UK
Equities: Value Bias	No
Other alts (exc commodities) as %	2.5

It is almost impossible to design a one-size-fits-all portfolio – each and
every one of us has our own attitude to risk, our own financial goals, our
own passions and hates. Yet the reality is that most investors tend to sit,
like most things in life, somewhere in the middle of any range of attitudes
and sensibilities. We nearly all want some element of risk in order to gain
greater rewards, but we don't want 'too much risk'. When pushed, most
would probably opt for some exposure to safer gilts and bonds, but they
have probably also heard that the 'future' is in something like emerging
market equities. The trade-off in potential for high returns and the desire
to protect a portfolio from large absolute losses is at the heart of any financial adviser's approach to constructing a portfolio.

But how do you translate these contrasting forces into a single portfolio? One example of an attempt to build the elusive middle-of-the-road, mid-risk portfolio comes in the shape of a revolutionary series of funds launched in the US by iShares. In 2008 the fund manager launched a set of target risk and target date 'all-in-one' funds that combined a number of different index tracking funds in one listed entity, giving investors access to everything from real estate to corporate bonds.

Perhaps the most popular of the 'risk'-based funds was an ETF called 'Moderate' – the composition of the index is in Table 11.1. What is immediately striking about this multi-ETF fund is that over 62 per cent of the total holdings were in US fixed-income securities, mostly government bonds (also known as T-bills). If you were to run the same exercise with most wealth-based advisers for instance in the UK – and the *FT Money* section does exactly this every year – you would get a very different answer, namely a 50–60 per cent allocation not to bonds but to 'riskier' equities. What is even more extraordinary about this US-based multi ETF is that it is overwhelmingly US focused – less than 11 per cent of the total funds are used to buy anything international, whereas most UK-based planners and advisers would probably consider foreign exposure of at least twice this level, if not closer to 50 per cent for equities.

Table 11.1 iShares Moderate Target Risk fund

iShares asset class breakdown as of 2/13/2009	
Asset class	% of fund
Domestic Fixed Income	62.55
Barclays Aggregate Bond Fund	26.25
Barclays Short Treasury Bond Fund	24.07
Barclays TIPS Bond Fund	12.24
Domestic Equity	22.86
S&P 500 Index Fund	17.87
S&P MidCap 400 Index Fund	3.02
S&P SmallCap 600 Index Fund	1.98
International Equity	11.93
MSCI EAFE Index Fund	10.86
MSCI Emerging Markets Index Fund	1.07
Domestic Real Estate	2.56
Cohen & Steers Realty Majors Index Fund	2.56
Individual Securities	0.11

Our own take on this challenge of trying to build a middle-of-the-road portfolio is outlined in Table 11.2. We have sided with most UK-based advisers and favoured a much more equity-based and internationally oriented portfolio. We have allocated only one third of the total portfolio to bonds – many academics might even suggest that this percentage is perhaps too low. Studies by the likes of Elroy Dimson and Paul Marsh at the LBS suggest that long-term returns from equities tend to average between 6 per cent and 8 per cent, with a 3–4 per cent risk premium, as it is called, over risk-free cash deposits, i.e. equities provide higher long-term returns albeit at the cost of greater volatility. That bias towards equities needs to be put in proper perspective however – over the last decade bonds have probably been a better investment idea and there are many periods in history where bonds have consistently beaten equities.

Table 11.2 Building a portfolio

Portfolio compositions:
Suggested

		2030 Medium
Devel Equity: UK (FTSE 100)	FTSE 100	0
Devel Equity: UK (FTSE ALL)	FTSE ALL	25.38
Devel Equity: World exc UK	MSCI WORLD exc UK	19
Devel Equity: Value Stocks UK	FTSE Div Plus or equity income fund	0
Devel Equity: Value Stocks Global	DJ Global Select Dividend	0
Devel Equity: Mid Caps	FTSE 250	0
Devel Equity: Small Cap	FTSE Small Cap	0
Emerging Markets	MSCI EM	6.38
Global Infrastructure and Utlities	FTSE Util/S&P Glob Infra	5
REITS	EPRA/NAREIT Global	4.25
Corporate Bonds: Sterling	iBoxx Sterling Corporate	10.83
Government Bonds: Conventional	FTSE All Stocks Gilt	10.83
Government Bonds: Index Linked	Barclays UK Index Linked	10.83
Alts: Commodities	DJ-AIG Composite	5
Other Alts	Credit Suisse Tremont Hedge	2.5
Total		100

Our other core focus is on international diversification – of the total 50 per cent plus exposure to equities, we have suggested a fairly even split between international and UK shares, with a particular focus on the equities of other developed world markets including the US and Europe. Emerging markets shares comprise just 6 per cent of the total value of the portfolio. This international diversification is in effect an insurance policy – we are not entirely convinced that the UK economy will be a very happy affair over the next few years and we would suggest that buying some US, Japanese and European investments might be a wise move.

There are also some deliberate omissions. We do not think it is appropriate for a mid-risk or middle-of-the-road investor to bias their portfolio for or against small caps or large mid caps. We have chosen the FTSE All Share index as our default index in part because it covers 98 per cent of the entire UK market capitalisation and includes both mid- and small-cap stocks (although it is still very large-cap heavy). We also think that any attempt to capture the 'value premium' is probably too risky for this portfolio – this term applies to the extensive research which suggests that 'cheaper', 'better-value' shares with decent balance sheets and higher yields provide better long-term returns. By and large we think the evidence does 'stack up' over the long term, but recent experience – where value stocks have underperformed the market – suggests that it is a risky and volatile strategy. We have also allocated just 5 per cent of the portfolio to real estate – we would suggest that exposure be to global real estate, not just UK assets – and we have suggested 5 per cent for commodities. One last thought: if the overall exposure to mainstream equities strikes you as too risky, you might want to consider upping the holdings of slightly less volatile utility and infrastructure shares. This fast-growing 'alternative equity' category tends to consist of companies with strong, regulated, asset-backed balance sheets, predictable cash flow profiles and decent yields – more cautious types might want to think about doubling their exposure to this category and cutting their FTSE All Share exposure.

5 The Adventurous Portfolio

Portfolio Name: ADVENTUROUS

Lifecycle Target Date: 2040 (probably in their thirties with 30 years or less to retirement)

Alternative assets bias

UK bias versus International

OVERWEIGHT – EQUITIES REST, i.e. equities, infrastructure and REITs

Low level of bonds – UNDERWEIGHT BONDS

BIAS towards size bias within equities i.e. focus on small caps

Value bias – 50%/50% within UK and developed world equities

Adventurous	
Bonds vs equities vis Alt Assets	70/20/10
Equities: Mainstream vs Rest ratio	3:1
Equities: UK vs International ratio	1.5:1
Int Equity: Dev vs EM	3:1
UK Equity: ALL vs Size bias	Size Bias: SC
Bonds: Govt vs Corp	4:1
Gilts: Conv vs Index L	1:1
Alt Assets: Commodit vs Other Alts	2:1
Bonds: Int vs UK	NO
Equities: Value Bias	Yes 50%/50%
Other alts (exc commodities) as %	10

Imagine that you are 30 years old. You have got between 35 and 40 years before you retire and you are suddenly starting to earn enough money to start a retirement fund. But you are faced with a huge question: how do you build a portfolio that will give you long-term growth without taking on too much risk? The core to building any portfolio is to balance risk and reward, even for younger investors. The riskiest assets tend to produce the biggest long-term gains, although over that long term the resulting volatility will be huge. Investors have become used to the idea that over the very long term equities are a great investment – the average over the last

100 years has been more than 6 per cent per annum in most major developed world markets. But no one actually saves for 100 years. Most investors face a more limited timeframe of between 20 and 40 years. That matters because over this time period volatility can make a huge difference.

US analyst and adviser John Mauldin looked at this in a paper called 'While Rome Burns'.[1] He examined the frequency of returns and the impact of volatility. He found that 'in the 103 years from 1900 through 2002, the annual change for the Dow Jones Industrial Average reflects a simple average gain of 7.2 per cent per year. During that time, 63 per cent of the years reflect positive returns, and 37 per cent were negative. Only five of the years ended with changes between +5 per cent and +10 per cent – that's less than 5 per cent of the time'. Mauldin reminds his readers that most of the years were far from average. Almost 70 per cent of the years were double-digit years, when the stock market either rose or fell by more than 10 per cent. He then goes on to examine actual returns in 88 20-year periods. According to Mauldin: 'Though most periods generated positive returns before dividends and transaction costs, half produced compounded returns of less than 4 per cent. Less than 10 per cent generated gains of more than 10 per cent.' He warns that 'the stock market rarely gives you an average year. The wild ride makes for those emotional investment experiences which are a primary cause of investment pain'.

Dividends smooth returns

But his overall message is that equities will deliver substantial compounded returns, especially if you focus on a number of variables, including dividends. A number of realities emerge from this long-term financial analysis. The first is that if you are consistent and have a long enough timeframe, then equities stand a very high chance of yielding greater long-term returns.

The next is that income and dividends matter. Accumulating returns from dividends comprise a large part of total returns, but there is also some evidence that over the long term the market misprices more value-orientated companies that tend to produce a decent yield. Work from economists such as Ken French and Eugene Fama at the University of Chicago suggests that smaller companies produce higher returns – called the scale premium – and you may be able to boost long-term returns by anything between 1 per cent and 3 per cent per annum.

All these concepts sit behind our latest portfolio, our Adventurous Portfolio. It is targeted at younger investors, but it could work for anyone willing to take on more risk. Crucially, though, it is very different from our equally ambitious and risky Global Growth Portfolio. It is not exclusively focused on equities (it contains some alternative assets as well as bonds) and it has a strong UK focus (see Figure 11.1). This portfolio is aimed at investors who want some diversification away from equities but not too much diversification away from the UK – when you retire you will probably have to live off sterling-based assets. Its small bias towards caution is reflected in some bonds exposure and in a bias towards slightly safer equity assets such as utilities and infrastructure companies.

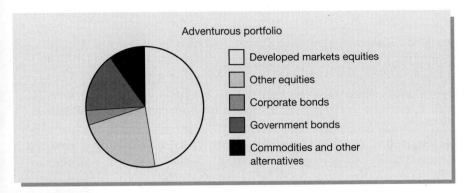

Adventurous portfolio

- Developed markets equities
- Other equities
- Corporate bonds
- Government bonds
- Commodities and other alternatives

Figure 11.1

There is one last key issue: the portfolio features plenty of value stocks. Within the bit of the portfolio that is equity based we have split our holding 50/50 between a strategy that simply tracks the major indices and a strategy that focuses on equity-income strategies.

Adventurous Portfolio breakdown

Developed market equities	Suggested Index	% of portfolio
UK (FTSE 100)	FTSE 100	12.5
UK (FTSE ALL)	FTSE ALL	0
World exc UK	MSCI WORLD exc Uk	8
Value Stocks UK	FTSE Div Plus or equity income fund	15.5
Value Stocks Global	DJ Global Select Dividend	8
Mid Caps	FTSE 250	2
Small Cap	FTSE Small Cap	1.5

Developed market equities	Suggested Index	% of portfolio
Other equities		
Emerging Markets	MSCI EM	5
Global Infrastructure and Utlities	FTSE Util/S&P Glob Infra	8.75
Real estate investment trusts	EPRA/NAREIT Global	8.75
Bonds		
Corporate Bonds: Sterling	iBoxx Sterling Corporates	4
Government Bonds: Conventional	FTSE All Stocks Gilt	8
Government Bonds: Index Linked	Barclays UK Index Linked	8
Alternative assets		
Alts: Commodities	DJ-AIG Composite	6.5
Other Alts	Credit Suisse Tremont Hedge	3.5

Sources for portfolios

FolioFN Model portfolios

Seven Investment Management portfolios

Marlborough iFunds active multi ETF funds

US-based Lazy Portfolios from *The Lazy's Person's Guide to Investing*[2]

S&P Target Risk Index series

iShares US-based Allocation funds

TDX Independence Target Date funds

Opportunistic Rebalancing

What do I do next? Where do the Essential 25 fit in?

In Table 11.3 you will see the list of all our *Investors Chronicle* master portfolios, with their core holdings. In the first two columns you will see the investment space and the underlying index, followed by five different model portfolios. If you sense that one of these model portfolios 'fits' your profile, start your own research.

The first step is to look at the index you are tracking. We feature all the indices below in our Essential 25. Look at what comprises the index (its main holdings) and the risks and potential rewards involved. Be certain that this is what you would like to track – as we have already said, all the big indices have their vulnerabilities and they are all liable to heavy holdings in the most popular sectors and companies. That's no bad thing – equity investing is, after all, a giant weighing machine that simply rewards the most successful companies. But remember that equity indices are volatile – some more than others – and that many big developed market indices are very closely correlated with each other. In our opinion it is no good putting all your money in a simple three-way split that involves a UK FTSE 100 index tracker, followed by an S&P 500 index tracker and a European index tracker – remember that good diversification is not just about national markets but also asset classes. Alternative assets like commodities have their value, as do bonds and gilts.

Once you have researched your index and looked at your suggested percentage allocation – and remember it is only a suggested allocation – start to think about which actual fund to invest in. We are not going to tell you this vital bit in this book (that would involve favouring one fund over another), but we do suggest which ETFs and index funds are on the market, their relative costs and their success at tracking the index (where data exist). You then have to make your own decisions – look at the fund in detail, using many of the ideas discussed in this book. In particular we would recommend focusing on:

- cost – anything above 1% is simply unacceptable;
- tracking error – anything more than 1 per cent per annum is a worry and more than 2.5 per cent is unacceptable;
- the asset manager and examine whether you are happy with the structure of the fund. Are there any counterparty risks;
- the index structure once more to see what risks you are taking using this fund. Are you buying into a small number of very big companies?
- how easy the index fund is to trade in and examine the bid–offer spread offered by a broker – don't accept any bid–offer spread above 1 per cent. Also be aware that some smaller ETFs in the US are very poorly traded and more than a few have shut up shop.

Once you have worked out your portfolio composition, go off and start buying your shares either in a lump sum or on a regular savings scheme on a monthly basis (the preferable option).

Once you are up and running we would suggest four simple portfolio management rules:

1 Do not check the portfolio more than once a week. Too much attention encourages overtrading.

2 We would recommend some form of rebalancing applied either on an annual basis or via some form of tolerance band system using the 20 per cent rule.

3 If you feel confident about your knowledge of the markets, think about using a simple market-timing system – we like the simple 200 Day moving average systems. If you do use a system, stick to it, through thick and thin, and do not overtrade. Only use your system for big signals that suggest a move out of all equities into cash and vice versa; likewise for other asset classes.

4 Diversify, diversify, diversify. Just focusing on equities may be a brilliant long-term strategy but it is really very risky. Be aware of that risk and contemplate some diversification away from equities, even if it is into commodities or even hedge funds. Equally within that broad category known as 'mainstream equities' seek out markets and niche markets that offer some form of diversification, i.e. utility stocks or infrastructure companies have some diversification benefits compared with mainstream equities.

Table 11.3 *Investors Chronicle master portfolios*

Lifecycle target date for retirement:	INDEX	2010 Income	2020 Low	2030 Medium	2040 Adv	2045 Global Growth
INVESTMENT SPACE						
Devel Equity: UK (FTSE 100)	FTSE 100	0	0	0	12.5	9
Devel Equity: UK (FTSE ALL)	FTSE ALL	5	16	25.38	0	0
Devel Equity: World exc UK	MSCI WORLD exc UK	2	8	19	8	27
Devel Equity: Value Stocks UK	FTSE Div Plus or equity income fund	6.5	0	0	15.5	0
Devel Equity: Value Stocks Global	DJ Global Select Divid	6	0	0	8	0
Devel Equity: Mid Caps	FTSE 250	0	0	0	2	4.5
Devel Equity: Small Cap	FTSE Small Cap	0	0	0	1.5	4.5
Emerging Markets	MSCI EM	0	0	6.38	5	27
Global Infrastructure and Utilities	FTSE Macquarie Global 100 or S&P Glob Infrastructure Index	12.5	5	5	8.75	9
REITS	EPRA/NAREIT Global Plus Index	3	4.5	4.25	8.75	9
Corporate Bonds: Sterling	iBoxx Sterling Corporate Bond Index	5	5	10.83	4	0
Government Bonds: Conventional	FTSE All Stocks Gilt	40	30	10.83	8	0
Government Bonds: Index Linked	Barclays UK Index Linked	20	25	10.83	8	0
Alts: Commodities	DJ-AIG Commodities Composite	0	4	5	6.5	6.5
Other Alts	Credit Suisse Tremont Hedge	0	2.5	2.5	3.5	3.5
Total		100	100	100	100	100

Appendix: The Essential 25

FTSE 100 – UK Equities

Volatility	1.21 (FTSE All Share Index is 1.11)
Weight of largest holding – as at March 13th 2009	BP – 15%
Weight of top ten largest holdings	52.41%
Yield:	5.81% As at March 2009

Returns

Index	2004	2005	2006	2007	2008
FTSE 100	6.7%	16.7%	10.7%	2.3%	−30.9%

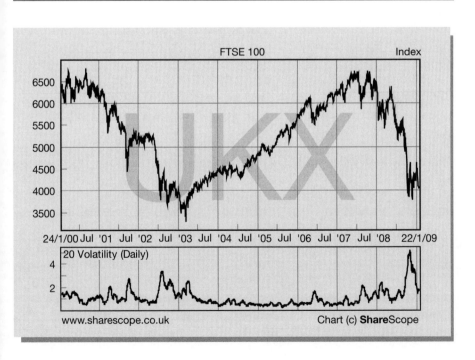

Region: Europe (not EuroZone)

ANALYSIS	
Likely Risk (High/Medium/Low)	Medium
Likely Volatility	Medium
Suitable for 'Simple' Investors i.e. small ISA investors	Yes
Diversification Risk with Top Holdings i.e. top three more than 20% of fund	Yes
Likely to be a core holding?	Yes
Market Cap based (MC)/Screened (S)	MC
Appeal to Income Investors?	Yes
Top 3 holding as % of total fund March 2009	23%
Country Breakdown: top 3 – March 2009	100% London listed but 60% of value of earnings sourced outside the UK
Sector Breakdown: top 3 – March 2009	Oil and Gas 23.2% Consumer Goods 13.25%
	Financials 17.9%

Highlighted ETFs

Details			
Fund	Lyxor FTSE 100	iShares FTSE 100	DBX FTSE 100
Ticker/EPIC	L100	ISF	XUKX
Issuer	Lyxor	iShares Barclays	Deutsche DBX
TER	0.30%	0.40%	0.30%

Comments

The FTSE 100 covers the largest companies by market cap, with the FTSE 250 covering the next 250 largest (i.e. those that do not make it into the FTSE 100). The composition of these indices changes regularly as companies move up and down between the relevant indices. According to the index owners, the FTSE Group, 'This index comprises the 100 most highly capitalised blue chip companies, representing approximately 81 per cent of the UK market. The FTSE 100 Index also accounts for 7.97 per cent of the world's equity market capitalisation (based on the FTSE All-World Index as at 31 December 2008). FTSE 100 constituents are all traded on the London Stock Exchange's SETS trading system.' The index is reviewed quarterly.

The weighting of shares in the index is a relatively simple exercise – the index is built around the market capitalisation of the constituent companies (all 100) so that the larger companies have a disproportionate impact on the value of the index, compared with a smaller (by market cap) company. So if HSBC, for instance, comprises 10 per cent of the index and its shares rise by 10 per cent, all things being equal with the other constituent companies, the index should rise by 1 per cent. This 'methodology' is called the free-float methodology for constructing an index and the basic formula for any index is, Index level = Σ (Price of stock* Number of shares)*free-float factor/ index divisor. The **free-float adjustment factor** represents the proportion of shares floated as a percentage of issued shares and then rounded up to the nearest multiple of 5 per cent for calculation purposes. To find the free-float capitalisation of a company, first find its market cap (number of outstanding shares × share price) then multiply its free-float factor. The free-float method, therefore, does not include restricted stocks, such as those held by company insiders.

The UK Blue Chip Index

The FTSE 100 is the big daddy of all UK-based indices. There are, it goes without saying, 100 stocks in the list and they comprise the largest quoted companies on the London Stock Exchange. It is also the main index for large, blue chip companies. Other key facts include:

1 Those 100 top stocks are valued at a total of £951bn – that's £951,000m.

2 The top 5 stocks are valued at a total of £33bn.

3 The top 10 stocks are valued at £13.4bn.

4 The bottom 50 stocks are valued at £105bn.

5 Some companies in this list have risen in value by more than 70 per cent in the last year, others have dropped by more than 80 per cent in the same year.

6 This volatility means that some stocks drop out of the FTSE 100 and some come in. This is done on a quarterly basis and means that the composition of the index is changing constantly.

7   The top stock, BP, comprises 9.6 per cent of the entire market cap while the bottom stock, investment group 3i, comprises just over 0.1 per cent of the entire market cap of the FTSE 100.

Should you track it? If you want to track the main market, with the largest, most liquid companies in the UK market, this is the index to use. But be aware that it is by its very nature heavily concentrated on the biggest companies, and many of those companies have a very strong foreign business presence. It is estimated that up to 60 per cent of the turnover of FTSE 100 companies is earned in either dollars or euros. Already you can see how certain distortions could affect your use of the index – it is clearly a mega-large-cap index where big companies dominate (think BP and HSBC, for instance) and foreign earnings are important. But if you aim to capture the bulk of the value of the UK market – and in particular its daily transaction value – nothing beats the FTSE 100. Crucially, you have also got a huge range of funds to invest in, mostly at very low cost.

Investors who want to access the FTSE 100 index face two main choices in terms of index tracking funds. The most popular and well-established route is to pick an index tracking unit trust. In the box below we have listed some of the main unit trust FTSE 100 trackers.

Fund	TER or annual management charge
F&C FTSE 100 Tracker 1	1%
Gartmore UK Index Ret Inc	1%
Halifax UK FTSE 100 Idx Tracking C	1.52%
HSBC FTSE 100 Index Ret Inc	1%
L&G UK 100 Index	0.84%
Marks & Spencer UK 100 Cos Inc	1%
Norwich Blue Chip Tracking 1	0.90%
RBS FTSE 100 Tracker ST	1%
Santander Stkmkt 100 Trk Gth	0.35%
Smith & Williamson Munro A Inc	0.75%
HSBC FTSE 250 Index Ret Inc	0.75%
Pru UK Index Tracker A Acc	1.64%

The other big alternative are the exchange traded funds – there are three main FTSE 100 index tracking ETFs, from iShares, Lyxor and Deutsche DBX. In our experience, both DBX and Lyxor tend to be cheaper in TER terms – we have broken out costs in the tables below – while iShares tends to run bigger, more established funds. By and large all the ETFs are cheaper than their unit trust siblings.

Fund	Lyxor FTSE 100	iShares FTSE 100	DBX FTSE 100
Ticker/EPIC	L100	ISF	XUKX
TER	0.30%	0.40%	0.30%

But cost is not the only factor – you also need to concern yourself with what the experts call tracking error. This is the difference between the underlying index and the fund returns. We have been measuring this closely and in the table below we have looked at the difference in returns over the 12 months to the beginning of March 2009. Over these 12 months, the FTSE 100 returned a loss of 35.74 per cent but underlying index trackers returned everything from –33.68 per cent to –36.83 per cent. The fund with the lowest tracking error was from iShares, with a tracking error or difference of just 0.21 per cent.

Name	Price % 1 year ago	Volatility	Difference
FTSE 100	**–35.74**	**1.21**	
ETF – Lyxor ETF FTSE 100	–34.7	2.05	1.04
ETF – iShares FTSE 100	–35.95	1.46	–0.21
Gartmore UK Index I	–35.23	1.78	0.51
Halifax UK FTSE 100 Idx Tracking C	–35.43	1.6	0.31
F&C FTSE 100 Tracker 1	–34.8	1.83	0.94
HSBC FTSE 100 Index Ret Inc	–36.83	1.83	–1.09
L&G UK 100 Index E Acc	–34.5	1.82	1.24
Liontrust Top 100	–35.85	1.8	–0.11
Marks & Spencer UK 100 Cos Inc	–34.89	1.93	0.85
Royal Bank of Scot FTSE 100 Trkr ST	–33.68	1.84	2.06
Santander Stkmkt 100 Trk Gth	–33.83	1.82	1.91

Funds to watch: You can also track the FTSE 100 using an inverse or bear tracker from Deutsche DBX Trackers, called XUKS, with a total expense ratio of 0.50 per cent. This is a simple tracker – for every 1 per cent move down in the index, you get a 1 per cent gain and vice versa, e.g. it makes money from a downwards move in the market. This is a potentially brilliant fund if you do not want the leverage of a covered warrant to make money on falling markets but still want to make money on the broad (downwards) directional move of the FTSE 100.

Investors might also be interested in a small UK unit trust tracker fund called The Munro Fund, run by a contributor to this book, Rob Davies. This tracks the constituents of the FTSE 100 but weights the shares in the portfolio by their total dividend payout, thus buying more shares in those paying out the most in dividends.

Fact File

The FTSE 100 – some handy facts

- The FTSE 100 is a market capitalisation-weighted index representing the performance of the 100 largest UK-listed large-cap or blue chip companies.

- All companies in the FTSE 100 must pass a test that looks at size in terms of market capitalisation and the availability or liquidity of their shares, i.e. only easy-to-purchase shares or investable shares are included. Constituents also need to have a full listing on the London Stock Exchange with a sterling- or euro-denominated price on the SETS electronic trading system. Most constituents must by law include the abbreviation 'plc' at the end of their name, indicating their status as a publicly limited corporation.

- The index represents just over 80 per cent of the entire market value of the various London-based stock exchanges.

- The index began on 3 January 1984 with a base level of 1000; the highest value reached to date is 6950.6, on 30 December 1999.

- The FTSE 100 is calculated in real time and the level of the index is published every 15 seconds. Trading lasts from 08.00–16.29 (when the closing auction starts), and closing values are taken at 16.35.

- The constituents of the index are determined quarterly. The larger companies in the adjacent index, the FTSE 250, are pushed up or promoted to the FTSE 100 index if they pass the tests above and their market cap goes above a certain level, which as I write (February 2009) is about £1.7bn in market cap.

FTSE All share

Volatility	1.11 (FTSE 100 1.21)
Weight of largest holding	BP 8.11%
Weight of top ten largest holdings	43.69%
Yield	4.8% as of March 2009

Returns

Index	2004	2005	2006	2007	2008
FTSE All Share	8.4%	18.02%	13.15%	2.03%	−32.78%

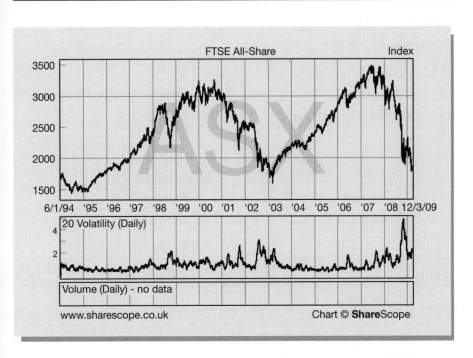

The Index – our analysis

ANALYSIS	
Likely Risk (High/Medium/Low)	Medium
Likely Volatility	Medium
Suitable for 'Simple' Investors i.e. small ISA investors	Yes
Diversification Risk with Top Holdings i.e. top three more than 20% of fund	No although top 3 companies comprise 19.73% of total index
Likely to be a core holding?	Yes
Market Cap based (MC)/Screened (S)	MC
Appeal to Income Investors?	Yes
Risk Factors?	Not enormously diversified and still blue chip focused
	High level of foreign earnings
Top 3 holding as % of total fund Mid March 2009	19.7%
Country Breakdown: top 3 – Mid March 2009	100% UK Listed but large foreign earnings for many companies in index
Sector Breakdown: top 3 – Mid March 2009	Oil and Gas 21.6%
	Healthcare 10.12%
	Banks 9%

Featured ETF funds

Details	ETF	ETF
Fund	Lyxor All Share	DBX FTSE All
Ticker/EPIC	LFAS	XASX
Issuer	Lyxor	Deutsche DBX
TER	0.40%	0.40%

Continued

Details	ETF	ETF
Annualised Tracking error % 2008	NA	NA
Currency	GBP	GBP
Launch Date	15/05/2007	18/06/2007

Featured unit trust tracker funds

Unit trust	Total expense ratio or annual management charge
Allianz RCM UK Index A	0.50%
AXA UK Tracker Ret Inc	1%
F&C FTSE All Share Tracker 1 Inc	0.39%
Fidelity Moneybuilder UK Index	0.28%
Gartmore UK Index I	0.50%
Halifax UK FTSE All Share Idx Trk C	1.50%
HSBC FTSE All Share Index A I Inc	0.64%
L&G (N) Tracker	1.00%
L&G UK Idx Tr Index	0.51%
M&G Index Tracker A Inc	0.46%
Norwich UK Index Tracking 1	0.90%
Threadneedle Navigator UK Index Trk	1.14%
Virgin UK Index Tracking	1%

Comments

The FTSE All-Share is perhaps the most important UK-based index. It is a market capitalisation-weighted index representing the performance of all eligible companies listed on the London Stock Exchange's main market, which pass a screening for size and liquidity. In total, the FTSE All-Share Index covers 689 companies – approximately 98 per cent of the UK's market capitalisation. The FTSE All-Share is also the aggregation of the

FTSE 100, FTSE 250 and FTSE small-cap indices. According to index developers FTSE group, 'The FTSE All-Share Index also accounts for 8.11 per cent of the world's equity market capitalisation.'

Many investors are confused by the FTSE 100 and the FTSE All Share index. They presume that the best way to track the broad market is via the FTSE 100 (the better-known index) whereas in fact the FTSE 100 index tracks the large-caps in the UK market. Which is not to say that the FTSE All-Share Index does not capture those large-caps as well – its composition is still weighted by the size of the market cap and the top 10 companies in the FTSE All Share comprise 43 per cent of the index as opposed to 52.4 per cent with the FTSE 100. So although the FTSE All casts a wider net, it is still very focused on mega-cap blue chips.

That said, the FTSE All index does capture a much broader range of companies and comprises the FTSE 100, the FTSE 250 and the members of the FTSE small-cap Index, but all weighted by market cap (which means that it is still dominated by the biggest FTSE 100 companies).

But there is another crucial point – the FTSE All is not actually ALL the market as the title implies. It does not include some really tiny companies that comprise the 'fag end' of the market, namely micro-caps in the FTSE Fledgling Index, i.e. really tiny companies valued at less than £10 million. There are many, many of these very small companies, but they do not really amount to much in 'economic size' or footprint so they are not covered by the FTSE All Share. So when you buy this index, do not think you are buying ALL the UK market – no one index captures that!

So FTSE 100 or FTSE All – which one should you invest in? If you want a broader market use the FTSE All, whereas if you want a more focused large-cap index go for the FTSE 100, but be aware that even the FTSE All is still, in reality, a large-cap index. Also, whatever you do *do not buy both* – you will be effectively duplicating a lot of the holdings and the FTSE All index tends to move in the same direction as the FTSE 100, so you will not get much diversification benefit.

As for the funds that track the index, they tend to split into two broad categories – a wide range of unit trust trackers and a small range of exchange traded funds. By and large, the ETFs tend to be cheaper and more effective at tracking the index, although the cheapest fund by far that tracks the FTSE All share is a unit trust index tracker from Fidelity, charging just 0.28 per cent per annum.

Name	Price % 1 year ago – March 2009	Volatility	Difference or tracking error in year to March 2009
FTSE All-Share	−36.61	1.11	
ETF – Lyxor All Share	−35.54	1.77	1.07
ETF – DBX Deutsche FTSE All Share	−36.61	2.09	0
F&C FTSE All Share Tracker 1 Inc	−37.62	1.73	−1.01
Fidelity Moneybuilder UK Index	−35.55	1.76	1.06
Halifax UK FTSE All Share Idx Trk C	−36.14	1.56	0.47
HSBC FTSE All Share Idx A Inc	−37.75	1.68	−1.14
Threadneedle Navigator UK Index Trk	−35.59	1.75	1.02
Virgin UK Index Tracking	−35.96	1.86	0.65

FTSE 250 – UK mid caps

Volatility	0.93 (FTSE All share index is 1.11) i.e. this index is less volatile than the FTSE All Share Index
Weight of largest holding	Foreign and Colonial Investment Trust at 1.27%
Weight of top ten largest holdings	10.59%
Yield % March 2009	3.84%

Returns

Index	2004	2005	2006	2007	2008
FTSE 250	18.9%	26.8%	27.1%	−5.8%	−40.3%

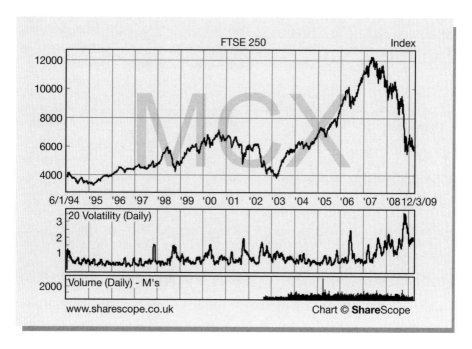

The index – our analysis

ANALYSIS	
Likely Risk (High/Medium/Low)	Medium
Likely Volatility	Medium
Suitable for 'Simple' Investors i.e. small ISA investors	Yes
Diversification Risk with Top Holdings i.e. top three more than 20% of fund	No – very well diversified
Likely to be a core holding?	Yes
Market Cap based (MC)/Screened (S)	MC
Appeal to Income Investors?	Yes
Risk Factors?	Very focused on the UK economy
Top 3 holding as % of total fund mid March 2009	3.5%

Continued

ANALYSIS

Country Breakdown: top 3 – mid March 2009	100% UK listed
Sector Breakdown: top 3 – mid March 2009	Financial Services 28%
	Industrials 25%
	Travel and Leisure 7.96%

Featured ETFs

Details

Fund	Lyxor FTSE 250	iShares FTSE 250	DBX FTSE 250
Ticker/EPIC	L250	MIDD	XMCX
Issuer	Lyxor	iShares Barclays	Deutsche DBX
TER	0.35%	0.40%	0.35%
Annualised Tracking error % last year	NA	0.48%	NA
Currency	GBP	GBP	GBP
Underlying Index	FTSE 250	FTSE 250	FTSE 250
Underlying currency risk	No	No	No
Number of holdings			
Fund value mid 2008 (M)			
Launch Date	15/05/2007	26/03/2004	18/06/2007

Featured unit trust tracker

Fund	*Annual management charge*
HSBC FTSE 250 Index Ret Inc	0.75%

Comments

The FTSE 250 Index is another of the big market capitalisation-weighted indices, this time covering the 'mid-capitalised companies' traded on the London Stock Exchange. According to its developers, the FTSE Group, 'the Index is designed to measure the performance of the mid-cap capital and industry segments of the UK market not covered by the large-cap FTSE 100 Index, which pass screening for size and liquidity' and represents approximately 15 per cent of the UK stock market capitalisation.

What are you buying when you invest in a FTSE 250 index fund? This hugely underrated and arguably under-reported index offers investors three big plays – the UK as an economy, growth companies and enormous diversification. It is also worth noting that over much of the first decade of the twenty-first century the index has also offered better returns with lower volatility. The FTSE 250 index is a crucial index in our view because it is very much focused on UK plc as an economy, with companies that will genuinely capture the future growth potential of the British economy, with sterling earnings. Obviously in a recession, that UK focus is something of a weakness and the larger-cap indices with their globally diversified components seem like a safer play, but many investors are unsure about what exactly it is they are buying with something like the FTSE 100. Is this large-cap index really capturing any broad trend except globalisation?

The FTSE 250 also tends to be jam packed with faster growing companies, many of them having risen from the FTSE small-cap index, with more than a few on their way up into the FTSE 100. Again that growth profile is also a weakness in bear markets as growth companies can find themselves going ex growth, with the inevitable consequences for the share price. We are also strongly attracted by the diversification on offer in this index – those 250 companies (actually many index trackers have 252 funds) include a huge range of companies and the top holdings comprise much less than 5 per cent of the total index value.

There are also some equally obvious weaknesses. It is very focused on financial companies and there are a large number of big investment trusts that tend to dominate the index alongside a chunky number of industrials. Should you buy it? Our feeling is that the FTSE 250 is one for more risk-friendly investors who do not mind taking on the potential for greater rewards. It tends to rise faster and fall faster than its bigger siblings (the FTSE 100 and the All-Share. As for funds, there is one major unit trust tracker from HSBC plus three cheaper ETFs from iShares, Lyxor and Deutsche, all less than 0.50 per cent.

FTSE All Stocks Gilt

Volatility	0.57
Weight of largest holding	5.45%
Weight of top ten largest holdings	44.69%
Yield as March 13th 2009 (flat yield)	4.3%

Returns

Index	2004	2005	2006	2007	2008
FTSE British Government All Stocks	6.60%	7.90%	0.70%	1.9%	7.5%

Note: this graph is only for the iShares ETF not for the index.

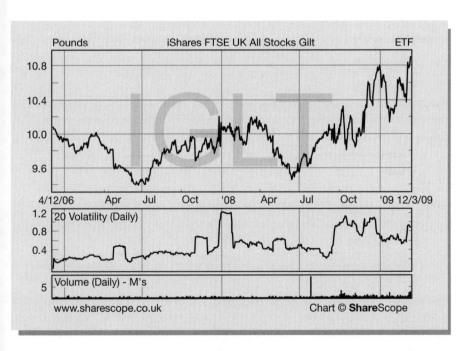

The index – our analysis

ANALYSIS	
Likely Risk (High/Medium/Low)	Low
Likely Volatility	Low
Suitable for 'Simple' Investors i.e. small ISA investors	Yes
Diversification Risk with Top Holdings i.e. top three more than 20% of fund	No
Likely to be a core holding?	Yes
Market Cap based (MC)/Screened (S)	MC
Appeal to Income Investors?	Yes
Risk Factors?	Very, very low risk of government default
Top 3 holding as % of total fund mid March 2009	15%
Country Breakdown: top 3 – mid March 2009	100% UK listed
Sector Breakdown: top 3 – mid March 2009	100% UK conventional gilts

Listed ETF

Details	
Fund	iShares FTSE UK All Stocks Gilt
Ticker/EPIC	IGLT
Issuer	iShares Barclays
TER	0.20%
Annualised Tracking error % in 2007	0.22%
Currency	GBP
Underlying currency risk	No
Number of holdings	30
Fund value March 2009 (M)	£330
Launch Date	01/12/2006

Top ten holdings in iShares ETF end March 2009

Gilt	Coupon %	Maturity	Price	% of index
TREASURY 8% 2021	8	07/06/21	148.76	5.45
TREASURY 5% Mar 7 2012	5	07/03/2012	108.75	4.9
TREASURY 5% Sep 7 2014	5	07/09/2014	114.86	4.59
TREASURY 4.25% Mar 7 2011	4.25	07/03/2011	105.66	4.57
TREASURY 4.5% Mar 7 2013	4.5	07/03/2013	108.94	4.55
TREASURY 4.75% Jun 7 2010	4.75	07/06/2010	104.72	4.3
TREASURY 5% Mar 7 2018	5	07/03/2018	117.97	4.28
TREASURY 4% Sep 7 2016	4	07/09/2016	110.44	4.05
TREASURY 4.75% Sep 7 2015	4.75	07/09/2015	114.85	4
TREASURY 4.75% Dec 7 2038	4.75	07/12/1938	114.75	4
Holdings by year				
15 years or more				**37.94%**
5 to 10 years				**31.99%**
5 years or less				**30.07%**

Source: iShares

Comments

This index's full title is actually the FTSE Actuaries Government Securities UK Gilts All Stock Index. It gives exposure to a diversified basket of UK government bonds, across all maturities, all in the conventional space, i.e. there are no index-linked holdings within this exclusively sterling-denominated fund. That makes this index a brilliant tool for buying into a diversified basket of what are called conventional government securities, otherwise known as gilts.

The index is not well known for sure and there is currently only one ETF that tracks it, but we view this as an absolutely core holding for all but the most adventurous investor. Why? If you want bonds exposure, your safest bet is probably gilts and if you want the best basket of sterling gilts this index gives you that in spades. What's even better is that the lonely iShares ETF that covers this index is incredibly cheap – the total expense ratio is just 0.20 per cent. You should not buy into this index if you think inflation is about to shoot up though – in that case the UK index-linked variant is probably a better idea.

The Wider iShares bond family

It is worth noting that iShares boasts a much wider range of bond/fixed-income security index tracking funds or ETFs, offering investors access to everything from global government inflation bonds to UK corporate bonds. In the box we have listed all the main ones available in Spring 2009.

Details			
Fund	iShares JPMorgan $ Emerging Markets Bond Fund	iShares $ Treasury Bond 1 – 3	iShares $ TIPS
Ticker/EPIC	SEMB	IBTS	ITPS
TER	0.45%	0.20%	0.25%
Annualised Tracking error % 2007	NA	0.25%	0.25%
Currency	GBP	GBP	GBP
Underlying Index	JPMorgan EMBI Global Core Index	Barclays US Treasury 1–3 year Index	Barclays US Government Inflation Linked Bond Index
Launch Date	15/02/2008	02/06/2006	08/12/2006

Details					
Fund	iShares Euro Inflation Linked Bond	iShares Global Inflation Linked Bond	iShares $ Corporate Bond	iShares Euro Corporate Bond	iShares £ Corporate Bond
Ticker/EPIC	IBCI	SGIL	IODE	IBCX	SLXX
TER	0.25%	0.25%	0.20%	0.20%	0.20%
Annualised Tracking error % 2007	0.08%	NA	NA	0.09%	0.59%

Continued

Details					
Currency	GBP	GBP	USD	Euro	GBP
Underlying Index	Barclays Euro Government Inflation Linked Bond Index	Barclays World Government Inflation Linked Bond Index	iBoxx USD Liquid Investment Grade Top 30	Markit iBoxx Euro Liquid Corporates Index	Markit iBoxx Sterling Liquid Corporate Long Dated Bond Index
Launch Date	10/11/2005	01/08/2008	16/05/2003	17/03/2003	26/03/2004

The indices used in the wider iShares Bond range – definitions

The **JPMorgan EMBI Global Core Index** represents debt obligations issued in US dollars (USD) by sovereign and quasi-sovereign entities of emerging market countries. The US dollar-denominated index is a highly recognised benchmark for sovereign and quasi-sovereign emerging market bonds including both fixed- and floating-rate instruments. The methodology of the index is designed to distribute the weights of each country within the index by limiting the weights of countries with higher debt outstanding and reallocating this excess to countries with lower debt outstanding.

The **Barclays US Government Inflation-linked Bond Index** (US TIPS) measures the performance of the TIPS market. It is the largest market in the Barclays Global Inflation-Linked Bond Index. Inflation-linked indices include only capital indexed bonds with a remaining maturity of one year or more. Bonds must be capital-indexed and linked to an eligible inflation index. They should be denominated in US dollars and pay coupon and principal in US dollars.

Barclays Euro Government Inflation Linked Bond Index measures the performance of the euro-zone government index-linked bond market with securities from Germany, France, Italy and Greece.

The **Barclays World Government Inflation-Linked Bond Index** measures the performance of the major government inflation-linked bond markets. The index is designed to include only those markets in which a global government linker fund is likely to invest. To be included, a market must have aggregate issuance of $4bn or more and have minimum rating of A3/A– for G7 and euro-zone issuers, Aa3/AA– otherwise. Markets included in the index, in the order of inclusion, are the UK, Australia, Canada, Sweden, the US, France, Italy, Japan, Germany and Greece.

The **iBoxx USD Liquid Investment Grade Top 30 Index** is a basket of 30 bonds, rebalanced quarterly following the close of the market on the last business day of February, May, August and November each year. It is designed to provide balanced representation of the US dollar investment-grade corporate market by the means of the most liquid corporate bonds available.

This range of corporate and government bond from iShares is market leading and hugely innovative – many if not most of them deserve to sit at the heart of any portfolio. Their biggest strength is their sheer range, taking in everything from index-linked government bonds through to sterling corporate bonds from the most reputable issuers. In particular, different funds will recommend themselves to different kinds of investors.

- As we have already noted, every investor should at least consider investing something in the FTSE All Stocks Gilts fund. It is an absolutely core holding in any mixed bonds/equity portfolio.

- Bearish investors worried by the growth of inflation in the future should opt for the index-linked funds, with most investors recommended to focus on either the UK variant or the global fund, which is also a great investment idea.

- Investors looking for a superior yield should look at the range of corporate bond funds and most probably the sterling variant. This is currently paying out a flat yield of over 67.85 per cent (spring 2009). Be aware though that corporate bonds can move in sympathy with equities and if corporate defaults gather pace this fund could be in for a hard time as capital values fall – it is not a great hiding place in a recession, unlike most traditional gilts.

- Investors looking for a slightly riskier bet may want to look at the emerging markets bond fund, which pays a chunky 7.86 per cent in flat yield (spring 2009). Emerging market bonds have shot up in value for prime low-risk countries in recent years and there is every chance that as the credit reputation of countries like Brazil and Russia improves, capital prices could go back up again.

This range of funds is also dirt cheap in our opinion – all but one of the funds charge less than 0.30 per cent. The only fund to charge above that level is the emerging markets fund, which is a tad expensive with a TER of 0.45 per cent, but even that is good value considering its range of investments in emerging markets bonds.

Risks? Of course there is no free lunch in modern investment and although these funds should by and large do well in bearish equity markets (with the exception maybe of corporate bond funds), they will all probably lag if shares start booming. Also be aware that if inflation does evaporate and turn into deflation, index-linked bonds may suffer.

UK small-cap

Volatility	0.67
Weight of largest holding	0.902%
Weight of top ten largest holdings	7%
Yield at March 13th 2009	

Returns

Index	2004	2005	2006	2007	2008
FTSE small-cap Index	11%	19.8%	18.2%	−12.9%	−48.80%

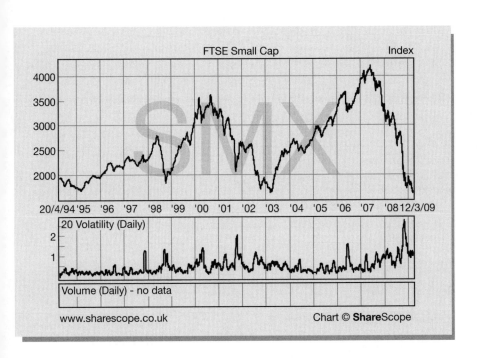

The index – our analysis

ANALYSIS	
Likely Risk (High/Medium/Low)	High
Likely Volatility	High
Suitable for 'Simple' Investors i.e. small ISA investors	Yes
Diversification Risk with Top Holdings i.e. top three more than 20% of fund	No
Likely to be a core holding?	Yes
Market Cap based (MC)/Screened (S)	MC
Appeal to Income Investors?	No
Top 3 holding as % of total fund Mid March 2009	Under 3%
Country Breakdown: top 3 – mid March 2009	100% UK Listed

Top ten holdings

Company	Weighting %
Thus Group	0.902
Cranswick	0.826
Dechra Pharma	0.724
Drewin Dolphin	0.719
Quintain Estates	0.713
Graphite Inv Trust	0.711
JPMorgan American Investment Trust	0.708
Redrow	0.706
SDL	0.706
Alternative Investment Strategies	0.701
TOTAL for TOP 10	7.416

Details as at 30th September 2008

Comments

The FTSE small-cap Index consists of companies outside the FTSE 350 Index – smaller companies – and represents approximately 2–3 per cent of the UK market capitalisation with an aggregate value of anything between £25bn and £50bn.

In the US, small-cap indices like the Russell 2000 are big business – dozens of funds (tracker or otherwise) follow the small-cap segment of the US market. In the UK, by contrast, small-cap investing is exclusively the preserve of actively managed funds – there are no small-cap index trackers in the UK and not one ETF or unit trust tracker follows the all-important FTSE small-cap Index or the FTSE Fledgling Index, which tracks really small companies that are not big enough to make it into the FTSE small-cap Index. This absence of small-cap tracker funds in the UK is a huge pity because small-cap investing works – academic evidence points to the fact that small-cap investing delivers superior returns over the long term despite the increased risks.

There is one niche fund worth examining before we look at that academic evidence – the Gartmore Fledgling Trust Ltd. This is an unusual creature. It is a listed investment trust that largely tracks the constituents of the FTSE Fledgling Index of tiny micro-cap stocks. This little-known index tracks any company that does not make it into the FTSE All Share because it is too small – companies in the index make up some £10bn by value of listed securities on the London Stock Exchange's main market and constitute 22 per cent by number of listed UK stocks. The Gartmore investment trust follows this index but then adds it own special twist – an actively managed overlay. At least 65 per cent of the portfolio is managed on an indexed basis while an active overlay is then applied to up to 35 per cent of the portfolio, including a maximum of 20 per cent invested in AIM stocks that meet the Fledgling market capitalisation criteria and were formerly traded on the main market. According to the fund managers, the active 'overlay overweights fledgling and AIM companies favoured by Gartmore's active investment process, as well as firms where directors have recently bought their own shares. Conversely, any Fledgling constituents that appear insolvent on a one-year view are not held'. This is a very unusual strategy and means that you are, in effect, buying into a hybrid passive index tracking/active small-cap fund, all with a relatively low expense ratio of just 0.8 per cent.

Why small-cap investing works

The most potent piece of evidence comes in the shape of a joint London Business School/ABN Amro study, run by Professors Elroy Dimson and Paul Marsh a few years back, on a rival small-cap index, called the HGSC index – the Hoare Govett small-cap – and its sister HG1000 index. The HGSC index (it represents the bottom 10 per cent by market cap) and the HG1000 (the bottom 2 per cent by market cap) have been 'live' for over 18 years, but Dimson and Marsh have pushed their analysis way back to 1955. Their conclusions are startling. Both the HGSC and the HG1000 have outperformed the FTSE All Share by 3.5 per cent and 5.7 per cent per annum respectively on an annualised return basis for more than 40 years. In simple terms that outperformance means that £1000 invested in the HGSC in 1955 would today be worth £1.8 million, vs £400,000 with the FTSE All-Share (with dividends reinvested in both cases). If you had opted for the HG1000 index your returns would be even greater – £4.6 million.

What seems to work in the UK also seems to work globally. James O'Shaughnessy in his research for 'What Works on Wall Street' found that really tiny stocks, measured by market value and called micro-stocks, deliver by far the biggest returns. In the 45 years between 1951 and 1996 these micro-caps delivered a compounded annual return of 35 per cent.

December 31 1996 value of $10,000 invested on December 31 1951 excl microcaps in millions		compounded annual returns	Sharpe adjusted risk return index by market cap 1951–1996 (higher is better)
All stocks	2.7	14.97%	49
Large stocks	1.6	13.11%	48
Small stocks	3.8	16.30%	50
S&P 500	1.7	13.39%	48
> $1 billion	1.6	13.18%	48
500m to 1 bn	1.9	14.04%	47
250–500m	3.4	15.90%	50
100m to 250m	3.4	16.51%	46
25m to 100m	7.8	19.75%	48
microcap	NA	35.93%	64

Source: 'What works on Wall Street', James O'Shaughnessy

Even after adjusting this return for the much greater risk taken on board (he uses a measure called the sharpe adjusted risk return) microcaps delivered the biggest return by far.

Small-caps grow faster

What is behind this consistent outperformance? The best answer is probably the simplest – it is much easier for a small company to grow really fast than a huge company. Call it the investing equivalent of gravity. The hard evidence comes in the table below from the CompanyREFs guide. It shows the average earnings growth rates of companies in different indices, ranging from the microcaps of the FTSE Fledgling through to the FTSE 100.

What is interesting is that small-cap shares consistently outperform both the FTSE 100 and FTSE 250 sectors both in projected earnings growth for the coming year and over the last three and five years. But the Fledgling index – the one that contains really very small companies – has produced much lower returns. These classic micro-caps have turned in some decent five-year EPS growth rates, but over the last five years, average EPS growth has been *negative*.

	All figures are median figures				
Measure	*Market*	*FTSE 100*	*Mid 250*	*Small-Cap*	*Fledgling*
Prospective EPS growth rate % current year	8.62	9.02	10.6	11.3	5.31
3 year EPS growth rate	14.7	11	8.68	12.9	11.3
5 year EPS growth rate	7.91	5.54	7.29	7.35	−1.33

Source: CompanyREFS – Hemington Scott

It's all about risk … and containing it

The huge variation in earnings growth between the small-caps index and those from the micro-caps is easily answered – risk. Micro-caps tend not to have an enormously proven business trading record and many fail completely – they simply vanish without trace.

Returns can also be hugely variable. Since the HGSC index went live there have been negative returns in five years and positive returns in thirteen. There are also some other less obvious problems with investing in small-caps. Small-caps suffer from a distinct sector bias. Because small-caps are by definition valued at no more than £500m in the UK there are no banks or tobacco companies. There are also remarkably few utility stocks and life assurers and there is even a paucity of oil and gas stocks. More importantly O'Shaughnessy himself has noted that the small-cap returns he obtained in his analysis can be 'chimera' because the only way to achieve those returns was to 'to invest a few million dollars in over 2000 stocks'.

That practical issue of capturing the small-cap effect suggests one reason why no one has yet to launch a UK small-cap ETF – it is simply too difficult and expensive to do.

FTSE World exc UK

Volatility	2.12
Weight of largest holding	2.66% (Exxon)
Weight of top ten largest holdings	11.12%
Yield	3.18%

Returns

Index	2004	2005	2006	2007	2008
FTSE World exc UK	NA	NA	6.38%	11.24%	−18.47%

Note: graph is Deutsche DBX Tracker FTSE world exc UK index ETF and not the actual index.

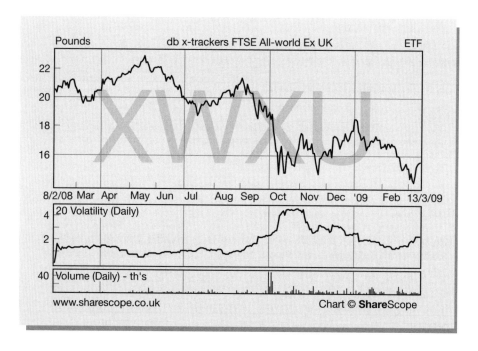

The index – our analysis

ANALYSIS	
Likely Risk (High/Medium/Low)	Low to Medium
Likely Volatility	Low
Suitable for 'Simple' Investors i.e. small ISA investors	Yes
Diversification Risk with Top Holdings i.e. top three more than 20% of fund	No
Likely to be a core holding?	Yes
Market Cap based (MC)/Screened (S)	MC
Appeal to Income Investors?	Yes
Risk Factors?	It invests in global equities and has no bond component
Top 3 holding as % of total fund March 2009	4.5%
Country Breakdown: top 3 – April 2009	US 46.6%
Japan 10%	
Sector Breakdown: top 3 – April 2009	Financials 18.8% Industrials 12.2% Consumer Goods 11.70%

Comments

Here is a simple idea – rather than buy lots of different developed world markets (the US, Europe and Japan, for instance), why not buy into one fund that tracks a big, well-known index of nearly all the developed world's stock markets? That's the idea behind a small band of ETFs that is a compelling proposition for private investors – you can buy the world developed markets outside of the UK and then add to that vast diversity of companies by investing in one of the UK main market trackers (FTSE 100 or FTSE All). With just two funds you would have access to the vast majority of the world's stock markets.

These global equity indices come in two guises. The most common is based around an index called the MSCI World Index, which includes the UK market (about 10 per cent of total holdings) and is focused on the world's developed exchanges. Its potentially more compelling rival is the FTSE World exc UK Index. This index excludes the UK, which is useful for investors looking to add diversity to their portfolios, although the net effect on the composition of the two indices is not that great. Note also that these indices track only equities – not bonds – and are focused on developed world markets and blue chips in particular.

Global Equity funds from iShares, Lyxor and DBX

ETF fund	ETF Ticker	Currency	TER	INDEX
DBX MSCI World	XMWO	GBP	0.45%	MSCI World
DBX FTSE All World Ex UK	XMXU	GBP	0.40%	FTSE World exc UK
Lyxor ETF MSCI World	LWOR	GBP	0.45%	MSCI World
iShares MSCI World	IWRD	GBP	0.50%	MSCI World

So, which of these global equities ETFs should you consider buying? As we have already noted above, our preference is to buy an ETF that invests globally but avoids the UK, which is why we like the DBX FTSE All World exc UK ETF with a TER of just 0.40 per cent. We think that most investors are already rather too biased towards UK stocks and so this fund should fit the bill. What is even better in our view is that all of these funds are very diversified – in both cases (the MSCI World and FTSE All World) you are buying into a portfolio of companies where the top three companies comprise only between 5 per cent and 9 per cent of the total holdings. There is one downside though – you are buying a heavy mix of US stocks which comprise between 40 per cent and 50 per cent of total holdings. This may worry some UK investors concerned about exposure to the US, although we would say it is simply a reflection of what happens on the global equity markets. If you want to buy exposure in a slightly more balanced way, you could assemble an ETF portfolio that included a FTSE All UK tracker, a Eurozone tracker (the DJ Eurostoxx 50) and the MSCI USA fund – all in equal portions.

Alternatively we think it is possible to build a very simple, four-fund portfolio using either of these global funds, a FTSE All Share Tracker, an MSCI

Emerging Markets index fund and a global government bonds fund. Bundle up these four funds and you would have a diversified multi-asset, international portfolio on the cheap – the combined expense should not be more than 0.4 per cent per annum.

FTSE World exc UK – Top Ten Holdings – Mid March 2009

Exxon Mobil	2.36%
Nestle SA	1.13%
Total	1.10%
Microsoft	1.04%
AT&T	1.00%
Wal-Mart Stores	1.00%
Johnson & Johnson	0.94%
Procter & Gamble	0.93%
Chevron	0.89%
IBM	0.84%

MSCI Top Ten World Holdings – Mid March 2009

Security	% Weight
EXXON MOBIL CORP	2.66
PROCTER & GAMBLE CO	1.08
JOHNSON & JOHNSON	0.99
NESTLE SA-REG	0.98
CHEVRON CORP	0.98
AT&T INC	0.94
BP PLC	0.94
MICROSOFT CORP	0.91
INTL BUSINESS MACHINES CORP	0.83
GENERAL ELECTRIC CO	0.81

DJ EuroStoxx 50 – European Shares

All data from March 2009

Volatility	30 day volatility at 34.12% as of 13th March 2009
Weight of largest holding	7.70% (Total)
Weight of top ten largest holdings	44%
Yield	4.41% as of March 2009

Returns

Index	2004	2005	2006	2007	2008
DJ EuroStoxx 50	6.90%	21.28%	15.12%	6.79%	–44%

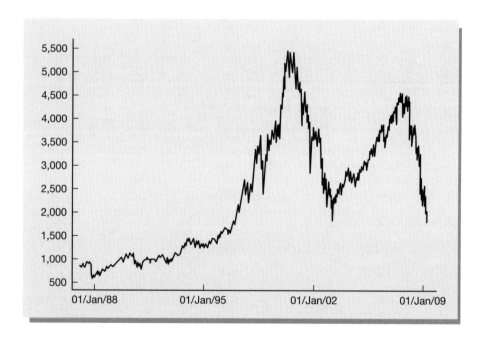

The index – our analysis

ANALYSIS	
Likely Risk (High/Medium/Low)	High
Likely Volatility	Medium to high
Suitable for 'Simple' Investors i.e. small ISA investors with small portfolios	Yes
Diversification Risk with Top Holdings i.e. top three more than 20% of fund	No
Likely to be a core holding?	Yes
Market Cap based (MC)/Screened (S)	MC
Appeal to Income Investors?	Yes
Risk Factors?	Euro zone markets, so some currency risk Underlying companies have strong export bias
Top 3 holding as % of total mid March 2009	17%
Country Breakdown: top 3 – mid March 2009	France 37% Germany 28% Spain 14.6%
Sector Breakdown: top 3 – mid March 2009	Banks 14% Telecoms 13% Oil and Gas 12.4%

Highlighted Europe (ETF) funds from iShares, Lyxor and DBX

Fund	EPIC	Currency	TER	Underlying Index
DBX EuroSTOXX 50	XESX	GBP	0.15%	DJ EuroSTOXX 50
DBX MSCI Europe	XMEU	GBP	0.30%	FTSE 250
iShares MSCI Europe	IMEU	GBP	0.35%	MSCI Europe

Continued

Fund	EPIC	Currency	TER	Underlying Index
iShares MSCI Europe exc UK	IEUX	GBP	0.40%	MSCI Europe exc UK
iShares DJ STOXX 50	EUN	GBP	0.35%	DJ STOXX 50
iShares DJ EuroSTOXX 50	EUE	GBP	0.15%	DJ EuroSTOXX 50
iShares FTSEurofirst 80	IEUR	GBP	0.40%	FTSEurofirst 80
iShares FTSEurofirst 100	IEUT	GBP	0.40%	FTSEEurofirst 100

Comments

The DJ EuroStoxx 50 has an ever so slightly snazzy-sounding ring to it, conjuring up images of smoky 1970s, Euro Disco, but the reality of this bellwether index is rather different. The DJ EuroStoxx 50 is the biggest and probably the most tracked European index for Eurozone blue chip outfits like Total or Siemens. According to index developer Dow Jones, 'it captures approximately 60 per cent of the free-float market capitalisation of the Dow Jones Euro Stoxx Total Market Index (TMI), which in turn covers approximately 95 per cent of the free-float market capitalisation of [Eurozone] countries'. It aims 'to provide a blue-chip representation of ... leaders in the Eurozone' and includes companies from Austria, Belgium, Finland, France, Germany, Greece, Ireland, Italy, Luxembourg, the Netherlands, Portugal and Spain.

Before working out whether you should buy (or short) this index as part of your portfolio, it is important to understand that the DJ EuroStoxx 50 is one of many popular blue chip indices on offer, with rival indices (and accompanying index tracking funds) from both the FTSE Group and MSCI. The first key distinction is between those like the MSCI Europe index and the FTSEurofirst 100 index that include countries such as the UK and Switzerland which sit outside the Euro zone. The DJ Eurostoxx 50 (alongside the FTSEurofirst 80 index) by contrast includes only companies from inside the Euro zone and excludes all UK and Swiss stocks (as well as nearly all Nordic companies). Just to confuse matters, the MSCI Europe excluding the UK index, used by ETF provider iShares, excludes the UK but includes all other European markets, including those outside the Eurozone. Our advice for most UK-based investors is to avoid any fund that is European by title but still invests in UK companies – you will probably already have a bias towards UK stocks in your portfolio and indices like the FTSEurofirst 100 will simply increase that bias if only because 41 per cent of the stocks in this European-wide index are British.

DJ EuroStoxx 50 composition as at end of February 2009

Sector Weightings %	
14.7	Banks
13.0	Telecommunications
12.4	Oil & Gas
12.4	Utilities
8.1	Insurance
6.3	Chemicals
5.1	Industrial Goods & Services
5.0	Technology
4.1	Food & Beverage
4.1	Health Care
3.8	Automobiles & Parts
3.6	Personal & Household Goods
2.2	Media
1.9	Construction & Materials
1.6	Retail
1.1	Basic Resources
0.7	Financial Services

Company Weight (%)	
TOTAL	7.70
TELEFONICA	5.90
SANOFI-AVENTIS	4.14
BCO SANTANDER	3.83
ENI	3.78
E.ON	3.68
FRANCE TELECOM	3.31
SIEMENS	3.22
GDF SUEZ	3.20
BAYER	2.85
NOKIA	2.79

Country Weightings %	
37.3	France
28.5	Germany
14.6	Spain
10.8	Italy
5.0	Netherlands
2.8	Finland
1.1	Luxembourg

Composition of related European indices as at Mid March 2009

FTSEurofirst 80	% weight	FTSEurofirst 100	% weight	MSCI Europe	% weight
TOTAL SA	7.11	BP PLC	4.6	NESTLE SA-REG	2.94
TELEFONICA SA	5.43	TOTAL SA	4.5	BP PLC	2.92
BANCO SANTANDER SA	3.17	TELEFONICA SA	3.43	TOTAL SA	2.4

Continued

FTSEurofirst 80	% weight	FTSEurofirst 100	% weight	MSCI Europe	% weight
GDF SUEZ	3.15	VODAFONE GROUP PLC	3.29	ROCHE HOLDING AG-GENUSSCHEIN	2.2
SIEMENS AG-REG	3.12	ROYAL DUTCH SHELL PLC-A SHS	3.1	VODAFONE GROUP PLC	2.18
SANOFI-AVENTIS	3.1	GLAXOSMITH-KLINE PLC	2.93	NOVARTIS AG-REG	2.15
ENI SPA	2.96	HSBC HOLDINGS PLC	2.67	GLAXOSMITH-KLINE PLC	2.13
E.ON AG	2.73	ROYAL DUTCH SHELL PLC-B SHS	2.29	HSBC HOLDINGS PLC	2.05
FRANCE TELECOM SA	2.71	BANCO SANTANDER SA	2.01	ROYAL DUTCH SHELL PLC-A SHS	1.93
NOKIA OYJ	2.46	GDF SUEZ	1.99	TELEFONICA SA	1.68

The next key distinction is in number of shares listed – the DJ Eurostoxx 50 is by definition focused on just the top 50 companies, the FTSEurofirst on the top 80 and the FTSEurofirst 100 on the top 100. That concentration on top companies matters because the top three stocks in the DJ Eurostoxx index account for just under 17 per cent of the fund whereas in the MSCI Europe exc UK Index they account for less than 8 per cent.

So, if you are after an index that tracks only Eurozone blue chips – and only the biggest – the DJ Eurostoxx 50 is probably the index for you. Luckily both iShares and DBX have funds that charge an impressive 0.15 per cent per annum for a basket of big blue chip shares with a strong French and German bias. These DJ Eurostoxx ETFs are a bargain compared with virtually any active fund manager who will probably own roughly the same set of companies and charge you at least an extra 1 per cent per annum for the privilege. It is also worth noting that there are a small number of unit trust-based funds that track Euroland companies but they all charge at least another 0.50 per cent per annum for the privilege of using a unit trust wrapper. It is also worth adding that if you want to stay focused on the Eurozone countries but with a slightly wider basket of shares that includes the 80 largest companies, you might want to consider looking at the iShares FTSEurofirst 80 ETF with a TER of just 0.4 per cent.

Money Market Funds

Volatility	0.50 – Very Low
Weight of largest holding	NR – see note below
Weight of top ten largest holdings	NR – see note below
Yield	NR – see note below

Returns

Index	*2004*	*2005*	*2006*	*2007*	*2008*
SONIA index	4.44%	4.70%	4.81%	5.76%	3.91%

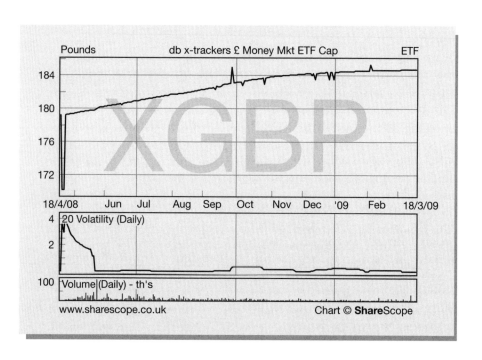

The index – our analysis

ANALYSIS	
Likely Risk (High/Medium/Low)	Low
Likely Volatility	Low
Suitable for 'Simple' Investors i.e. small ISA investors	Yes
Diversification Risk with Top Holdings i.e. top three more than 20% of fund	No
Likely to be a core holding?	Yes
Market Cap based (MC)/Screened (S)	MC
Total return or pays income? TR/Inc	TR – rolls up into index and the ETF
Appeal to Income Investors?	No – does not make a payout

Comments

It is very unlikely that many private investors will have heard of an index called SONIA, which is a pity because it is a supremely important index if you happen to be in the banking game. The SONIA index is absolutely critical to the working of the UK financial system because it tells investors – and banks – what interest they can expect from overnight holdings of sterling cash. In essence, it is a proxy for the return on cash – or as the academics might say, it is the risk-free rate of return because it is the return from offering your cash overnight to the banks (though that may not strike all readers as an absolutely risk-free exercise, given the recent banking collapse). In technical terms the SONIA Total Return Index 'reflects a daily rolled deposit earning the SONIA rate (the Sterling Overnight Index Average), which is the short-term money market reference in the UK', according to ETF provider Deutsche DBX Trackers. 'The Sterling Overnight Index Average is the weighted average rate of all unsecured sterling overnight cash transactions brokered in London … with all counter parties in a minimum deal size of £25 million. SONIA is sponsored by the Wholesale Markets Brokers' Association (WMBA).'

You may also have noticed two key extra words in the index title – total returns. This index of returns from overnight sterling cash does not pay an income – the sterling deposits tracked by this index are compounded (reinvested) daily and the compounding is done every day during the year. So, do not buy into any vehicle that tracks this index expecting to receive an income – you will receive that income, but that return will come from capital gains rolled up over the period of your holding.

Why invest in a product that tracks this index? In simple terms, this is an alternative to holding cash in your portfolio. You do not have to rely on your investment provider working out what laughable rate they will pay you – you get the market return they would get if they invested their money on the markets. Banks borrow from each other if they do not have the exact funds and they use the SONIA index as their reference point. It also moves up and down with interest rates – when interest rates are low, this index will offer a low return and vice versa.

Currently there is only one fund provider with an ETF that tracks this index – Deutsche DBX Trackers, with details in the box below.

Details	
Fund	DBX Sterling Money Market ETF
Ticker/EPIC	XGBP
Issuer	Deutsche DBX
TER	0.15%
Currency	GBP
Underlying Index	SONIA Total Return Index
Launch Date	09/04/2008

As ETFs go, this Deutsche fund is a great idea, but with one big proviso – it cannot be used in an ISA. We really like this ETF because of its simplicity – Deutsche uses derivatives and options to mimic the underlying action of buying into a basket of short-term deposit accounts (money market accounts) and then pays out the return to holders of the ETF.

Obviously there are two big provisos, worth repeating. The first is that point about total returns – the interest is paid out as part of the total market value of the fund (which goes up every day in value because of that accrued inter-est), not as dividend cheque. The second key point to consider is that this cannot be used in a maxi ISA – it can be used only in a mini-cash ISA because of the tax rules, which is a real shame in our humble opinion. Nevertheless, if you are looking for a cash alternative to hold some reserves, or an alternative vehicle to gilts funds, this is definitely one to consider. It is also worth noting that there is an equivalent US dollar money market ETF. According to Deutsche this separate index reflects a daily rolled deposit earning the federal funds effective rate, which is the short-term money market reference in the US. The federal funds rate is decided at Federal Open Market Committee (FOMC) meetings. Again the interest paid is compounded – according to DB the deposits compounded (reinvested) daily and the compounding is done on a 360-day-per-year convention.

MSCI Emerging Markets

Volatility	2.22
Weight of largest holding	4.37% (Brazilian oil company Petrobas)
Weight of top ten largest holdings	20.36%
Yield	3.69%

Returns

Index	*2004*	*2005*	*2006*	*2007*	*2008*
MSCI Emerging Markets	22.4%	30.3%	29.2%	36.5%	−54.5%

Graph below is for iShares ETf and not the index.

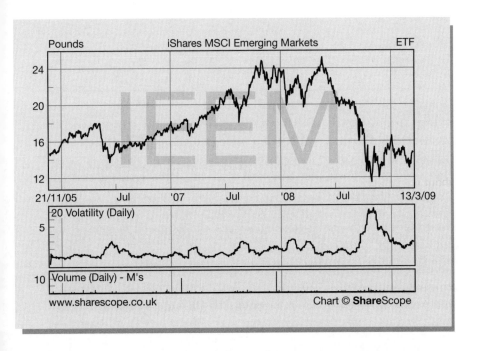

The index – our analysis

ANALYSIS	
Likely Risk (High/Medium/Low)	High
Likely Volatility	High
Suitable for 'Simple' Investors i.e. small ISA investors	Yes
Diversification Risk with Top Holdings i.e. top three more than 20% of fund	No
Likely to be a core holding?	Yes
Market Cap based (MC)/Screened (S)	MC
Appeal to Income Investors?	Yes
Risk Factors?	Political Risk Volatile markets
Top 3 holding as % of total fund March 2009	8%
Country breakdown: top 3 – March 2009	China 17%
South Korea 14%	
Brazil 12%	
Sector breakdown: top 3 – March 2009	Financials 23% Energy 14.5% Telecoms 14%

Comments

Investors have always harboured a strange dichotomy in their minds, involving a stark contrast between value and growth. Value is all about cheap stuff. It is boring, it is sensible, it is safe and it is the kind of stuff you would buy at a Morrisons or Asda if they sold shares, and it sort of does what it says on the tin i.e. provide good value. Ranged against this is something called growth – faster-growing, sexier stuff that is a bit more expensive but worth the extra cost because it predicts a great future, provided the managers can deliver on the hope and the market position.

This hugely simplified dichotomy has usually been applied to developed world equities – there are even indices in the UK and US dedicated to only value or growth stocks. But this division can also be applied on a much grander level to all assets and investment ideas – increasingly large stock markets like ours in the UK and the US are, in effect, value markets, full of boring utilities, overweight oil mega-corporations and tobacco companies puffing out cash profits. The growth 'bits' of the globalised markets tend increasingly to belong to emerging markets in the developing world – places like India or China or even Russia (on a good day) are seen as much more exciting, much faster growing, more 'with it' in the new order of things.

The big problem for most ordinary mortals is one of accessibility – how on earth can investors hope to buy into the dozens of markets that comprise this fast-growing new investment universe (emerging markets as an asset class only really emerged in the 1980s)? Luckily there is an answer – the well-established MSCI Emerging Markets Index or MSCI EM for short. It is widely used by the institutions as a benchmark index and comprises all the world's main emerging stock markets in one composite index, although it's worth adding that you can also buy into the various different components (regional or national) on an individual basis if you so choose.

Over the last 20 or so years, returns from this index have been spectacular, even after the mauling of 2007 and 2008.

% returns from MSCI EM index

Index Level: Currency: Date	Price USD EM (EMERGING MARKETS) % change
1988	34.9
1989	59.2
1990	−13.8
1991	56.0
1992	9.0
1993	71.3
1994	−8.7
1995	−6.9
1996	3.9
1997	−13.4

Continued

Index Level: Currency: Date	Price USD EM (EMERGING MARKETS) % change
1998	−27.5
1999	63.7
2000	−31.8
2001	−4.9
2002	−8.0
2003	51.6
2004	22.4
2005	30.3
2006	29.2
2007	36.5
2008	−54.5
Copyright MSCI Inc.	

Before we look at the various funds that track this investment space, let's look at the index in a little more detail. According to index builders MSCI Barra, the 'MSCI Emerging Markets Index is a free-float-adjusted market-capitalisation index that is designed to measure equity market performance of emerging markets. As of June 2007 the MSCI Emerging Markets Index consisted of the following 25 emerging market country indices: Argentina, Brazil, Chile, China, Colombia, Czech Republic, Egypt, Hungary, India, Indonesia, Israel, Jordan, Korea, Malaysia, Mexico, Morocco, Pakistan, Peru, Philippines, Poland, Russia, South Africa, Taiwan, Thailand, and Turkey'. The top ten companies within the index are in the box opposite – it is a smattering of Chinese and Taiwanese technology giants, Russian and Brazilian oil companies and the odd Israeli drugs company.

Top ten holdings 30/01/09 Security	Country	% Weight
CHINA MOBILE LTD	Hong Kong	3.14
SAMSUNG ELECTRONICS CO LTD	Korea (South)	2.5
PETROBRAS – PETROLEO BRAS	Brazil	2.24
PETROBRAS – PETROLEO BRAS-PR	Brazil	2.13
TEVA PHARMACEUTICAL IND LTD	Israel	2.11
OAO GAZPROM-REG S ADS	Russian Federation	1.96
AMERICA MOVIL SAB DE CV-SER L	Mexico	1.68
TAIWAN SEMICONDUCTOR MANUFAC	Taiwan	1.66
CIA VALE DO RIO DOCE-PREF A	Brazil	1.52
CHINA LIFE INSURANCE CO-H	China	1.42
Currency: USD		20.36

The MSCI EM index comprises a number of smaller, more specific regional and national indices, nearly all of which are tracked by separate ETFs. There are also a number of related smaller indices that do not quite fit inside the MSCI Emerging Markets mother ship but overlap. Chief among them is the MSCI AC (All Country) Far East ex Japan Index, which is a free-float-adjusted market-capitalisation weighted index that is 'designed to measure the equity market performance of the Far East, excluding Japan and comprises China, Hong Kong, Indonesia, Korea, Malaysia, Philippines, Singapore, Taiwan, and Thailand', i.e. emerging Asia. You may also notice MSCI AC Far East Ex-Japan SmallCap which is a variation of the emerging Asia index and tracks small-cap stocks.

The featured emerging markets (EM) ETF funds

Details						
Fund	iShares MSCI Emerging Markets	DB MSCI Emerging Markets EM	Lyxor ETF MSCI Emerging Markets	Lyxor ETF MSCI AC Asia Pacific ex Japan	iShares MSCI AC Far East ex Japan small-cap	DB MSCI EM Asia TRN

Details						
Ticker/ EPIC	IEEM	XMEM	LEME	LASP	ISFE	XMAS
Issuer	iShares Barclays	Deutsche DBX	Lyxor	Lyxor ETF	iShares Barclays	Deutsche DBX
TER	0.75%	0.65%	0.65%	0.65%	0.74%	0.65%
Currency	GBP	GBP	GBP	GBP	GBP	GBP
Underlying Index	MSCI Global Emerging Markets Index	MSCI global Emerging Markets Index	MSCI global Emerging Markets Index	MSCI AC Far East exc Japan	MSCI AC Far East exc Japan small-cap	MSCI EM Asia
Launch Date	17/11/2005	22/06/2007	14/01/2008	18/10/2007	08/05/2008	21/06/2007

The most obvious choice for mainstream investors looking to buy into the emerging markets investment space is to start with the mother ship index, namely the MSCI EM index, tracked by Lyxor, DBX and iShares. All these global EM ETFs are cheap, fairly diversified across different countries (although resources do tend to figure heavily) and biased towards the biggest and best companies in the global emerging markets space. We would recommend these global funds over any of the more country- or region-specific funds – ETFs that concentrate on just Russia or China, for example, are just too risky and volatile for most simple, basic investors.

Returns from emerging markets

Market:	Emerging Markets (EM)			
As Of:	March 13th, 2009			
Currency:	USD			
Regional Performance				
MSCI Index	**1 Yr**	**3 Yr**	**5 Yr**	**10 Yr**
BRIC	−54.120%	−7.840%	7.900%	9.760%
EM (EMERGING MARKETS)	−51.990%	−11.520%	2.490%	5.110%
EM ASIA	−48.950%	−10.410%	−0.050%	3.310%
EM EASTERN EUROPE	−69.390%	−24.900%	−3.900%	8.630%
EM EMEA Eastern Europe, Middle East, Africa	−57.190%	−18.440%	0.210%	4.330%
EM FAR EAST	−47.500%	−10.000%	−0.570%	3.070%
EM LATIN AMERICA	−53.030%	−5.080%	12.860%	10.900%
Country Performance				
MSCI Index	**1 Yr**	**3 Yr**	**5 Yr**	**10 Yr**
CHINA	−40.640%	4.630%	8.560%	4.600%
INDIA	−57.540%	−12.780%	4.920%	7.390%
INDONESIA	−58.910%	−5.710%	8.250%	10.600%
KOREA	−53.170%	−18.320%	−1.210%	7.030%
TAIWAN	−48.570%	−14.430%	−9.040%	−4.410%
THAILAND	−55.270%	−13.760%	−5.100%	3.040%
EM ASIA	−48.950%	−10.410%	−0.050%	3.310%
BRAZIL	−54.390%	−2.180%	17.940%	14.120%
POLAND	−66.560%	−20.820%	−2.410%	0.860%
RUSSIA	−70.820%	−26.400%	−5.730%	14.620%
SOUTH AFRICA	−41.940%	−13.190%	3.730%	6.000%

Source: MSCI Barra

The big question – index or passive?

Our broader concern with global EM index funds is whether a passive fund is necessarily the best approach to investing. One particularly trenchant critic of the index route is Dr Slim Feriani, veteran manager of Advance Developing Markets (ADD), one of the most successful emerging markets investment trusts. 'Particularly in the case of emerging markets,' says Dr Feriani, 'you do not want to invest in ETFs because they are structurally biased towards larger markets and larger companies. Therefore, you'd be missing out on some of the best investment opportunities in this asset class, which are often in smaller countries and the small and mid-cap space. These are best exploited by good, specialist and active stick pickers. We strongly believe that investing in emerging markets is for specialists, because of the complexity of investing in 25–40 different countries. You certainly should not go with single-country funds. Indeed, trying to play the 'emerging markets' theme through a single-country ETF is like putting all your eggs in one basket. If you did invest in an Indian ETF early this year (XNIF), you'd have lost a third of your money by now.'

Supporters of index tracking emerging markets funds point out that specialist, active fund managers may be able to provide market-timing and risk-management skills, but that their expertise comes at a cost. Most actively managed, diversified emerging markets funds charge at least 1.5 – 2 per cent a year in management fees plus an initial charge that can amount to 5 per cent. ETFs from the likes of iShares, Lyxor and DBX charge between 0.5 per cent and 0.8 per cent a year, giving investors an automatic 1 per cent or more extra return a year.

ETF supporters also argue that index funds are simpler and cleaner. They claim that most active fund managers fail to hit their benchmark returns whereas with an ETF you are simply buying the market. But Dr Feriani begs to differ. 'Even if you were to try to go for a more diversified ETF like a global emerging markets ETF, then it's no guarantee that it's actually going to track its index. Indeed, the iShares emerging markets ETF (EEM) was 6 per cent behind the MSCI emerging markets index in 2007. That's a huge tracking error. Many good active managers did a lot better than that last year.'

The numbers tell a slightly more balanced story. Over some periods active fund managers such as Dr Feriani and Dr Mark Mobius at Templeton Emerging Markets Investment Trust have beaten the benchmark index. But in the first half of 2008, for example, Templeton's flagship fund was down 11 per cent (compared with a 12 per cent loss on the benchmark), whereas the iShares fund was down only 8.9 per cent.

Investing in small-caps

By and large we would accept that there is a strong case to be made for tracking emerging markets cheaply and effectively at a global level, although investors may want to top up their holdings with a more specialised actively managed fund from the likes of Progressive or Templeton. We cannot – by contrast – see any rationale for investing in specific national markets, bar perhaps China or Latin America. We believe that country-specific index tracking funds in the developing world are just too risky and specialised for the ordinary investor. Your best bet with specific countries is to either use a specialised active fund manager who can take those judgement calls for you or stick with a global EM index fund.

The one big exception to this rule of staying out of specialist markets comes with small-caps. iShares offers two very specialist EM funds that we think are compelling for more adventurous types. The first is called the iShares Asia ex Japan Small Cap Fund. It is hugely diversified on a number of levels, with a great variety of nations and different sectors (Taiwan 29 per cent, South Korea 22 per cent, Hong Kong 13 per cent and China 12 per cent; financials, industrials, technology all fairly evenly represented). Crucially the focus on smaller caps is very welcome, especially when you consider that the average PE ratio of the 900-plus companies held in the portfolio is relatively low.

Clearly this is not a fund for risk-averse, inexperienced investors, but if you are willing to live with the likely increased volatility, this could be a great investment idea. We also like the idea of the iShares MSCI Emerging Markets Small Cap fund. The index providers define this segment of their wider EM index as any company in a 'country's equity universe whose total market capitalisation lies between $200m and $1.5bn'. This little-known index started in 1998 and by its peak in 2007 had quadrupled in value, but in the bear market of 2007 and 2008, the index crashed back in value, although it is still well ahead of its starting levels in 1998, with an annualised return of just under 4 per cent. Crucially, at the time of writing, it appears to be offering great value – the index sports an average price to earnings ratio of only 6.90, with most companies valued at three quarters of book value and producing an overall yield of 5.41 per cent. The top ten holdings are in the box overleaf.

Top ten holdings13/03/09

Security	Country	% Weight
GUINNESS ANCHOR BHD	Malaysia	1.03
SKYWORTH DIGITAL HLDGS LTD	Bermuda	0.85
NAMPAK LTD	South Africa	0.85
MEDI-CLINIC CORP LTD	South Africa	0.82
SPAR GROUP LIMITED/THE	South Africa	0.7
SUN INTERNATIONAL LTD	South Africa	0.64
DAISHIN SECURITIES CO LTD	Korea (South)	0.6
CHEIL WORLDWIDE INC	Korea (South)	0.6
THAI UNION FROZEN PROD PUB	Thailand	0.58
MIRLE AUTOMATION CORP	Taiwan	0.57
Currency: USD		
COUNTRY COMPOSITION		
Taiwan		20%
South Korea		15%
China		12.5%

What about BRIC funds?

There is one last emerging markets investment idea worth considering –
why not invest in an emerging markets index that focuses on the top
companies (50 of them) in Brazil, Russia, India and China, otherwise
known as the BRIC countries? iShares offers one such fund that tracks a
FTSE index imaginatively called the FTSE BRIC 50. This tracks the 50
largest companies in the developing world and includes outfits like
Petrobas from Brazil and Gazprom from Russia – companies that some
analysts call the mega-caps of tomorrow. It is a potentially brilliant idea for
an investor looking for a very focused investment, but there are some
potentially big flaws.

Details	
Fund	iShares FTSE BRIC 50
Ticker/EPIC	BRIC
Issuer	iShares Barclays
TER	0.74%
Currency	GBP
Underlying Index	FTSE BRIC 50
Launch Date	23/04/2007
Region/Global	Global

Well over 60 per cent of the fund's investment is accounted for by big Russian and Brazilian companies, with India and China comprising a rather measly 38 per cent between them. To be fair to iShares and the FTSE, this index does precisely what it claims to, namely track the world's top 50 largest quoted companies based in the developing world, and it just so happens that these are mainly Russian and Brazilian mega caps.

This makes us nervous. What we think you may be capturing here is not the emerging markets story you think you are catching – you are actually buying into a very small number of hugely successful Russian, Chinese and Brazilian oil companies (Gazprom, Lukoil, Vale and Petrobas account for just under 40 per cent of the fund), plus a smattering of successful Brazilian conglomerates.

You are also buying into a fund whose top three holdings account for just over 30 per cent of the fund – the top ten account for just under 60 per cent. That makes this fund highly concentrated (not unexpected in a mega-cap fund, to be fair) and not necessarily the most diversified we have seen.

All in all this is another great idea that might make rather a good investment if a) oil starts rising in price, and b) Russia does not turn even nastier, and c) Brazil carries on growing fast. All of these eventualities could come to pass, but we wouldn't count on it – in our humble opinion the iShares BRIC 50 fund is just too risky for our main Essential 25 list.

Japan – The TOPIX, MSCI Japan and the Nikkei 225

Volatility	
Weight of largest holding	Toyota in MSCI Japan at 5% and 4% in TOPIX
Weight of top ten largest holdings	22% for MSCI Japan and 20% for TOPIX
Yield %	1.8%

Returns

Index	1997	1998	1999	2000	2001	2002	2003	2004	2005	2006	2007	2008
MSCI Japan	24.6	4	61.9	−28.9	−29.9	−10.7	34.3	15	24.2	5.1	−6.4	−29

Index	2008	2007	2006	2005	2004
Nikkei 225®	−42.12	−11.13	6.92	40.24	7.61

Featured ETFs

ANALYSIS		
Index	TOPIX	MSCI Japan
Likely Risk (High/Medium/Low)	Medium	Medium
Likely Volatility	Medium	Medium
Suitable for 'Simple' Investors i.e. small ISA investors	Yes	Yes
Diversification Risk with Top Holdings i.e. top three more than 20% of fund	No	No
Likely to be a core holding?	Yes	Yes
Market Cap based (MC)/ Screened (S)	MC	MC

Continued

ANALYSIS

Appeal to Income Investors?	No	No
Risk Factors?	Long-term bear market in Japan	Long-term bear market in Japan
	Currency risk of investing in non-sterling market	Currency risk of investing in non-sterling market
Top 3 holding as % of total fund March 2009	9%	11.5%
Sector Breakdown: top 3 – March 2009	Industrials 16% Banks 10%	Industrials 18% Consumer Goods 18%
	Automotive 10%	Financials 17%

Featured ETFs

Details

Fund	Lyxor ETF Japan	DBX MSCI Japan TRN Index	iShares MSCI Japan SmallCap
Ticker/EPIC	LTPX	XMJP	ISJP
Issuer	Lyxor	Deutsche DBX	iShares Barclays
TER	0.50%	0.50%	0.59%
Currency	GBP	GBP	GBP
Underlying Index	TOPIX Tokyo Index	MSCI Japan	MSCI Japan Small Cap
Launch Date	25/09/2007	08/01/2007	08/05/2008

Comments

When most investors hear about Japan they usually hear about the price movements in something called the Nikkei 225 index. It is the most widely used measure of Japanese stock markets by the global media but bizarrely it is not tracked by any major ETFs in the UK. The most widely used index is a subset of the MSCI World index, called the MSCI Japan index, although Lyxor also uses a locally developed index, operated by the Tokyo Stock Exchange, called the TOPIX. This latter index is also known as the Tokyo Stock Price Index, and it is a fairly conventional capitalisation-weighted index of all companies listed on the First Section of the Tokyo Stock Exchange. The index is supplemented by the subindices of the 33 industry sectors. The MSCI index is also a market-capitalisation basis index comprising 85 per cent of the constituents of the Tokyo Stock Exchange. The small-cap variation of the MSCI index comprises the smallest 40 per cent of that index group, with market cap in the range of $200–1500m.

This index is widely used by institutional investors and is also popular with structured product providers. It covers much the same kind of companies as the Nikkei but with a wider spread of companies and sectors, i.e. it is slightly less concentrated than the Nikkei. The MSCI Index does not track an actual market by the same name as such – it is an institutional construct based on the widely used MSCI index series and includes virtually all the companies found on the TOPIX index.

As to which index or fund to use if you want to track Japan, the truth is that there is not a huge difference. Both ETF funds charge the same expense ratio, with the DBX MSCI fund showing slightly more bias towards financials and banks. It is also worth noting that the DBX fund is a total return fund, which means that any dividend yield from holding the underlying stocks is rolled up into the return, i.e. you will not get an income from dividends as you do with the Lyxor fund.

More adventurous types may want to take a closer look at a specialist Japanese small-cap fund from iShares based on that MSCI index – the wider MSCI Japan fund trades at about 1.8 times book as we write, whereas the smaller caps trade at 1.4 times book value. To be fair the smaller cap index of the MSCI has been having a torrid time in recent years, but the potential for a value-induced recovery is huge. We also like the fact that you are not paying an awful lot in terms of expenses for this specialised fund – its TER is a very reasonable 0.59 per cent per annum.

Adventurous types may also want to have a look at a specialist 'value' fund from Powershares called the Dynamic Japan fund – details below.

Details	
Fund	PowerShares Dynamic Japan Fund
Ticker/EPIC	PSDJ
Issuer	Powershares
TER	0.75%
Currency	USD
Underlying Index	QSG Active Japanese Equity Index
Underlying currency risk	Yes
Launch Date	15/09/2008

According to Powershares, 'the QSG Active Japanese Equity Index is a liquidity-adjusted market-capitalisation index designed to select and report the 250 equity securities with highest likelihood of future outperformance from a broader universe of the 1000 largest Japanese companies (by liquidity-adjusted market capitalisation). The equity securities are selected and weighted using a proprietary multi-factor model based on the following measures of expected outperformance: balance sheet strength, capital structure, leverage, earnings growth, earnings quality, and price momentum.'

Over the last decade Japan has been a horrible place to invest in, especially in the value space. Many great investing minds have come unstuck trying to figure out what exactly works, but it looks like the quantitative investing types might have come up with the outline of an answer in the shape of this new Powershares fund based on a QSG index. This brand new index uses a value-driven screening approach that has been tested on Japan only from 2008. Crucially, the research firm behind the index – QSG – has redesigned its value index specifically for Japan. Rather than just apply the same measures across global markets and then simply isolate the Japanese stocks identified, the researchers started with the most liquid Japanese market and reworked their screening process from the bottom up, to fit local circumstances. In particular, QSG tried to pinpoint the combination of measures that could identify a financially sound company whose shares might attract investor interest in spite of the overall bearishness of the market. The resulting screening process – the combination of factors it uses is proprietary – was then backtested through to 1990 and the 'passing' companies have been built into an index of 125 stocks that are equally weighted and rebalanced every quarter. All the usual objections apply, of course: it is a black box, it is proprietary, and it has been tried only in a backtest, which is not the real world.

But at least the index is not capitalisation weighted, which avoids an undue concentration of holdings in a few big companies that could implode. It also has a value bias, which we sense is the way to go in Japan. More importantly, we think the results speak for themselves. Over nearly every time scale, the QSG index has beaten the *Topix* index. Over five years, the QSG index is up 95 per cent against 71 per cent for the *Topix* and over the last year the QSG index is down 10.4 per cent, against minus 13 per cent for the *Topix*.

DJ-AIG Agriculture

Volatility	
Weight of largest holding	Soybeans 25%
Weight of top ten largest holdings	NR
Yield %	NR

Returns

Index	2004	2005	2006	2007	2008
	NA	NA	NA	NA	NA

The index – our analysis

ANALYSIS	
Likely Risk (High/Medium/Low)	Medium to high
Likely Volatility	Medium to high
Suitable for 'Simple' Investors i.e. small ISA investors	No
Large/mid/small-cap bias?	NR
Diversification Risk with Top Holdings i.e. top three more than 20% of fund	NR
Likely to be a core holding?	Yes

Continued

ANALYSIS

Market Cap based (MC)/Screened (S)	MC
Appeal to Income Investors?	No
Risk Factors?	Very specific sector
	Risk of falling agriculture prices
Appeal to investors looking to short main markets	No

Featured ETFs

Details

Fund	ETFS Agriculture DJ-AIGCI	Powershares Global Agriculture NASDAQ QMX
Ticker/EPIC	AIGA	PSGA
Issuer	ETF Securities	Powershares
TER	0.49%	0.75%
Annualised Tracking error % last year	NA	NA
Currency	USD	USD
Underlying Index	Dow Jones AIG Agriculture DJ-AIGCI	NASDAQ OMX Global Agriculture Index
Underlying currency risk	Yes	Yes
Launch Date	01/09/2008	15/09/2008
Asset Class	Commodities	Equities

Comments

If you want to capture the agriculture investment theme you have two basic choices – either track the agricultural commodities themselves (via their futures-based markets) or invest in the companies that supply the agriculture sector. In the pure commodities space that means focusing on an index called the Dow Jones AIG Agriculture sub index – also known as AIGA. This tracks a basket of agricultural commodities and is a sub-index of the wider DJ-AIG All Index.

For agriculture companies the best bet is something called the NASDAQ OMX Global Agriculture Index, which is designed to measure the overall performance of globally traded securities of the largest and most liquid companies involved in agriculture and farming-related activities.

Top Holdings in 'Powershares' Agriculture Fund (July 2009)

Monsanto Co.   10.99%

Syngenta AG   8.65%

Potash Corp. of Saskatchewan Inc. 8.24%

Archer Daniels Midland Co.   7.26%

Mosaic Co.   6.89%

Top Holdings in ETF Securities Fund

Soybeans 25%

Corn 19%

Wheat 16%

Cotton 11%

Sugar 10%

Coffee 10%

Soybean oil 9%

Both of these indices – and their accompanying ETFs – are potentially excellent ideas for investors looking to build some exposure to the global agriculture space. They access this space in two very different ways:

■ The Powershares fund invests in all companies (big companies) that supply the world's farming sector. That list includes fertiliser companies (Potash), biotech companies (Monsanto), tractor and plant machinery (Deere) and agricultural agents and suppliers.

■ The ETF Securities fund is more focused on just agricultural commodities and invests in a range of futures-based contracts in everything from soybeans (the main constituent) to coffee and wheat (but no livestock, which is a separate ETC).

The attractions of both funds together is that you could pretty much buy global access to all things farming related with the exception maybe of land (for this you could buy one of the putative listed farm land funds, with Braemar asset management likely to launch the first fund at some point in 2009). The bigger question is perhaps whether you want to have any access at all to agriculture.

Bulls of 'soft commodities' – agricultural products to you and I – advance a number of key arguments, including the following:

■ Agricultural commodities outperformed most other asset classes in the bear market of 2008 and 2009.

■ Agriculture has a relatively low level of correlation to the business cycle and to other asset classes.

■ A growing world population and rising per capita incomes are likely to fuel growing demand for certain key softs including livestock, rice and grains.

■ The supply of land is obviously fairly constrained, made worse by diminishing water resources.

■ According to ETF Securities investors also need to be aware that 'tight supply relative to growing demand has caused inventories of many agricultural products to fall to near 50-year lows, making prices highly sensitive to negative supply events'.

■ Agricultural products are a strong hedge against inflation.

■ Last but by no means least, government efforts to combat climate change and increase biofuel usage have fed through into increasing pressure on grains.

The case for investing in agricultural products and companies is not a one-way street though – soft commodities are hugely volatile in price and many economists point to the long-term relative decline in real prices for most food commodities. Despite all the rhetoric about 'they ain't making enough land any more', crop yields and agricultural productivity have increased substantially over the very long term, making most farmers in the West for instance dependent on income from government subsidies, from selling valuable land and from ancillary activities including tourism.

FTSE UK Dividend Plus Index

Volatility	1.57 (FTSE All Share index is at 1.11) i.e. it is more volatile
Weight of largest holding	5.39% (Brit Insurance)
Weight of top ten largest holdings	41.56%
Yield as at 13th March 2009	11.32%

Returns

Index	2004	2005	2006	2007	2008
UK Dividend Plus Index	29.6%	22%	19%	−16%	−49%

Note: graph below is the iShares UK Dividend Plus Index ETF and NOT the index

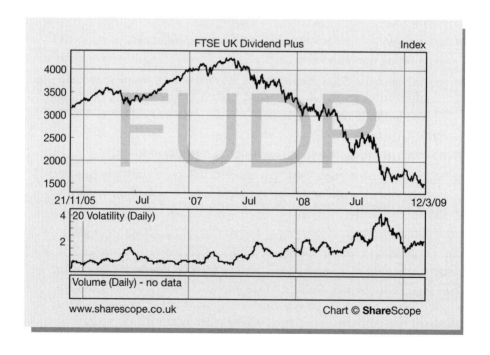

The index – our analysis

ANALYSIS	
Likely Risk (High/Medium/Low)	High
Likely Volatility	High
Suitable for 'Simple' Investors i.e. small ISA investors	Yes
Diversification Risk with Top Holdings i.e. top three more than 20% of fund	No
Likely to be a core holding?	Yes
Market Cap based (MC)/Screened (S)	Screened for yield
Appeal to Income Investors?	Yes
Risk Factors?	Mid and small-cap biased – also has been too reliant on financial services companies Very volatile
Top 3 holding as % of total fund March 2009	15%
Country Breakdown: top 3 – March 2009	100% UK Listed
Sector Breakdown: top 3 – March 2009	Financials 25% Consumer services 23% Industrials 19%

Featured ETF from iShares

Details	
Fund	iShares FTSE UK Dividend Plus
Ticker/EPIC	IUKD
Issuer	iShares Barclays
TER	0.40%
Annualised Tracking error % in 2007	0.29%

Continued

Details

Currency	GBP
Underlying Index	FTSE UK Dividend Plus
Number of holdings	43
Fund value mid March 2009	£145m
Launch Date	04/11/2005

Comments

As indices go, this is not one of the best known – it gives investors exposure to around 43 UK companies which pay out the highest forecasted dividend yields in the FTSE 350. It is designed to select high dividend-paying stocks using just one specialist index. According to the index developers, the FTSE Group, 'The FTSE UK Dividend+ Index selects the top 50 stocks by one-year forecast dividend yield. The constituents' weightings within the index are determined by their dividend yield as opposed to market capitalisation. The FTSE UK Dividend+ Index was created to allow investors to capture the long-term effect of higher compounding returns, and benefit from the lower correlations to traditional market cap weighted indices.'

Investors may want to pay attention to that last sentence in the index defi-nition – 'the long-term effect of higher compounding returns'. The key here is that dividends matter – an awful lot – and especially if you then reinvest the dividends in shares. Sadly, capturing that dividend effect is rather trick-ier – lots of companies pay a juicy dividend and any investor trying to build a portfolio might find themselves inundated with shares. The FTSE UK Dividend Plus index is designed to give investors an alternative – track the highest-yielding FTSE 350 stocks based on their forecast payout.

In theory, this is a promising idea and the academic literature certainly suggests that this is potentially a brilliant long-term investment idea, but the reality in the last few years has been rather less positive – returns in bear markets from this kind of index have been utterly dreadful. Countless tens of millions of pounds of investors' money poured into the iShares ETF that tracks this index in the years after 2004 and much of that money flooded back out again in the later part of the decade as the market sav-agely turned against value stocks. And that is the key point – by default most value stocks pay out a good yield, which means that any strategy that captures high-yielding stocks catches value stocks and value stocks are more volatile and much riskier in a bear market.

The reverse of this is also true – value stocks and in particular high-yielding stocks may be a bad idea in bear markets, but in bull markets returns can be spectacular. The point here is the length of the investment – invest for only a few years and time that purchase of the index poorly and you could be looking at colossal losses. By contrast, your profits could be huge if you time that purchase well and then hold over ten, twenty or even longer periods *and* reinvest the yield.

Dividends really matter

The academic literature – backed up by a mountain of analysis from City strategists such as Andrew Lapthorne at SocGen – suggests that dividends benefit investors over the long term in a number of different ways.

The first and perhaps most obvious is the regular dividend payment as a contributor to what are called total shareholder returns (the capital returns plus the income yield), but the magic of dividends does not stop there. There is some evidence that a strategy of buying the right kind of dividend payers (reliable or progressive dividend payers with a decent balance sheet) will actually deliver better returns in and of itself, i.e. the market itself tends to highly rate reliable dividend payers and gives those companies' shares a higher rating. The reason for this market preference is obvious in retrospect – dividends are easy to calculate and involve simple, hard numbers made in regular payments as opposed to profits and earnings which can be overstated and hugely volatile. Dividends also tend to be much more stable over time compared with earnings (annual earnings growth has historically been 2.5 times more volatile than dividend growth according to bank SocGen), while the discipline of making the regular dividend payout encourages a more focussed management, determined to conserve the financial resources of the firm. As Lapthorne at SocGen reminds us: 'The retention of a too high proportion of earnings can encourage unnecessary mergers and acquisition (and often wasteful) investment in the pursuit of higher earnings growth.' As an example of this discipline and focus it is worth noting that very few companies ever set their management teams a dividends target as a way of calculating their bonuses – the cynic might note how difficult it is too manipulate the dividends stats compared with earnings.

The long-term case for dividends and their importance to private investors rests on a combination of all these factors – the dividend payout itself, the rating attached to a high-yielder and growth in the dividend payout over time. But there is one last, vital element to reckon with: the reinvestment of these dividend payouts.

The hard spade work for this analysis into dividend reinvestment comes from London Business School Professors Elroy Dimson, Paul Marsh and Mike Staunton, featured regularly in their Credit Suisse Global Investment Returns Yearbooks. Like many analysts, they break down the long-term returns from equities into four components:

- the actual yield itself (usually compared to the risk-free rate of return from holding cash or index-linked gilts);

- the growth rate of real dividends (increased dividends above the inflation rate);

■ the way the market rewards a company because of its dividend, i.e. the rating it will give the shares via a measure like the price to dividend ratio; and last but no means least

■ the reinvestment of the dividend using schemes like the dividend reinvestment investment plans or DRIPs.

According to Dimson et al 'the dividend yield has been the dominant factor historically' and they add that 'the longer the investment horizon, the more important is dividend income'. Dimson's point is that the long-term real dividend growth rate is actually only about 1 per cent per annum and thus cannot make that big a difference while the rerating of stocks based on its multiple to dividends is also very variable over time and does not make that much of a difference – as the authors note, 'dividends and probably earnings have barely outpaced inflation'.

But the actual payout is dwarfed by the importance of reinvesting dividends. Looking at the 109 years since 1900 Dimson et al. suggest that the average real capital gain in just stocks plus the dividend payout is about 1.7 per cent per annum (an initial $1000 would have grown six fold), but over the same period dividends reinvested would have produced a total return of 6 per cent per annum (or a total gain of 582 times the original $1000).

Andrew Lapthorne and his quantitative team at SocGen have looked at the same territory over a slightly smaller, more recent time period. They decomposed the returns of equities since 1970 in the major developed world markets including the UK, and discovered a slightly different picture to the LBS study. They reckon that the actual dividend yield represented just 30 per cent of the nominal returns versus 70 per cent for dividend growth, with their analysis suggesting that real dividend growth has been closer to 1.2 per cent over the period. Looking at the UK the SG team reckon that of total annualised equity returns since 1970 of 11.4 per cent, the actual dividend yield accounted for 4.3 per cent per annum, dividend growth 8 per cent per annum and multiple expansion (a higher or lower share price to dividend yield) −1.1 per cent i.e. high-yielding shares were actually rated lower by the market.

Lapthorne's analysis contains a number of other hugely important insights. His team's analysis looked at the relationship between earnings – profits – and dividends, for instance. Most people commonly assume that there is a very close relationship between profits and dividends, but that relationship is not in reality that strong. The SG team looked at the volatility of earnings growth, for instance, and dividend growth – earnings were hugely more volatile. Crucially, when they used a measure called beta to look at the sensitivity of dividends to earnings, they discovered relatively low numbers (0.00 indicates no sensitivity while 1 implies absolute sensitivity) of between 0.12 and 0.50 for nearly all major equity sectors with the exception of healthcare, building and construction, and travel and leisure. The point here is that dividends do not change as much as earnings and that markets value that consistency.

The wider range of value/dividend funds

Most UK investors in high-yield equity funds have tended to focus only on the UK Dividend plus index, but there is a much greater range of global high-yield equity funds available. They are listed in the table opposite and include one for Europe, a global one and one for Asia/Pacific. At the time of writing (March 2009) all are paying running yields in double figures.

Details				
Fund	iShares DJ Asia Pacific Select Dividend	DBX DJ STOXX Global Select Dividend 100	iShares DJ Euro STOXX Select Dividend	DBX EuroSTOXX Select Dividend 30
Ticker/EPIC	IAPD	XGSD	IDVY	XD3E
Issuer	iShares Barclays	Deutsche DBX	iShares Barclays	Deutsche DBX
TER	0.59%	0.50%	0.40%	0.30%
Annualised Tracking error % 2007	0.83%	NA	1.83%	NA
Currency	GBP	GBP	GBP	GBP
Underlying Index	Dow Jones Asia Pacific Select Dividend 30 Index	DJ STOXX Global Select Dividend 100		DJ EuroSTOXX Select Dividend 30
Launch Date	02/06/2006	01/06/2007	28/10/2005	01/06/2007
Asset Class	Equities	Equities	Equities	Equities
Region/Global	Asia	Europe	Europe	Europe

Yields on wider range of equity yield exchange traded funds

Fund	Yield – iShares data from mid March 2009
UK Dividend Plus	11%
DJ Asia/Pacific Select Dividend	14.11%
DJ EuroSTOXX Select Dividend 30	11.63%

The wider range of dividend indices – definitions

The Dow Jones regional indices – Asia, Europe and Global – are all based on dividends. According to the provider each index includes a fixed number of components, ranging from 20 to 100 depending on the size of the market. To be eligible for selection to the indices, stocks must pass screens for dividend quality and for liquidity in most markets. Stocks are then selected to the indices based on dividend yield. For the Dow Jones STOXX regional indices, a stock's dividend performance is evaluated relative to its home market. Index constituents are dividend weighted rather than market capitalisation-weighted. The weights of individual securities are capped to prevent one or several components from dominating the indices. The composition of each index is reviewed on an annual basis.

S&P Global Water

Volatility	
Weight of largest holding	Veolia 10%
Weight of top ten largest holdings	50%
Yield %	2.53%

Returns

Index	2008	2007	2006	2005	2004
S&P Global Water 50 Index	–39.03	14.13	37.87	19.45	33.74

The index – our analysis

ANALYSIS	
Likely Risk (High/Medium/Low)	Medium
Likely Volatility	Medium
Suitable for 'Simple' Investors i.e. small ISA investors	Yes
Diversification Risk with Top Holdings i.e. top three more than 20% of fund	Yes
Likely to be a core holding?	Yes

Continued

ANALYSIS

Market Cap based (MC)/Screened (S)	MC
Appeal to Income Investors?	No
Risk Factors?	Highy volatile and specialised equity sector
Appeal to investors looking to short main markets	No
Top 3 holding as % of total fund March 2009	21%
Country Breakdown: top 3 – March 2009	US 42%, UK 19%, France 11.5%
Sector Breakdown: top 3 – March 2009	Utilities 42% Industrials 37% Materials 9%

Featured ETFs

Details

Fund	iShares S&P Global Water	Lyxor World Water	Powershares Palisades Global Water Fund
Ticker/EPIC	IH2O	LWAT	PSHO
Issuer	iShares	Lyxor ETF	Invesco Powershares
TER	0.65%	0.60%	0.75%
Currency	GBP	GBP	Euro
Underlying Index	S&P Global Water Index	SocGen World Water Index (SAM)	Palisades Global Water Index
Launch Date	16/03/2007	13/03/2008	

Comments

We believe an investment in the global water sector is possibly one of the best niche ideas we have ever heard of. In fact, we prefer the idea of global water over, say, clean energy or even global infrastructure because it is much more targeted and precise – you are buying companies that will benefit from the huge global wave of investment in water as a sector. Here is a range of compelling facts supporting the case for the water industry.

- Less than 1 per cent of the world's fresh water (about 0.007 per cent of all water on earth) is readily accessible for human use.
- 884 million people, around 13 per cent of the world's population, lack access to safe drinking water, whilst 2.5 billion people worldwide lack access to basic sanitation.
- Global consumption of water is doubling every 20 years – more than twice the rate of human population growth.
- By 2025 two-thirds of the world's population will be living with serious water shortages or water scarcity.
- 88 per cent of all diseases are caused by unsafe drinking water, inadequate sanitation and poor hygiene.

A recent report from fund management group Henderson's, one of the best SRI teams in the business, drew attention to the huge business potential of this sector:

- The global water market addressing municipal and industrial water/ wastewater equipment and services is estimated to be US$ 425bn.
- Wastewater use and recycling is increasingly seen as the fastest and lowest-cost way of procuring more water.
- 60 per cent of all water main pipes in the US will be classified as substandard by 2020. Estimates for water infrastructure replacement and upgrades range from US$ 300bn to US$ 1tn.
- Agriculture accounts for 70 per cent of world fresh water usage and an estimated 31 per cent of this is wasted.

All in all we agree with Henderson's assessment of the potential here but we would add one other crucial strength – steady cash flow. By and large, the companies in this sector operate in fairly regulated markets (the utilities certainly do) and that means that they will never grow at a phenomenal rate, but they will grow sustainably with strong profits. It is in the interest of regulators to let these companies invest in new capacity and improve the service and that means more profits in the long term. Add this all up and we think you have the perfect investment case, even for cautious investors with a suspicion of equity markets. Crucially, these investment pluses have not gone unnoticed in recent years – the table below shows returns from holding the main indices on offer via ETFs. The bottom line: water has been a great investment space – until 2008, of course, when water utilities like everything else went into freefall.

Index provider	Palisades Global Water Glb Wtr	S&P Global Water Global Water	SocGen World Water Index
ETF provider	Powershares	ishares	Lyxor
Holdings	37	50	20
2001	−0.43		
2002	−8.83	−9.15	
2003	51.86	30.5	
2004	34.05	30.66	39
2005	21.55	16.77	28.8
2006	32.98	35.3	24.7
2007	26.9	12.17	−4
H1 2008	−12.3	−9.3	−18.7
5 yr vol	**15.06%**	**12.43%**	
3 yr vol			**16.20%**
Benchmark- S&P 500			
5 yr vol	7.58%		
3 yr vol	10.23%		

The problems start when you try to work out which index or fund to invest in. There are three main options, detailed in the table below. All invest in companies that have a substantial investment in water, but some (the Palisades index, for instance) are much more biased towards companies that make equipment for the water sector. Others, like the SocGen index (followed by Lyxor) and the S&P Index, are weighted more heavily towards water utilities (the S&P Index is invested 42 per cent in utilities). You also need to be aware that the funds have a bias towards US stocks and that, by and large, they are all more volatile than holding a basket of ordinary stocks like the S&P 500. More cautious investors may tend to favour the Lyxor/SocGen fund with its heavy utility bias, while more adventurous investors may gravitate towards the Powershares/Palisades fund and the iShares fund. Overall, on balance we like the look of the S&P Global Water index as the best way of capturing both utility firms and water specialists.

(All figures below from July 2008)

Palisades Water Index		SG World Water Index		S&P Global Water	
Name	*% holding*	*Name*	*% Holding*	*Name*	*% holding*
Tetra Tech Inc.	4.41%	Severn Trent	10.41%	Suez	11.33%
Impregilo S.p.A.	4.22%	Veolia	9.72%	Veolia	6.88%
Stantec Inc.	4.04%	Geberit	8.94%	Geberit	6.50%
Veolia Environnement S.A.	3.87%	Pennon	8.88%	Kurita	6.08%
Valmont Industries Inc.	3.71%	United Utilities	8.18%	United Utilities	5.87%
Utilities	24.50%	20 companies		Utilities	42%
IT	8%	Annualised perf. since launch	10.60%	Industrials	42%
Industrials	60%	Volatility since launch	24.80%	Materials	10%
		Max Drwadown	36%		
average PE	13	Launched 31 August 2006		50 companies	

Continued

Palisades Water Index		SG World Water Index		S&P Global Water	
Name	% holding	Name	% Holding	Name	% holding
average market cap $bn	6.6			Standard Deviation 3yr	18.83%
number of companies	37	perf. Since launch Feb 2006	3.5% (pa)	Standard Deviation 5 yr	24%
		Launched 3 February 2006		PE	22.79
US	24%	2007 performance	−5.37%	3 yr EPS growth	24%
Japan	9.35%	H1 2008	−18.73%	Net Margin	7%
Italy	9.06%			Yield	2.45%
Canada	7.68%				
Austria	7.53%			US	40%
Finland	6.08%			France	18%
				UK	7%

FTSE NAREIT Developed Markets (Global) Property Index Series

Volatility (GLOBAL index)	
Weight of largest holding	SUN HUNG KAI PROPERTIES at 6%
Weight of top ten largest holdings	30%
Yield %	6.6% Spring 2009

Returns

Index	2008	2007	2006	2005	2004
GLOBAL PROPERTY INDICES					
FTSE EPRA/NAREIT Developed Asia Dividend+ Index	−55.35	25.41	40.75	8.66	33.59
FTSE EPRA/NAREIT Developed Dividend+ Index	−46.61	−4.24	41.62	10.84	35.4
FTSE EPRA/NAREIT Developed Europe ex UK Dividend+ Index	−36.18	−19.63	50.48	29.2	39.53
FTSE EPRA/NAREIT UK Index	−46.12	−36.27	47.96	19.34	45.99
FTSE EPRA/NAREIT United States Dividend+ Index	−38.68	−16.94	36.25	11.52	32.03

ANALYSIS	
Likely Risk (High/Medium/Low)	Medium to low
Likely Volatility	Medium to low
Suitable for 'Simple' Investors i.e. small ISA investors	Yes
Diversification Risk with Top Holdings i.e. top three more than 20% of fund	No
Likely to be a core holding?	Yes
Market Cap based (MC)/Screened (S)	MC
Appeal to Income Investors?	Yes
Risk Factors?	Sector risk
	Very American and Anglo Saxon markets biased (55% of index including USA, UK and Australia)
Appeal to investors looking to short main markets	Yes – 6.6% Spring 2009

Continued

ANALYSIS

Top 3 holding as % of total fund end July 2008	14%
Country Breakdown: top 3 – March 2009	USA 37%, Australia 10%, Hong Kong 17%
Sector Breakdown: top 3 – end July 2008	100% Property Funds

Featured ETFs – the iShares Property funds

Details

Fund	iShares FTSE EPRA/NAREIT US Property Yield	iShares FTSE EPRA/NAREIT Developed Markets Property Yield Fund	iShares FTSE /EPRA European Property Index	iShares FTSE EPRA/NAREIT UK Property Fund	iShares FTSE EPRA/NAREIT Asia Property Yield
Ticker/ EPIC	IUSP	IWDP	IPRP	IUKP	IASP
Issuer	iShares Barclays	iShares Barclays	iShares Barclays	iShares Barclays	iShares Barclays
TER	0.40%	0.59%	0.40%	0.40%	0.59%
Underlying Index	FTSE EPRA/ NAREIT US Dividend Plus Index	FTSE EPRA/ NAREIT Global Dividend Plus Index	FTSE EPRA/ NAREIT Europe exc UK Dividend Index	FTSE EPRA/ NAREIT UK Property Index	FTSE EPRA/ NAREIT Asia Dividend Plus Index
Launch Date	03/11/2006	20/10/2006	04/11/2005	16/03/2007	20/10/2006

Comments

Property, and especially commercial property, has emerged over the last decade as perhaps the single most important alternative asset class, helped in part by the boom (until recently) in capital prices and the increasing number of specialist, tax-efficient real estate investment trusts (REITs). That growth has opened the space for a multitude of funds that take an active approach to accessing the sector, but in recent years a number of international indices have emerged that give investors more 'passive exposure'. The most important comes via the FTSE Group in alliance with a trade group called NAREIT.

Their FTSE EPRA/NAREIT Global Real Estate Index Series is designed to track the performance of listed real estate companies and REITs worldwide. According to the FTSE Group they launched the FTSE EPRA/NAREIT Global Dividend+ Index as a 'market cap-weighted index designed to measure the performance of global higher yielding stocks within the developed universe of the EPRA/NAREIT Global Index, excluding Greece'. The yield bias of the index refers to the requirement for stocks to have a one-year forecast dividend yield of 2 per cent or greater. The index is then weighted by market capitalisation in line with the free float-adjusted EPRA/NAREIT Global Index. The Developed Markets version of the fund covers most of the world, including Japan, the UK, the US and Europe, but excludes emerging markets property companies. The index series is then broken down into regional sub-indices including one for the UK, for Europe and for the US (each in turn tracked by an iShares fund).

On paper we would recommend this small range of iShares funds as a core investment for all investors. It offers a number of not insubstantial advantages:

- It allows you to diversify across national and regional markets.
- It allows access to global commercial property markets, from offices through to industrial estates.
- The funds are usually invested in core REIT holdings which are tax efficient – REITs must pay most of their income stream as a dividend to investors (free of tax).
- They produce a useful dividend yield.
- They also offer investors a way of diversifying risk against core equity holdings. Most of the funds on offer boast correlations with the FTSE All Share of less than 0.5, while the US version is also fairly lowly correlated with the US equity markets at 0.405 (over five years against the FTSE US index).

The biggest advantage, of course, is that this asset class has stormed ahead over the last decade – the average annual gain for the Global version is a fantastic 25 per cent per annum bar 2008 But those stunning gains up until 2007 need to be put into perspective – prices collapsed in 2007 and 2008 and the rate of decline showed little sign of abating in 2009. The main Developed Markets index, for instance, was down 46 per cent in 2008 (as was the UK index), although the Asia index was down a whopping 55 per cent.

Beyond these short-term price weakness issues, we are slightly concerned by a number of other factors:

1 Dangerous concentrations. These funds look highly diversified across national markets but once you dig a bit deeper you discover that you are betting on just six key national property markets. In the Asia fund, Australia and Hong Kong account for a huge percentage of the total holdings, while in Europe France and Holland account for over 60 per cent. Turning to the Global fund, the US accounts for a staggering 37 per cent of the total investments, followed by Australia again with 10 per cent and Hong Kong at 17 per cent.

2 There is potential for the tracking error to be fairly noticeable with these funds. Tracking errors on these funds have ranged from a minuscule 0.1 per cent through to a whopping 1.6 per cent per annum (in 2007).

3 The TER for two of the funds – Asia and Global – is rather high at 0.59 per cent. That is not expensive compared with actively managed property funds but it is not exactly cheap for such a liquid range of underlying holdings.

The bottom line? We do have some concerns with these funds but we think they really do deserve a place in most long-term portfolios. They are still a cheap and easy way of buying access to the best commercial real estate companies and they also pay out a cracking yield – see the table below for the chunky payouts. So this is a great series of products to buy if you want to access the global commercial property markets. The Global product is less interesting in our book because of it is strong US bias – we would favour picking up, say, the US and the newish UK fund as a starter.

Spring 2009 yields on iShares property funds

Fund	Yield – iShares
UK fund	6.25%
Global fund	6.63%
US fund	8.38%
Asian fund	5.5%
European fund	5.5%

China and the HSCEI Index

Volatility	3.48 (high)
Weight of largest holding	13.7% (China Construction Bank)
Weight of top ten largest holdings	68% (Very high – only 43 stocks in the index)
Yield % (as at March 2009)	2.69%

Returns

Index	2004	2005	2006	2007	2008
HSCEI China Index	NA	12.42%	94%	56%	–51%

Graph – This graph is not for the index but for the Lyxor fund which tracks that index

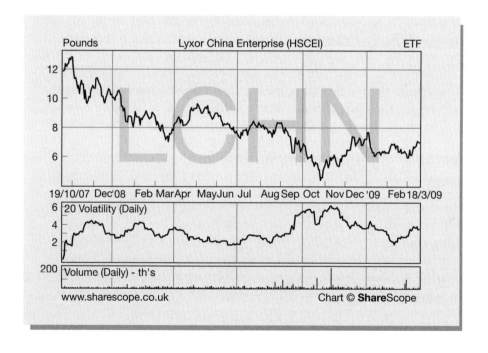

The index – our analysis

ANALYSIS	
Likely Risk (High/Medium/Low)	High
Likely Volatility	High
Suitable for 'Simple' Investors i.e. small ISA investors	No
Diversification Risk with Top Holdings i.e. top three more than 20% of fund	Yes
Likely to be a core holding?	No
Market Cap based (MC)/Screened (S)	MC
Appeal to Income Investors?	No
Risk Factors?	Political Risk – it's a communist state with high levels of political interference

A very volatile market |
| Top 3 holding as % of total March 2009 | 37% |
| Country Breakdown: top 3 – March 2009 | 100% Chinese based but Hong Kong listed |
| Sector Breakdown: top 3 – March 2009 | Banks 39%
Insurance 17%
Oil and Gas 15% |

Comments

The idea of investing in individual national emerging markets is a tricky subject. Many adventurous types love focusing on a specific nation and then going aggressively long, but we think the risks are just too great and that investors do not realise just how volatile these individual national markets really are. But even we accept that a case can be made for investing in China as an individual market over the long term – unlike other BRIC countries, such as Russia and Brazil, it is not an obvious resources play and its private sector is growing much faster than rival India. More importantly China is already a huge economy, a growing part of the global trade and financial system and its size alone makes it equivalent to most emerging markets regions.

The big issue is which index to focus on. There are a number of different ways of buying into big Chinese mega-caps plus the odd few small-cap options. Our preference is for an index called **the Hang Seng China Enterprises Index,** which is, according to its developers, 'a free float capitalisation-weighted index comprised of H-Shares listed on the Hong Kong Stock Exchange and included in the Hang Seng Mainland Composite Index. As of 15 January 2008, the constituents comprised 43 H-shares'.

Share classes

A shares – these are companies incorporated in mainland China and traded on the mainland A-share markets. The prices of A shares are quoted in Renminbi (the Chinese currency) and currently available only to mainlanders, although selected foreign institutional investors are allowed to trade A shares.

B shares – these are companies incorporated in mainland China and are traded in the mainland B-share markets (Shanghai and Shenzhen). B shares are quoted in foreign currencies. In the past, only foreigners were allowed to trade B shares. Since March 2001, mainlanders can also trade B shares, although they must trade with legal foreign currency accounts.

H shares – these are companies incorporated in mainland China and listed on the Hong Kong Stock Exchange and other foreign stock exchanges.

All this jargon about H shares needs some explaining. The key principle to grasp is that China is not really like other countries. On paper it is a capitalist's paradise but in reality most of the very big companies are largely owned – and certainly controlled through their management – by **the state, aka the Chinese Communist Party.** One of the ways that the state/the CPC exercises control is via different classes of equity, with some available only for local Chinese nationals and quoted on the local Chinese exchanges (Shanghai principally), alongside other classes (H shares) that are available to foreigners through well-established exchanges such as the Hong Kong market. This Hong Kong dimension adds another complication – there are some very successful Chinese companies that are based on the Hong Kong exchange, which have nearly all their operations in China, but are not in reality properly Chinese companies. Confused? So are most institutional investors. To make matters even worse, you will also encounter some rival indices, chief among them the **FTSE/Xinhua China 25 Index,** which tracks shares of the most widely followed 25 mainland enterprises available to offshore investors, which are traded on the Stock Exchange of Hong Kong Limited (SEHK). On paper it is very similar to the

HSCEI but it tracks a smaller number of companies and is much less diversified. This variety of indices – and we are not including the main Hong Kong index, the Hang Seng, in this quick overview – is duplicated in a number of competing exchange traded funds on the London market.

The highlighted funds

Details			
Fund	Lyxor ETF China Enterprise	DBX FTSE Xinhua China 25	iShares FTSE Xinhua China 25
Ticker/EPIC	LCHN	XX25	IDFX
Issuer	Lyxor ETF	Deutsche DBX	iShares Barclays
TER	0.65%	0.60%	0.74%
Currency	GBP	GBP	GBP
Underlying Index	HSCEI index of H or Hong Kong listed shares	FTSE Xinhua China 25	FTSE Xinhua China 25
Launch Date	18/10/2007	20/06/2007	21/10/2004

All three funds offered are a potentially excellent way of buying into the big Chinese growth story, although our preference is for the HSCEI index tracked by the Lyxor ETF. All three funds buy into huge Chinese megacaps that list certain classes of their shares on the main Hong Kong market, the Hang Seng. Most of these companies are ultimately state owned with major holdings in the oil/gas sector, mobile telecoms and banking – you will not see that many purely privately owned companies in any of these ETFs. If you are after smaller cap Chinese shares you are better off looking to the US ETF market and the China small-cap ETF HAO offered by Alphashares.

Investors also need to be aware that the underlying shares owned by these three large-cap funds are usually classes exclusively for foreigners and do not grant ultimate power or control over the companies concerned. Also, it is worth noting that all three funds concentrate on a small number of very big companies – 43 for the China Enterprises Index and 25 for the FTSE index.

The only really big difference – and it is not even that big – is in cost. The iShares fund is the most expensive with a TER of close to 0.75 per cent, while the Deutsche DBX shares are the cheapest with a TER of 0.60 per cent.

Private investors looking to invest in any of these funds also need to be aware of the much broader risks of investing in China. Apart from the political control we mentioned above, Chinese equities are enormously volatile and liable to fluctuate madly, with many frequent busts. Also, compared with many emerging markets Chinese shares are highly rated – as this is written (Spring 2009), the average PE for the FTSE Xinhua 25 is a choppy 11.5, a good 30–40 per cent above most developed world markets, even though that figure is at the very low end of recent valuations (in recent years the Chinese market has traded close to 20–30 times earnings). These high ratings are perhaps deserved given the phenomenal growth prospects of the Chinese economy, but investors need to be aware that this potential high growth comes at the cost of high volatility and high valuations compared with peer markets.

Macquarie Global 100 Index

Volatility	1.57
Weight of largest holding	6.23% (GDF Suez)
Weight of top ten largest holdings	34%
Yield (March 2009)	5.15%

Returns

Index	2004	2005	2006	2007	2008
Macquarie Global 100 index	NA	NA	39.52%	23.19%	−38.98%

Graph – this graph is for the DBX ETF of the index and not the actual index

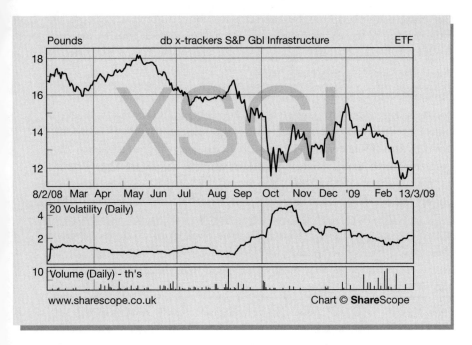

The index – our analysis

ANALYSIS	
Likely Risk (High/Medium/Low)	Medium
Likely Volatility	Medium
Suitable for 'Simple' Investors i.e. small ISA investors	Yes
Diversification Risk with Top Holdings i.e. top three more than 20% of fund	No
Likely to be a core holding?	Yes
Market Cap based (MC)/Screened (S)	MC
Appeal to Income Investors?	Yes
Risk Factors?	Many companies subject to regulatory oversight and thus vulnerable to political pressure
	Deflation could be a risk to margin structures

Continued

ANALYSIS	
Top 3 holding as % of total fund March 2009	14%
Country Breakdown: top 3 – March 2009	USA 22% Canada 9% Spain 9%
Sector Breakdown: top 3 – July 2008	Utilities 42% Transportation 39% Energy 17%

The highlighted funds – infrastructure funds

Details			
Fund	DB S&P Global Infrastructure	iShares S&P Emerging Markets Infrastructure	iShares FTSE/ Macquarie Global Infrastructure 100
Ticker/EPIC	XSGI	IEMI	INFR
Issuer	Deutsche DBX	iShares Barclays	iShares Barclays
TER	0.60%	0.74%	0.65%
Currency	GBP	GBP	GBP
Underlying Index	S&P Global Infrastructure index	S&P Emerging Markets Infrastructure Index	FTSE/Macquarie Global Infrastructure 100
Launch Date	15/01/2008	14/02/2008	20/10/2006

The infrastructure space has been one of the fastest growing bits of the investment universe over the last decade, fuelled in part by the growth of a number of competing global and regional indices. The two main indices come courtesy of the FTSE Group and rival S&P. The S&P Global Infrastructure Index series includes 75 large, liquid infrastructure stocks from around the world, with one-fifth of the constituents emerging market stocks with a liquid, developed market listing (NYSE ADRs, LSE GDRs or Hong Kong listings of Chinese stocks). To ensure diversified exposure across different infrastructure clusters, S&P makes sure that the 75 constituents are distributed at each rebalancing as follows:

- energy 15–20 per cent
- transportation 30–40 per cent
- utilities 30–40 per cent.

Constituent weights are driven by size, with no single stock having a weight of more than 5 per cent in the index at rebalancing.

S&P Global Infrastructure Index – top holdings (July 2009)	
TransCanada Corporation	5.11%
Abertis Infraestructuras	4.96%
Gaz de France (GDF SUEZ)	4.37%
Autostrade Spa	4.15%
Enbridge Inc	4.04%
E.ON AG	3.77%
Iberdrola	3.19%
Transurban Group	3.11%
Spectra Energy Corp	2.97%
RWE AG St.	2.88%

The other main index comes from rival outfit FTSE, namely the FTSE Macquarie. The Macquarie Global Infrastructure Index (MGII) Series is calculated by FTSE and is designed to 'reflect the stock performance of companies worldwide within the infrastructure industry, principally those engaged in management, ownership and operation of infrastructure and utility assets. The infrastructure industry is now one of the world's fastest growing asset classes with a current market value of over US$1,600 billion and the FTSE Macquarie Global Infrastructure Index itself has seen a 200 per cent increase in market capitalisation from July 2000 to the end of January 2006'. The main index in the series is the Macquarie Global Infrastructure 100 Index, which includes the top 100 constituents from developed and advanced emerging countries of the main Global Infrastructure Index series. In practice, this index focuses on utilities-based businesses, with 55 per cent of the holdings in electricity-based companies and another 37 per cent in utilities (gas and water mainly).

FTSE Macquarie Global Infrastructure Index – top ten holdings (July 2009)

MGII Top 10 Security	Country	% Weight
GDF SUEZ	France	6.23
E.ON AG	Germany	5.41
IBERDROLA SA	Spain	3.89
EXELON CORP	United States	3.34
RWE AG	Germany	3.05
TOKYO ELECTRIC POWER CO INC	Japan	3.02
SOUTHERN CO	United States	2.51
ENEL SPA	Italy	2.41
NATIONAL GRID PLC	United Kingdom	2.28
FPL GROUP INC	United States	2.23

There is one last index worth noting. It is called the S&P Emerging Markets Infrastructure Index and it provides liquid and tradable exposure to 30 of the largest publicly listed emerging market companies in the global infrastructure industry. The index follows a modified market capitalisation-weighted scheme that reduces single-stock concentration and balances exposure across the three clusters. At rebalancing, the transportation, energy, and utilities clusters have weights of 20 per cent, 40 per cent and 40 per cent, respectively.

The investment case for infrastructure assets

According to the FTSE Group, infrastructure and utility assets are essential for all investors. They cite the following positives for the investment space:

- Essential and irreplaceable services with inelastic demand means exposure to infrastructure provides adequate gearing for growth in portfolio.
- Global trend towards PPPs and privatisation of traditionally public-funded assets is driving rapid growth of infrastructure with expectations for continued development in the three diverse areas of roads, airports and telecommunications.
- Strong cash flows characterised by low volatility and average correlation with other asset classes make infrastructure an excellent toll for properly diversifying a portfolio.
- Strong record of market index outperformance.

All three of these indices and accompanying funds are hugely innovative and potentially very useful for investors – they give you access to the world's leading utility and public infrastructure companies. Thankfully they are all rather different in emphasis. The iShares Emerging Markets fund does what it says on the tin and focuses on less developed markets, although it is still rather focused on Hong Kong/China alongside South America, while the sibling iShares FTSE/Macquarie 100 fund is much more focused on first-world utility companies, with a particular emphasis on electricity companies.

Deutsche DBX trackers focus on the S&P Global Infrastructure index. The resulting DBX ETF is the cheaper of the two global index tracking trackers and it is less concentrated in its holdings than the two iShares funds, with the top three holdings (in company terms) accounting for just 13 per cent of the fund. Also US-based companies account for just 24 per cent of top holdings, which is much lower than the iShares FTSE MacQuarie fund. On balance though we slightly prefer the Macquarie 100 Index as it strikes us as more defensive in tone, with high-quality utility-based assets sitting at the core of the portfolio.

We do have some doubts regarding the iShares Emerging Markets fund, mainly because its top three holdings account for no less than 25 per cent of the fund's holdings, which is rather worrying in our view. On the plus side, though, this fund is likely to deliver much higher returns over the long term – the economies in the underlying countries are growing faster – alongside probable high volatility.

MSCI Latin America

Volatility	4.24 (very high)
Weight of largest holding	10.23% (Petrobas)
Weight of top ten largest holdings	44.12%
Yield	2.25%

Returns

Index	2004	2005	2006	2007	2008
MSCI Latin America Index	34.8%	44.9%	39.3%	46.9%	−52.8%

Note graph below is from iShares ETF and not the index.

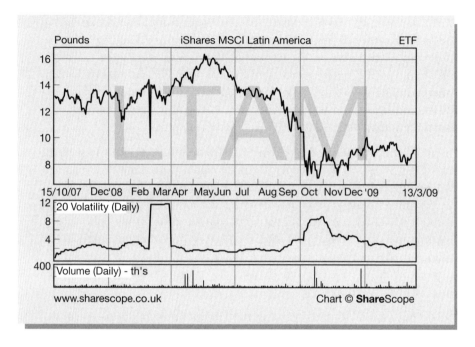

The index – our analysis

ANALYSIS	
Likely Risk (High/Medium/Low)	High
Likely Volatility	High
Suitable for 'Simple' Investors i.e. small ISA investors	No
Diversification Risk with Top Holdings i.e. top three more than 20% of fund	Yes – 22.5%
Likely to be a core holding?	No
Market Cap based (MC)/Screened (S)	MC
Risk Factors?	Political risk and national dependence on commodities
	Volatile market

Continued

ANALYSIS

Top 3 holding as % of total March 2009	22.5%
Country Breakdown: top 3 – March 2009	62% Brazil 25% Mexico 6% Chile
Sector Breakdown: top 3 – March 2009	Mining 21.5% Telecoms 14.3% Financial 14%

Comments

Our general advice is to stay clear of specific countries and regions within the fast-expanding emerging markets investment universe – we feel that the risks are just too great even though some countries like India or even Russia do present enormous opportunity. Our view is that your exposure to these growth markets is best achieved through a general MSCI Emerging Markets index tracker. But there are two notable exceptions to this rule – China and Latin America.

The sudden emergence of Latin America and especially Brazil on to the investment landscape in this century is nothing short of extraordinary. Growth in countries like Brazil and Mexico and even Chile and Peru has been translated into some astonishing stock market gains and a number of world beating, mega-corporations have emerged – names like Petrobas from Brazil (a massive oil company) and America Movil (a Mexican mobile phone giant) are increasingly forces to be reckoned with.

We think adventurous investors should seriously consider some sort of investment in this region, although we would caution that its heightened volatility and bias towards the resource sector will probably put off more conservative investors who are risk averse. Also we would recommend exposure to the whole region and not just to Brazil – most Latin American funds tend to have massive exposure to Brazil anyway, but you also get the benefit of some diversification into interesting economies like Mexico and Chile.

Top holdings of iShares Latin America ETF at end of January 2009

Company	Country	% Weight
PETROBAS	Brazil	10.23
AMERICA MOVIL SAB DE CV-SER L	Mexico	7.4
CIA VALE DO RIO DOCE	Brazil	5.09
CIA VALE DO RIO DOCE-PREF A	Brazil	5.04
BANCO BRADESCO -PREF	Brazil	4.24
BANCO ITAU HOLDING FIN-PREF	Brazil	3.46
UNIBANCO-UNITS	Brazil	2.28
CIA SIDERURGICA NACIONAL SA	Brazil	2.22
CIA DE BEBIDAS DAS AME-PREF	Brazil	2.2
WALMART MEXICO	Mexico	1.96

The funds

Until just a few years ago, any investors wanting to invest in Latin America as a specific region would have had very few choices – basically only a few specialist investment trusts operated in this new investment space. Now we have three ETFs all tracking the same regional index, which includes massive outfits like Petrobas as well as minnows from countries like Colombia and Peru plus the odd outfit from once mighty markets including Argentina. What is even better is that these funds are all fairly cheap, charging between 0.65 per cent and 0.74 per cent.

Selected Latin American funds

Details			
Fund	iShares MSCI Latin America	DB MSCI EM Latin America TRN	Lyxor ETF MSCI Latin America
Ticker/EPIC	LTAM	XMLA	LLAT
Issuer	iShares Barclays	Deutsche DBX	Lyxor ETF
TER	0.74%	0.65%	0.65%
Underlying Index	MSCI EM Latin America Index	MSCI EM Latin America Index	MSCI EM Latin America
Launch Date	16/10/2007	22/06/2007	14/01/2008

MSCI Latin American Index: returns since inception

Year	Index Value	% change
1988	170.003	70.0
1989	252.833	48.7
1990	220.825	−12.7
1991	539.620	144.4
1992	602.256	11.6
1993	907.404	50.7
1994	898.564	−1.0
1995	763.016	−15.1
1996	907.500	18.9
1997	1,164.664	28.3
1998	721.582	−38.0
1999	1,121.893	55.5
2000	915.634	−18.4
2001	876.163	−4.3
2002	658.941	−24.8
2003	1,100.848	67.1
2004	1,483.584	34.8
2005	2,149.973	44.9
2006	2,995.669	39.3
2007	4,400.409	46.9
2008	2,077.684	−52.8

Brazilian funds

You could, of course, just go straight to the source of much of the biggest returns of recent years and invest directly in a Brazilian index tracking fund. There are two main indices worth following in Brazil. The most common comes from the ubiquitous MSCI Barra and is called the **iShares**

MSCI Brazil Index Fund. It tracks nearly all the most liquid stocks on the Brazilian market and is a subset of the wider MSCI EM Latin American index. The other main choice is based on the main local market and is called the **Bovespa Index**, which is an index of about 50 stocks traded on the Sao Paulo Stock Exchange (**BO**lsa de **V**alores do Estado de São **PA**ulo). According to the index developers, 'the index is composed by a theoretical portfolio with the stocks that accounted for 80 per cent of the volume traded in the last 12 months [on the Sao Paulo Stock Exchange] .... comprises 70 per cent of the all the stock value traded' on the exchange. In sum, it is the local, smaller equivalent of our FTSE 100. All three of these ETFs are potentially a brilliant way of playing the Brazilian success story.

Details

Fund	Lyxor ETF Brazil (Bovespa)	iShares MSCI Brazil	DBX MSCI Brazil TRN Index
Ticker/EPIC	LBRZ	IBZL	XMBR
Issuer	Lyxor ETF	iShares Barclays	Deutsche DBX
TER	0.65%	0.74%	0.65%
Underlying Index	Bovespa	MSCI Brazil Index	MSCI Brazil TRN Index
Launch Date	18/10/2007	18/11/2005	22/06/2007

Brazil is obviously a resource play first and foremost and investors need to understand that bias – holdings in this broad sector account for between 40 per cent and 60 per cent of these fund holdings. In particular these ETFs are a big bet on the giant Brazilian private oil company Petrobas (23 per cent), alongside a gamble on the Brazilian iron ore company (Vale at 26 per cent of the iShares fund) plus the odd huge bank like Bradesco – all the other sectors on the Brazilian market are dwarfs by comparison. Crucially you are not over-paying for the companies in these portfolios – as we write (spring 2009) the average PE ratio for this basket of companies is only about 11 times current earnings.

So, which Brazilian ETF to buy? If pushed we would probably go for the Lyxor fund because it is cheaper and slightly less concentrated on any particular sector or company, although in truth all three funds are a decent bet on Brazil. But our earlier point still holds true – we would prefer to buy a Latin American fund to add some diversification.

MSCI World Islamic Index

Volatility (GLOBAL index)	
Weight of largest holding	EXXON MOBIL at 4%
Weight of top ten largest holdings	20%
Yield %	1.99%

Returns

Short-term returns in 2008 and 2009

Index	Apr–09	Mar–09	Feb–09	Jan–09	2008
ISLAMIC INDICES					
MSCI Emerging Markets Islamic Index	15.72	14.46	–4.38	–4.85	–55.36
MSCI USA Islamic Index	5.6	7.27	–9.43	–4.56	–30.69
MSCI World Islamic Index	7.51	7.09	–9.05	–6.1	–35.08

Featured ETFs

Details

Fund	iShares MSCI World islamic	iShares MSCI Emerging Markets Islamic	iShares MSCI USA Islamic
Ticker/EPIC	ISWD	ISEM	ISUS
Issuer	iShares Barclays	iShares Barclays	iShares Barclays
TER	0.60%	0.85%	0.50%
Underlying Index	MSCI World Islamic	MSCI EM Islamic	MSCI USA
Number of holdings	302	200	251
Fund value mid 2008 (M)	$19	$4	$10
Launch Date	10/12/2007	10/12/2007	
Region/Global	Global	Global	USA

ANALYSIS

Likely Risk (High/Medium/Low)	Medium to low
Likely Volatility	Medium to low
Suitable for 'Simple' Investors i.e. small ISA investors	Yes
Diversification Risk with Top Holdings i.e. top three more than 20% of fund	No
Likely to be a core holding?	Yes
Market Cap based (MC)/Screened (S)	MC but ethically screened
Appeal to Income Investors?	No
Risk Factors?	Still very biased towards energy and materials
	Biased to US markets
Appeal to investors looking to short main markets	No
Top 3 holding as % of total fund March 2009	8%
Country Breakdown: top 3 – March 2009	US 54%
	UK 10%
	Japan 8%
Sector Breakdown: top 3 – March 2009	Energy 22%
	Healthcare 18%
	IT 13%

Comments

The MSCI Islamic Index Series (the 'Islamic Indices') follows something called Sharia investment principles. This 'screened' index is based on an MSCI equity index (or any combination of MSCI equity indices), but excludes all the non-'compliant' securities. Following the Sharia investment principles, MSCI excludes securities using two types of criteria: business activity and financial ratios. The first category means that the index provider must exclude any company that derives more than 5 per cent of its revenue (cumulatively) from any of the following activities:

- alcohol: distillers, vintners and producers of alcoholic beverages, including producers of beer and malt liquors, owners and operators of bars and pubs;

- tobacco: cigarettes and other tobacco products' manufacturers and retailers;

- pork-related products: companies involved in the manufacture and retail of pork products;

- financial services: commercial banks involved in retail banking, corporate lending, investment banking; companies involved in mortgage and mortgage-related services; providers of financial services, including insurance, capital markets and specialised finance; credit agencies; stock exchanges;

- Gambling/casino: owners and operators of casinos and gaming facilities, including companies providing lottery and betting services;

- music: producers and distributors of music, owners and operators of radio broadcasting systems;

- hotels: owners and operators of hotels;

- cinema: companies engaged in the production, distribution and screening of movies and television shows, owners and operators of television broadcasting systems and providers of cable or satellite television services;

- adult entertainment: owners and operators of adult entertainment products and activities.

Sharia investment principles also do not allow investment in companies deriving significant income from interest or companies that have excessive leverage. MSCI uses the following three financial ratios to screen for these companies:

- total debt over total assets;
- sum of a company's cash and interest-bearing securities over total assets;
- accounts receivables over total assets.

While the two first financial ratios may not exceed 33.33 per cent, the third ratio may not exceed 70 per cent.

The Islamic sector has been growing at an astonishing rate in recent years. Part of that is down to strong demand from a large number of immigrant and non-immigrant Muslims for Sharia-compliant financial services and transactions. But that is not the whole picture – another key factor has been growing oil wealth, with demand for suitable investments soaring in the Gulf GCC region. Crucially these demand-led factors have been helped by the growth of new financial structures that let Islamic investors mix belief with profit. The fact that Islamic laws prohibit paying and receiving interest does not imply that they frown on making money or encourage reverting to an all-cash or barter economy. Received religious opinion simply demands that all parties in a financial transaction share the risk and profit or loss of the venture. Depositors in Islamic banking are closer in form to shareholders, for instance, who can earn dividends when the bank makes a profit or lose part of their savings if the bank posts a loss. The idea is to link the return in an Islamic contract to productivity and the quality of the project, thereby ensuring a more equitable distribution of wealth. Looking at the legal framework, Islamic financial instruments take the form of contracts between providers and users of funds to manage risk. On the asset side, Islamic banks engage in investment and trading activities according to the various contracts available while deposits, for instance, are usually based on a *Mudaraba* contract or an interest-free loan contract (*Qard Al Hasan*).

With Islamic banking growing fast, it was inevitable that the asset management boys would follow. In fact, the concept of stock indices compliant with the beliefs of Islam is not new. The first Shariah-compliant indices from a major index provider were launched by Dow Jones Indexes in 1999, and FTSE followed suit with its own family in 2000. The iShares ETF platform is based in turn on a relatively new entrant to the market (2007), MSCI. A report released by S&P last year put estimates of current Shariah-compliant assets at $400bn, and estimated the potential market for Islamic financial services to be in the area of $4tn. Like rival index provider S&P, MSCI works with a consulting firm, Kuwait-based Ratings Intelligence Partners, to ensure that the indices are Shariah-compliant. Crucially, it is important that investors understand that not all Islamic indices are created in the same way – the S&P index, for instance, screens out those companies that engage in the trading of gold and silver as cash on a deferred basis. MSCI screens out companies involved in the music industry (including radio broadcasting), hotels and the film and television industry (including television broadcasters, cable providers and theatres).

With these ethically strict screening techniques in place, it comes as no surprise to learn that some social (SRI) investors who are not Muslims have started taking these funds seriously. There is a real paucity of ethical index funds, after all, and these funds do a good job of removing some of the more sinful companies on the main developed markets. Many Christian investors, for instance, would probably share many if not most of the same ethical views as Islamic investors – the only key difference seems to be that these Islamic funds do not exclude weapons manufacturers, but they do exclude banks which tend to pass most SRI tests.

Looking at the funds in detail you need to be aware that the decision to exclude financials does have one major effect – you are likely to increase your exposure to energy and resource stocks. Holdings of these kind of stocks range between 34 per cent (US fund) and 48 per cent for the emerging markets fund. Healthcare also becomes important in these funds, which in bear markets may be something of a plus as most healthcare stocks are fairly defensive. Investors in the Emerging Markets fund will also have to contend with the moral implications of investing 15 per cent of the fund in Russia (its invasion of Afghanistan is hardly a bright spot in Islamic/Russian relations) and 14 per cent in technically communist and thus heathen China.

S&P Global Forestry and Timber

Volatility	2.47
Weight of largest holding	9%
Weight of top ten largest holdings	65%
Yield	6%

Returns

Index	2004	2005	2006	2007	2008
S&P Global Forestry and Timber	23.55	−5.59	16.73	13.13	−49

Note: this is not the graph of the index but of the iShares ETF.

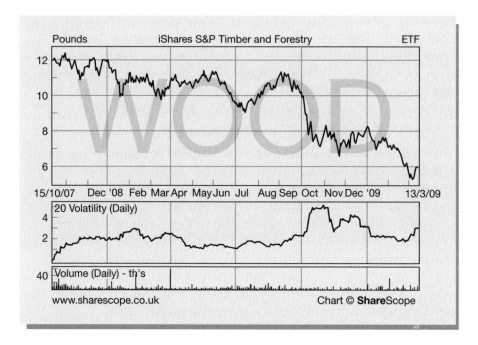

The index – our analysis

ANALYSIS	
Likely Risk (High/Medium/Low)	High
Likely Volatility	High
Suitable for 'Simple' Investors i.e. small ISA investors	No
Diversification Risk with Top Holdings i.e. top three more than 20% of fund	Yes (26%)
Likely to be a core holding?	Yes but only for adventurous investors
Market Cap based (MC)/Screened (S)	MC
Appeal to Income Investors?	Yes

Continued

ANALYSIS	
Risk Factors?	Highly volatile
	Very focused on US and Canadian companies
Top 3 holding as % of total March 2009	26%
Country Breakdown: top 3 – March 2009	US 40% Canada 18% Finland 9.5%
Sector Breakdown: top 3 – March 2009	100% timber related

Featured ETF

Details	
Fund	iShares S&P Global Timber and Forestry
Ticker/EPIC	WOOD
Issuer	iShares Barclays
TER	0.65%
Currency	GBP
Underlying Index	S&P Global Timber and Forestry Index
Launch Date	15/10/2007

Comments

Timber and forestry is one of the newest of the various alternative asset classes to have emerged in the last decade or so. Big name investors like David Swensen, head of Yale's hugely successful endowment investment fund, have made substantial profits by investing in global forestry and as news of those profits has spread, investors have been keen to find some way of accessing a very specialised niche. Unsurprisingly, a large number of funds and indices have sprung up to take part in this new alternative assets land grab and one of the most successful new indices to emerge has come from Standard & Poor's. Its S&P Global Timber & Forestry Index comprises 25 of the largest publicly traded companies engaged in the ownership, management or upstream supply chain of forests and timberlands. According to the index developers, 'these may be forest products companies, timber REITs, paper products companies, paper packaging companies, or agricultural product companies that are engaged in the ownership, management or the upstream supply chain of forests and timberlands'.

Index constituents exhibit the following characteristics:

- **weighting** – modified capitalisation weighted;
- **market capitalisation** – US$250m;
- **liquidity** – Three month average daily volume of at least US$2m;
- **reconstitution** – annual.

What emerges out of this index is a varied bunch of logging companies, and timber-based real estate investment trusts or REITs including names like Plum Tree (a US timber REIT), and the giant Canadian forestry and paper company Sino-Forest Corporation. Currently there is one ETF that tracks the index – from iShares – but for some strange reason, this new fund has received a rather subdued welcome from the UK market and financial press, for no good cause in our view. For more adventurous investors, we reckon that this is a first-rate index and the accompanying ETF gives investors the opportunity to invest in a sector that is genuinely different.

Why do we like this product so much? Performance has certainly not been wonderful – the index was down over 40 per cent in 2008, for instance. The biggest plus in our books is that this asset class is almost completely uncorrelated with wider equity markets. Run any analysis of markets and you will see timber companies constantly cropping up as lowly correlated with indices like the FTSE 100. And, of course, there is a good reason for this – the mechanics of the forestry sector (like some similarly uncorrelated agricultural products) is driven more by environment, weather and tax breaks rather than globalisation or liquid capital flows.

We also like the fact that this ETF is not too concentrated on say just a few big companies. The top three companies account for less than 28 per cent of the total holding (of only 25 companies) and there seems to be a good mix of paper packagers, forestry products directly and specialist timber land owners. The only major risk in our book is that this fund is highly concentrated on the American continents, with the US and Canada accounting for just under 70 per cent of all holdings.

There are, of course, some big, chunky risks. There is no getting away from the fact that this index has been very volatile in recent years and returns have been dreadful. But if you buy the long-term investment argument for paper –

constrained global supply, increased global demand via industrialisation –
and for established forestry land companies in well-regulated parts of the
world, then those poor returns could be reversed in the coming decades. If
nothing else you are buying a bunch of companies with double-digit operating margins, heavy asset backing (the US REITs are frequently land
revaluation plays) and a yield that, as of writing, stands close to 6 per cent pa.
Our bottom line is that the strong long-term secular trends that favour the
forestry sector and its low correlation/decent return profile make this a cracking investment which should appeal beyond the high net worth/
sophisticated investor segment this sector has traditionally been targeted at.

Top ten holdings in March 2009	
Plum Creek Timber Co. 8.99%	United States
Rayonier Inc. 8.91%	United States
Oji Paper Co. 7.78%	Japan
Potlatch Corp. 6.75%	United States
Weyerhaeuser Corp. 6.49%	United States
Sino-Forest Corporation 6.48%	Canada
West Fraser Timber 6.01%	Canada
UPM-Kymmene Oyj 4.92%	Finland
Canfor Corporation 4.78%	Canada
SCA – Svenska Cellulosa AB 4.64%	Sweden

S&P Global Clean Energy

Volatility	3.81
Weight of largest holding	7.28% (Iberdrola)
Weight of top ten largest holdings	53.45%
Yield	1.25%

Returns

Index	2004	2005	2006	2007	2008
S&P Global Clean Energy	11%	24.89%	43.03%	76.5%	−51%

Note: this graph is not the index but the iShares ETF which tracks the index

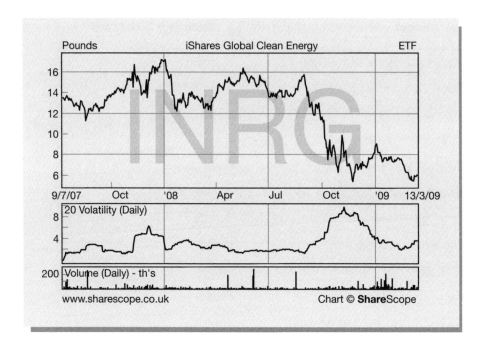

The index – our analysis

ANALYSIS	
Likely Risk (High/Medium/Low)	Very High
Likely Volatility	High
Suitable for 'Simple' Investors i.e. small ISA investors	Yes
Diversification Risk with Top Holdings i.e. top three more than 20% of fund	Yes (but only 20.5%)

Continued

ANALYSIS

Likely to be a core holding?	No
Market Cap based (MC)/Screened (S)	MC
Total return or pays income? TR/Inc	Inc
Appeal to Income Investors?	No
Risk Factors?	Technology focused and vulnerable to changes in energy prices US focused
Top 3 holding as % of total fund March 2009	21%
Country Breakdown: top 3 – March 2009	USA 29% China 21% Spain 12%
Sector Breakdown: top 3 – March 2009	Industrials 69% Utilities 22% IT 8%

The highlighted funds – Green Energy ETFs

Details

Fund	iShares S&P Global Clean Energy	Lyxor ETF New Energy TF	Powershares Global Clean Energy Fund
Ticker/EPIC	INRG	LNEW	PSDW.L
Issuer	iShares	Lyxor ETF	Invesco Powershares
TER	0.65%	0.60%	0.75%
Currency	GBP	GBP	Euro
Underlying Index	S&P Global Clean Energy	SG World Alternative Energy Index	The WilderHill New Energy Global Innovation Index
Launch Date	09/07/2007	13/03/2008	

Comments

Green investing has been a fabulous investment category in the last few years – investors have piled into clean energy companies pushing up prices to amazing levels. In the table below we have broken out returns from before the crash. As you will see, the returns were amazing, but those returns had been at the expense of some pretty choppy volatility (the matching table below gives some data on volatility). All of the underlying indices were star performers, but all have returned volatile returns way in excess of what you would expect from buying, say, an S&P 500 index fund.

Year performance	WilderHill Energy	S&P Global Clean Energy	SocGen World Energy (euro)
ETF provider Holdings	Powershares 50	iShares 30	Lyxor 20
2001	−23.12		
2002	−19.97		
2003	54.87		
2004	20.37	11.02	37.4
2005	21.04	24.89	81
2006	34.82	43.03	20.6
2007	59.02	76.5	52
H1 2008	−12.44	−16.17	22.5
5 yr vol			
3 yr vol	21.45%	26.81%	24%
Benchmark- S&P 500			
5 yr vol	7.58%		
3 yr vol	10.23%		

Note: all figures below from July 2008

Comparison of holdings in clean energy ETFs					
iShares		Lyxor		Powershares	
Wind	26.00%	Wind power	46%	Wind	27%
Solar	46%	Solar	33%	Solar	27%
Hydro	15%	Hydro	10.50%	Energy efficiency	20%
Biofuels	7%	Efficiency/power	7.67%	Biofuels	13%
Geothermal	2.37%	Fuel cell	1.37%	Power storage	3%
30th June 2008		**31st July 2008**		**30th June 2008**	

What all this price data tells us is that the whole new energy space (which obviously includes solar power and wind power plus all the other 'also run' technologies including wave power and waste conversion technology) is capable of extraordinary gains, but at the cost of extraordinary volatility. By the end of 2008, for instance, the S&P index was down a scary 51 per cent in one year. That does not mean that investors should not use these indices and their accompanying funds as part of a long-term plan, it is just that they should be careful about timing a large lump-sum purchase – we would suggest this investment space is a great long-term monthly savings investment idea.

But what exactly are you buying into with a green or clean energy index tracking fund? The crucial point to understand is that these funds do not invest in the same thing, even though they all track clean energy indices. At the end of 2008, for instance, the Lyxor SocGen fund had 46 per cent of its total holdings in wind power companies by our calculations whereas the iShares S&P fund had just 26 per cent. Hydro is a big component of the iShares and the Lyxor fund but a tiny component of the Powershares fund where biofuels is a much bigger play (oh dear!). Of course, these percentages will change month on month but they should tell you a bigger story – what constitutes a green energy fund will vary hugely. With this huge discrepancy – what exactly is your index investing in? – you may face a much tougher question, namely whether the passive approach is right. Should you be looking to invest using an active fund manager instead? Impax, for instance, has a hugely successful investment trust that tracks a lot of the themes mentioned above but holds a much more interesting and unique range of assets, yet its TER is just over 1 per cent, which is not much more than 30 basis points above these passive ETF funds. Impax in particular is very knowledgeable about this sector and has been building its own index with the FTSE that tracks clean energy stocks – in the table overleaf.

If you do decide that the passive approach is best for you, which index and which fund should you choose? All three of the big ETFs in this space will give you exposure to the sector (notwithstanding our comments about different holdings), but we would suggest that more adventurous types might look at the S&P index while more cautious types might look at the Powershares ETF, which tracks a less well-known index called WilderHill New Energy Index. It is slightly less volatile, although it has also produced some very decent returns until the great crash of 2008.

Name	EPIC	Price	2008	2nd half 08	Jan 1st to March 15th 2009	Volatility
PowerShares Gbl Clean Energy Fund	PSBW	3.295	−48.8	−39.3	−16.3	2.75
iShares Global Clean Energy	INRG	6.0351	−51.5	−41.2	−26.7	3.81
Lyxor ETF New Energy	LNEW	1.4975		−34	−19.9	3.54
FTSE All-Share	ASX	1899.25	−32.4	−20.6	−14	1.11

FTSE ET50 Index

Pure Play Environmental Technology Companies
50 companies
31st December 2007

2007	72%
5 years annualised	31%
Vestas	11.34%
Suntech	7.25%
First Solar	6.03%
Gamesa	4.99%
Iberdrola Renovables	4.08%
USA	41%
Denmark	15%
Spain	10.57%

Different clean energy index compositions at the end of 2008

WilderHill New Energy		SG Index World Alt Energy Index		S&P Global Clean Energy	
Name	*% holding*	*Name*	*% holding*	*Name*	*% holding*
Acciona	2.01%	Renewable Energy Corp	5.65%	Vestas	8.01%
Babcock & Brown Wind Partners	2.01%	Ceres Power Holdings	5.58%	First Solar	6.79%
EDF Energies Nouvelles	2.01%	First Solar	5.50%	Gamesa	5.91%
EDP Renovaveis	2.01%	Ballard Power Systems	5.49%	Cemig	5.90%
Gamesa	2.01%	FuelCell Energy	5.47%	Cia Paranaense	5.25%
Solar	27%	20 constituents		30th June 2008	
Wind	27%	North America	36%	30 companies	
Energy Efficiency	20%	Europe	45%	1st half 2008	−15%
Biofuels	13%	Asia	5%	Standard Deviation	26.87%
Power Storage	3%			PE	31.22
		solar	33%	3 yr EPS Growth	55%
Europe	46%	wind power	46%	Dividend Yield	0.76%
Americas	33%	hydro	10.50%		
Asia	20.30%	efficiency/power	7.67%	USA	33%
		fuel cell	1.37%	Spain	13.9%
				Germany	12%
				Brazil	11%

S&P 500

Volatility	1.31
Weight of largest holding	Exxon Mobil 4.8%
Weight of top ten largest holdings	21.5%
Yield	2.12%

Returns

Index	2004	2005	2006	2007	2008
S&P 500	9.3%	3%	13.6%	3.5%	−37%
Dow Jones	3.6%	−0.6%	16.3%	6.4%	−32.7%
NASDAQ Comp	8.4%	1.4%	9.5%	9.8%	−39%

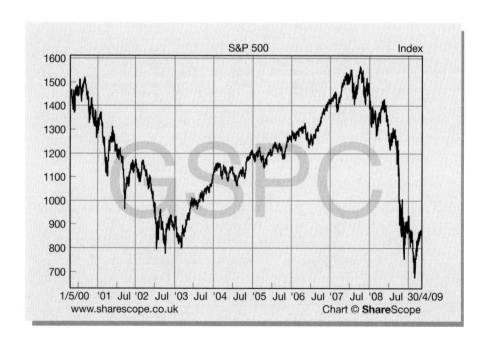

The index – our analysis

ANALYSIS	
Likely Risk (High/Medium/Low)	Medium
Likely Volatility	Medium
Suitable for 'Simple' Investors i.e. small SA investors	Yes
Diversification Risk with Top Holdings i.e. top three more than 20% of fund	No
Likely to be a core holding?	Yes
Market Cap based (MC)/Screened (S)	MC
Appeal to Income Investors?	No
Risk Factors?	Currency Risk
Top 3 holding as % of total fund – March 2009	9%
Country Breakdown: top 3 – March 2009	100% US Listed
Sector Breakdown: top 3 – March 2009	Basic Resources 25.5% Oil and Gas 16.4% Banks 13%

The highlighted funds

Details				
Fund	iShares S&P 500	iShares S&P SmallCap 600	Lyxor ETF Dow Jones IA GBP	Lyxor ETF MSCI USA GBP
Ticker/EPIC	IUSA	ISP6	LIND	LMUS
Issuer	iShares	iShares	Lyxor ETF	Lyxor ETf
TER	0.4%	0.4%	0.50%	0.35%
Underlying Index	S&P 500	S&P small-cap Index	Dow Jones Industrial Average	MSCI USA
Launch Date	15/03/02	12/05/08	13/03/08	13/03/08

Details

Fund	Lyxor ETF NASDAQ 100 GBP	Deutsche DBX MSCI USA TRN INDEX ETF	Deutsche DBX S&P 500 SHORT ETF	ETF Russell 1000 Fund	ETFS Russell 2000 Fund
Ticker/EPIC	LNSQ	XMUS	SPXTS	RONE	RTWO
Issuer	Lyxor ETF	Deutsche DBX	Deutsche DBX	ETF Securities	ETF Securities
TER	0.3%	0.3%	0.50%	0.35%	0.45%
Underlying Index	NASDAQ 100	S&P 500	S&P 500 (inverse of index)	Russell 1000	Russell 2000
Launch Date	13/03/08	08/01/2007	15/01/2008	November 2008	November 2008

Comments

We would suggest that any internationally diversified portfolio should have some exposure, no matter how small, to the US – that could be done indirectly through a world developed markets index, which would have a heavy US weighting, or directly through a fund that tracks a major US index.

If you decide to track a major US index you will be spoilt for choice. There is an almost bewildering array of ETFs based on major US indices, both large-cap and small-cap. These include the following:

■ The major one – and our preferred index – the S&P 500, which is a value-weighted index published since 1957 of the prices of 500 large-cap liquid stocks actively traded in the US. The stocks included in the S&P 500 are those of large publicly held companies that trade on either of the two largest American stock markets, the New York Stock Exchange and NASDAQ. Almost all of the stocks included in the index are among the 500 American stocks with the largest market values or capitalisations.

■ The Dow Jones Industrial Average, which is a price-weighted average of blue-chip stocks and the oldest index by far. The index covers all industries with the exception of Transportation and Utilities. The index has been a widely followed indicator of the stock market since 1 October 1928.

■ The Russell 1000® Index, which measures the performance of the large-cap segment of the US equity universe. It is a subset of the Russell

3000® Index and includes approximately 1000 of the largest US securities. According to ETF Securities, 'The Russell 1000® represents approximately 92 per cent of the US equity market vs. only 66 per cent for the S&P 500. Russell Indexes are used by more US institutional investors than all other index providers combined.'

- THE MSCI USA Index. This is based around the hugely popular MSCI World Developed markets index and covers almost 98 per cent of all the stocks – large and small – listed on the US stock markets (including the NASDAQ and the NYSE).

- The iShares S&P SmallCap 600 reflects the total return performance of the S&P SmallCap 600 Index. The index comprises 600 small-capitalisation companies in the US and covers approximately 3–4 per cent of the US equity market. S&P generally defines the small-cap segment of a country's equity universe as being securities whose total market capitalisation lies between $300m to $2bn.

- The Russell 2000 Index measures the performance of the small-cap segment of the US equity universe. The Russell 2000® index measures the performance of the 2000 smallest companies in the Russell 3000 Index, which represents approximately 8 per cent of the total market capitalisation of the US equity market vs. 3–4 per cent for the S&P 600

Which index to use? Given this huge range we would stick with perhaps the best known of the large-cap indices, namely the S&P 500 index, which is tracked in turn by ETFs from both iShares and Deutsche DBX (the Deutsche fund is slightly cheaper with a TER of just 0.3 per cent). It is also worth noting that Deutsche DBX offers a short S&P 500 fund – its ticker is SPXTS and it pays 1:1 on the downside. If you are looking for a slightly more comprehensive index that includes small-caps, we would suggest looking at the MSCI USA index, while the Russell 2000 is our preferred index for capturing the vibrant small-cap segment in the US markets.

S&P Frontiers

Volatility	1.96
Weight of largest holding	National Bank of Kuwait at 9%
Weight of top ten largest holdings	26%
Yield	NA

Returns

Index	2004	2005	2006	2007	2008
	NA	NA	NA	NA	NA

Note: graph below is of DBX Tracker fund not index.

The index – our analysis

ANALYSIS	
Likely Risk (High/Medium/Low)	High
Likely Volatility	High
Suitable for 'Simple' Investors i.e. small ISA investors	No
Diversification Risk with Top Holdings i.e. top three more than 20% of fund	Yes
Likely to be a core holding?	Yes for adventurous investors

Continued

ANALYSIS

Market Cap based (MC)/Screened (S)	MC
Appeal to Income Investors?	No
Risk Factors?	Political Risk Volatile national markets
Top 3 holding as % of total fund March 2009	27%
Country Breakdown: top 3 – march 2009	Kuwait 32% UAE 18.6% Colombia 18.6%

Featured ETF

Details

Fund	S&P SELECT FRONTIER ETF
Ticker/EPIC	SPNFN
Issuer	Deutsche DBX
TER	0.95%
Underlying Index	S&P Select Frontiers Index
Launch Date	15/01/2008

Comments

Frontier markets comprise roughly 1bn people and about $2.4tn of global capital. Defined loosely by international bodies like the World Bank, frontier markets are high-risk, low-income countries. They typically:

■ are difficult to access for outside investors;

■ are fairly risky on the political (and economic) front;

■ have the potential for huge returns and even bigger declines.

According to analysts at S&P – they have their own frontier indices – frontier market economies have been growing at a 'brisk pace since 2000'. Over this time, frontier markets' GDP has grown at an annualised rate of

5.6 per cent, outpacing the growth of both emerging and developed markets. According to S&P, 'frontier market GDP growth has been higher than that of emerging and developed markets for every year since 2001'.

To be fair, this huge growth is primarily because the countries concerned started from a much lower base – the GDP per capita of much of the developed world is roughly $37,500 compared with just $1845 for Frontier markets (and $2390 for emerging markets). That relative economic under-achievement is also marked in their financial services sector – most frontier markets do have stock markets (there is the odd exception such as Cambodia) but they are typically fairly difficult to invest in if you are a foreigner, heavily protected, over-regulated and subject to massive volatility. Still, the potential is obvious – obvious enough, in fact, for economists at Goldman Sachs to speculate on the countries most likely to follow in the path of the mighty BRIC economies of today. Their top candidates – called the Next 11 – included Egypt, Pakistan, Vietnam, Turkey and even Iran (which is notoriously difficult to access for foreigners).

Are frontier markets a good investment?

The big problem with all of these grand-sounding global investment narratives is that frequently they are precisely just that, broad stories and huge global narratives with little actual investment logic. Economies like Pakistan or Cambodia may be growing like gang-busters, but will any of that rapid economic growth actually a) trickle down to local stock markets, and b) ever make it out of the country into the investment portfolios of investors who have financed this growth?

The risks here are fairly obvious. The biggest and nastiest risk is of national economic meltdown – think Zimbabwe. You will be familiar with terms like 'bread basket of Africa' and 'economic powerhouse of southern Africa', but prior to the meltdown inspired by its leader Robert Mugabe, Zimbabwe had a fairly robust stock market, open to foreign investors since 1993. In the last decade this market slumped, as economic paralysis infected all parts of the economy – national GDP is half of what it was in 2000, and is declining for the eighth consecutive year. Ever since President Mugabe's disastrous land-reform campaign, the country's farming, tourism, and gold sectors have collapsed.

If you take one step back from Zimbabwe and examine this frontier sector as a whole, you can begin to see some quite powerful potential investment opportunities. Over the last 12 years, since December 2005, $100 invested in frontier markets would now be worth just under $600 compared with

$400 for emerging markets and just over $300 for developed markets. Frontier markets also provide one other crucial advantage – until recently they have been poorly correlated with developed world stock markets. Economic theory suggests that frontier markets, with their heavy commodity bias and their startup industrial exposure (refining, basic materials processing, etc.) should provide low correlation to the S&P.

How to invest

Investing in frontier markets directly is almost impossible for private investors in the UK. There are a few companies listed on the London exchange that do give you some exposure to markets like Cambodia and Nigeria, but they are few and far between. The more sensible alternative is to invest across the board in a wide range of countries, so that you can balance out the potential risks.

Many emerging markets fund managers are beginning to enter this space in a small way. Emerging markets guru Mark Mobius, for instance, has started buying into frontier markets through his various small-cap Templeton funds. There is also a specialist frontiers market investment trust run out of London by Progressive Fund Management – it is called the Advance Frontiers market fund and it takes a very active fund-of-fund approach.

The other alternative is to invest in the one and only frontiers market ETF in the UK, managed by Deutsche BX. The most popular index (the Select Frontier Index) comes from S&P. This index is actually a subset of something called the S&P/IFCG Extended Frontier 150, and comprises 40 of the largest and most liquid stocks from countries that have smaller economies or less developed capital markets than traditional emerging markets and are, therefore, excluded from most emerging market benchmarks and investment funds.

To be eligible for the Index a stock must have a minimum free-float market capitalisation of US$100m, an average daily value traded over six months greater than US$2m, and a minimum of 15 days traded over each of the previous six months. The top 30 stocks are then ranked by market capitalisation and those that meet these inclusion criteria are chosen for the Index, subject to the constraint that a maximum of five stocks from any particular country can be included. The Index is free-float market cap weighted with adjustments to ensure that no country has a weight over 30 per cent, no stock has a weight over 10 per cent and a minimum daily basket trade based on average trading history over the last six months of US$200m assuming 100 per cent participation. The Index is rebalanced on a semi-annual basis in January and July of each year.

Countries in the index include Bahrain, Bulgaria, Colombia, Croatia, Jordan, Oman, Pakistan, Romania, Sri Lanka, UAE and Vietnam. The Deutsche DBX ETF tracks this index – and sits alongside the firm's already extensive range of specialist emerging market index trackers (it has also recently launched a specific Vietnam FTSE ETF (TFVTTU)). These ETFs allow investors to accurately track the most liquid stocks, at a relatively low cost, ranging between 0.85 per cent and 0.95 per cent per annum, with no initial up-front charge. But investors need to be aware that the frontier space more than most asset classes does require a huge amount of caution and risk control – skills that may require a more active fund management approach. ETFs may be terrifically efficient and cheap, but if they operate in intrinsically inefficient markets that are busily going nowhere, your investment could suffer. In particular investors need to know what they are investing in with such a fund – a strong Gulf States bias (plus Colombia) and a strong focus on banks and telecom companies plus the odd property giant.

Brent Oil

Volatility	2.51 (high)
Weight of largest holding	NR
Weight of top ten largest holdings	NR
Yield	NR

Returns

Index	2004	2005	2006	2007	2008
Brent Crude Oil composite	36.7%	44.4%	1%	61%	–53%

Graph

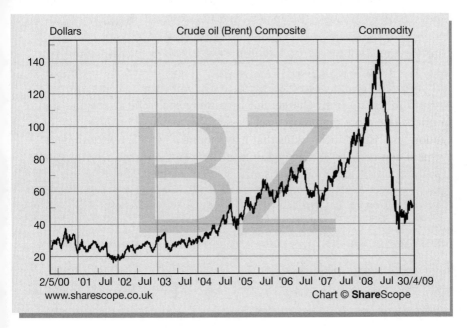

Crude oil (Brent) Composite — Dollars / Commodity

www.sharescope.co.uk
Chart © **Share**Scope

The index – our analysis

ANALYSIS	
Likely Risk (High/Medium/Low)	High
Likely Volatility	High
Suitable for 'Simple' Investors i.e. small ISA investors	No
Diversification Risk with Top Holdings i.e. top three more than 20% of fund	No
Likely to be a core holding?	Possibly for Adventurous Investors

The highlighted funds from ETF Securities

Energy	Exchange	Physically Backed or Collateralised	Exchange Code	Currency	TER
ETFS Petroleum DJ-AIGCI[SM]	London Stock Exchange	Collateralised	AIGO	USD	0.49%
ETFS Forward Petroleum DJ-AIGCI-F3[SM]	London Stock Exchange	Collateralised	FPET	USD	0.49%
ETFS Short Petroleum DJ-AIGCI[SM]	London Stock Exchange	Collateralised	SPET	USD	0.98%
ETFS Leveraged Petroleum DJ-AIGCI[SM]	London Stock Exchange	Collateralised	LPET	USD	0.98%
ETFS Brent 1mth	London Stock Exchange	NO	OILB	USD	0.49%
ETFS Brent 1mth £	London Stock Exchange	NO	OLBP	GBX	0.49%
ETFS Brent 1yr	London Stock Exchange	NO	OSB1	USD	0.49%
ETFS Brent 2yr	London Stock Exchange	NO	OSB2	USD	0.49%
ETFS Brent 3yr	London Stock Exchange	NO	OSB3	USD	0.49%
ETFS Crude Oil	London Stock Exchange	Collateralised	CRUD	USD	0.49%
ETFS Short Crude Oil	London Stock Exchange	Collateralised	SOIL	USD	0.98%
ETFS Leveraged Crude Oil	London Stock Exchange	Collateralised	LOIL	USD	0.98%
	Deutsche Borse (Xetra)	Collateralised	4RT6	EUR	0.98%
ETFS Gasoline	London Stock Exchange	Collateralised	UGAS	USD	0.49%
ETFS WTI 2mth	London Stock Exchange	NO	OILW	USD	0.49%
ETFS WTI 2mth £	London Stock Exchange	NO	OLWP	GBX	0.49%
ETFS WTI 1yr	London Stock Exchange	NO	OSW1	USD	0.49%
ETFS WTI 2yr	London Stock Exchange	NO	OSW2	USD	0.49%
ETFS WTI 3yr	London Stock Exchange	NO	OSW3	USD	0.49%

Comments

Oil seems to have become everyone's favourite commodity after gold – barely a day goes by without a national newspaper or specialist magazine making a bold prediction on the future direction of oil prices. We have absolutely no idea if oil is likely to shoot up through $100 a barrel again or crash below $10.

What we do understand is that many investors are tempted by the defensive qualities of oil – it is almost like gold, a backup commodity in case of financial meltdown. The global economy may grind to a halt with expensive oil, but investors in long oil funds are likely to be richly rewarded. There are also the long-term oil bulls with their peak oil theories to contend with – many maintain that we have already gone past the point at which extra demand for oil is increasing at a faster rate than the growth in supply.

Again we have no idea if this is the case – what does slightly alarm us is that oil and oil-based funds have become so popular that there is some evidence (hotly contested to be sure) that financial speculation is beginning to overwhelm some markets. Big US oil ETFs based on futures prices have begun to heavily influence the direction of futures-based markets as fund managers have to buy up positions to maintain the fund's exposure.

Our sense is that if you really must buy access to an individual commodity in your portfolio, you are probably best off focusing on just two – oil and gold. The trickier question is how to buy that access – do you invest in a fund that tracks something called WTI or Brent. In the box below we have outlined the differences between these two types of oil – the basic difference is that Brent is slightly heavier than its West Texas cousin (WTI) and tends to trade $1 and $2 lower in price.

But this distinction between Brent and WTI is just the start of the process of working out how to invest – your next challenge is to decide whether you want to invest in a broad crude oil index, a specific Brent/WTI fund and whether you want to track futures prices. Just to add to the confusion you can also make money on price falls in oil – by investing in an inverse short ETC – or gear up your exposure to oil increases by investing in a leveraged oil ETC. The full list of oil-based options from ETF Securities is in the box above.

If we had a preference we would suggest the Brent Oil 1 month futures ETC – sterling based – which, as the name suggests, invests in one-month futures-based contracts based on spot Brent Oil prices.

Definitions of different types of oil from the Energy Information Administration in the US

West Texas Intermediate

West Texas Intermediate (WTI) crude oil is of very high quality and is excellent for refining a larger portion of gasoline. Its API gravity is 39.6 degrees (making it a 'light' crude oil), and it contains only about 0.24 per cent of sulphur (making a 'sweet' crude oil). This combination of characteristics, combined with its location, makes it an ideal crude oil to be refined in the United States, the largest gasoline-consuming country in the world. Most WTI crude oil gets refined in the Midwest region of the country, with some more refined within the Gulf Coast region. Although the production of WTI crude oil is on the decline, it still is the major benchmark of crude oil in the Americas. WTI is generally priced at about a $5–6 per-barrel premium to the OPEC Basket price and about $1–2 per-barrel premium to Brent, although on a daily basis the pricing relationships between these can vary greatly.

Brent

Brent Blend is actually a combination of crude oil from 15 different oil fields in the Brent and Ninian systems located in the North Sea. Its API gravity is 38.3 degrees (making it a 'light' crude oil, but not quite as 'light' as WTI), while it contains about 0.37 per cent of sulphur (making it a 'sweet' crude oil, but again slightly less 'sweet' than WTI). Brent blend is ideal for making gasoline and middle distillates, both of which are consumed in large quantities in Northwest Europe, where Brent blend crude oil is typically refined. However, if the arbitrage between Brent and other crude oils, including WTI, is favorable for export, Brent has been known to be refined in the United States (typically the East Coast or the Gulf Coast) or the Mediterranean region. Brent blend, like WTI, production is also on the decline, but it remains the major benchmark for other crude oils in Europe or Africa. For example, prices for other crude oils in these two continents are often priced as a differential to Brent, i.e., Brent minus $0.50. Brent blend is generally priced at about a $4 per-barrel premium to the OPEC Basket price or about a $1–2 per-barrel discount to WTI, although on a daily basis the pricing relationships can vary greatly.

Gold

Volatility	1.28 (relatively low)
Weight of largest holding	NR
Weight of top ten largest holdings	NR
Yield	NR

Returns

Index	2004	2005	2006	2007	2008
Gold Bullion (LBM)	5.5%	17.3%	21%	30%	0.4%

Graph

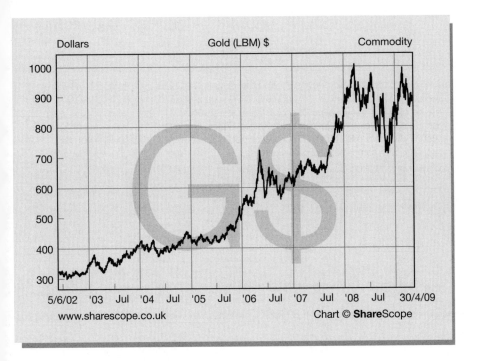

The index – our analysis

ANALYSIS	
Likely Risk (High/Medium/Low)	Medium to Low
Likely Volatility	Medium
Suitable for 'Simple' Investors i.e. small ISA investors	Yes
Diversification Risk with Top Holdings i.e. top three more than 20% of fund	No – not relevant
Likely to be a core holding?	Yes

The highlighted funds

Energy	Exchange	Physically backed or collateralised	Exchange Code	Currency	TER
Gold Bullion Securities	London Stock Exchange	Physically Backed	GBS	USD	0.40%
Gold Bullion Securities £	London Stock Exchange	Physically Backed	GBSS	GBX	0.40%
ETFS Precious Metals DJ-AIGCI	London Stock Exchange	Collateralised	AIGP	USD	0.49%
ETFS Short Precious Metals DJ-AIGCI	London Stock Exchange	Collateralised	SPMT	USD	0.98%
ETFS Leveraged Precious Metals DJ-AIGCI	London Stock Exchange	Collateralised	LPMT	USD	0.98%
ETFS Physical Gold	London Stock Exchange	Physically Backed	PHAU	USD	0.39%
ETFS Physical Gold £	London Stock Exchange	Physically Backed	PHGP	GBX	0.39%
ETFS Physical PM Basket	London Stock Exchange	Physically Backed	PHPM	USD	0.43%
ETFS Physical PM Basket £	London Stock Exchange	Physically Backed	PHPP	GBX	0.43%
ETFS Gold	London Stock Exchange	Collateralised	BULL	USD	0.49%
ETFS Gold £	London Stock Exchange	Collateralised	BULP	GBX	0.49%
ETFS Short Gold	London Stock Exchange	Collateralised	SBUL	USD	0.98%
ETFS Leveraged Gold	London Stock Exchange	Collateralised	LBUL	USD	0.98%

Comments

Gold is a peculiar investment class – even those investors with absolutely no interest in commodities generally will tend to have more than a passing interest in the shiny stuff, if only because of its safe haven status and redoubtable qualities against inflation and financial Armageddon.

We do not tend to favour investing in individual commodities but we can understand why investors might want to gain access to gold in times of distress. To be honest, we are not convinced of the investment benefits of gold beyond this distressed imperative – although there are users of gold in industry and especially jewellery, as a commodity its only real value is as a store of ... value!

Nevertheless, our slight scepticism with gold is not shared by the millions of investors who have pumped countless tens of billions into US and UK-based gold funds and especially ETCs. Assets in gold ETCs rose to over $30bn by 3Q 2008, up from less than $5bn only three years ago. Flows into ETCs have continued to build even during periods when the gold price was falling, indicating that strategic investors are increasingly using ETCs to build long-term positions in gold.

Part of that increased interest is a function of easier access via various ETC and ETF-based platforms – investors now have the choice to invest in gold both short and long and as part of a wider basket of precious metals. They can also invest in futures-based forward prices and in spot prices. Crucially, they can also invest in actual physical-holdings of gold, not futures-based rolling contracts – these physical-backed ETCs have proved hugely popular. If we had to express a preference we'd suggest that a physical-based gold fund like PHGP (a sterling-based tracker) would probably be the safest bet for ultra-cautious investors looking to profit from any increase in financial volatility.

iBoxx Sterling Corporate Bonds

Volatility	0.58 (relatively low)
Weight of largest holding	4.4% Walmart
Weight of top ten largest holdings	36%
Yield	Flat Yield 7.21% Gross Redemption Yield 8.43%

Returns

Index	2004	2005	2006	2007	2008
iBoxx £ Liquid Corporates Long Dated Index	NA	4.3%	−5.2%	−6.6%	−10.5%

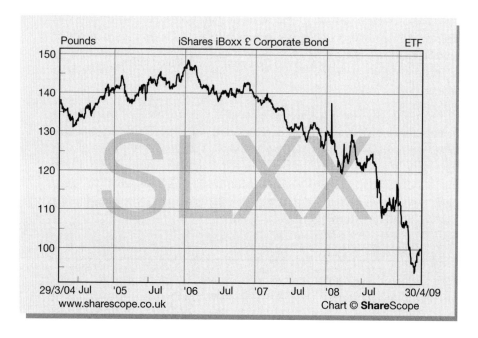

The index – our analysis

ANALYSIS	
Likely Risk (High/Medium/Low)	Low to Medium
Likely Volatility	Low to medium
Suitable for 'Simple' Investors i.e. small ISA investors?	Yes
Diversification Risk with Top Holdings i.e. top three more than 20% of fund	No
Likely to be a core holding?	Yes
Market Cap based (MC)/Screened (S)	MC
Appeal to Income Investors?	Yes

The featured ETF

Details	
Fund	**iShares £ Corporate Bond**
Ticker/EPIC	SLXX
Issuer	iShares
TER	0.2%
Underlying Index	iBoxx £ Liquid Corporates Long Dated Index
Launch Date	26/03/04

Details of Index

Fixed Income Information

No. of Holdings 48

Weighted Avg. Maturity (years) 16.37

Weighted Avg. Coupon (%) 6.38

Inclusion criteria for index

Bond types: Fixed coupon, step-ups, rating-driven bonds and callable hybrid capital

Min. time to maturity: 1.5 years at the rebalancing date

Minimum rating: BBB- from FITCH or S&P or Baa3 from Moody's (The lowest available rating is taken)

Amount outstanding: £250m

Maximum age since issuance: 2 years

Max # bonds per issuer: 1

Comments

Virtually every major listed company issues some form of fixed income debt – the most popular form is something called a corporate bond. Like government bonds or gilts, this promises to pay the holder a fixed income coupon regularly until the bond is redeemed.

Unlike most Western governments though, there is a major default risk – no major OECD country has ever defaulted on its debt but plenty of corporations have. That risk, an extra risk, is quantifiable and is expressed in the yield – the riskier the company, the higher the yield. Crucially, it is important to understand that not every high-yielding, high-risk bond-issuing company goes bust – the vast majority carry on paying their interest coupons. But it is also true that the highest quality, most blue-chip companies – especially those given the term investment grade, for the very lowest potential risk – are the least likely to go bankrupt and stop paying their debts.

In recent years that investment grade status has been taken to bizarre lengths – in 2009, for instance, corporations like McDonald's possessed better-rated debt than some Western countries. Italy may be forced out of the Euro but global hamburger specialists will probably continue paying their interest coupons.

All of these relatively simple challenges and debates – plus many more – form the background to why so many investors like investing in corporate bonds. They like the higher yield (bar McDonald's) as compared to government debt – they also appreciate the fact that most of these big debt issues are very liquid and easy to trade in.

Sadly, though, there is a big problem facing most ordinary private investors –big corporations issue their bonds in big bundles requiring an initial outlay of £50,000 or more. Direct ownership of corporate bonds by private investors is unsurprisingly, very low as a consequence.

Step forward corporate bond funds and indices. These aggregate the most liquid, most popular bond issues into one structure – in this case an index produced by a specialist markets firm called MarkIt. Only the most liquid bonds get into this fund – although it is important to say that not all the bonds in the fund are of the highest 'risk grade'. Investors use ratings firms to assess the potential risk of default and the safest companies tend to get the coveted AAA rating with the lowest rating (outside junk bonds) getting BBB ratings.

This index, and the accompanying iShares ETF, invests only in these popular, liquid, BBB and above-rated bonds – and it produces a yield which is substantially in excess of any government bond. But there is a real risk – corporate bonds are issued mostly by quoted, listed companies and when these companies are in distress, their bonds tend to fall in value as investors fret about bankruptcy and default. And they are right to worry about that risk – the financial meltdown of the once mighty Detroit car firms involved bond holders taking a massive hit on their investments. If you believe that corporate failure is likely to increase as a result of economic distress, you should avoid corporate bonds like the plague – their prices will fall as investors demand a higher risk premium via the yield which will, in turn, increase. If, on the other hand, you believe that corporate financial health is about to substantially improve, then corporate bonds could be the perfect place to receive a decent yield plus some capital uplift.

References

Chapter 1

[1] Jensen, M. (1968) 'The performance of mutual funds in the period 1945–1964', *Journal of Finance*, Vol, 23, May.

[2] Gruber, M.J. (1996) 'Another puzzle: the growth in actively managed mutual funds', *Journal of Finance*, Vol. 51, pp. 783–810.

[3] Carhart, M.M. (1997) 'On persistence in mutual fund performance', *Journal of Finance*, Vol. 52, pp. 57–82.

[4] Elton, E., Gruber, M.J., Das, S. and Hlavka, M. (1993) 'Efficiency with costly information: a reinterpretation of evidence from managed portfolios', The Review of Financial Studies, http://ideas.repec.org/a/oup/rfinst/v6y1993i1p1-22.html.

[5] Elton, E., Gruber, M. and Blake, C. (1995) 'Fundamental economic variables, expected returns, and bond fund performance', *Journal of Finance*, Vol. 50.

[6] Clements, J. (1999) 'Stock funds just don't measure up', *The Wall Street Journal*, 5 October.

[7] Fletcher, J. (1997) 'An examination of UK unit trust performance with the Arbitrage Pricing Theory framework', *Review of Quantitative Finance and Accounting*.

[8] See note 4.

[9] Cuthbertson, K., Nitzsche, D. and O'Sullivan, N. (??) 'False discoveries: winners and losers in mutual fund performance', *European Financial Management*.

[10] Booth, D. (2001) 'Index and enhanced index funds', www.dfaus.com/library/articles/index_enhanced_funds/.

[11] French, K.R. (2008) 'The cost of active investing', http://ssrn.com/abstract=1105775.

Chapter 2

[1] Fama, E. (1965) 'Random walks in stock market prices', *Financial Analysts Journal*, September–October.

[2] Dimson, E. and Mussavian, M. (1998) 'A brief history of market efficiency', *European Financial Management*, Vol. 4, No. 1, pp. 91–193.

[3] Quoted in Dimson and Mussavian (1998).

[4] Malkiel, B. (1973) *A Random Walk Down Wall Street*, W. W. Norton & Co., London.

[5] Samuelson, P. (1965) 'Proof that properly anticipated prices fluctuate randomly', *Industrial Management Review*, Vol. 6, No. 2.

[6] Fama (1965).

[7] Fama, E. (1970) 'Efficient capital markets: a review of theory and empirical work', *The Journal of Finance*, Vol. 25, No. 2.

[8] Fama, E. (2003) 'The Efficient Market Hypothesis and its critics', *Journal of Economic Perspectives*.

[9] Fama, E., Fisher, Lawrence, Jensen, M. and Roll, R. (1969) 'The adjustment of stock prices to new information', International Economic Review, Vol. 10, pp. 1–21.

[10] Jensen, M. (1968) 'The performance of mutual funds in the period 1945–1964', *Journal of Finance*, Vol, 23, pp. 389–416.

[11] Dimson and Mussavian (1998).

[12] Lo, A.W. and MacKinlay, A.C. (1999) A Non-Random Walk Down Wall Street, Princeton University Press,

[13] Malkiel, B. (2003) 'The Efficient Market Hypothesis and its critics', CEPS Working Paper No. 91, Princeton University, New Jersey, NJ.

[14] Shiller, R.J. (2000) *Irrational Exuberance*, Princeton University Press, New Jersey, NJ.

[15] Vanguard (2003) 'Sources of portfolio performance: the enduring importance of asset allocation', July, https://institutional.vanguard.com/iip/pdf/icr_asset_allocation.pdf.

[16] Malkiel (2003).

[17] Fama, E.F. and French, K.R. (1992) 'The cross-section of expected stock returns', *Journal of Finance*, Vol. 47, No. 2, pp. 427–465.

[18] www.dfaus.com/philosophy/dimensions/.

[19] DeBondt, W.F.M. and Thaler, R. (1995) 'Financial decision-making in markets and firms: a behavioural perspective', in Jarrow, R.A., Maksimovic, V. and Ziemba, W.T. (eds) *Handbooks in Operations Research and Management Science: Finance*, Elsevier, Amsterdam, pp. 385–410.

[20] Quoted in Malkiel, B. (2003) 'The Efficient Market Hypothesis and its critics', *Journal of Economic Perspectives*, Vol. 17, No. 1, pp. 59–82.

[21] As note 20.

[22] Fama, E. (2000) 'The new indexing', at www.dfaus.com/library/articles/new_indexing/.

[23] As note 13.

[24] Fluck, Z. Malkiel, B. And Quandt, R. (1997) 'The predictability of stock returns: a cross-sectional simulation', *Review of Economics and Statistics*, Vol. 79, No. 2, pp. 176–183.

[25] Schwert, G.W. (2001) 'Anomalies and market efficiency', University of Rochester Simon School Working Paper No. FR 02-13.

[26] Roll and Shiller (1992)

[27] Tryenor, J. (1981) *Financial Analysis Journal*.

[28] Lummer, S. and Riepe, M. (1994) 'The role of asset allocation in modern portfolio management', in Lederman, J. and Klein, R.A. (eds) *Global Asset Allocation: Techniques for Optimizing Portfolio Management*, John Wiley and Sons, Chichester.

[29] Brinson, G.P., Singer, B.D. and Beebower, G.L. (1991) Determinants of portfolio performance II: an update', *The Financial Analysts Journal*, Vol. 47, No. 3, p. 40.

Chapter 3

[1] Abstract—The Case for Indexing: European- and Offshore-Domiciled Funds, Vanguard Investment Counseling & Research, https://advisors.vanguard.com/iwe/pdf/ICRICIS.pdf.

[2] Malkiel, B. (1973) *A Random Walk Down Wall Street*, W. W. Norton & Co., London.

[3] Quoted at www.ifa.com/book/book_pdf/02_nobel_laureates.pdf.

[4] Fama, E. (2000) 'The new indexing', http://www.dfaus.com/library/articles/new_indexing/.

[5] Burgess, G., 'Are equal weighted indexes better than market cap weighted indexes?' at http://www.dfaus.com/library/articles/new_indexing/.

[6] Richards, A. (2002) *All About Exchange Traded Funds*, McGraw-Hill.

[7] www.amex.com.

[8] 'The choice between ETFs and conventional index fund shares', Vanguard Investment Counseling & Research paper, www.vanguard.com/pdf/s563.pdf?2210036900.

Chapter 4

[1] Rogers, J. (2004) *Hot Commodities*, Random House.

Chapter 6

[1] Siegel, J. (2009) 'The stock market's little shop of horrors: and you thought the aftermath of 1929 was grim', *The Journal of Investing*, Vol. 18, No. 2, pp. 6–12.

[2] Smith, T. (1996) *Accounting for Growth: Stripping the Camouflage from Company Accounts*, Century Business.

[3] Siegel, J. (1994) *Stocks for the Long Run, The Definitive Guide to Financial Market Returns and Long-term Investment Strategies*, Irwin Professional Publishing, Burr Ridge, IL.

[4] Arnott, R.D., Hsu, J.C. and West, J.M. (2008) *The Fundamental Index: A Better Way to Invest*, Wiley.

Chapter 8

[1] Keynes, J.M. (1936) *The General Theory of Employment, Interest and Money*, Harcourt Brace and Co., New York.

Chapter 10

[1] Merriman, P. and Buck, R., available online at www.fundadvice.com/articles/market-timing/one-portfolio-for-life.html.

[2] Smith Barney, 'The art of rebalancing: How to tell when your portfolio needs a tune-up', available online at www.asaecenter.org/files/ArtofRebalancing.pdf.

[3] Vanguard, 'Portfolio rebalancing in theory and practice', available online at https://institutional.vanguard.com/iip/pdf/ICRRebalancing.pdf.

[4] Available at www.seekingalpha.com.

[5] DeMuth, P. and Stein, B. (2009) *Yes, You Can Supercharge Your Portfolio!*, Hay House.

[6] Daryanani, G. (2008) 'Opportunistic rebalancing: a new paradigm for wealth managers', *Journal of Financial Planning*, January.

[7] Schwab Center for Investment Research (2000) 'The costs and benefits of waiting to invest', Vol. 3, No. 1.

[8] Graham, J.R. and Harvey, C.R. (1995) 'Market timing ability and volatility implied in investment newsletters' asset allocation recommendations', available at http://ssrn.com/abstract=6006.

[9] Morningstar article available at www.ifa.com/archives/articles/staff_20020315_morningstar_study_confirms_virtues_of_buy_and_hold_in_bear market.asp.

[10] Graham, B. (1986)*The Intelligent Investor: A Book of Practical Counsel*, Harper & Row.

[11] Pesaran, H. and Timmermann, A. (2000) 'A recursive modelling approach to predicting UK stock returns', *The Economic Journal, January*.

[12] Hendry, H. (2008), available at http://uk.reuters.com/article/idUKLNE4AK05B20081121.

[13] Mauldin, J., 'While Rome Burns', available online at www.investorsinsight.com/blogs/thoughts_from_the_frontline/archive/2009/02/20/while-rome-burns.aspx.

[14] Faber, M. (2007) 'A quantitative approach to tactical asset allocation', *Journal of Wealth Management*, Spring.

[15] Bond, T. (2008) Barclays Equity Gilt Study.

[16] Britton, J., quoted in *Investors Chronicle*.

[17] See www.share.com.

[18] Source: FTSE data available through Sharescope.

[19] Available at https://advisors.vanguard.com/iwe/pdf/ICRIBM.pdf.

[20] Farrell, P. (2004) *The Lazy Person's Guide to Investing*, Warner Business Books.

[21] Bernstein, W. (2002) *The Four Pillars of Investing: Lessons for Building a Winning Portfolio*, McGraw-Hill.

[22] Lowell, J. (2006) *What Every Fidelity Investor Needs to Know*, Wiley.

[23] Schultheis, B. (2005) *The CoffeeHouse Investor*, Palouse Press.

[24] https://institutional.vanguard.com/iam/pdf/IAM_Lifecycle_funds.pdf.

[25] www.cpmkts.com/.

[26] www.mscibarra.com/products/indices/us/index.jsp.

[27] As note 1 above.

Chapter 11

[1] Mauldin, J., 'While Rome Burns', available online at www.investorsinsight.com/blogs/thoughts_from_the_frontline/archive/2009/02/20/while-rome-burns.aspx.

[2] Farrell, P. (2004) *The Lazy Person's Guide to Investing*, Warner Business Books.

Index

Page numbers in *italics* denote a table/diagram